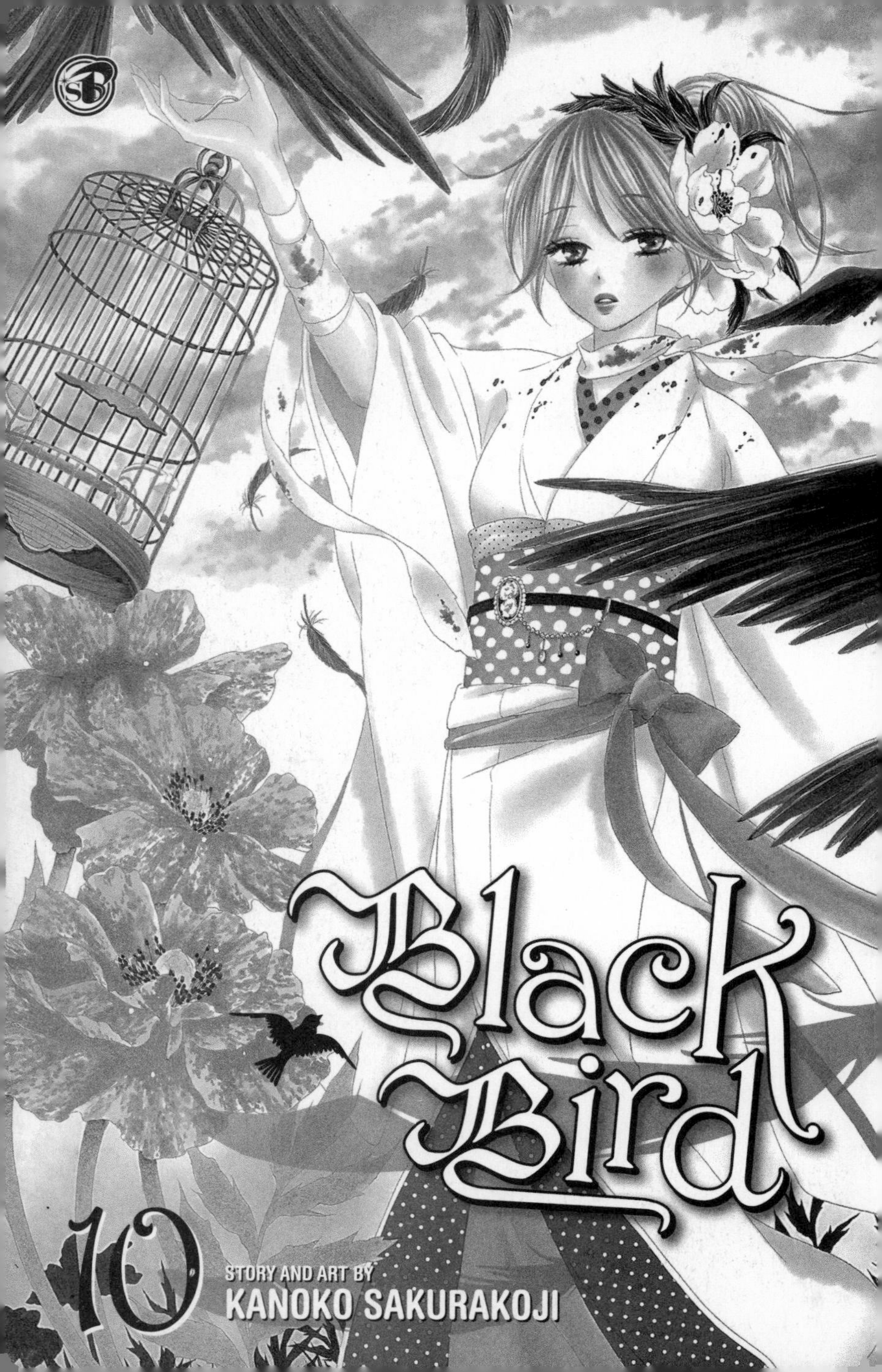
Black Bird
10
STORY AND ART BY
KANOKO SAKURAKOJI

Black Bird

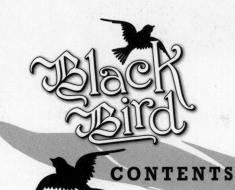

CONTENTS

CHARACTERS

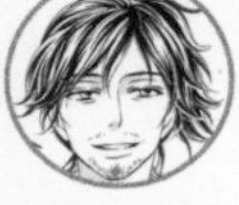

YOH USUI
Kyo and Sho's father. He was the former leader of the tengu clan.

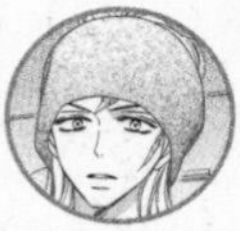

RAIKOH WATANABE
Like Misao, he can see demons and spirits. However, he refuses to believe that humans and demons can live in harmony and uses his abilities to destroy them.

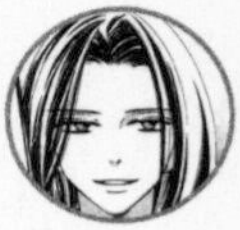

SHO USUI
Kyo's older brother and a ex-member of the Eight Daitengu. He is also know as Sojo. His attempted cou failed and his whereabou are currently unknown.

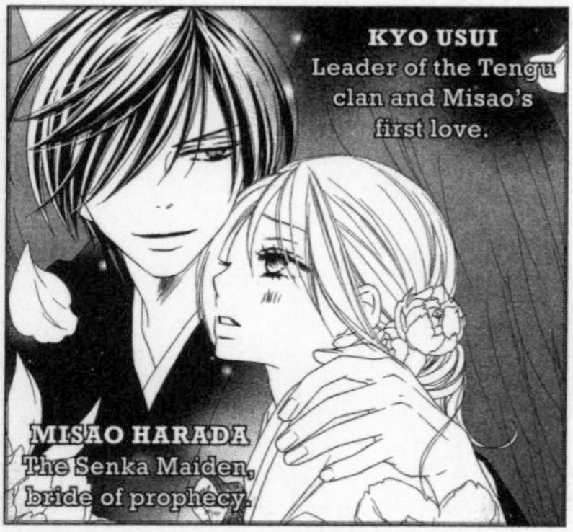
KYO USUI
Leader of the Tengu clan and Misao's first love.
MISAO HARADA
The Senka Maiden, bride of prophecy.

THE EIGHT DAITENGU
Kyo's bodyguards. Their names designate their official posts.

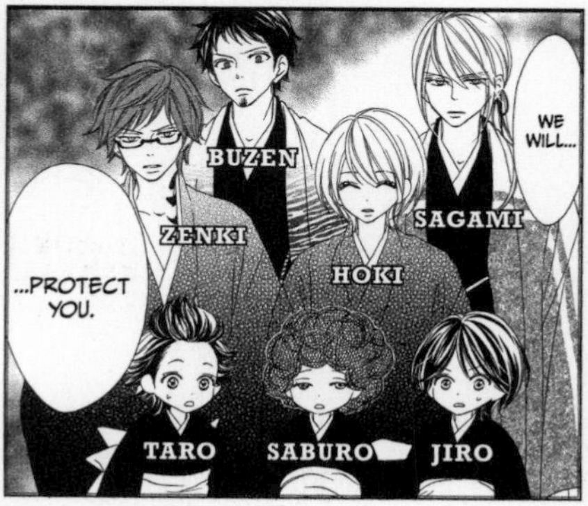
WE WILL...
...PROTECT YOU.
BUZEN
SAGAMI
ZENKI
HOKI
TARO
SABURO
JIRO

STORY THUS FAR

Misao can see spirits and demons, and her childhood sweetheart Kyo has been protecting her since she was little.

"Someday, I'll come for you, I promise." Kyo reappears the day before Misao's 16th birthday to tell her, "Your 16th birthday marks 'open season' on you." She is the Senka Maiden, and if a demon drinks her blood, he is granted a long life. If he eats her flesh, he gains eternal youth. And if he makes her his bride, his clan will prosper...And Kyo is a *tengu*, a crow demon, with his sights firmly set on her.

So far, Kyo has avoided sleeping with Misao because he knows that sex with a demon is somehow dangerous for the Senka Maiden. But when Raikoh's treachery leaves Kyo hovering near death, he finally gives in and takes Misao.

Now Kyo's powers have no equal, so other demon clans begin a campaign of indiscriminate attacks on humans to pressure Kyo by working on Misao's sense of guilt. Realizing this, Kyo begins to suspect there is a traitor leaking the information that Misao is his weak point. In the midst of all this trouble, Kyo's father, who hasn't been heard from in years, suddenly shows up...!

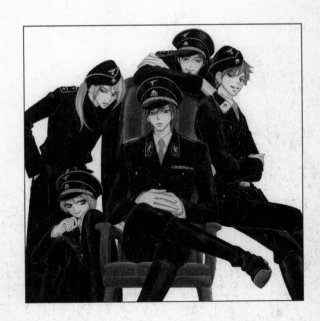

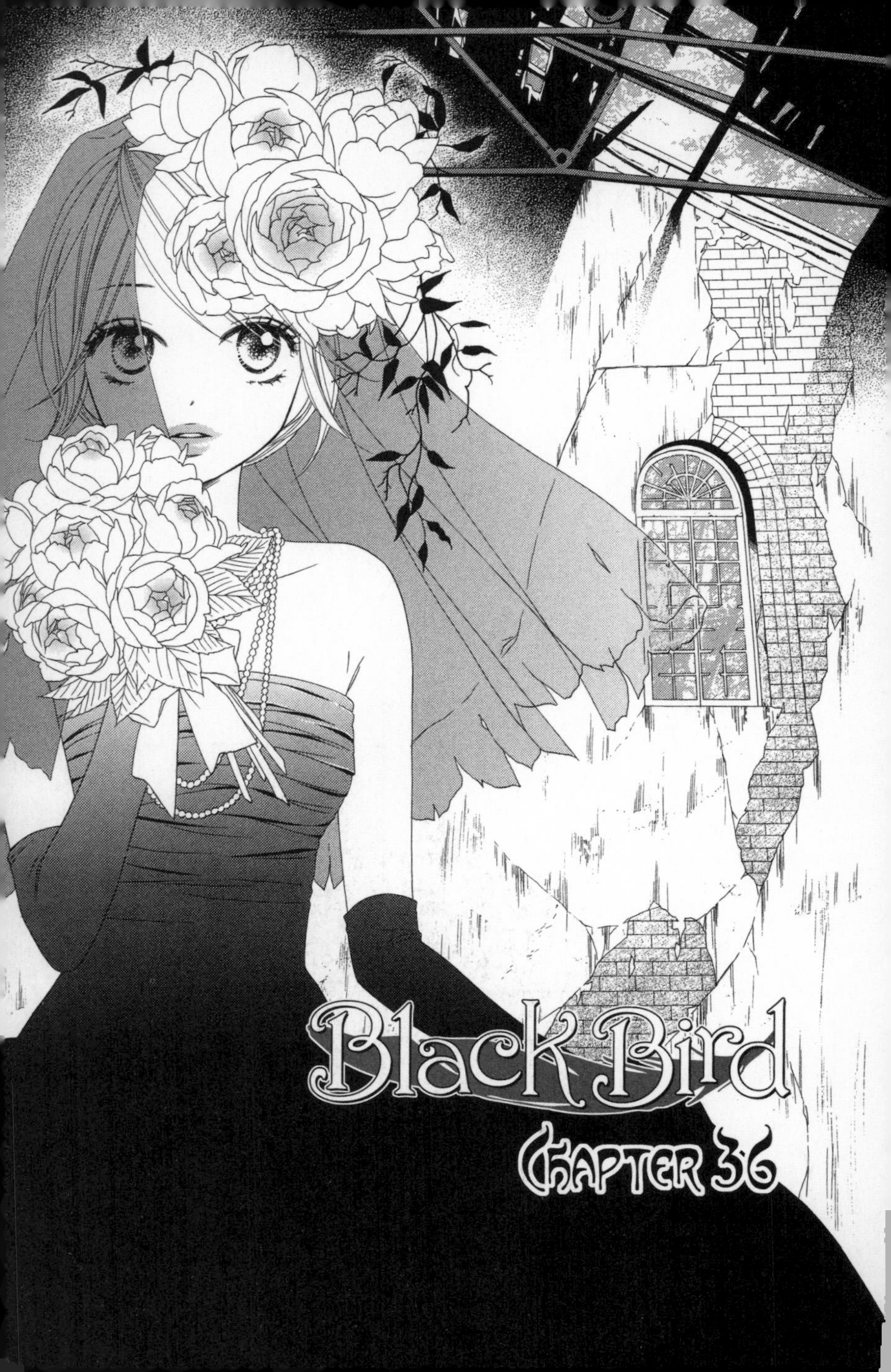
Black Bird
Chapter 36

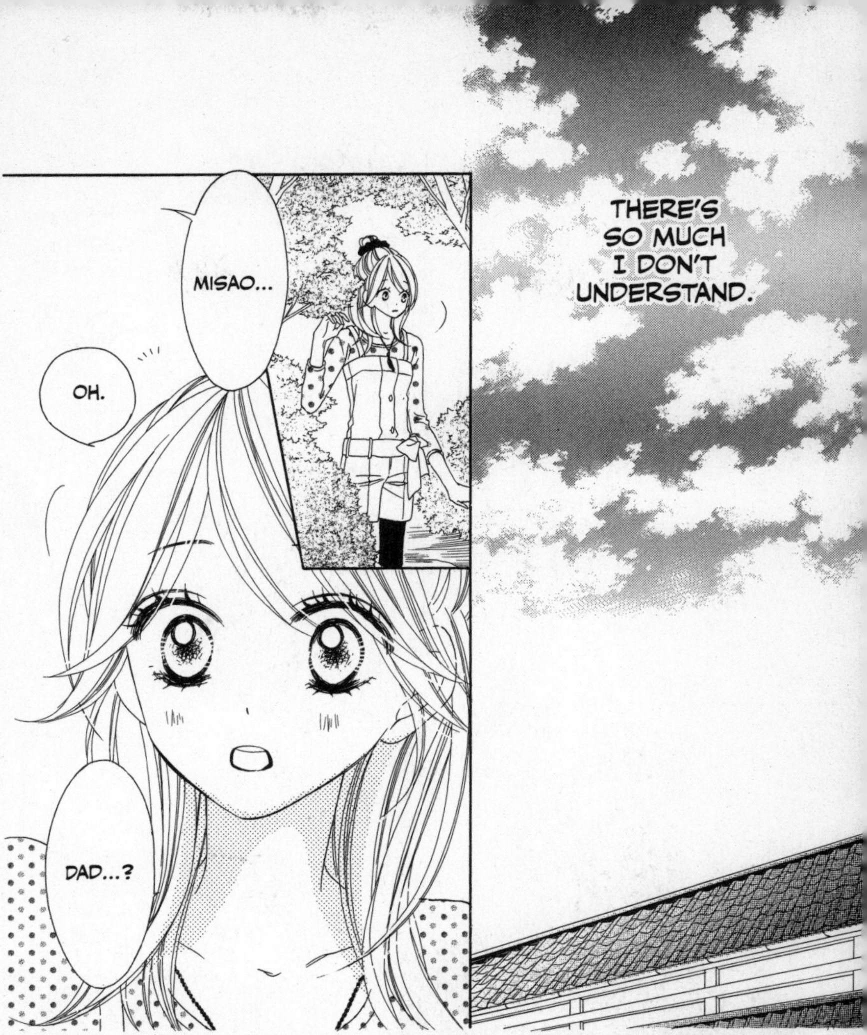
THERE'S SO MUCH I DON'T UNDERSTAND.
MISAO...
OH.
DAD...?

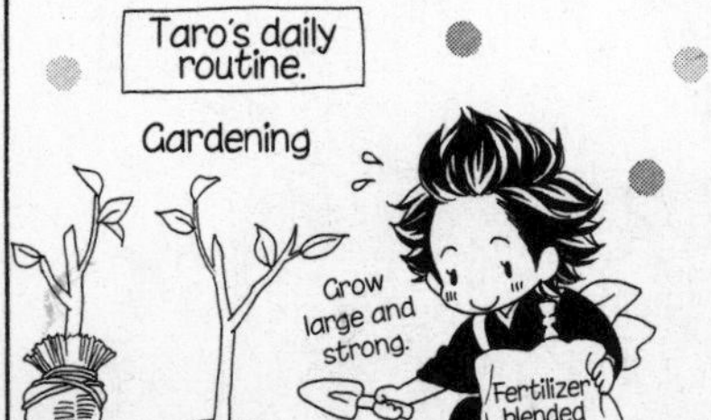
Taro's daily routine.
Gardening
Grow large and strong.
Fertilizer blended by Taro.

Hello, I'm Kanoko Sakurakoji.
Black Bird has finally
reached its 10th volume!
It's unbelievable!
This is all thanks to you,
my readers. ♡ ♡

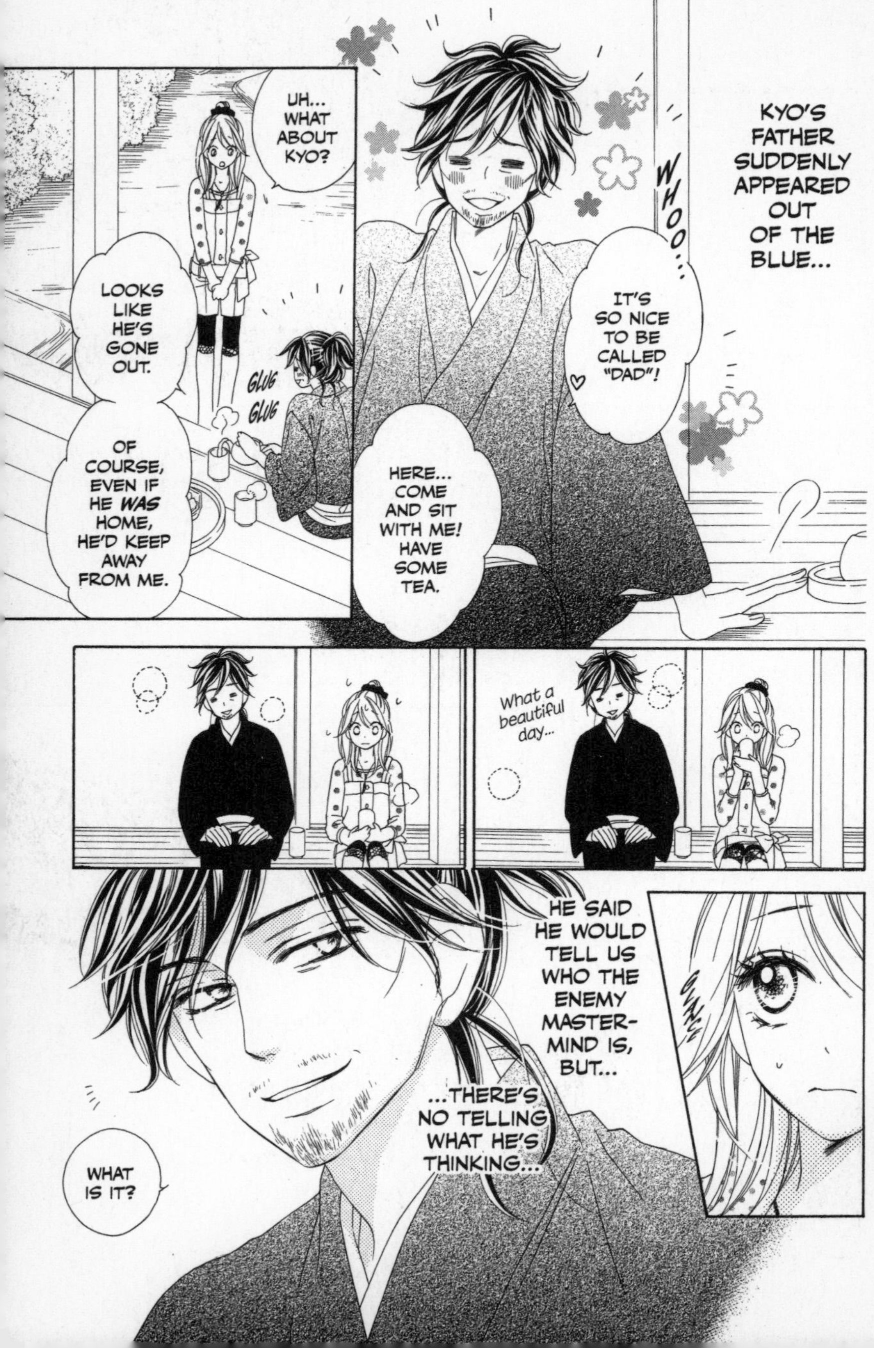
KYO'S FATHER SUDDENLY APPEARED OUT OF THE BLUE...
WHOOO...
IT'S SO NICE TO BE CALLED "DAD"!
HERE... COME AND SIT WITH ME! HAVE SOME TEA.
UH... WHAT ABOUT KYO?
LOOKS LIKE HE'S GONE OUT.
GLUG GLUG
OF COURSE, EVEN IF HE *WAS* HOME, HE'D KEEP AWAY FROM ME.
What a beautiful day...
HE SAID HE WOULD TELL US WHO THE ENEMY MASTER-MIND IS, BUT...
...THERE'S NO TELLING WHAT HE'S THINKING...
WHAT IS IT?

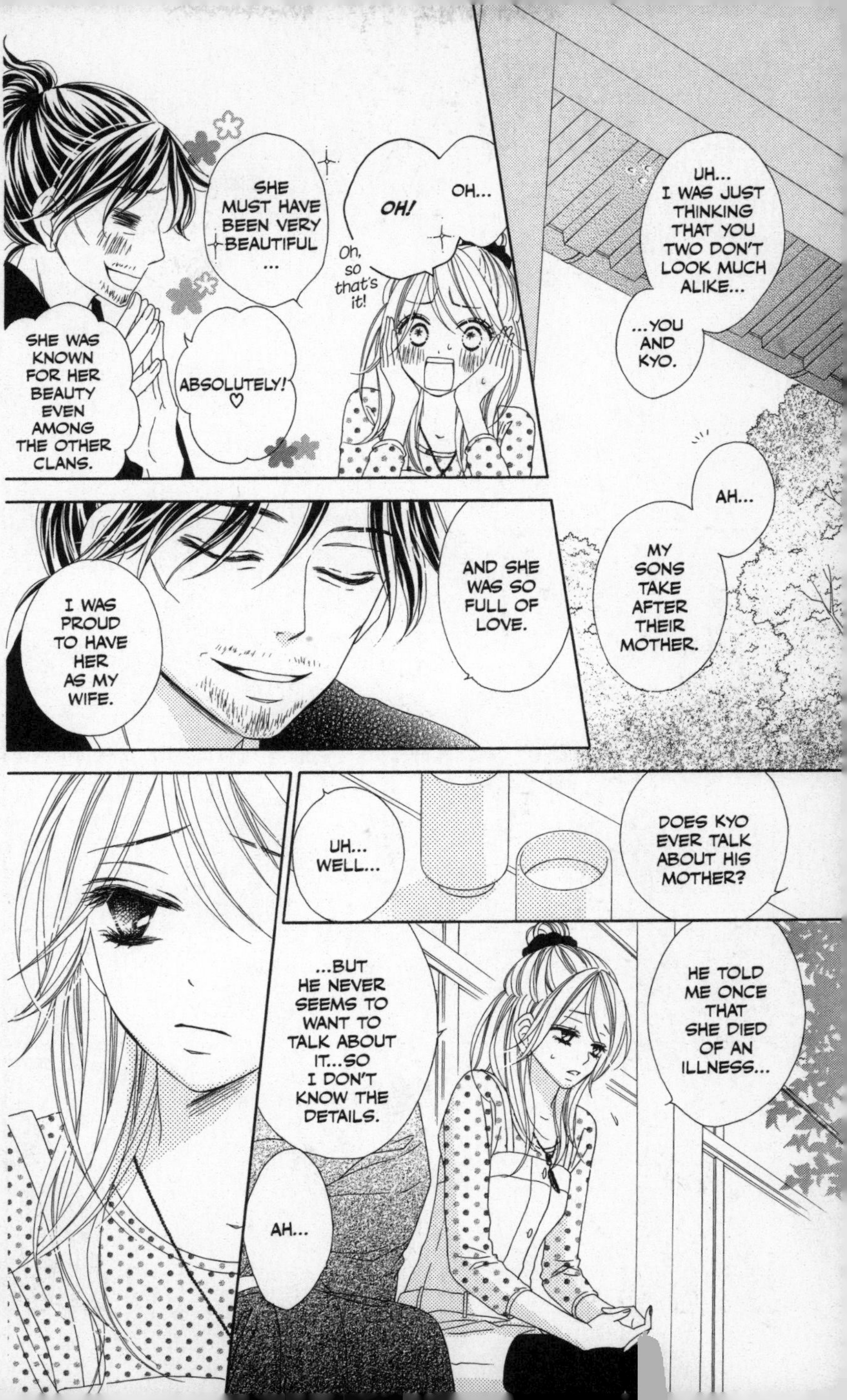
UH... I WAS JUST THINKING THAT YOU TWO DON'T LOOK MUCH ALIKE...
...YOU AND KYO.
AH...
MY SONS TAKE AFTER THEIR MOTHER.
OH...
OH!
Oh, so that's it!
SHE MUST HAVE BEEN VERY BEAUTIFUL ...
ABSOLUTELY! ♡
SHE WAS KNOWN FOR HER BEAUTY EVEN AMONG THE OTHER CLANS.
AND SHE WAS SO FULL OF LOVE.
I WAS PROUD TO HAVE HER AS MY WIFE.
DOES KYO EVER TALK ABOUT HIS MOTHER?
UH... WELL...
HE TOLD ME ONCE THAT SHE DIED OF AN ILLNESS...
...BUT HE NEVER SEEMS TO WANT TO TALK ABOUT IT...SO I DON'T KNOW THE DETAILS.
AH...

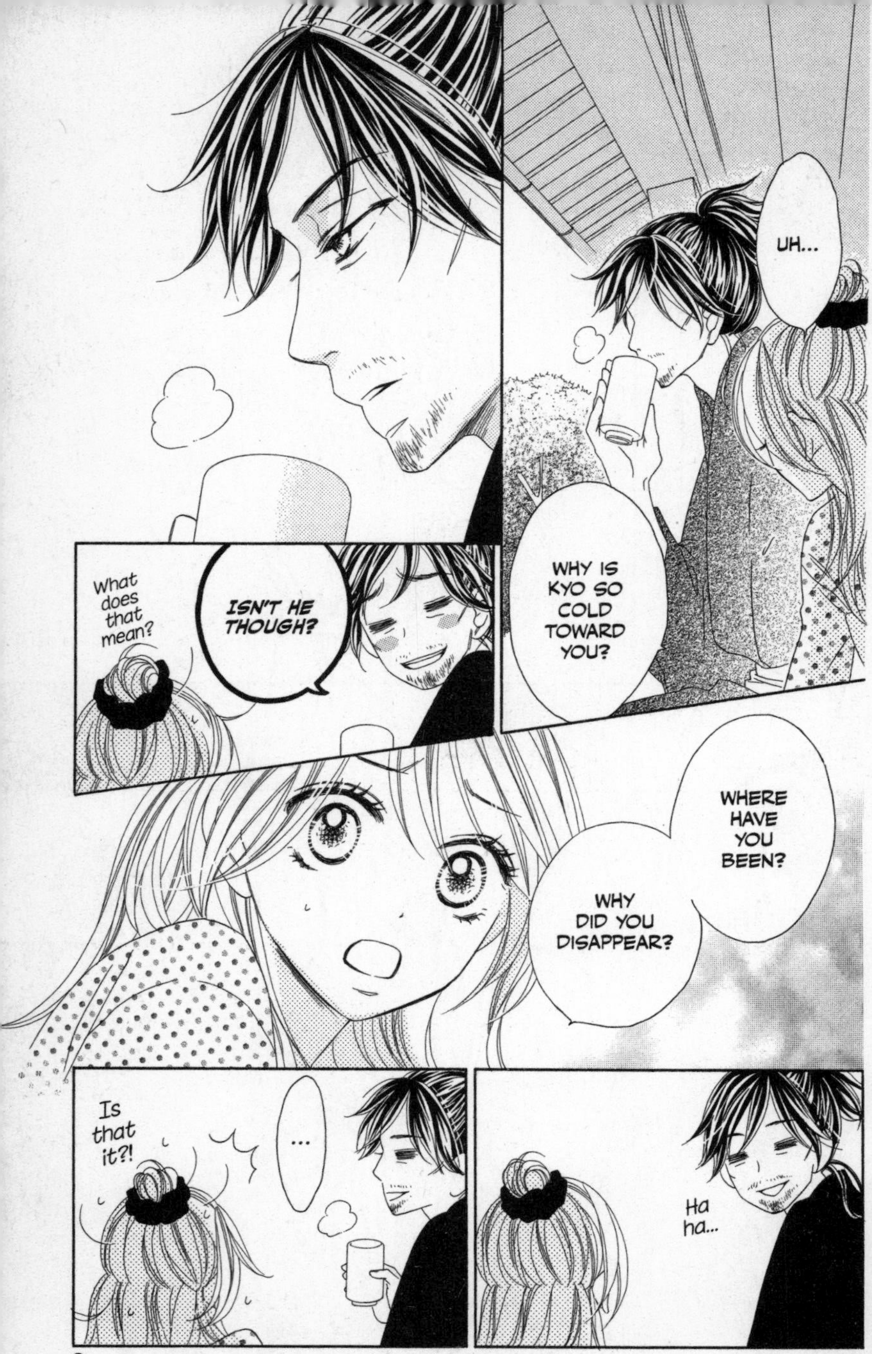
UH...
WHY IS KYO SO COLD TOWARD YOU?
ISN'T HE THOUGH?
What does that mean?
WHERE HAVE YOU BEEN?
WHY DID YOU DISAPPEAR?
Ha ha...
...
Is that it?!

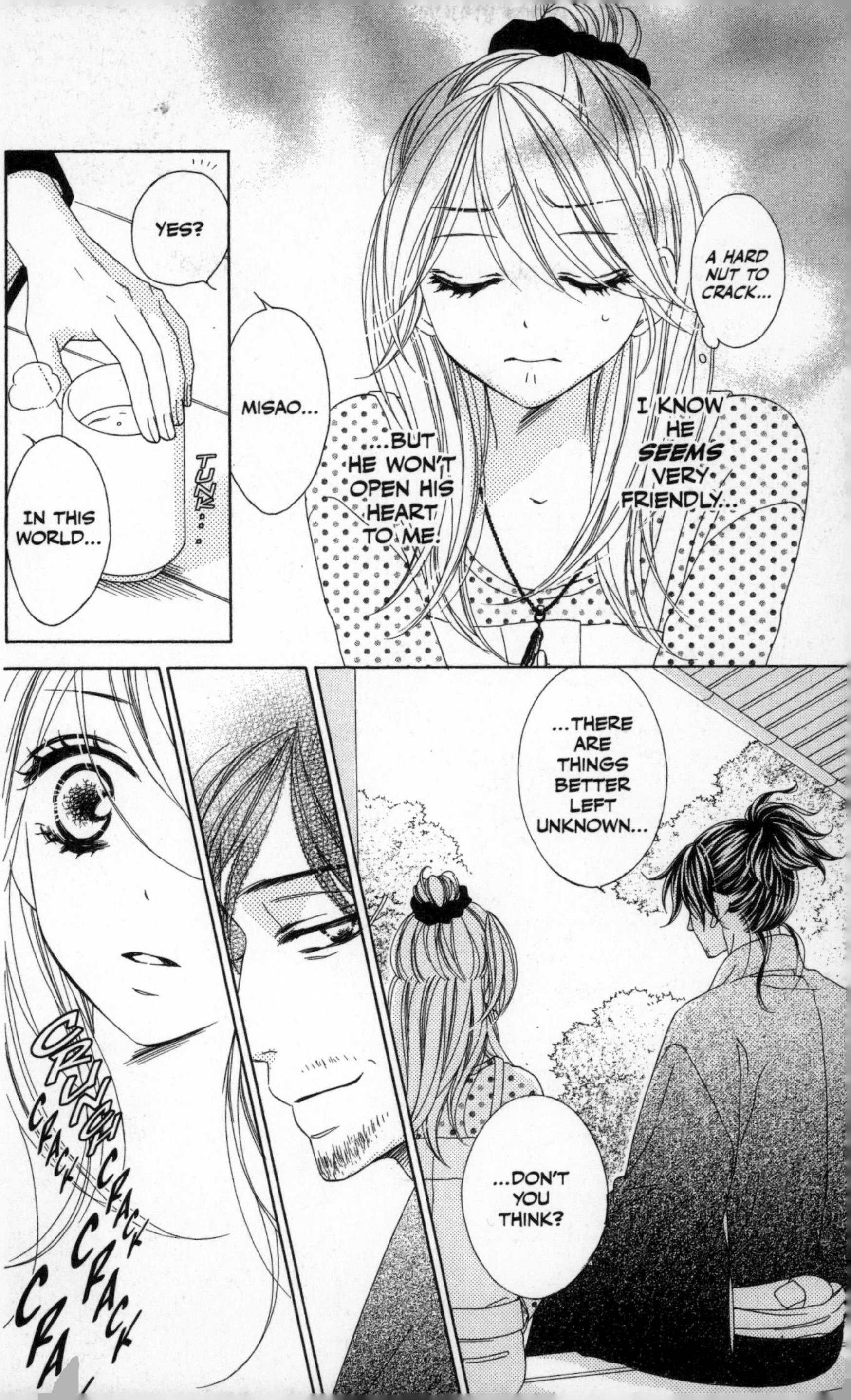
A HARD NUT TO CRACK...
I KNOW HE SEEMS VERY FRIENDLY...
...BUT HE WON'T OPEN HIS HEART TO ME.
MISAO...
YES?
TUNK...
IN THIS WORLD...
...THERE ARE THINGS BETTER LEFT UNKNOWN...
...DON'T YOU THINK?
CRUNCH
CRACK
CRACK
CRACK
CRACK
CRA

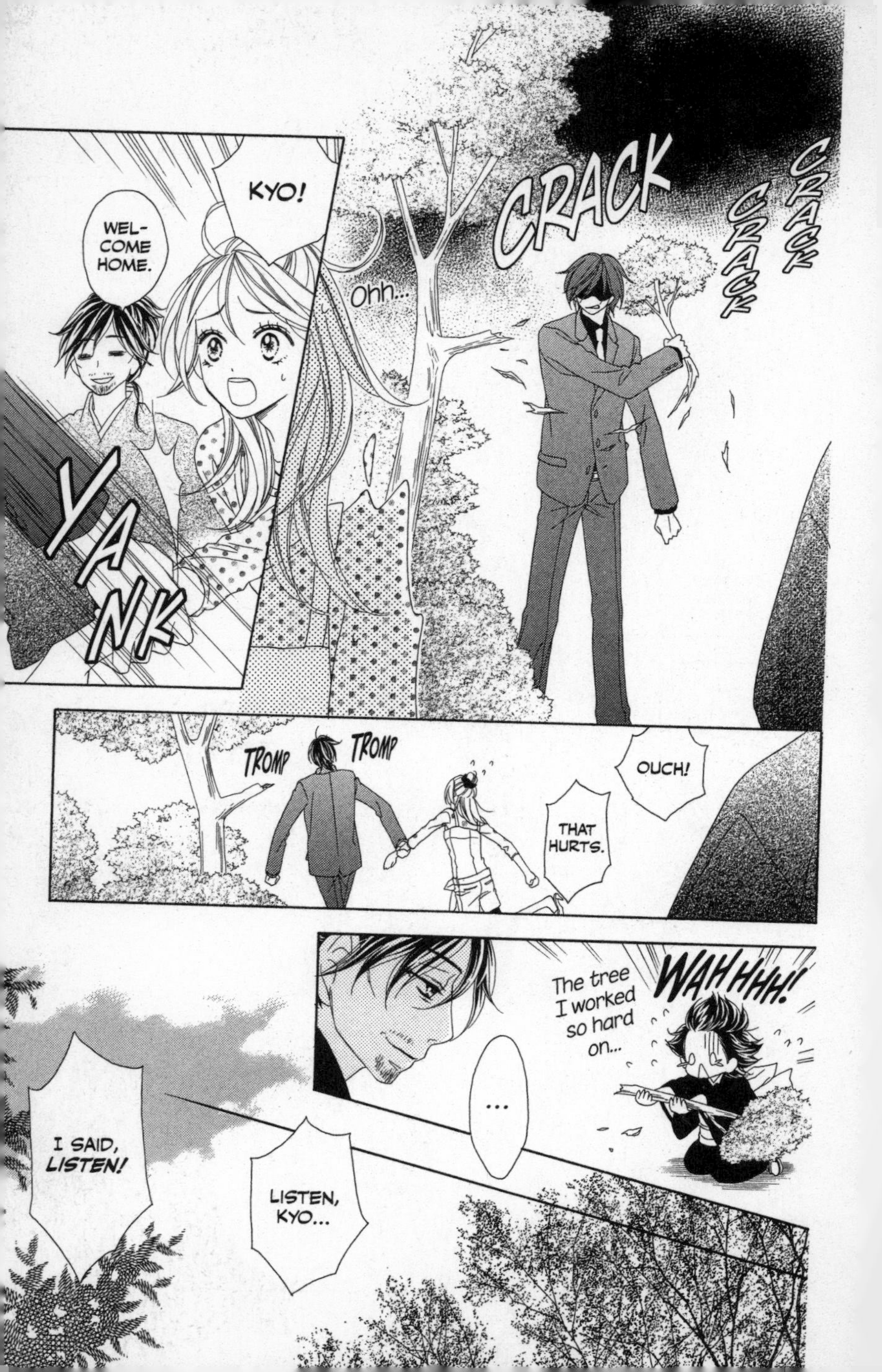
CRACK
CRACK
CRACK
Ohh...
KYO!
WEL-COME HOME.
YANK
OUCH!
THAT HURTS.
TROMP
TROMP
WAHHHH!
The tree I worked so hard on...
...
LISTEN, KYO...
I SAID, LISTEN!

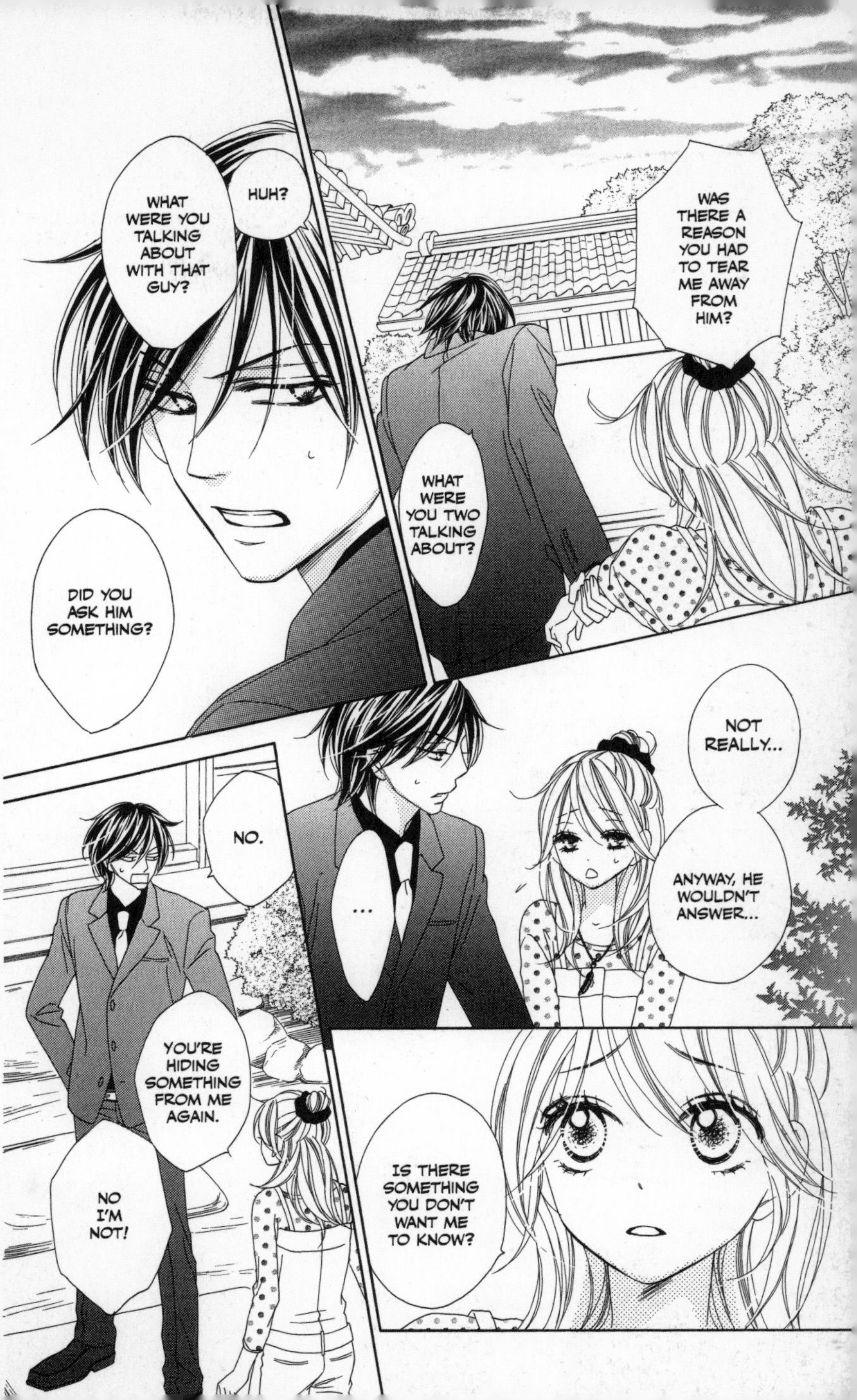
WAS THERE A REASON YOU HAD TO TEAR ME AWAY FROM HIM?
WHAT WERE YOU TWO TALKING ABOUT?
HUH?
WHAT WERE YOU TALKING ABOUT WITH THAT GUY?
DID YOU ASK HIM SOMETHING?
NOT REALLY...
ANYWAY, HE WOULDN'T ANSWER...
...
IS THERE SOMETHING YOU DON'T WANT ME TO KNOW?
NO.
YOU'RE HIDING SOMETHING FROM ME AGAIN.
NO I'M NOT!

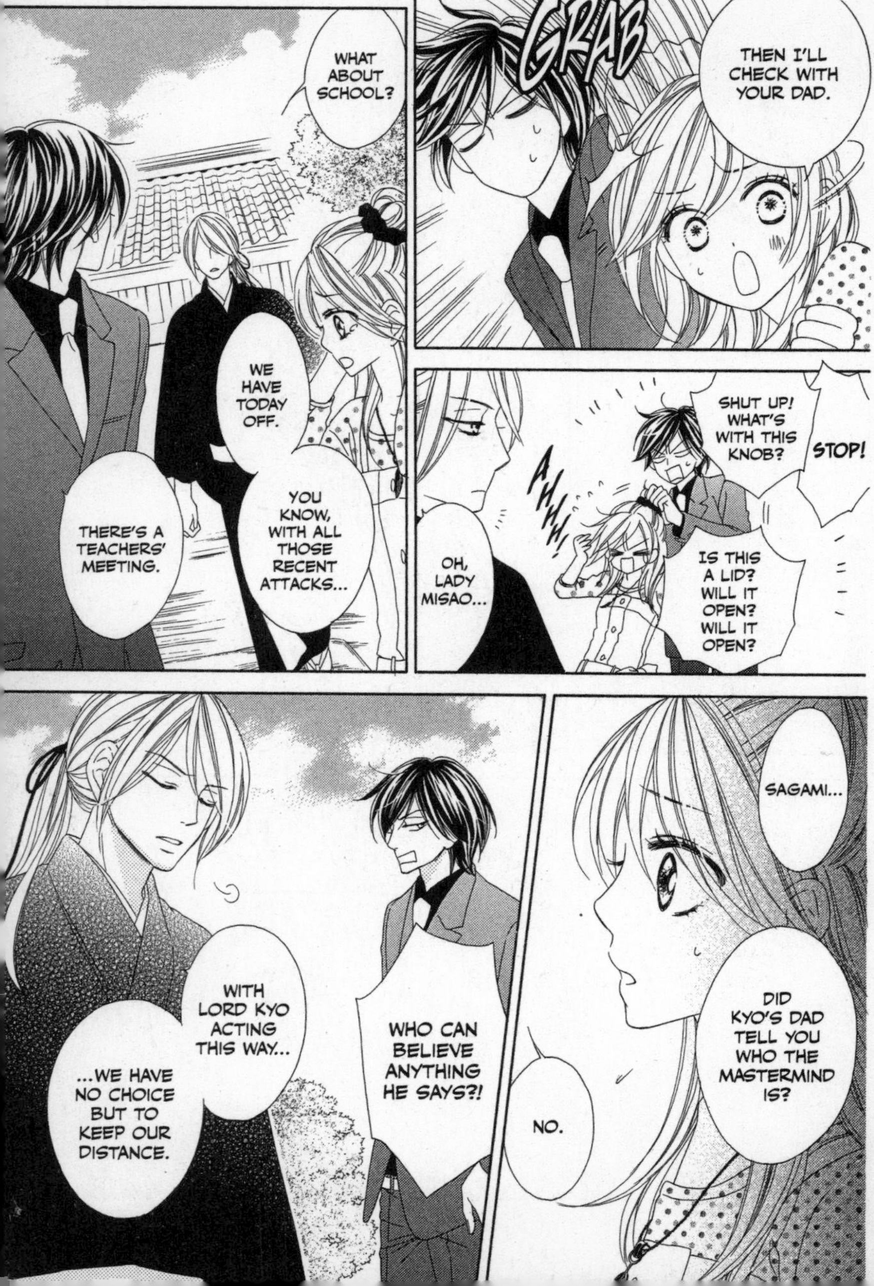
THEN I'LL CHECK WITH YOUR DAD.
GRAB
STOP!
SHUT UP! WHAT'S WITH THIS KNOB?
IS THIS A LID? WILL IT OPEN? WILL IT OPEN?
AHH!
OH, LADY MISAO...
WHAT ABOUT SCHOOL?
WE HAVE TODAY OFF.
YOU KNOW, WITH ALL THOSE RECENT ATTACKS...
THERE'S A TEACHERS' MEETING.
SAGAMI...
DID KYO'S DAD TELL YOU WHO THE MASTERMIND IS?
NO.
WHO CAN BELIEVE ANYTHING HE SAYS?!
WITH LORD KYO ACTING THIS WAY...
...WE HAVE NO CHOICE BUT TO KEEP OUR DISTANCE.

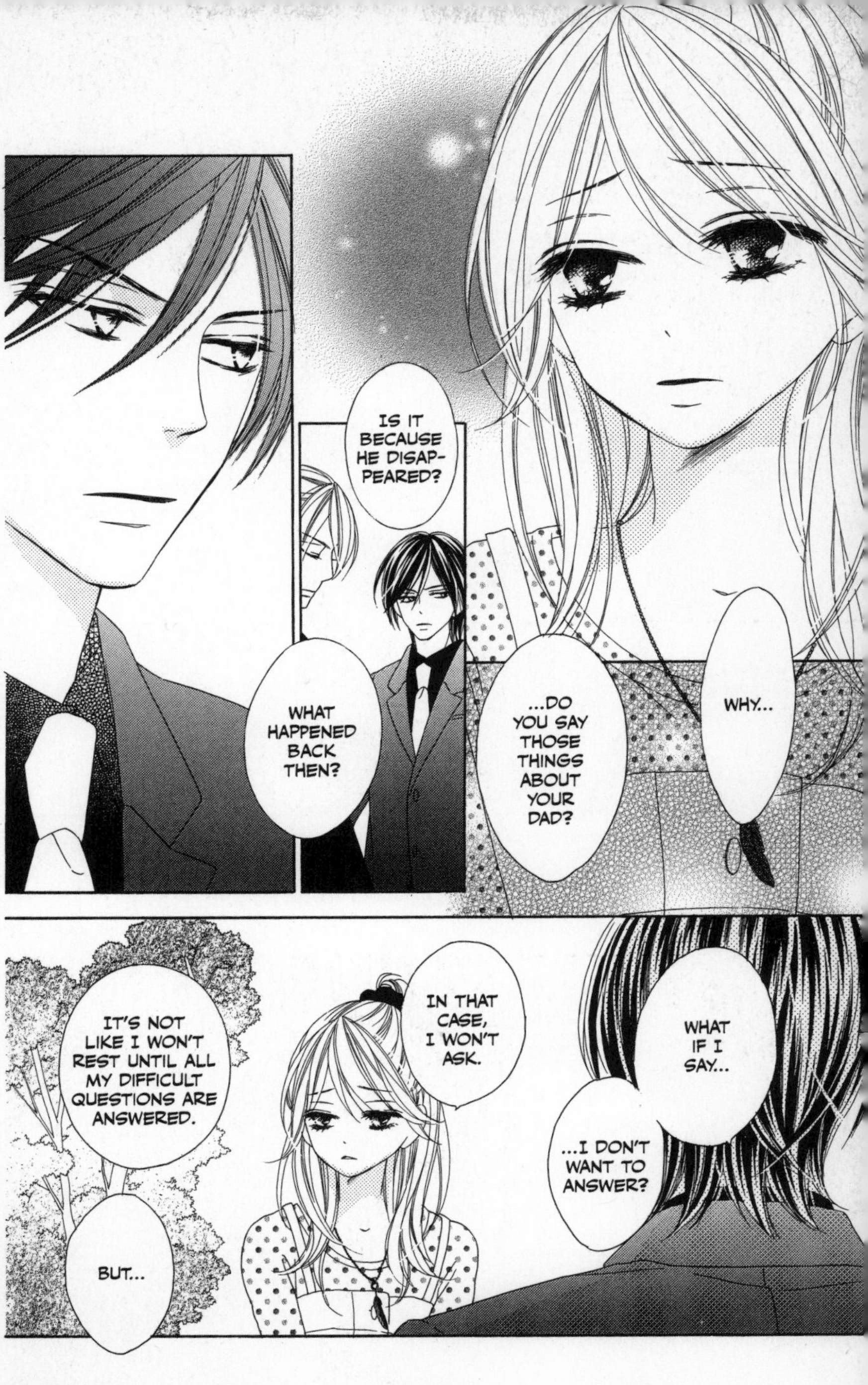
WHY...
...DO YOU SAY THOSE THINGS ABOUT YOUR DAD?
IS IT BECAUSE HE DISAPPEARED?
WHAT HAPPENED BACK THEN?
WHAT IF I SAY...
...I DON'T WANT TO ANSWER?
IN THAT CASE, I WON'T ASK.
IT'S NOT LIKE I WON'T REST UNTIL ALL MY DIFFICULT QUESTIONS ARE ANSWERED.
BUT...

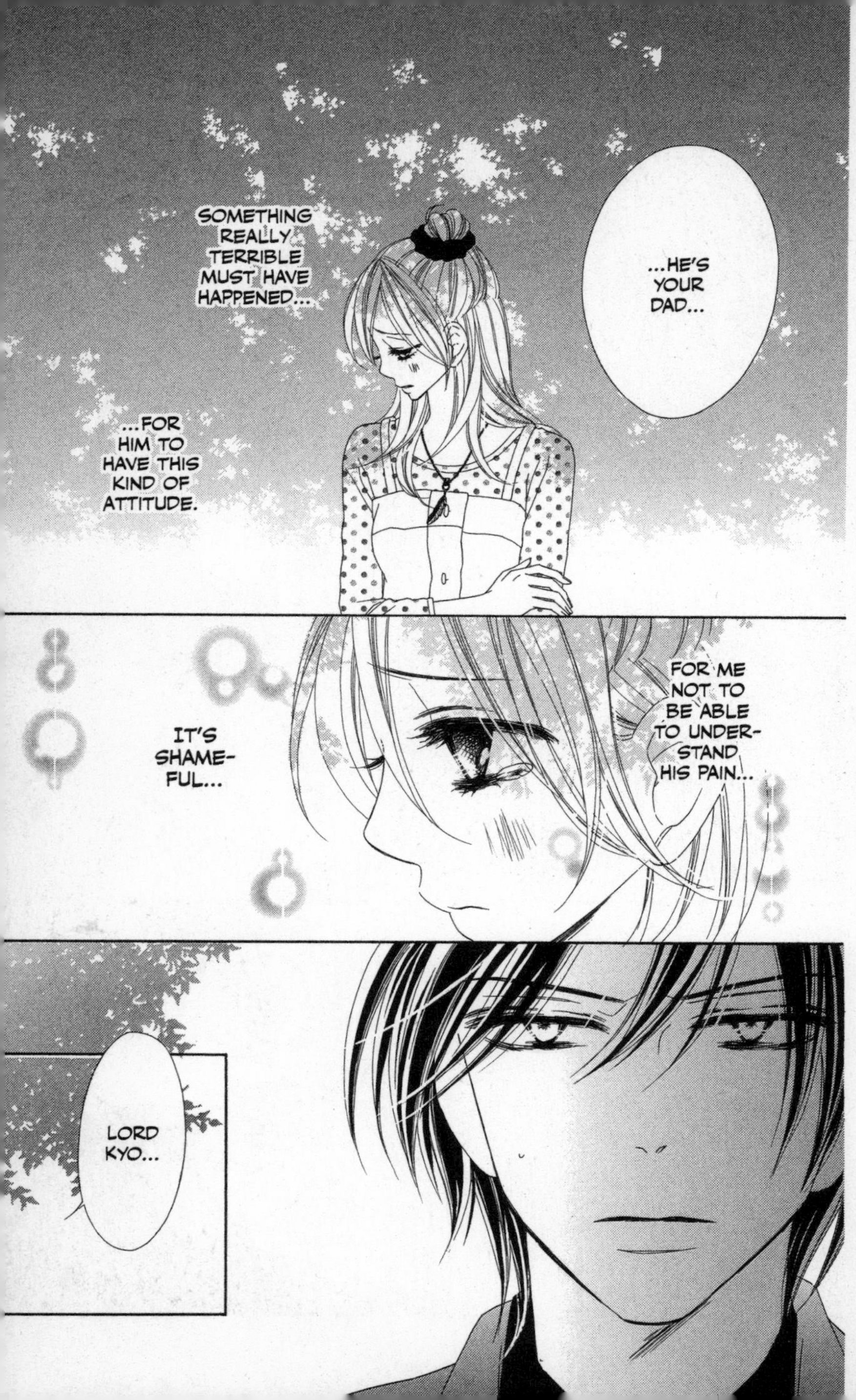
...HE'S YOUR DAD...
SOMETHING REALLY TERRIBLE MUST HAVE HAPPENED...
...FOR HIM TO HAVE THIS KIND OF ATTITUDE.
FOR ME NOT TO BE ABLE TO UNDER-STAND HIS PAIN...
IT'S SHAME-FUL...
LORD KYO...

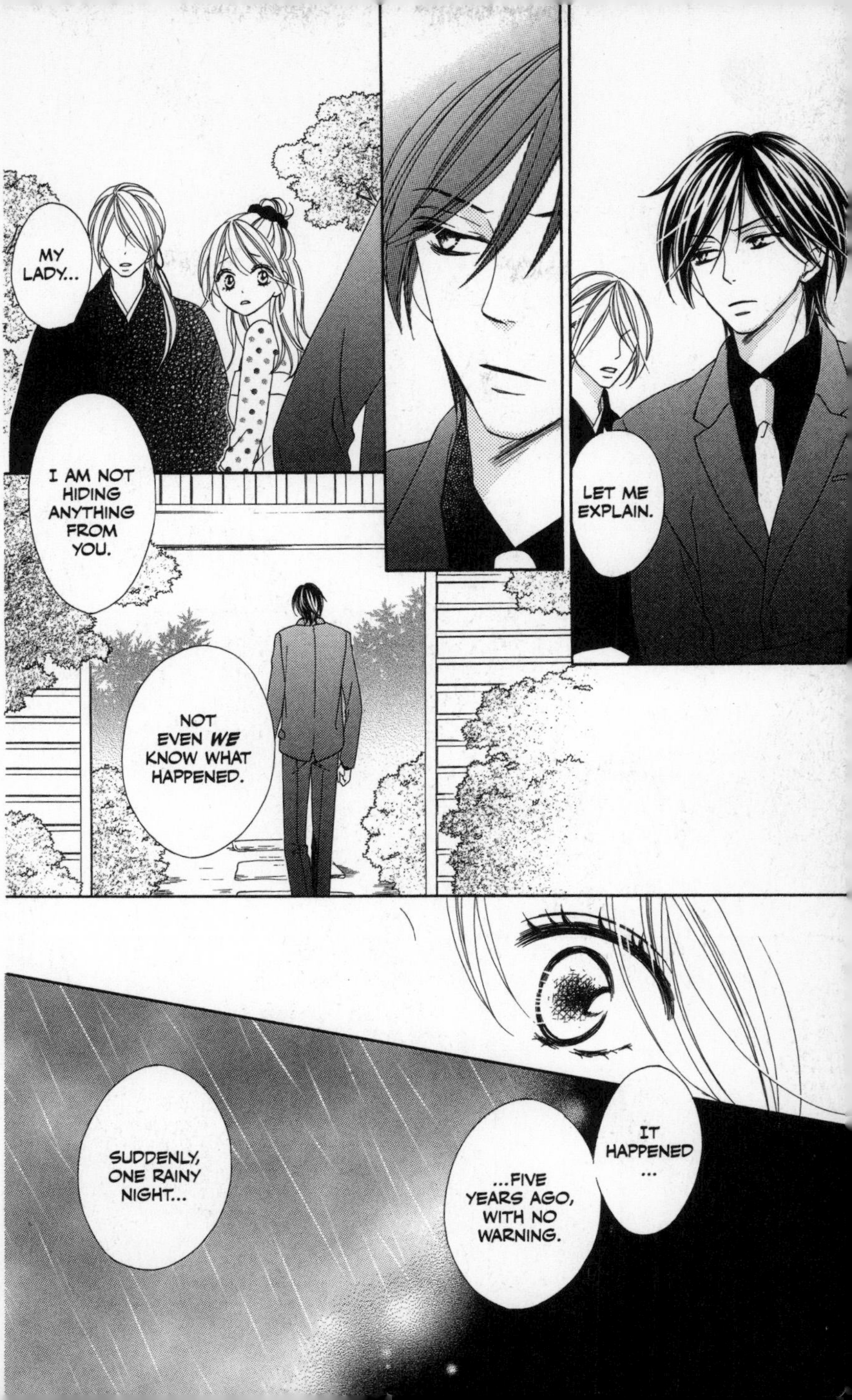
LET ME EXPLAIN.
MY LADY...
I AM NOT HIDING ANYTHING FROM YOU.
NOT EVEN *WE* KNOW WHAT HAPPENED.
IT HAPPENED...
...FIVE YEARS AGO, WITH NO WARNING.
SUDDENLY, ONE RAINY NIGHT...

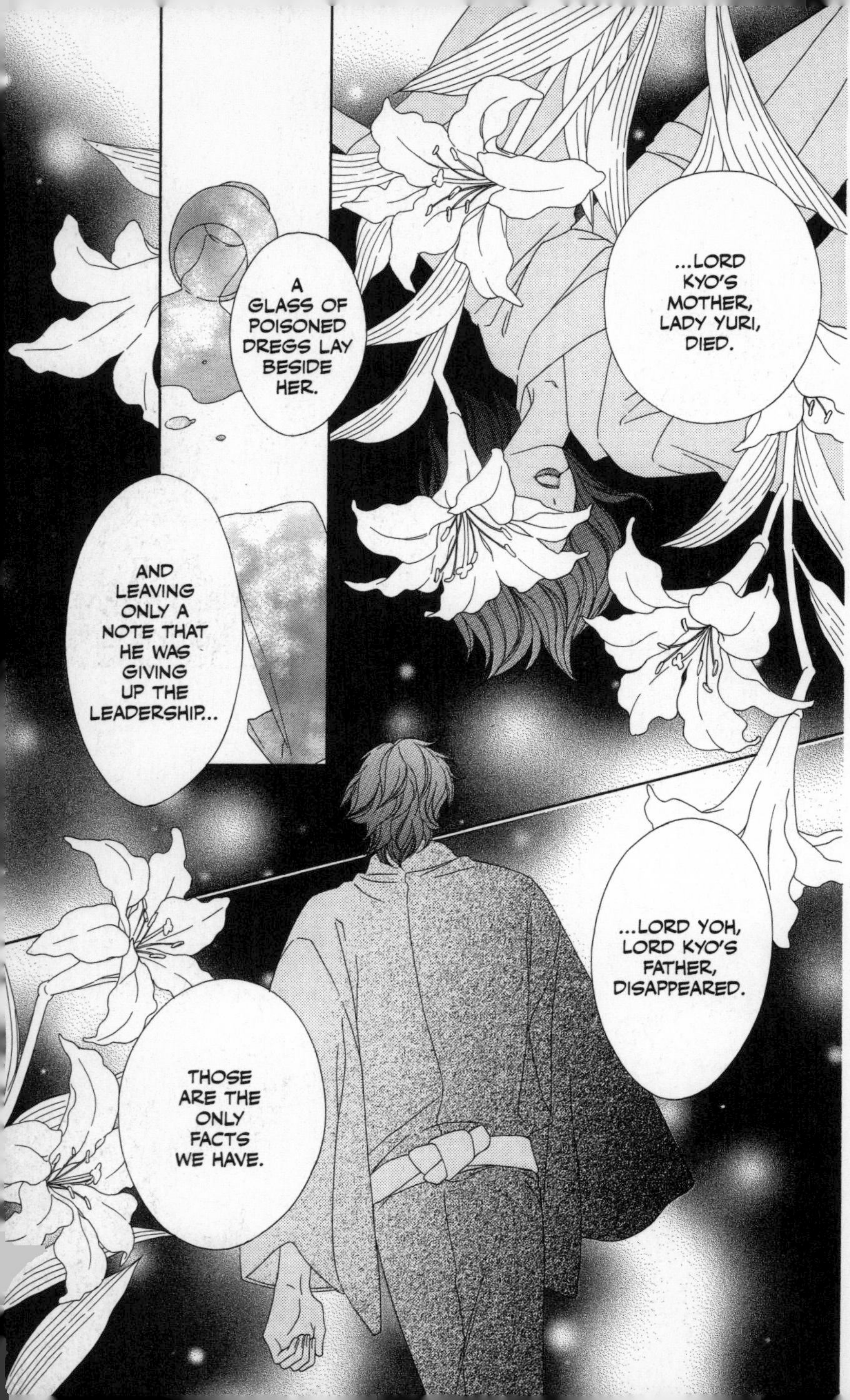
...LORD KYO'S MOTHER, LADY YURI, DIED.
A GLASS OF POISONED DREGS LAY BESIDE HER.
AND LEAVING ONLY A NOTE THAT HE WAS GIVING UP THE LEADERSHIP...
...LORD YOH, LORD KYO'S FATHER, DISAPPEARED.
THOSE ARE THE ONLY FACTS WE HAVE.

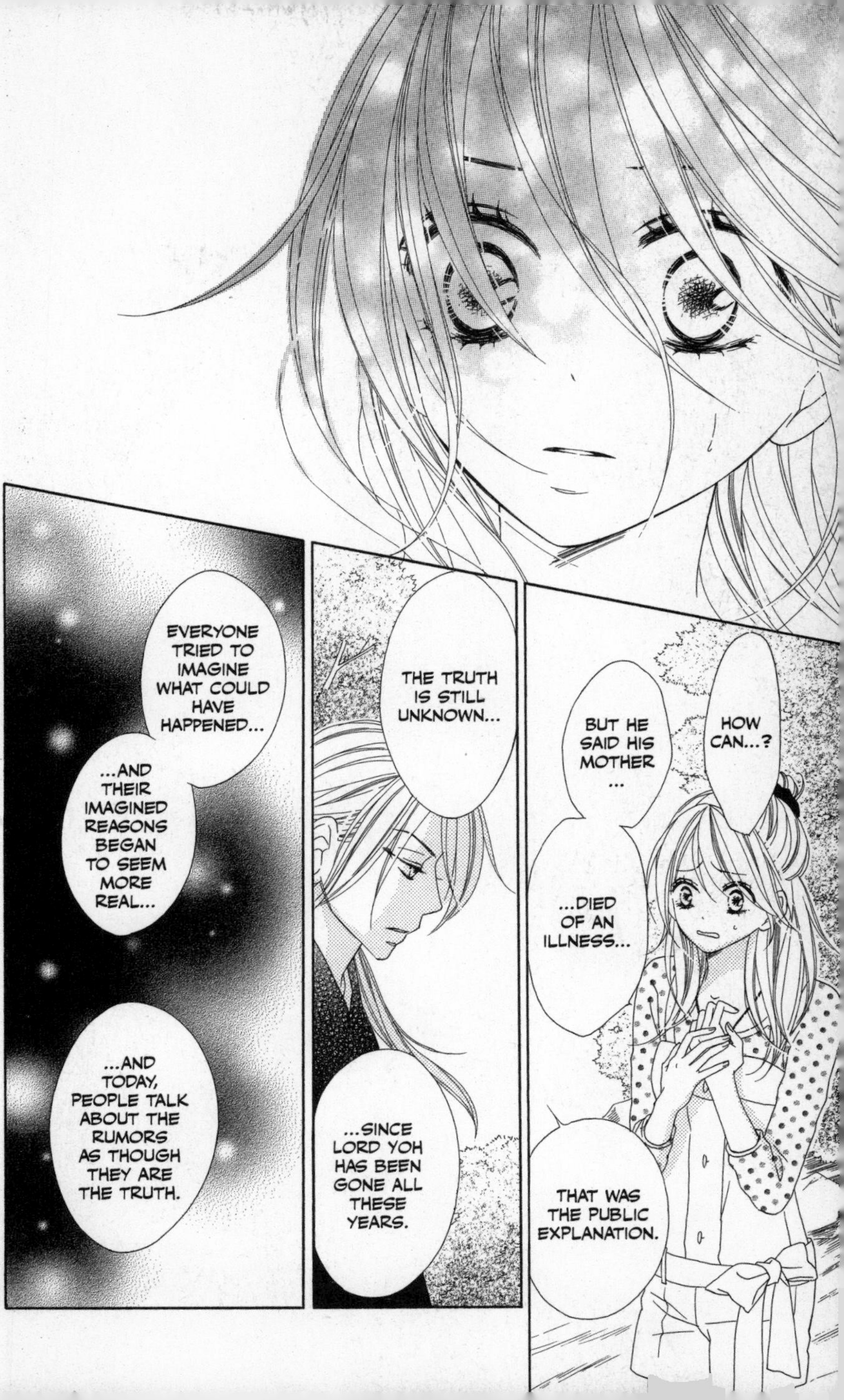
HOW CAN...?
BUT HE SAID HIS MOTHER ...
...DIED OF AN ILLNESS...
THAT WAS THE PUBLIC EXPLANATION.
THE TRUTH IS STILL UNKNOWN...
...SINCE LORD YOH HAS BEEN GONE ALL THESE YEARS.
EVERYONE TRIED TO IMAGINE WHAT COULD HAVE HAPPENED...
...AND THEIR IMAGINED REASONS BEGAN TO SEEM MORE REAL...
...AND TODAY, PEOPLE TALK ABOUT THE RUMORS AS THOUGH THEY ARE THE TRUTH.

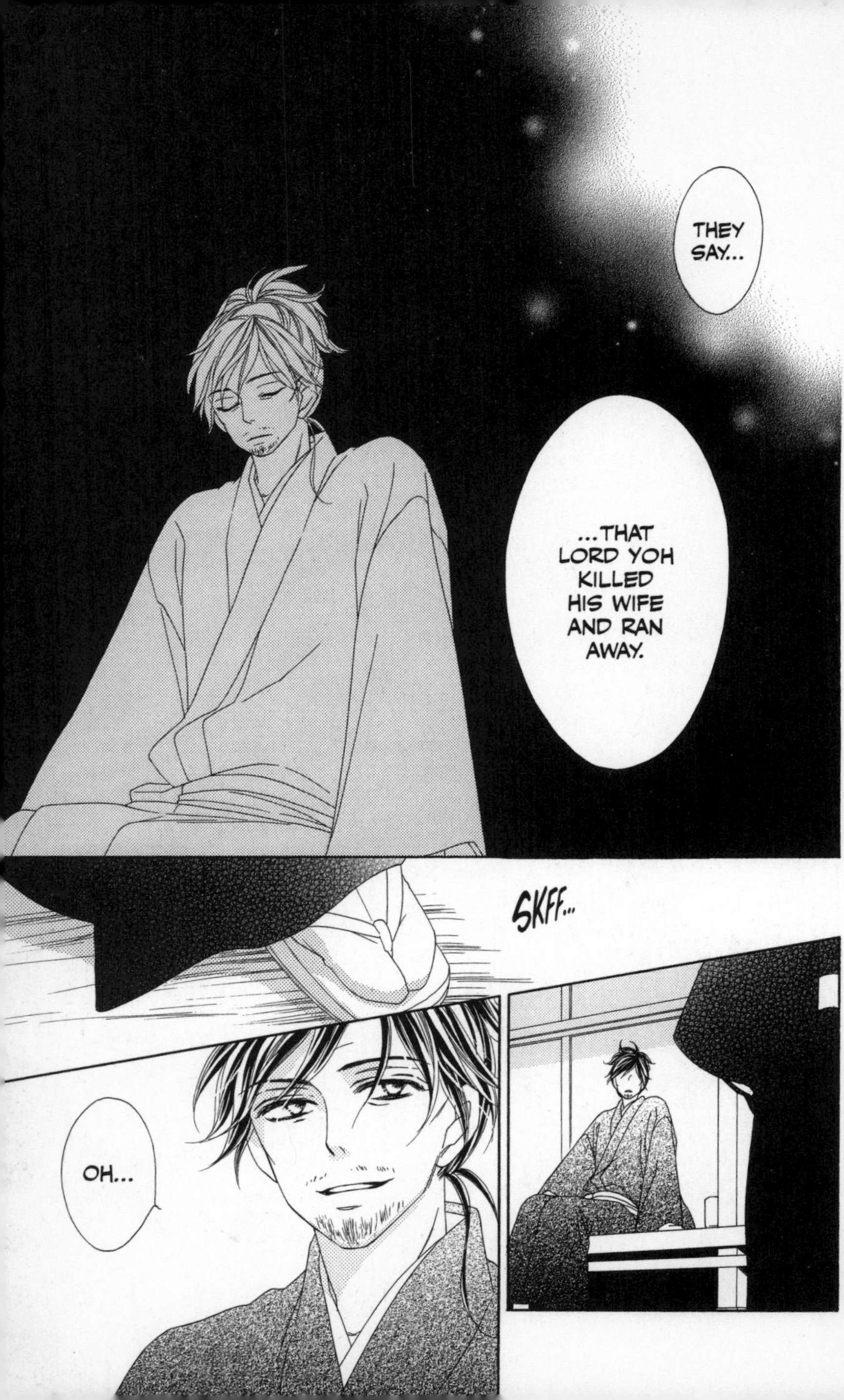
THEY SAY...
...THAT LORD YOH KILLED HIS WIFE AND RAN AWAY.
SKFF...
OH...

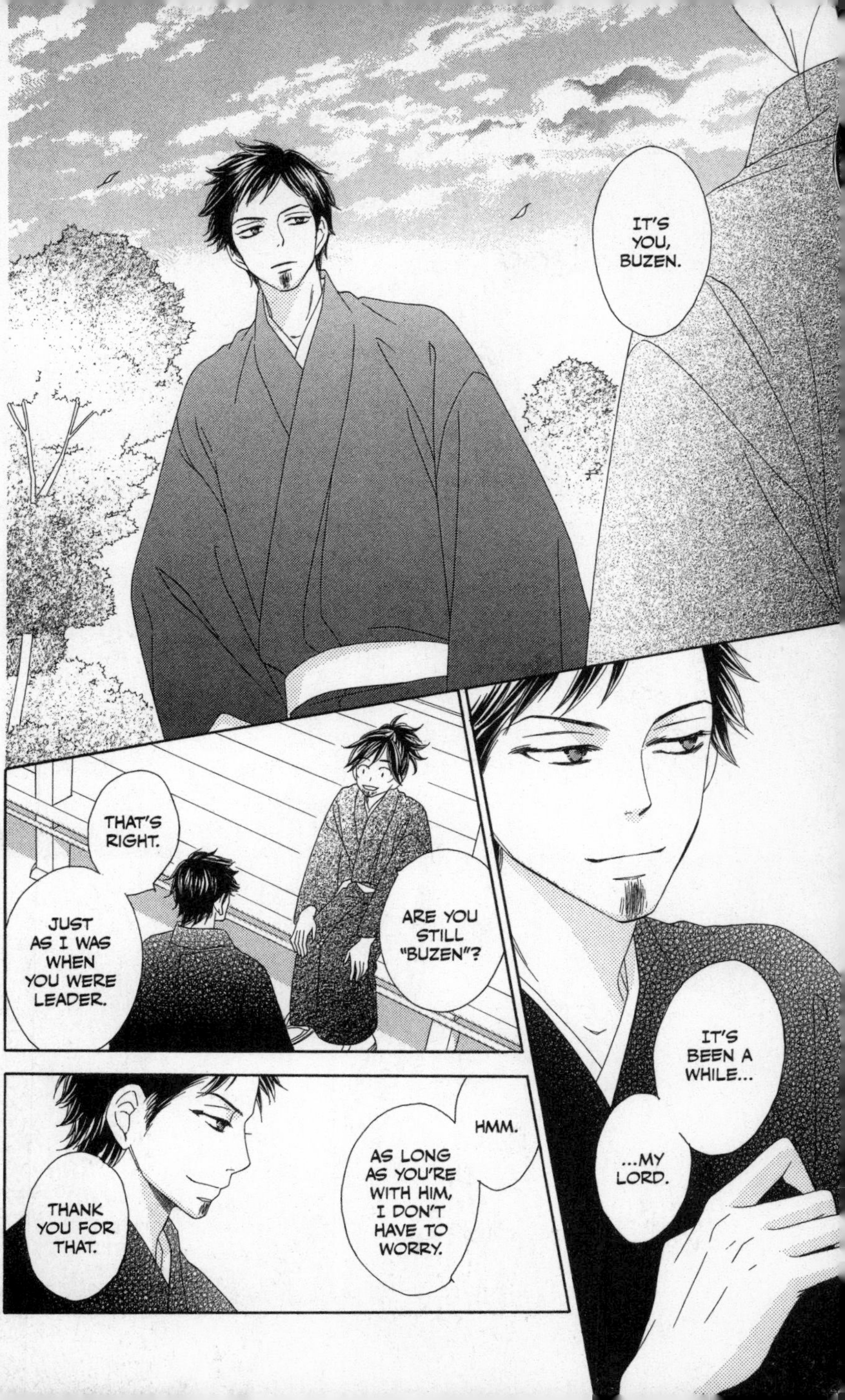
IT'S YOU, BUZEN.
IT'S BEEN A WHILE...
...MY LORD.
ARE YOU STILL "BUZEN"?
THAT'S RIGHT.
JUST AS I WAS WHEN YOU WERE LEADER.
HMM.
AS LONG AS YOU'RE WITH HIM, I DON'T HAVE TO WORRY.
THANK YOU FOR THAT.

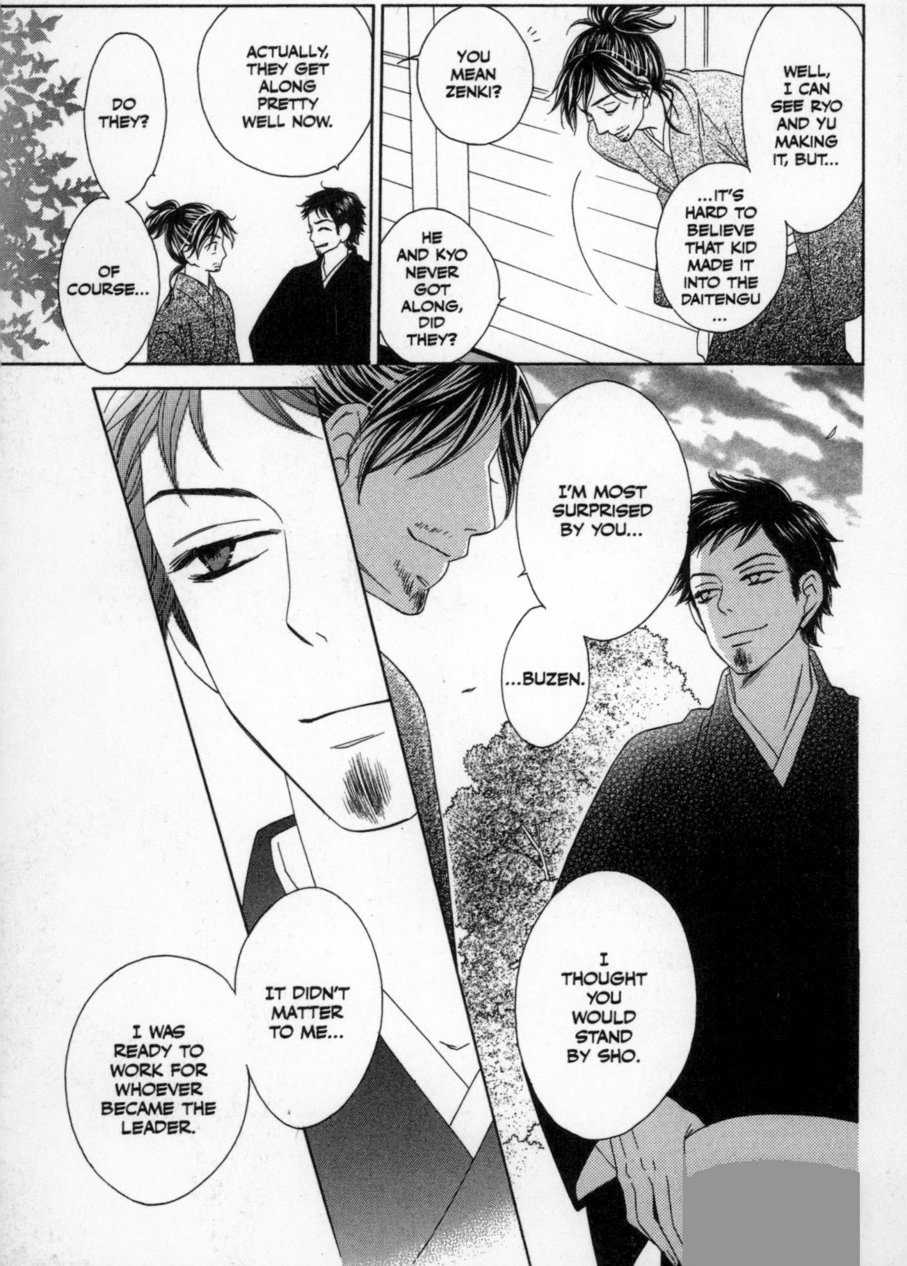
WELL, I CAN SEE RYO AND YU MAKING IT, BUT...
...IT'S HARD TO BELIEVE THAT KID MADE IT INTO THE DAITENGU...
YOU MEAN ZENKI?
HE AND KYO NEVER GOT ALONG, DID THEY?
ACTUALLY, THEY GET ALONG PRETTY WELL NOW.
DO THEY?
OF COURSE...
I'M MOST SURPRISED BY YOU...
...BUZEN.
I THOUGHT YOU WOULD STAND BY SHO.
IT DIDN'T MATTER TO ME...
I WAS READY TO WORK FOR WHOEVER BECAME THE LEADER.

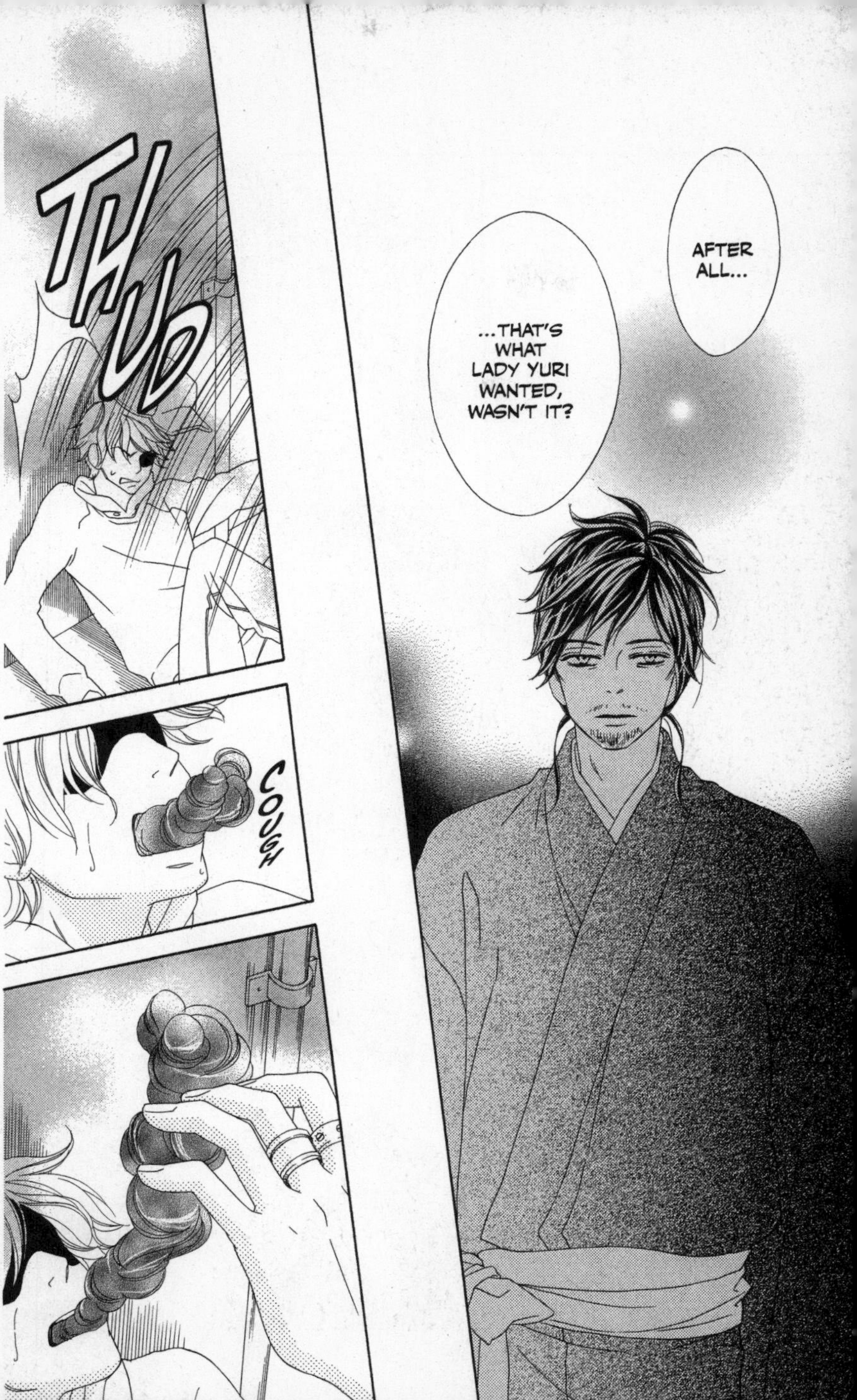
AFTER ALL...
...THAT'S WHAT LADY YURI WANTED, WASN'T IT?
THUD
COUGH

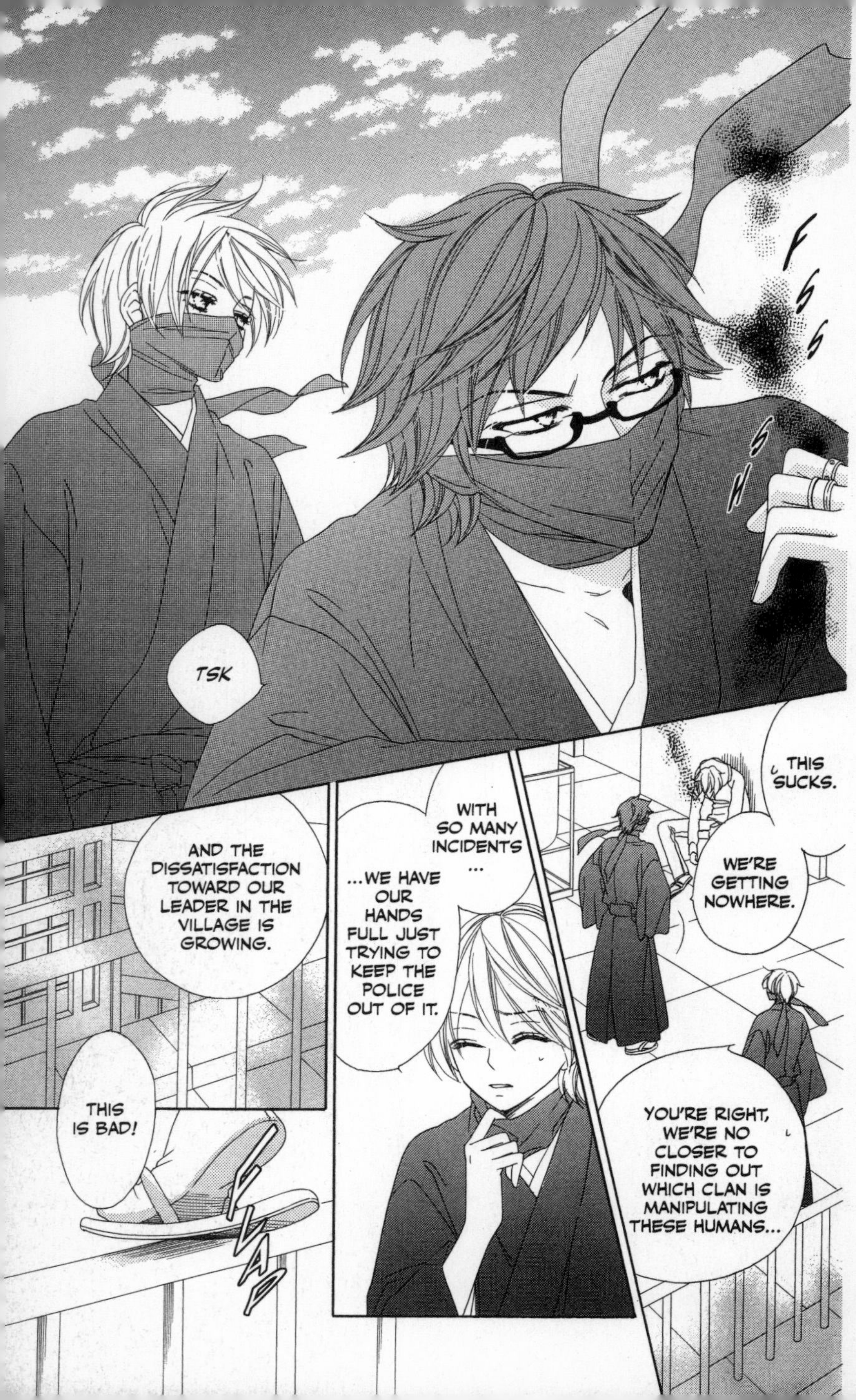
FSSSH
TSK
THIS SUCKS.
WE'RE GETTING NOWHERE.
YOU'RE RIGHT, WE'RE NO CLOSER TO FINDING OUT WHICH CLAN IS MANIPULATING THESE HUMANS...
WITH SO MANY INCIDENTS...
...WE HAVE OUR HANDS FULL JUST TRYING TO KEEP THE POLICE OUT OF IT.
AND THE DISSATISFACTION TOWARD OUR LEADER IN THE VILLAGE IS GROWING.
THIS IS BAD!
FWAP

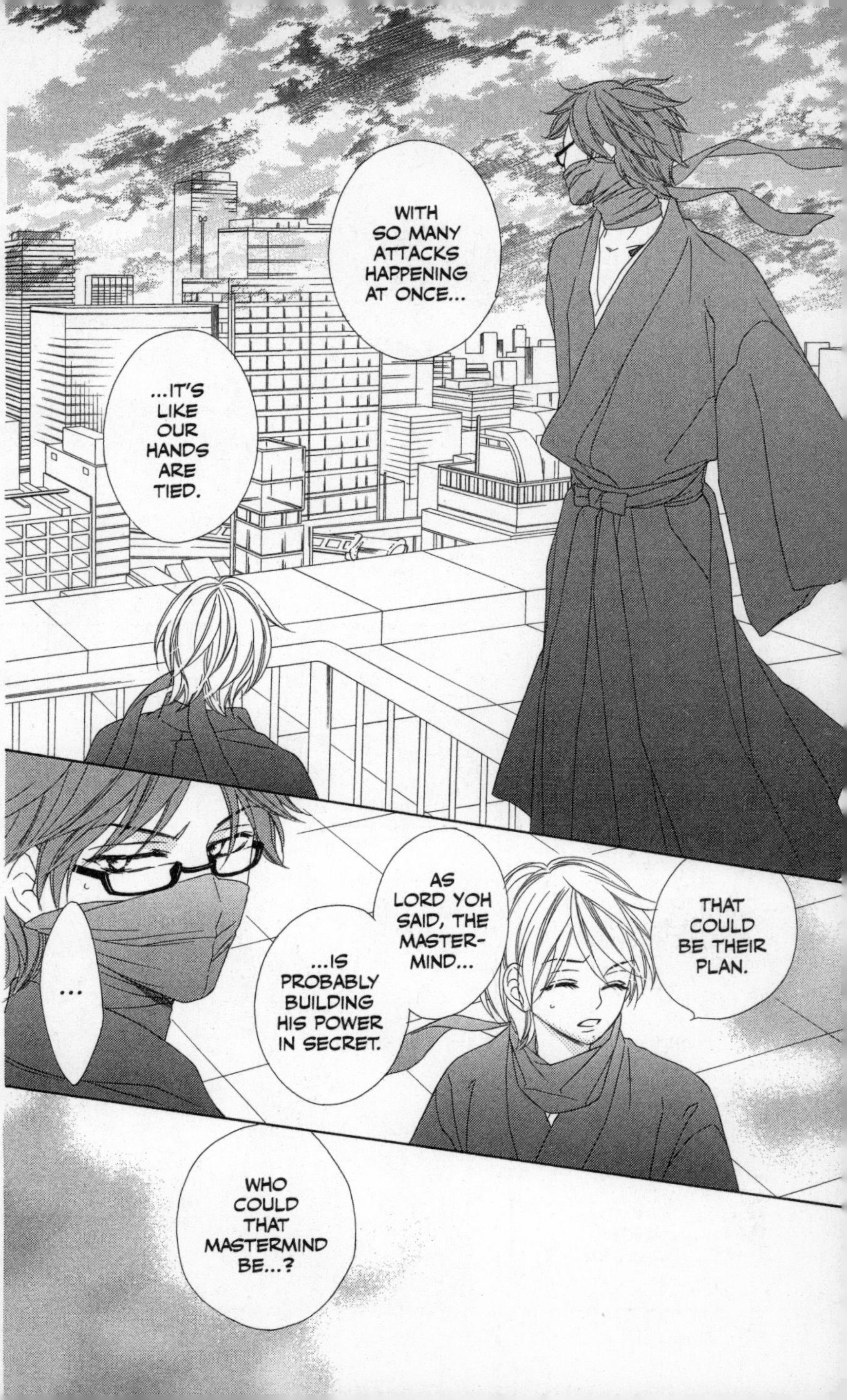
WITH SO MANY ATTACKS HAPPENING AT ONCE...
...IT'S LIKE OUR HANDS ARE TIED.
THAT COULD BE THEIR PLAN.
AS LORD YOH SAID, THE MASTER-MIND...
...IS PROBABLY BUILDING HIS POWER IN SECRET.
...
WHO COULD THAT MASTERMIND BE...?

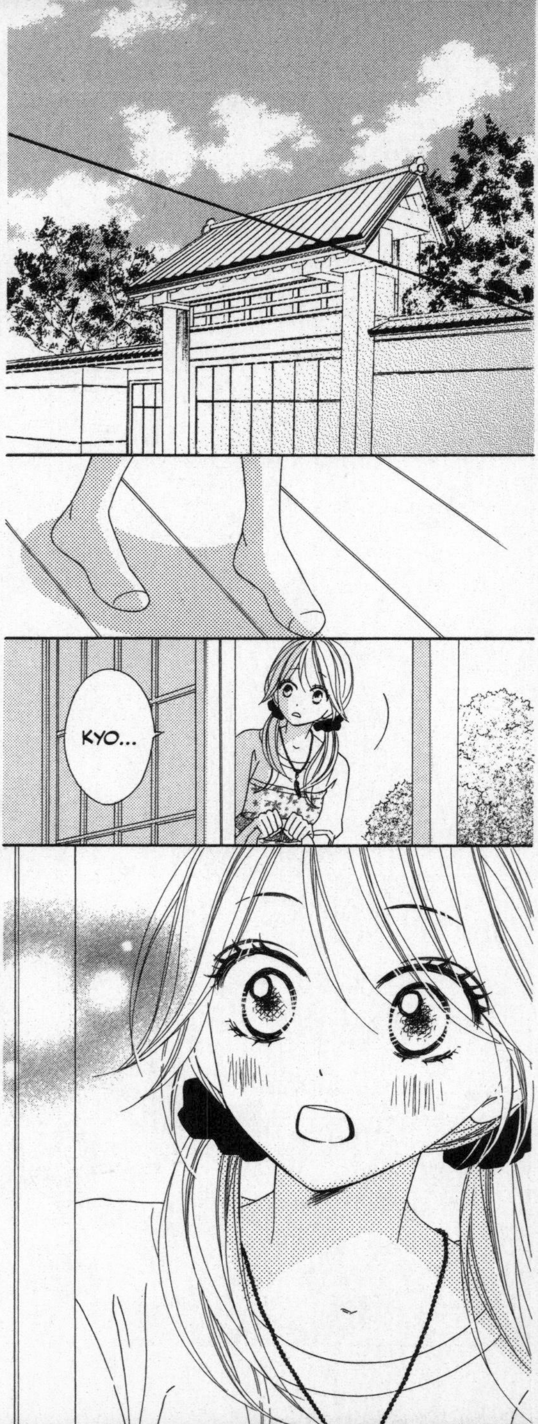
KYO...

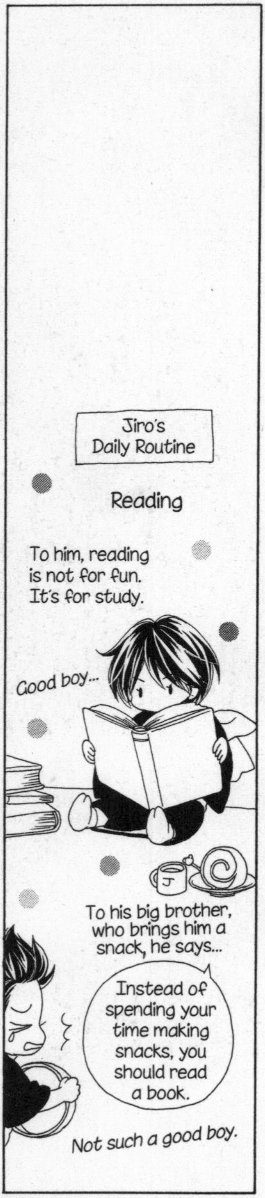
Jiro's
Daily Routine
Reading
To him, reading is not for fun. It's for study.
Good boy...
To his big brother, who brings him a snack, he says...
Instead of spending your time making snacks, you should read a book.
Not such a good boy.

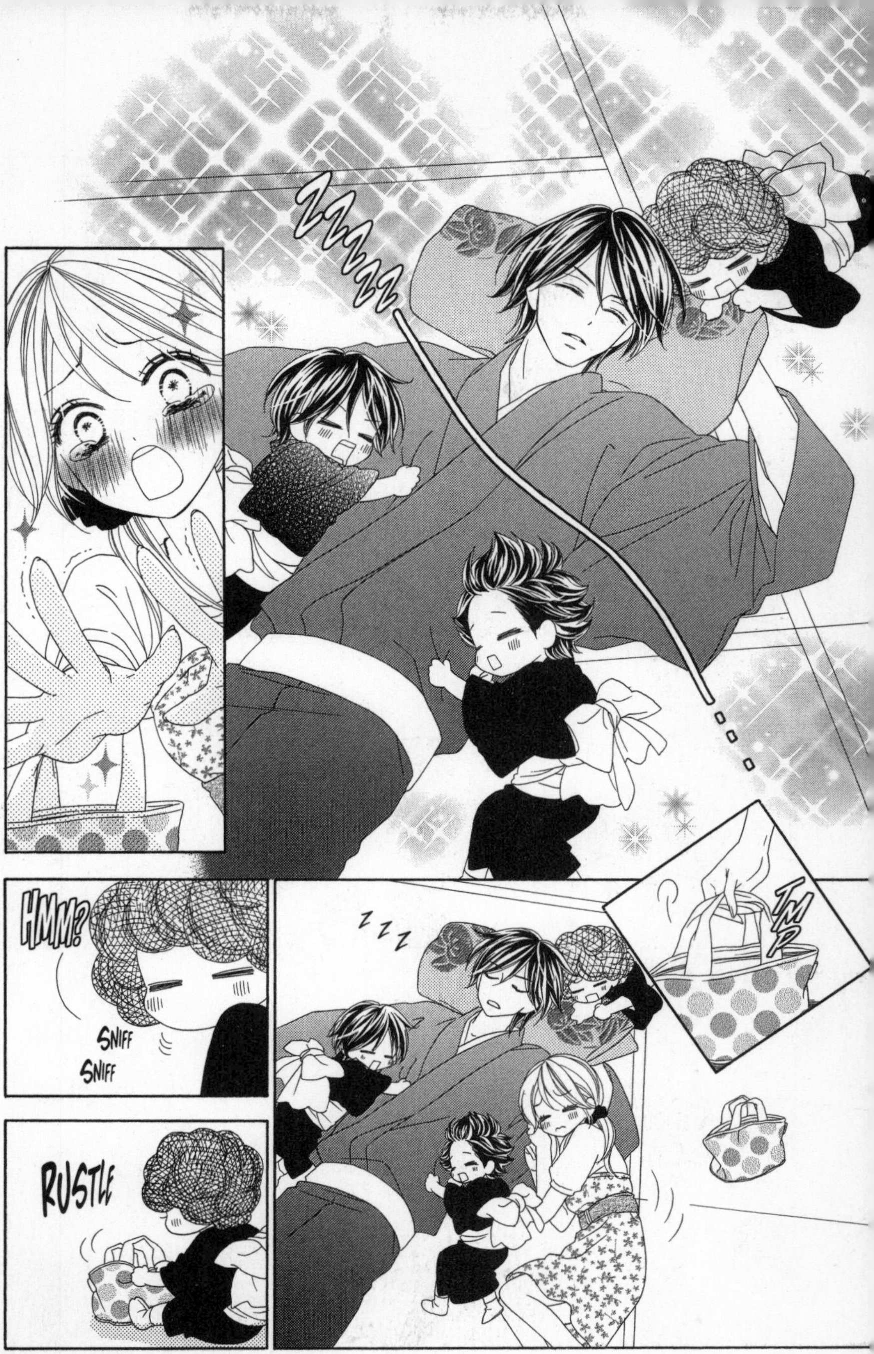
ZZZZZ
...
TMP
ZZZ
HMM?
SNIFF
SNIFF
RUSTLE

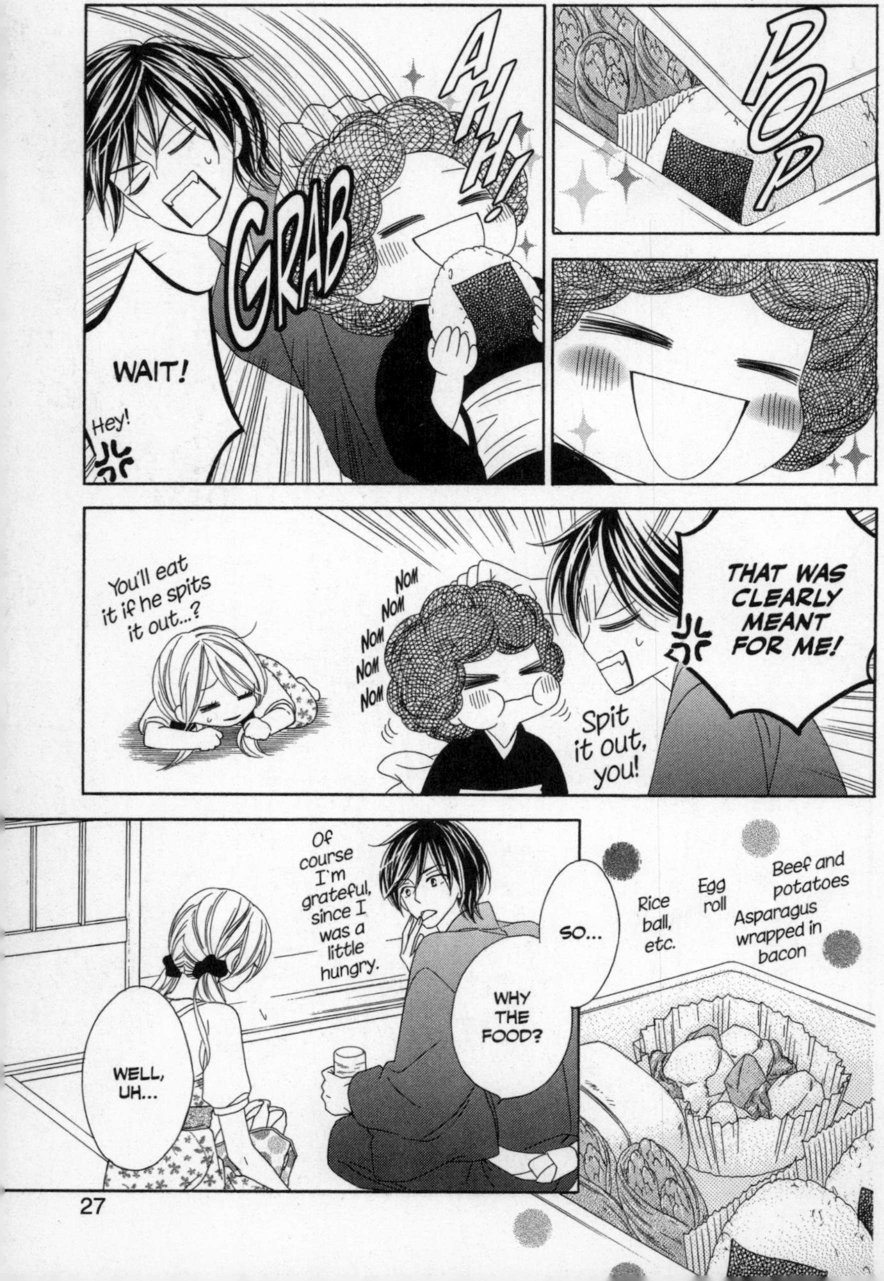

POP
AHH!
GRAB
WAIT!
Hey!
THAT WAS CLEARLY MEANT FOR ME!
Spit it out, you!
NOM NOM NOM NOM NOM NOM
You'll eat it if he spits it out...?
Beef and potatoes
Asparagus wrapped in bacon
Egg roll
Rice ball, etc.
SO...
WHY THE FOOD?
Of course I'm grateful, since I was a little hungry.
WELL, UH...

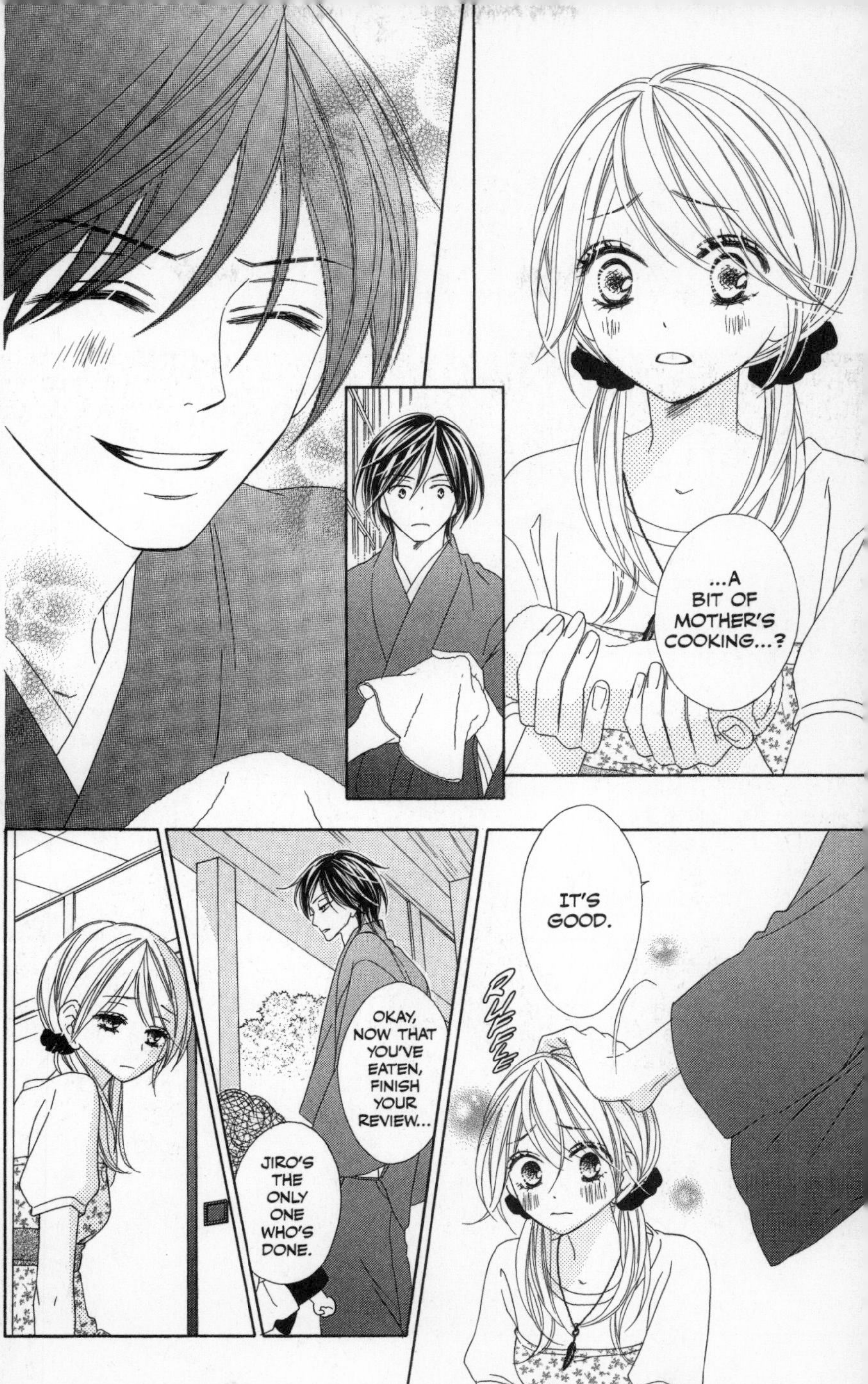
...A BIT OF MOTHER'S COOKING...?
IT'S GOOD.
RUFFLE
OKAY, NOW THAT YOU'VE EATEN, FINISH YOUR REVIEW...
JIRO'S THE ONLY ONE WHO'S DONE.

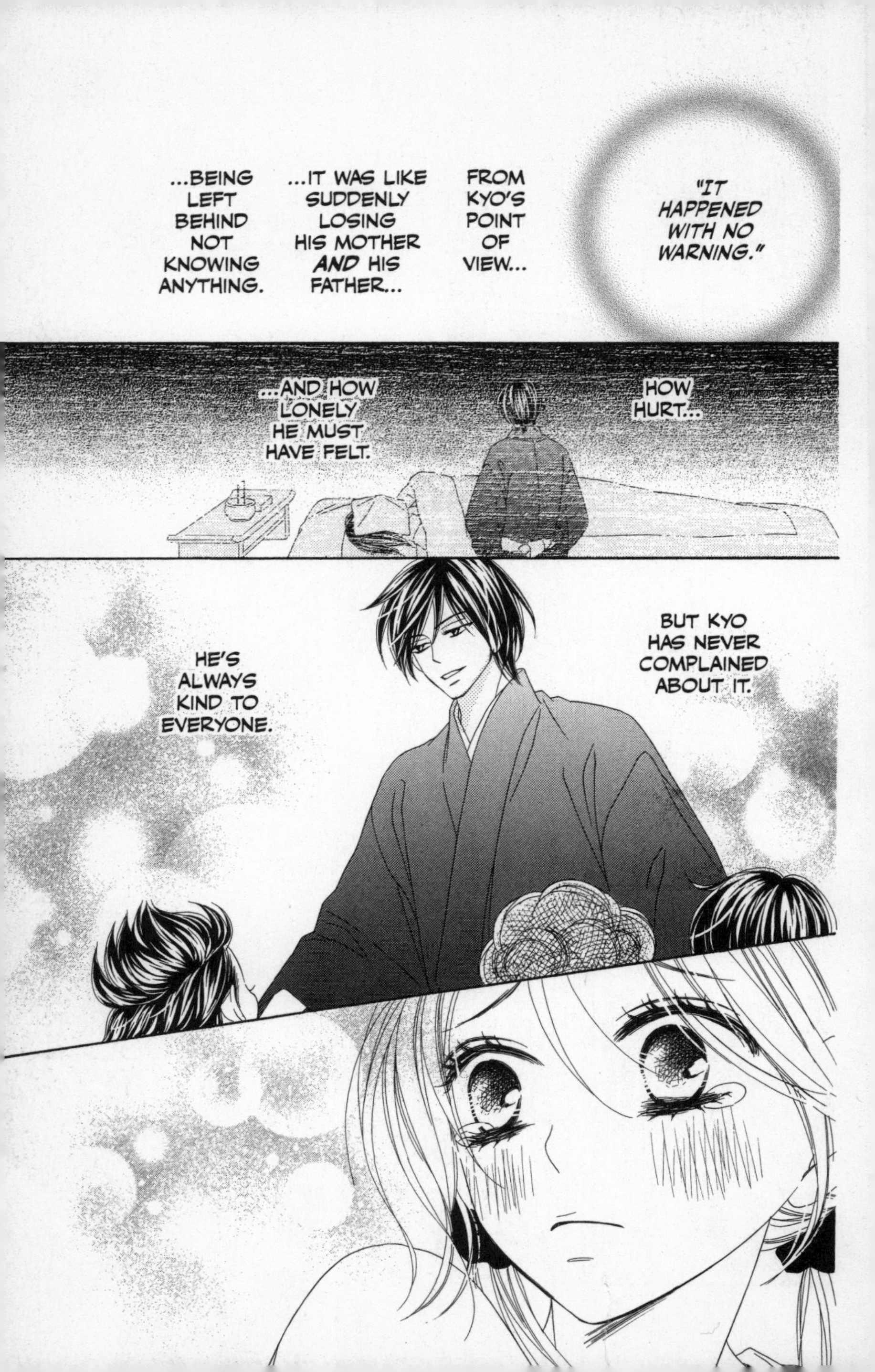
"IT HAPPENED WITH NO WARNING."
FROM KYO'S POINT OF VIEW...
...IT WAS LIKE SUDDENLY LOSING HIS MOTHER *AND* HIS FATHER...
...BEING LEFT BEHIND NOT KNOWING ANYTHING.
HOW HURT...
...AND HOW LONELY HE MUST HAVE FELT.
BUT KYO HAS NEVER COMPLAINED ABOUT IT.
HE'S ALWAYS KIND TO EVERYONE.

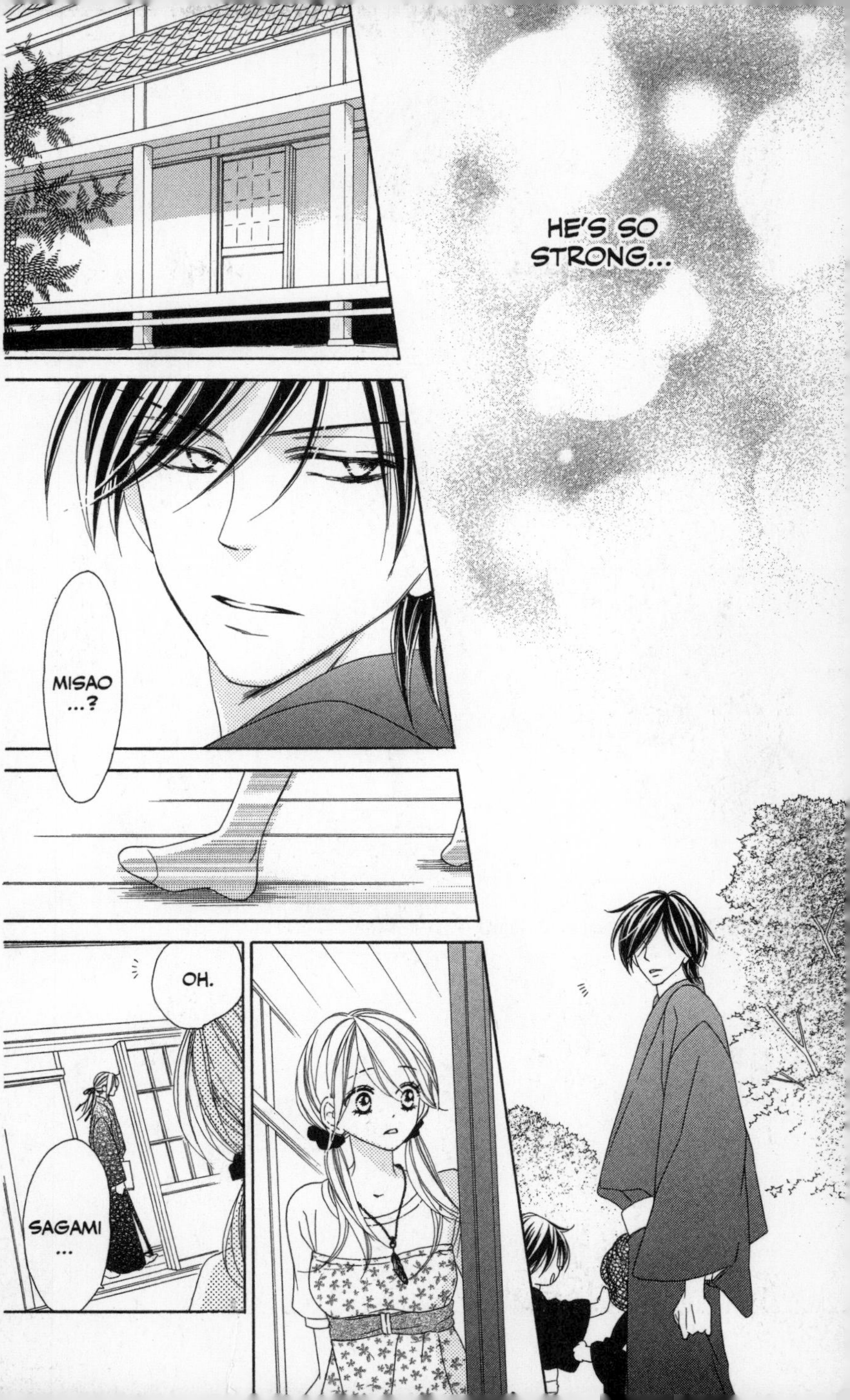
HE'S SO STRONG...
MISAO ...?
OH.
SAGAMI ...

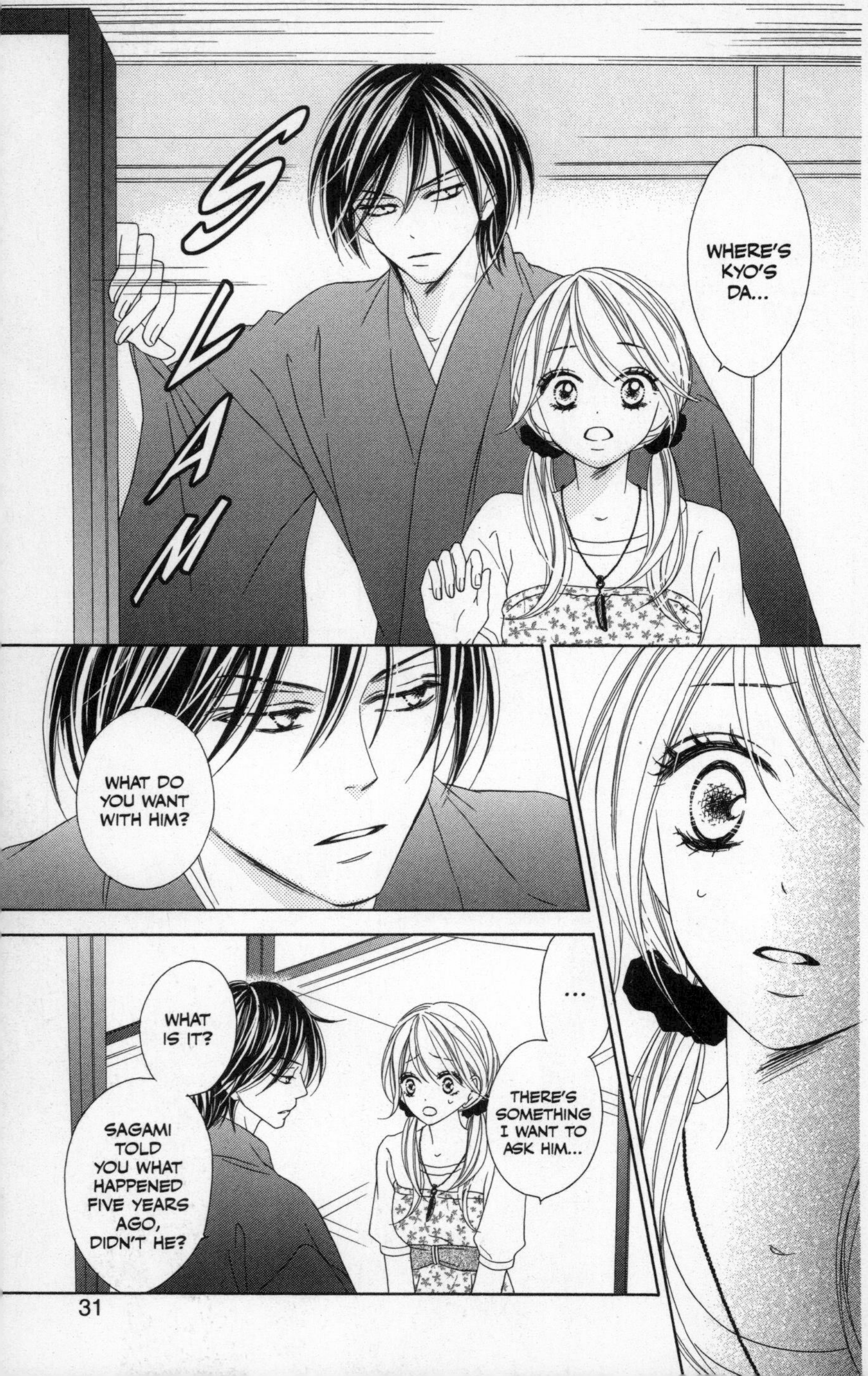
WHERE'S KYO'S DA...
SLAM
WHAT DO YOU WANT WITH HIM?
...
THERE'S SOMETHING I WANT TO ASK HIM...
WHAT IS IT?
SAGAMI TOLD YOU WHAT HAPPENED FIVE YEARS AGO, DIDN'T HE?

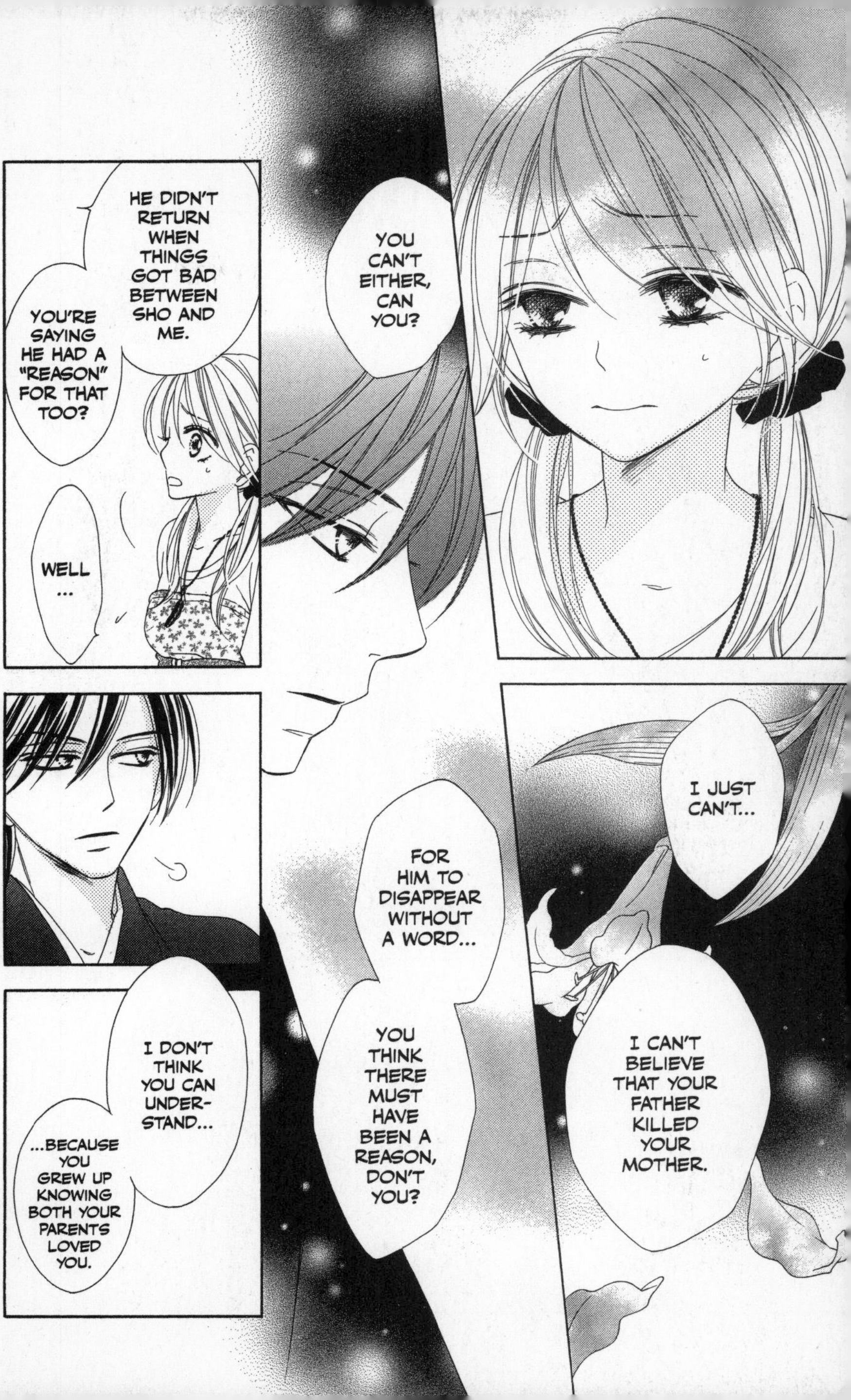
YOU CAN'T EITHER, CAN YOU?
I JUST CAN'T...
I CAN'T BELIEVE THAT YOUR FATHER KILLED YOUR MOTHER.
FOR HIM TO DISAPPEAR WITHOUT A WORD...
YOU THINK THERE MUST HAVE BEEN A REASON, DON'T YOU?
HE DIDN'T RETURN WHEN THINGS GOT BAD BETWEEN SHO AND ME.
YOU'RE SAYING HE HAD A "REASON" FOR THAT TOO?
WELL...
I DON'T THINK YOU CAN UNDER-STAND...
...BECAUSE YOU GREW UP KNOWING BOTH YOUR PARENTS LOVED YOU.

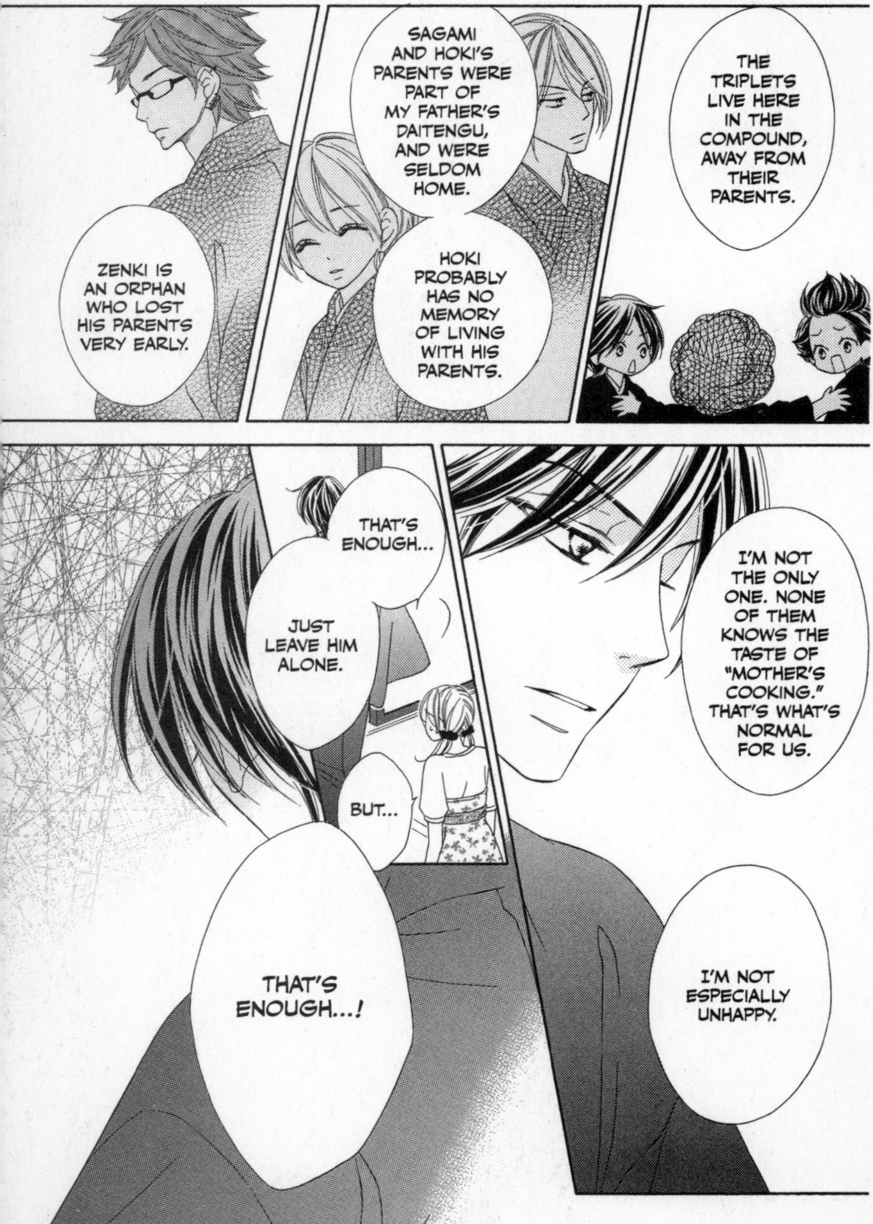
THE TRIPLETS LIVE HERE IN THE COMPOUND, AWAY FROM THEIR PARENTS.
SAGAMI AND HOKI'S PARENTS WERE PART OF MY FATHER'S DAITENGU, AND WERE SELDOM HOME.
HOKI PROBABLY HAS NO MEMORY OF LIVING WITH HIS PARENTS.
ZENKI IS AN ORPHAN WHO LOST HIS PARENTS VERY EARLY.
I'M NOT THE ONLY ONE. NONE OF THEM KNOWS THE TASTE OF "MOTHER'S COOKING." THAT'S WHAT'S NORMAL FOR US.
I'M NOT ESPECIALLY UNHAPPY.
THAT'S ENOUGH...
JUST LEAVE HIM ALONE.
BUT...
THAT'S ENOUGH...!

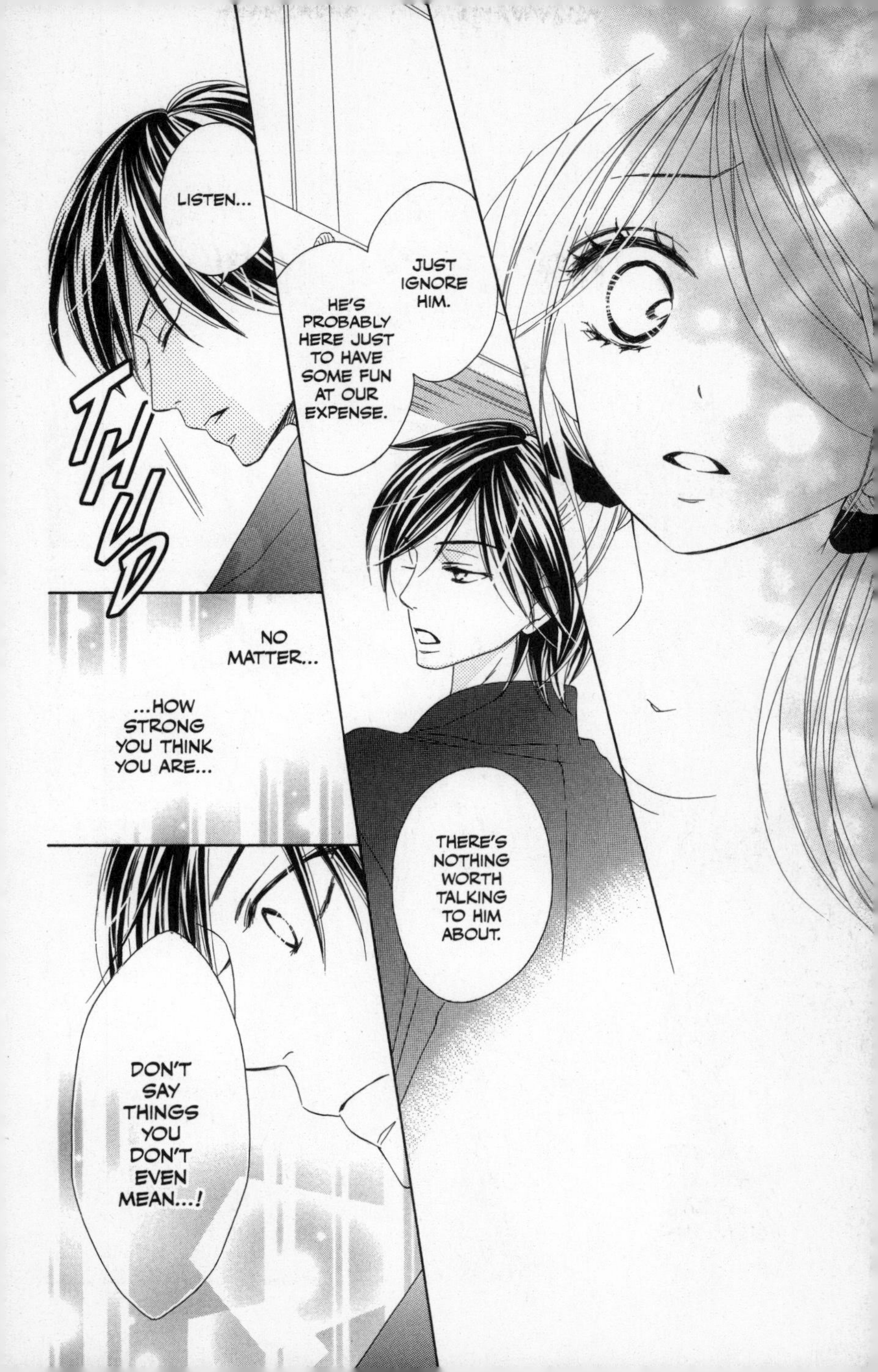
JUST IGNORE HIM.
HE'S PROBABLY HERE JUST TO HAVE SOME FUN AT OUR EXPENSE.
THERE'S NOTHING WORTH TALKING TO HIM ABOUT.
LISTEN...
THUD
NO MATTER...
...HOW STRONG YOU THINK YOU ARE...
DON'T SAY THINGS YOU DON'T EVEN MEAN...!

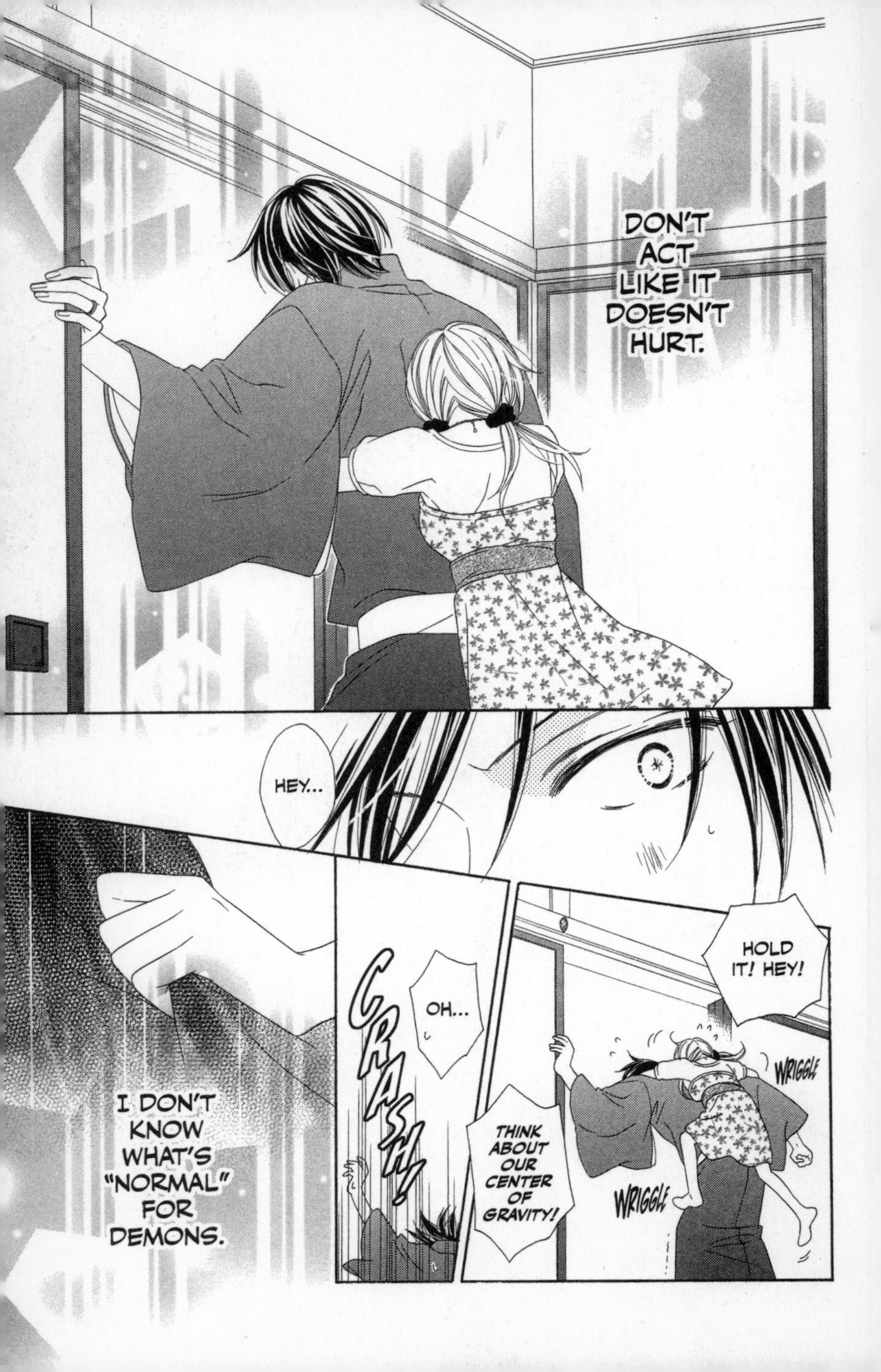
DON'T ACT LIKE IT DOESN'T HURT.
HEY...
HOLD IT! HEY!
WRIGGLE
WRIGGLE
THINK ABOUT OUR CENTER OF GRAVITY!
OH...
CRASH!
I DON'T KNOW WHAT'S "NORMAL" FOR DEMONS.

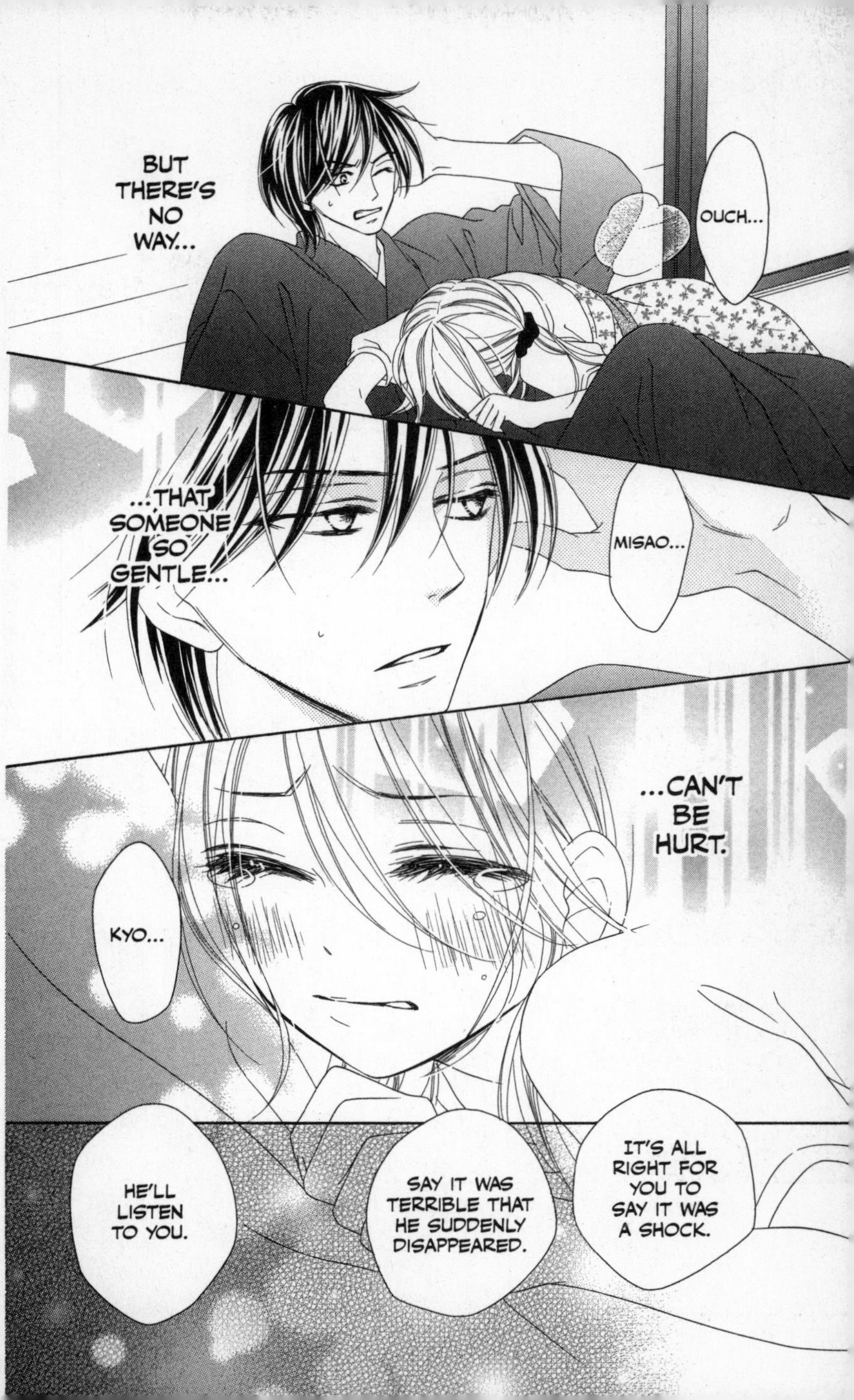
OUCH...
BUT THERE'S NO WAY...
MISAO...
...THAT SOMEONE SO GENTLE...
...CAN'T BE HURT.
KYO...
IT'S ALL RIGHT FOR YOU TO SAY IT WAS A SHOCK.
SAY IT WAS TERRIBLE THAT HE SUDDENLY DISAPPEARED.
HE'LL LISTEN TO YOU.

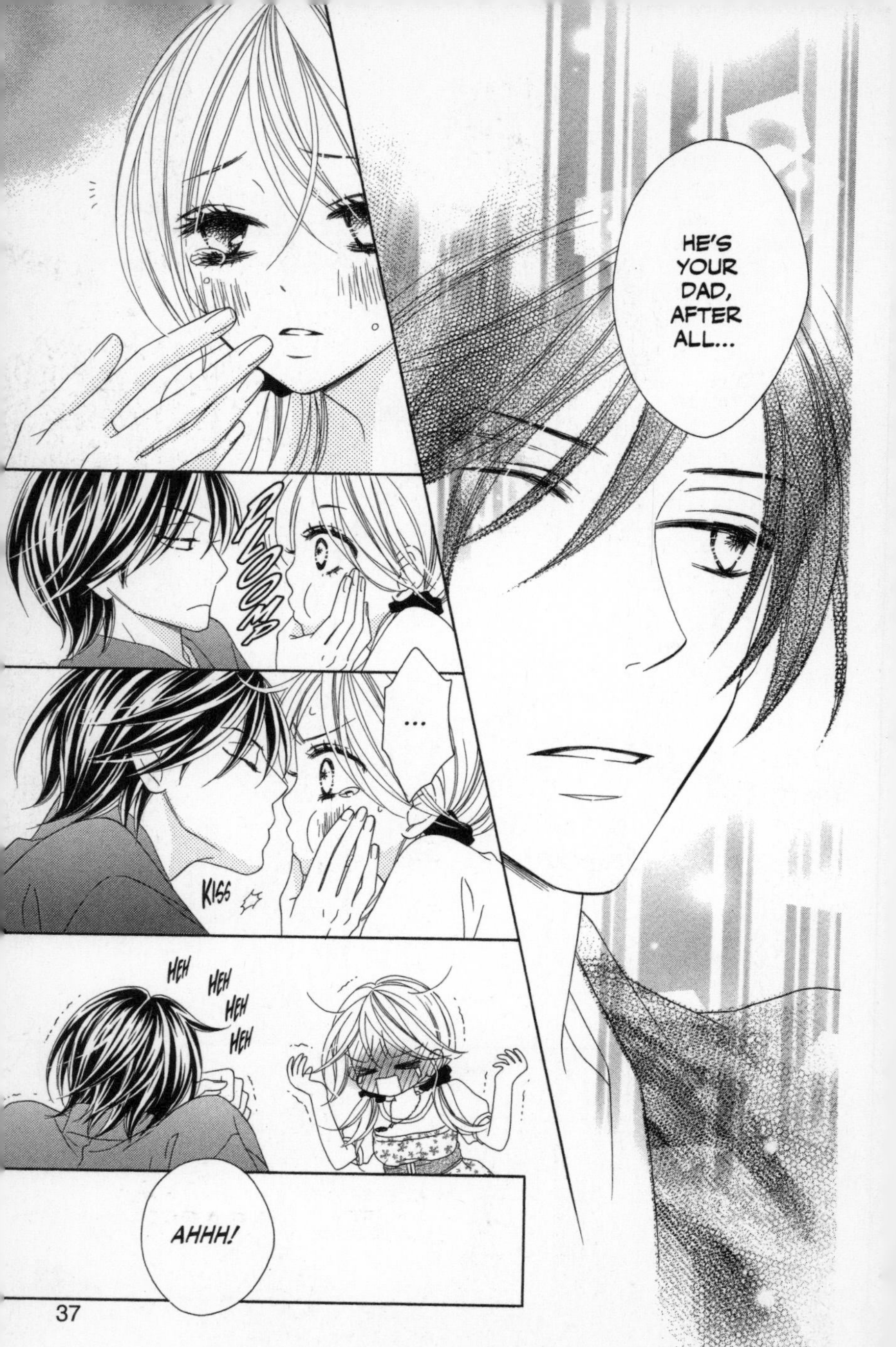
HE'S YOUR DAD, AFTER ALL...
PLOOMP
...
KISS
HEH HEH HEH HEH
AHHH!

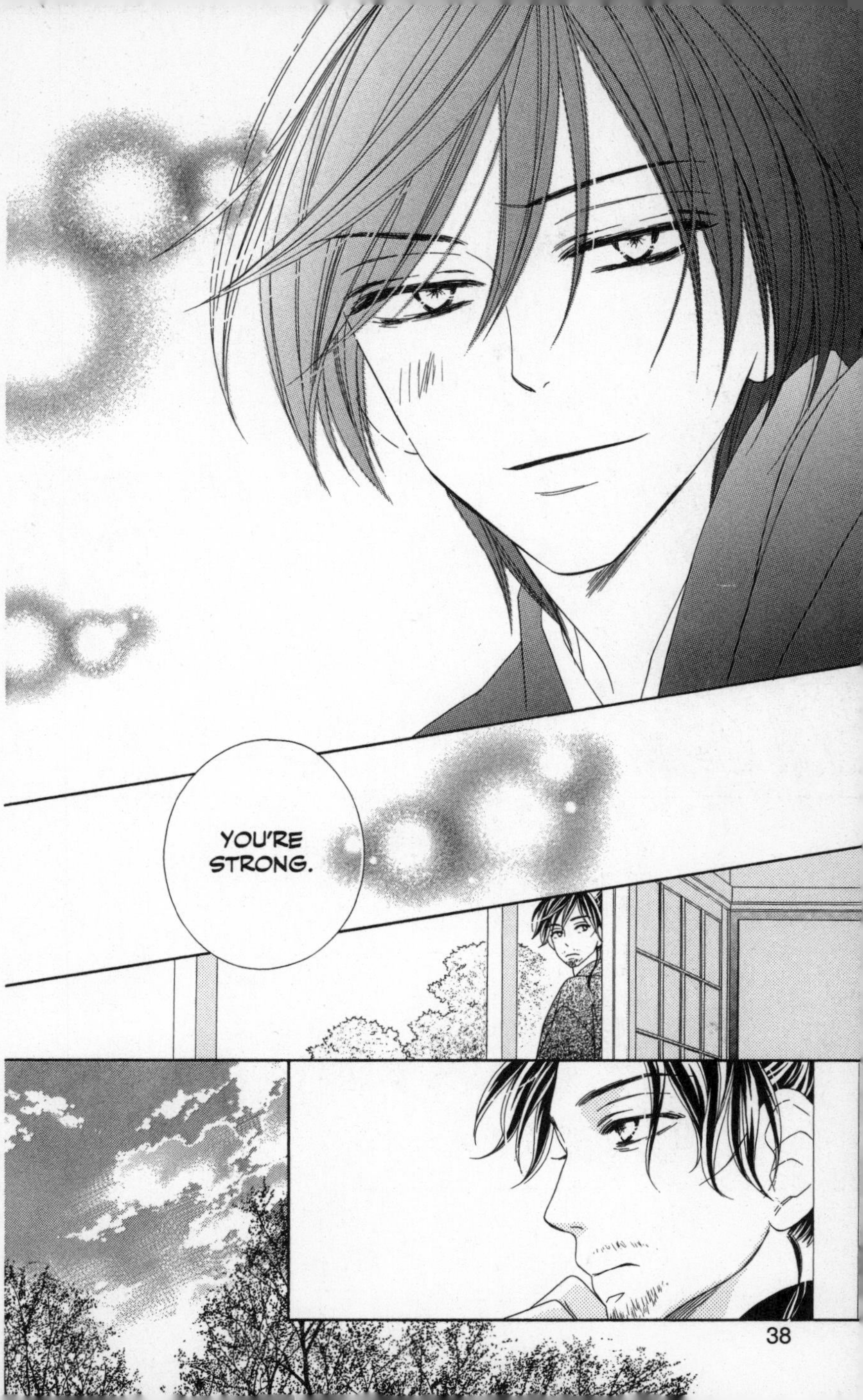
YOU'RE
STRONG.

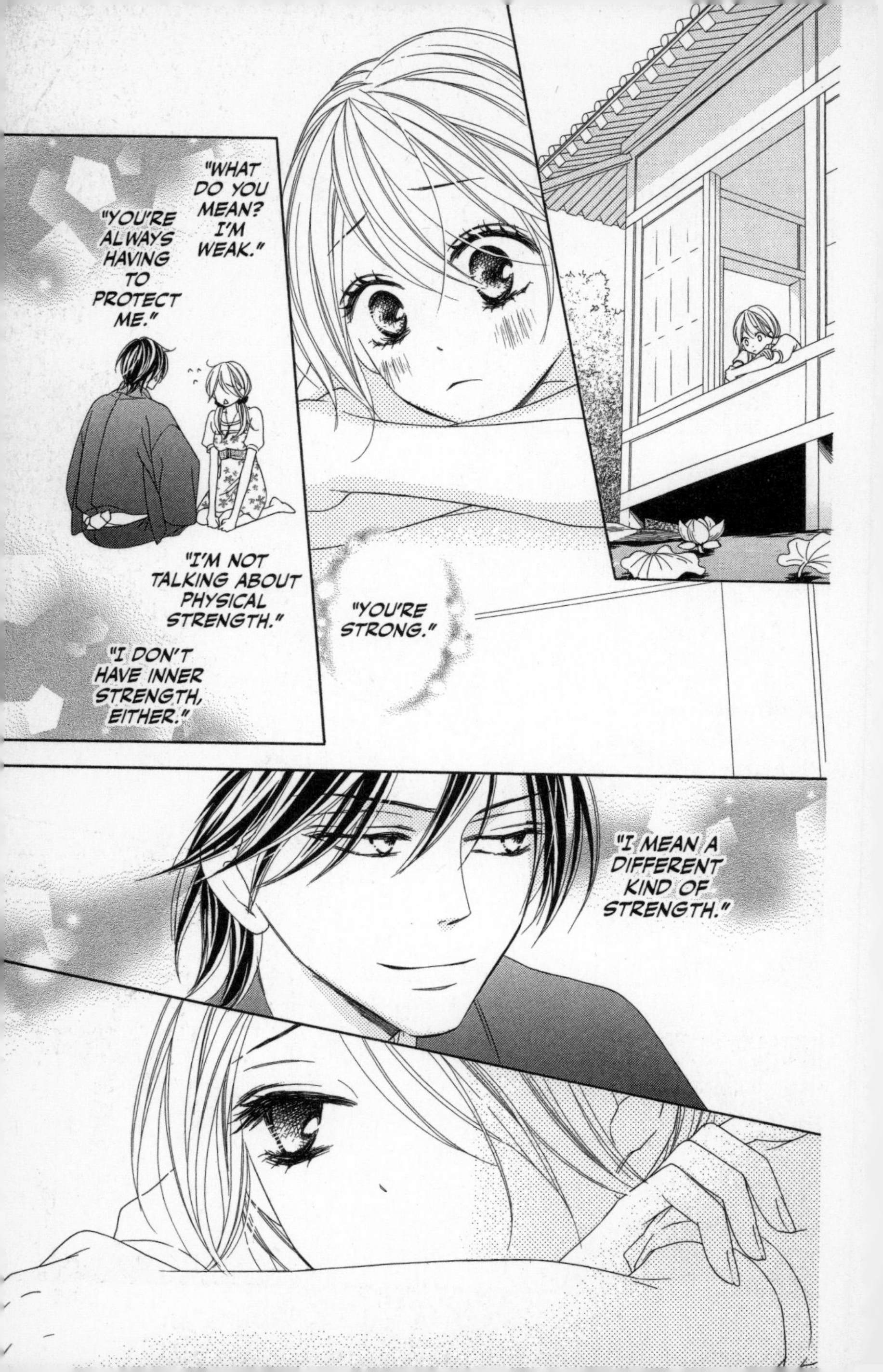
"YOU'RE STRONG."
"WHAT DO YOU MEAN? I'M WEAK."
"YOU'RE ALWAYS HAVING TO PROTECT ME."
"I'M NOT TALKING ABOUT PHYSICAL STRENGTH."
"I DON'T HAVE INNER STRENGTH, EITHER."
"I MEAN A DIFFERENT KIND OF STRENGTH."

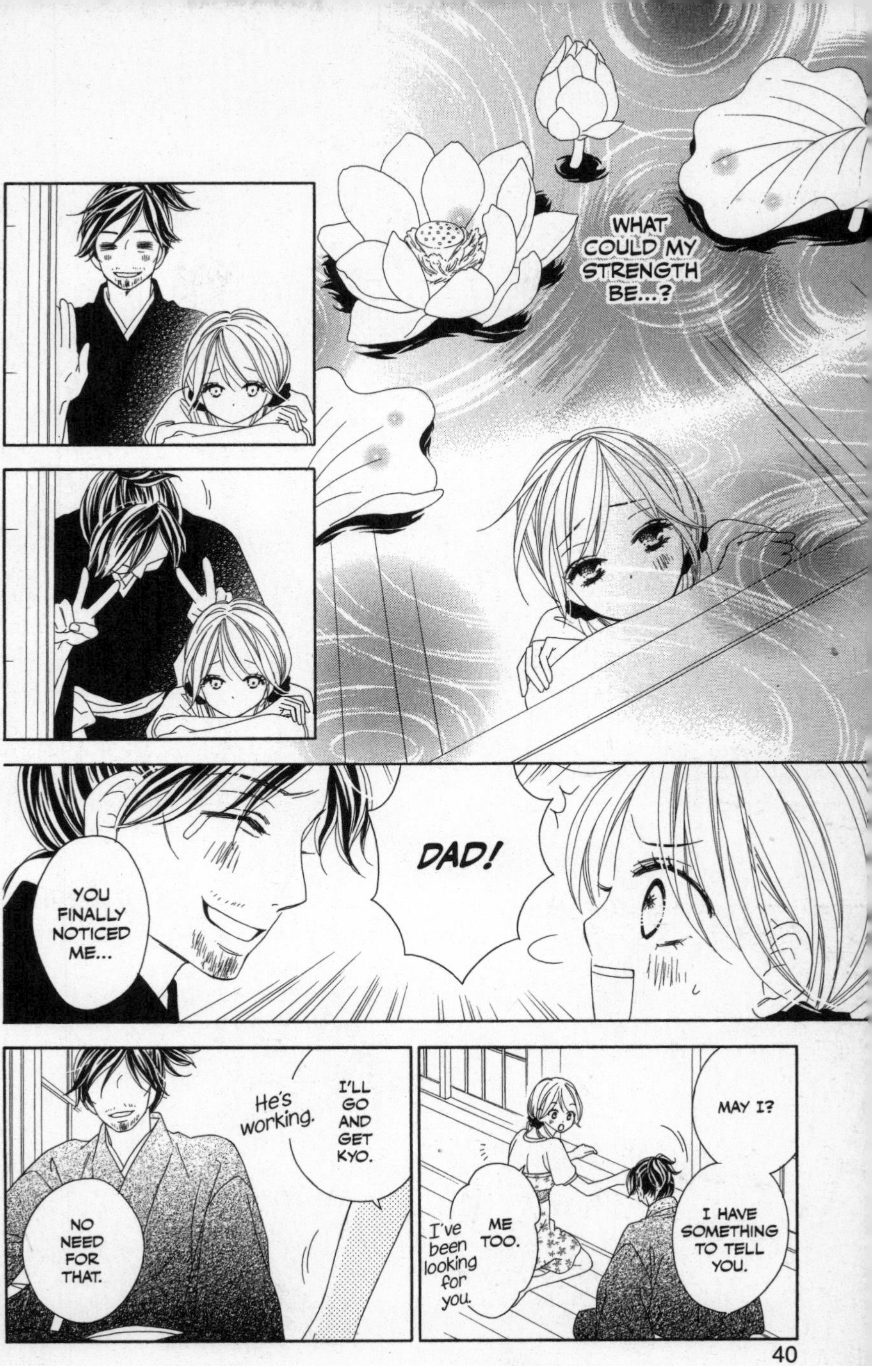
WHAT COULD MY STRENGTH BE...?
DAD!
YOU FINALLY NOTICED ME...
MAY I?
I HAVE SOMETHING TO TELL YOU.
ME TOO.
I've been looking for you.
I'LL GO AND GET KYO.
He's working.
NO NEED FOR THAT.

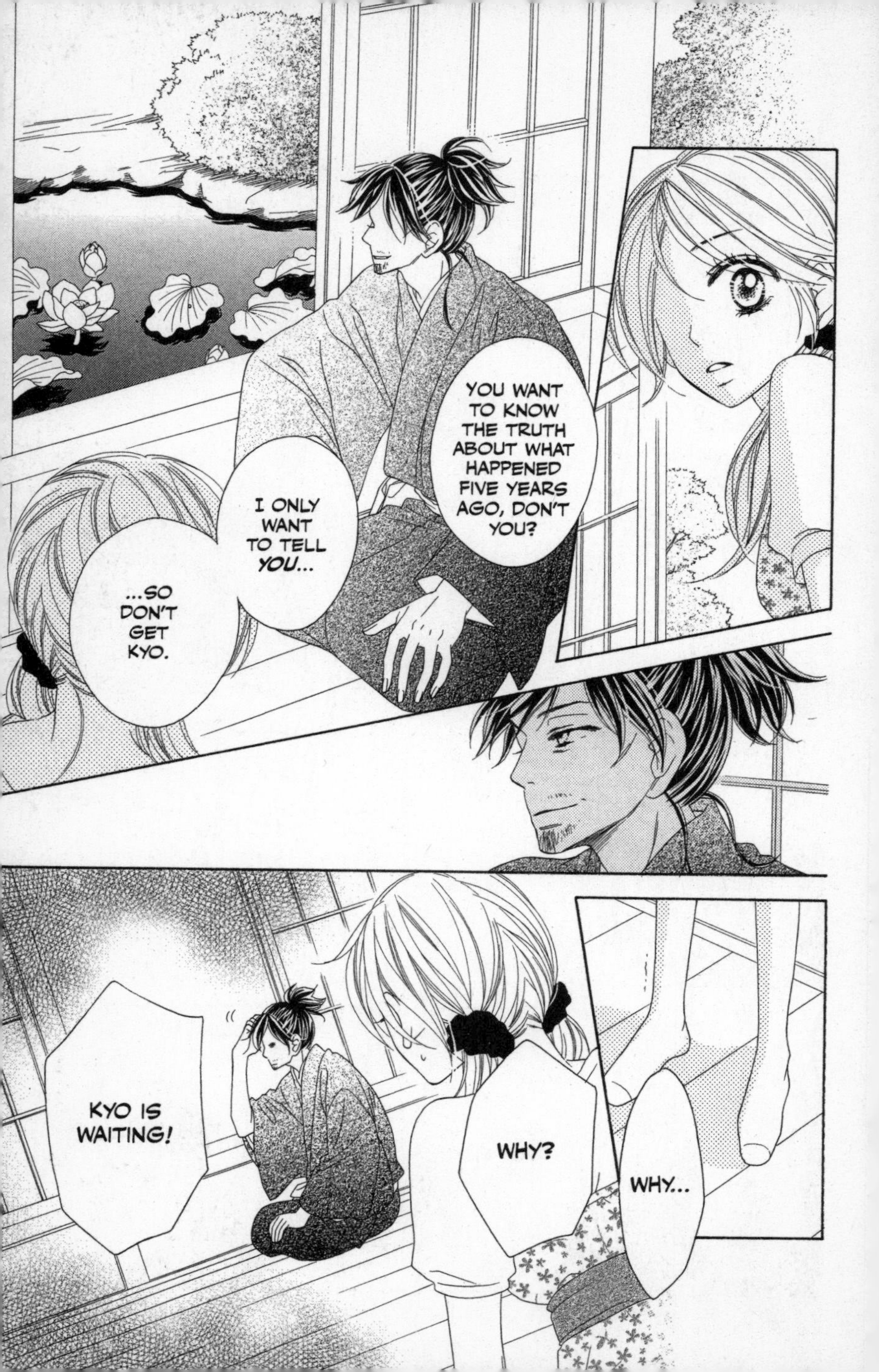
YOU WANT TO KNOW THE TRUTH ABOUT WHAT HAPPENED FIVE YEARS AGO, DON'T YOU?
I ONLY WANT TO TELL *YOU*...
...SO DON'T GET KYO.
WHY...
WHY?
KYO IS WAITING!

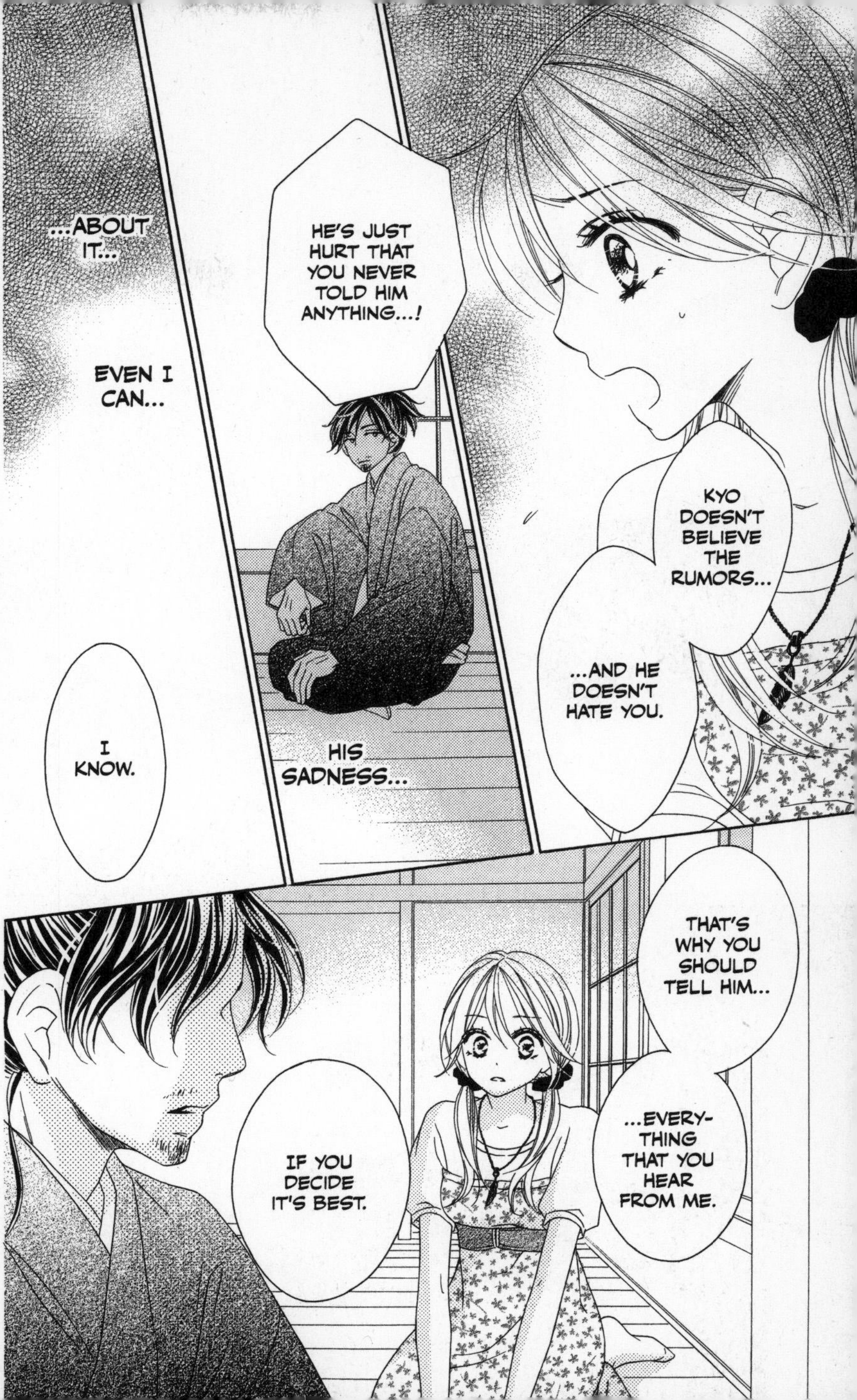
KYO DOESN'T BELIEVE THE RUMORS...
...AND HE DOESN'T HATE YOU.
HE'S JUST HURT THAT YOU NEVER TOLD HIM ANYTHING...!
HIS SADNESS...
...ABOUT IT...
EVEN I CAN...
I KNOW.
THAT'S WHY YOU SHOULD TELL HIM...
...EVERY-THING THAT YOU HEAR FROM ME.
IF YOU DECIDE IT'S BEST.

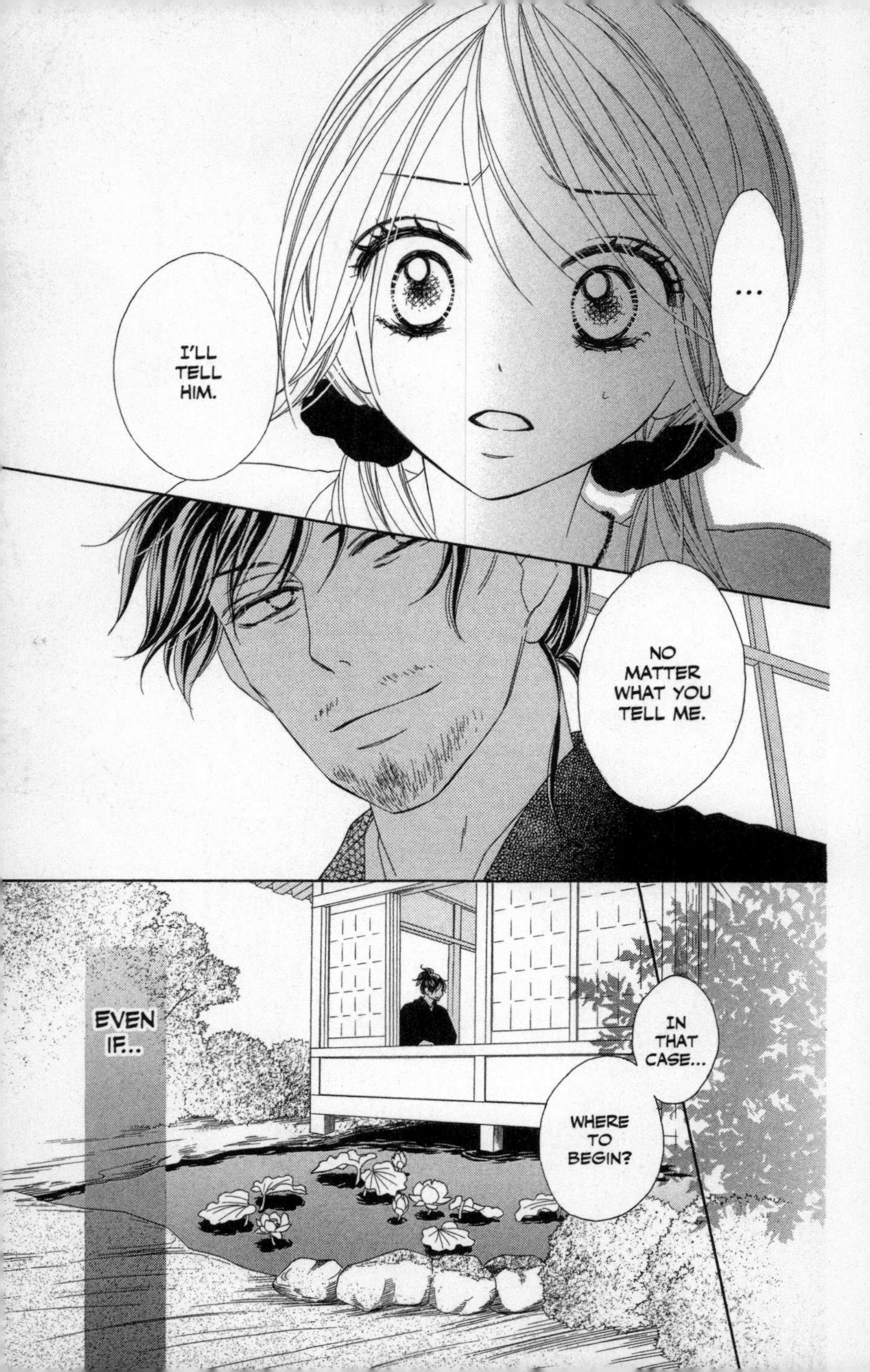
...
I'LL TELL HIM.
NO MATTER WHAT YOU TELL ME.
IN THAT CASE...
WHERE TO BEGIN?
EVEN IF...

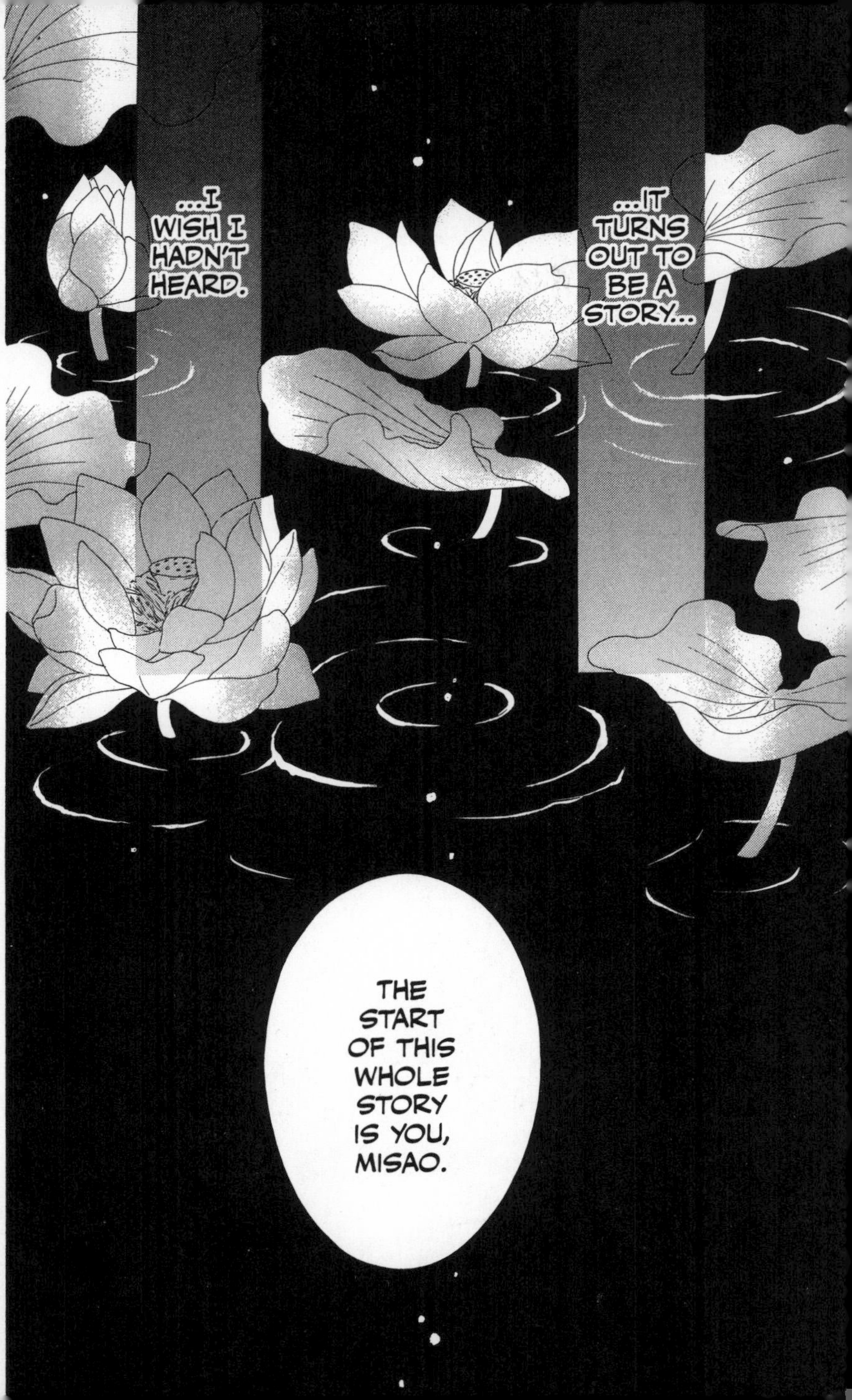
...IT TURNS OUT TO BE A STORY...
...I WISH I HADN'T HEARD.
THE START OF THIS WHOLE STORY IS YOU, MISAO.

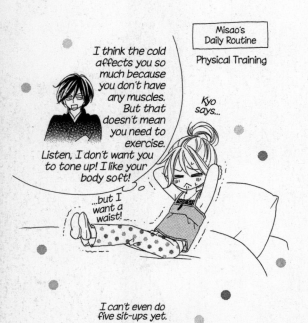

Misao's Daily Routine

Physical Training

I think the cold affects you so much because you don't have any muscles. But that doesn't mean you need to exercise. Listen, I don't want you to tone up! I like your body soft!

Kyo says...

...but I want a waist!

I can't even do five sit-ups yet.

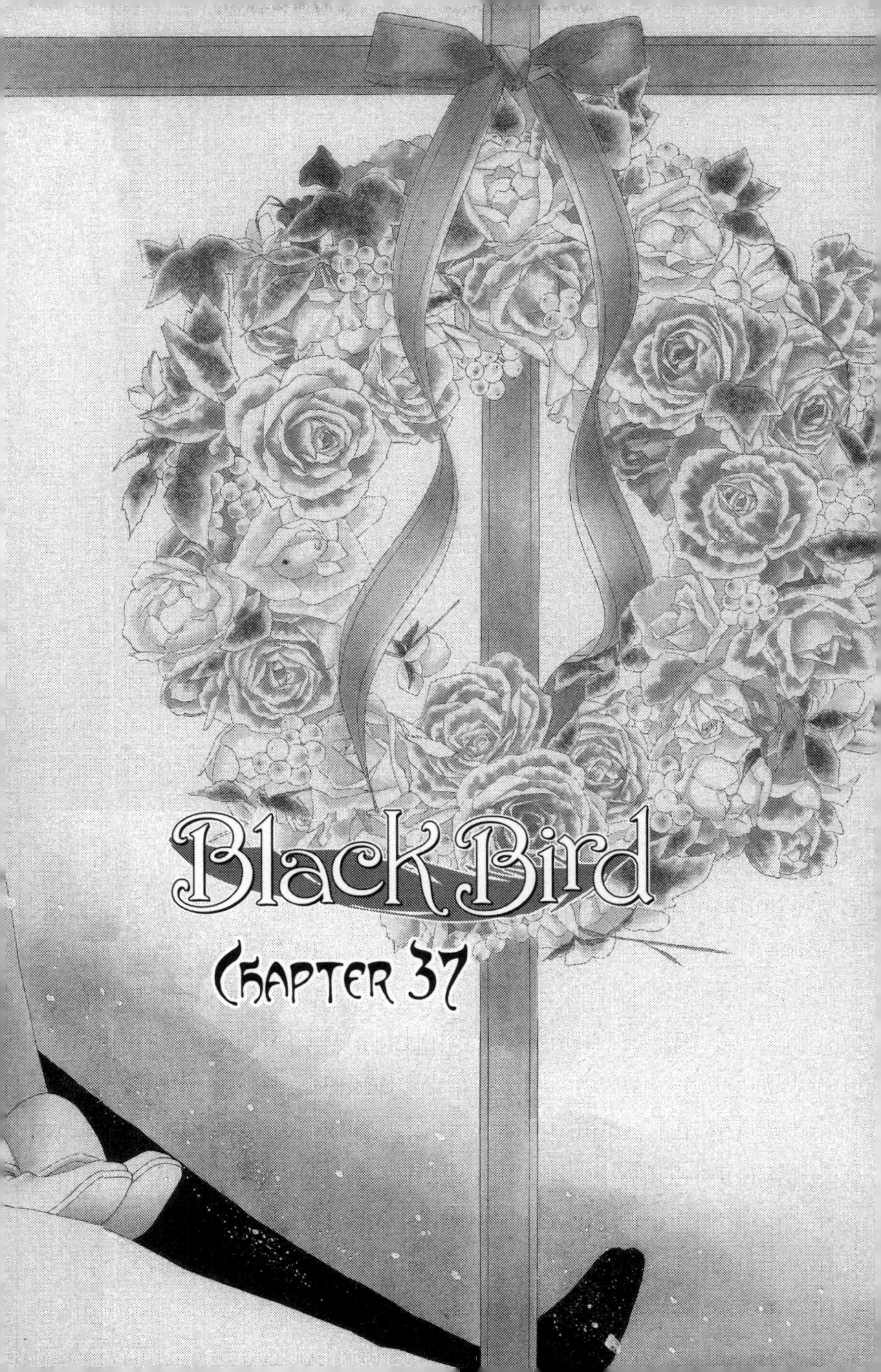
Black Bird
Chapter 37

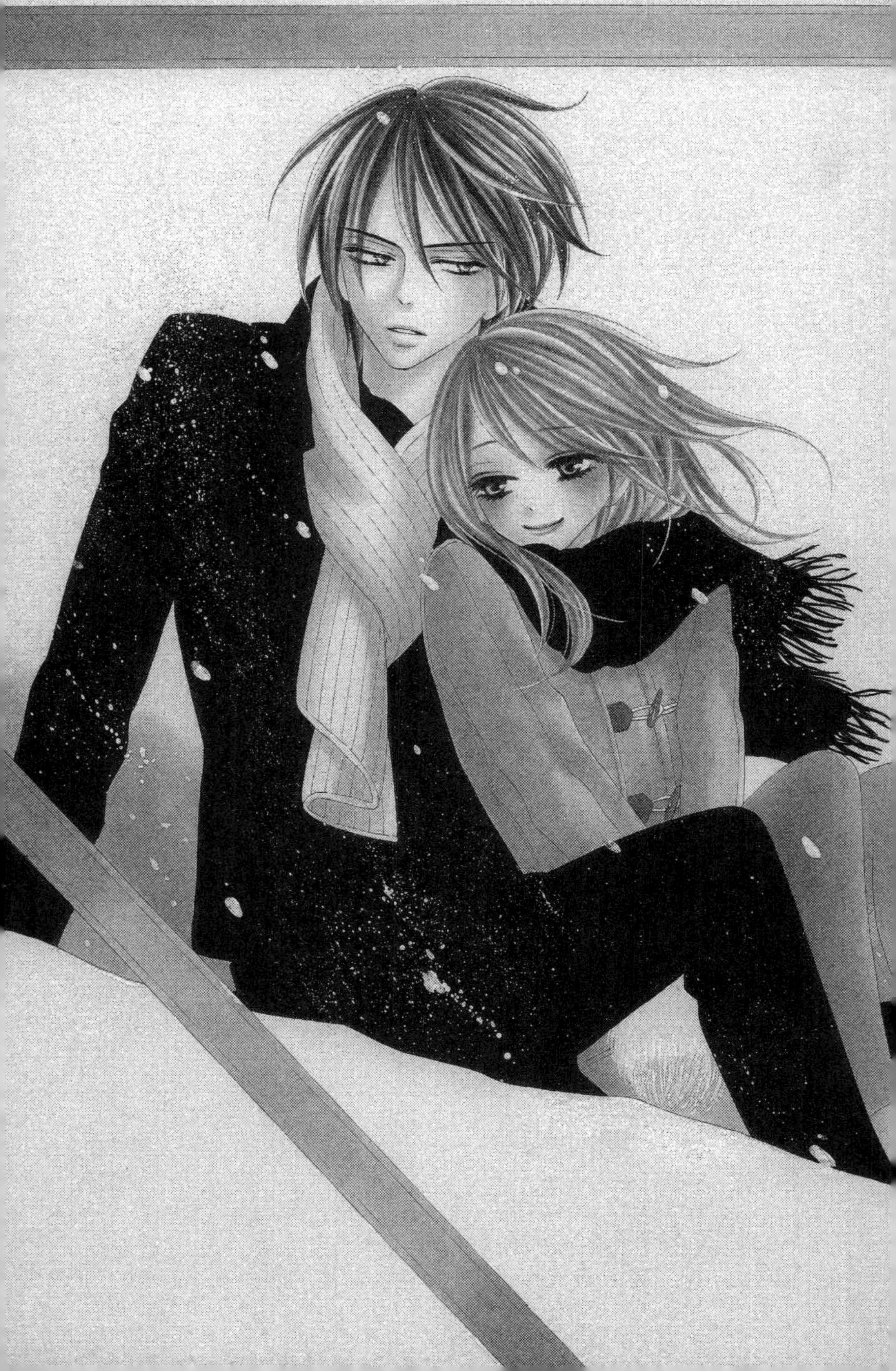

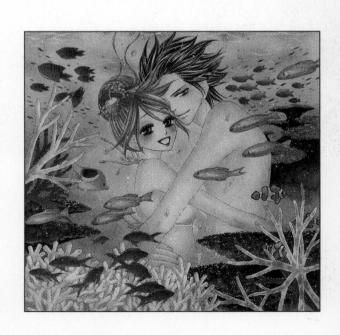

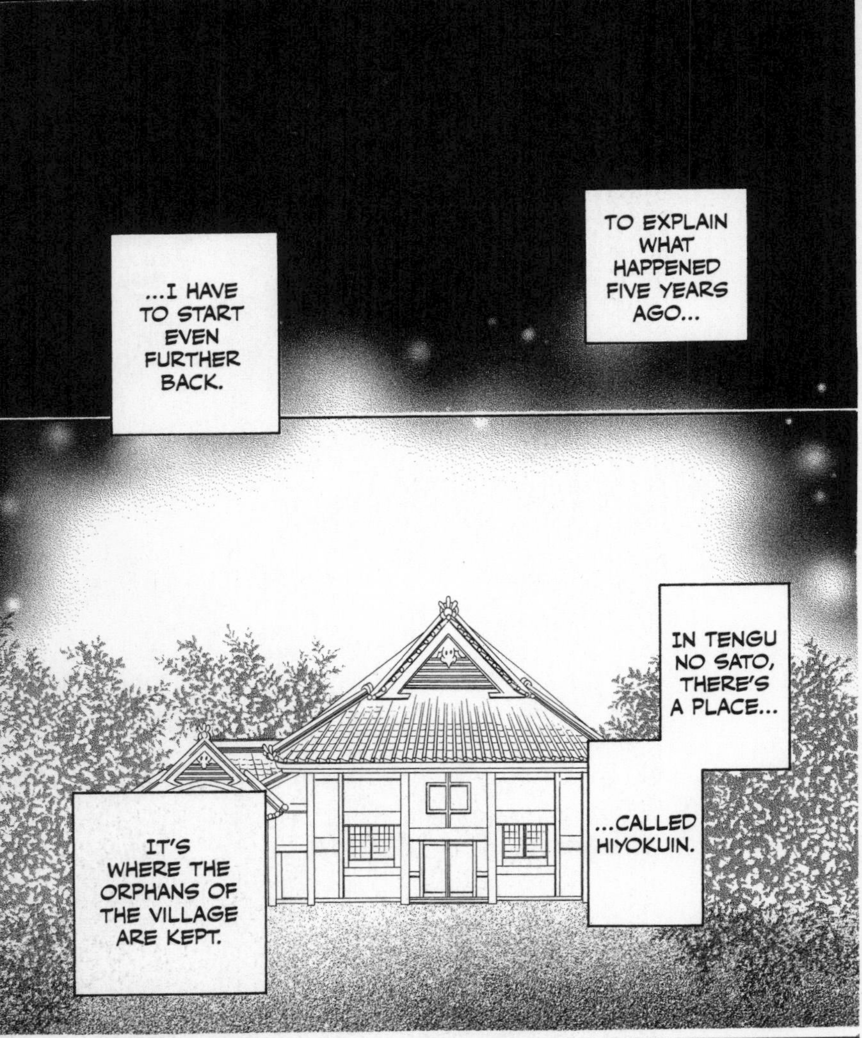
TO EXPLAIN WHAT HAPPENED FIVE YEARS AGO...
...I HAVE TO START EVEN FURTHER BACK.
IN TENGU NO SATO, THERE'S A PLACE...
...CALLED HIYOKUIN.
IT'S WHERE THE ORPHANS OF THE VILLAGE ARE KEPT.

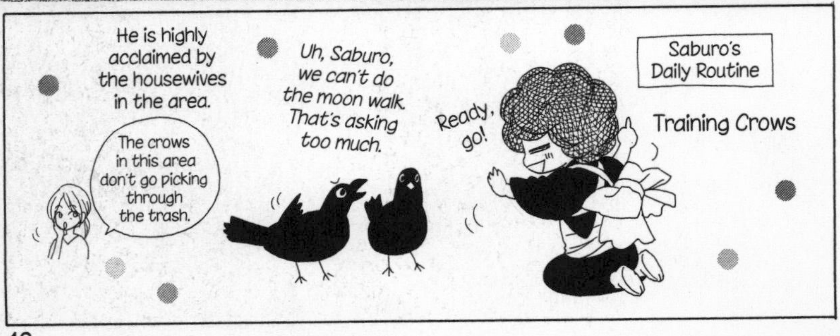
Saburo's Daily Routine
Training Crows
Ready, go!
Uh, Saburo, we can't do the moon walk. That's asking too much.
He is highly acclaimed by the housewives in the area.
The crows in this area don't go picking through the trash.

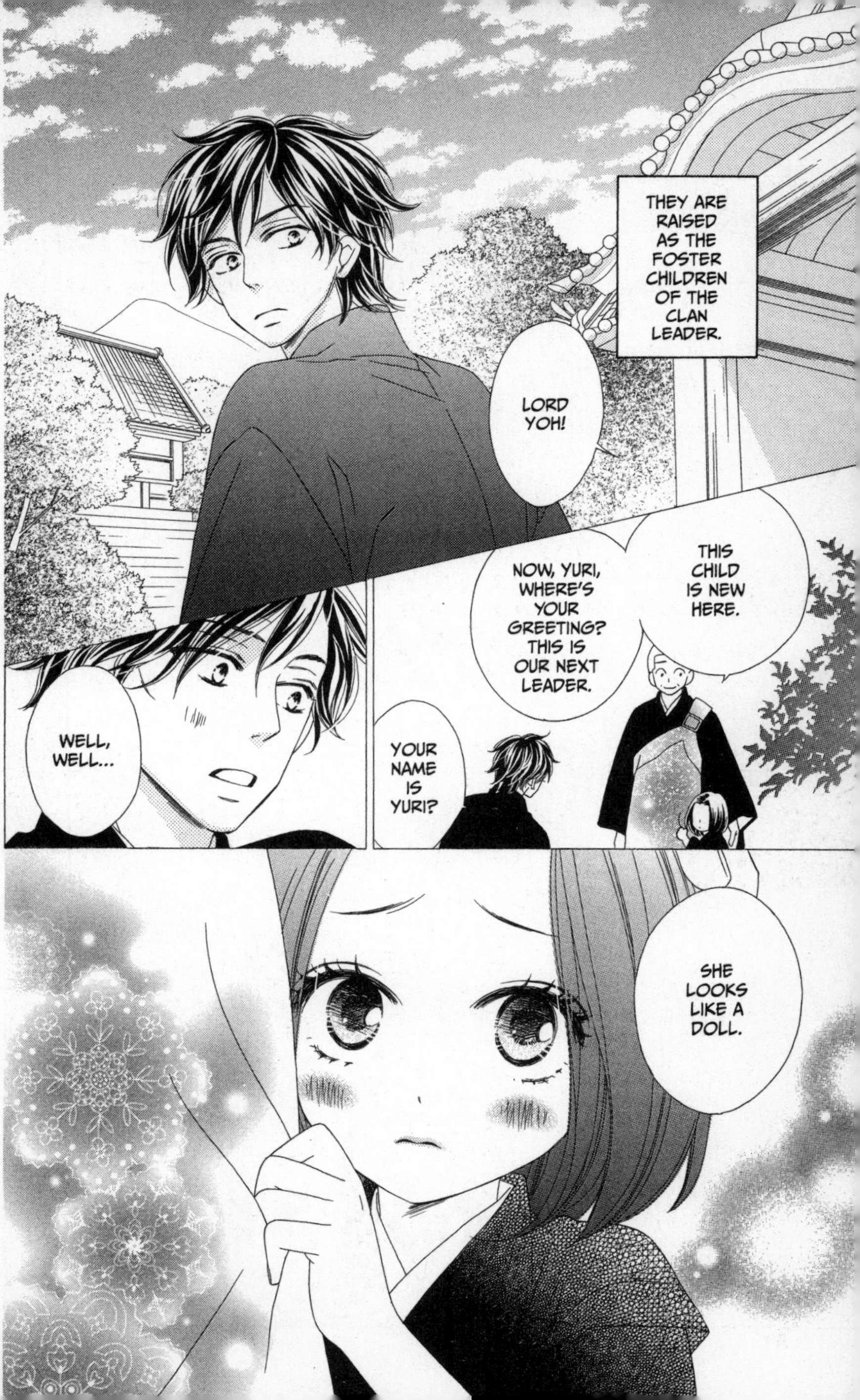
THEY ARE RAISED AS THE FOSTER CHILDREN OF THE CLAN LEADER.
LORD YOH!
THIS CHILD IS NEW HERE.
NOW, YURI, WHERE'S YOUR GREETING? THIS IS OUR NEXT LEADER.
YOUR NAME IS YURI?
WELL, WELL...
SHE LOOKS LIKE A DOLL.

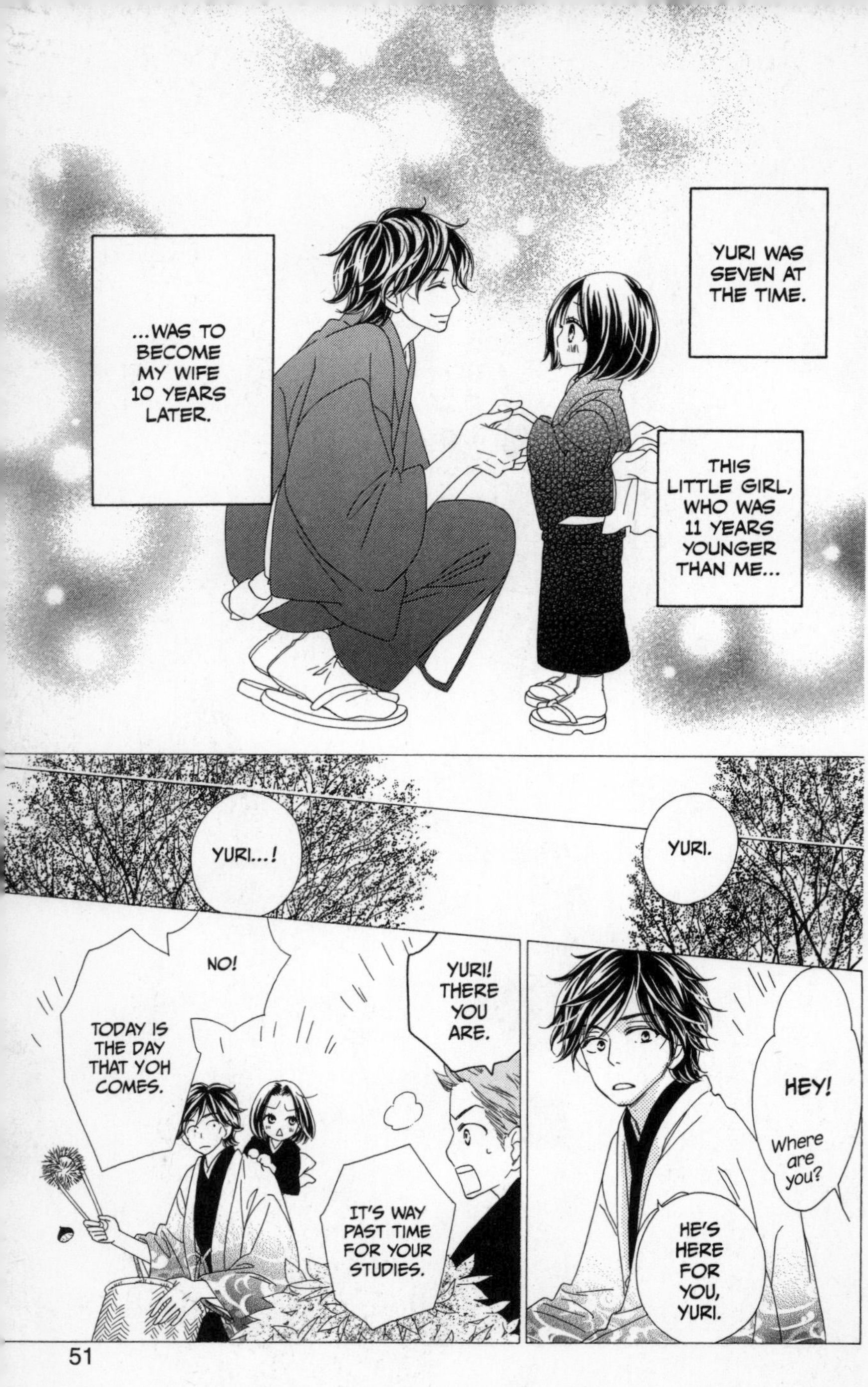
YURI WAS SEVEN AT THE TIME.
THIS LITTLE GIRL, WHO WAS 11 YEARS YOUNGER THAN ME...
...WAS TO BECOME MY WIFE 10 YEARS LATER.
YURI.
YURI...!
HEY!
Where are you?
HE'S HERE FOR YOU, YURI.
YURI! THERE YOU ARE.
IT'S WAY PAST TIME FOR YOUR STUDIES.
NO!
TODAY IS THE DAY THAT YOH COMES.

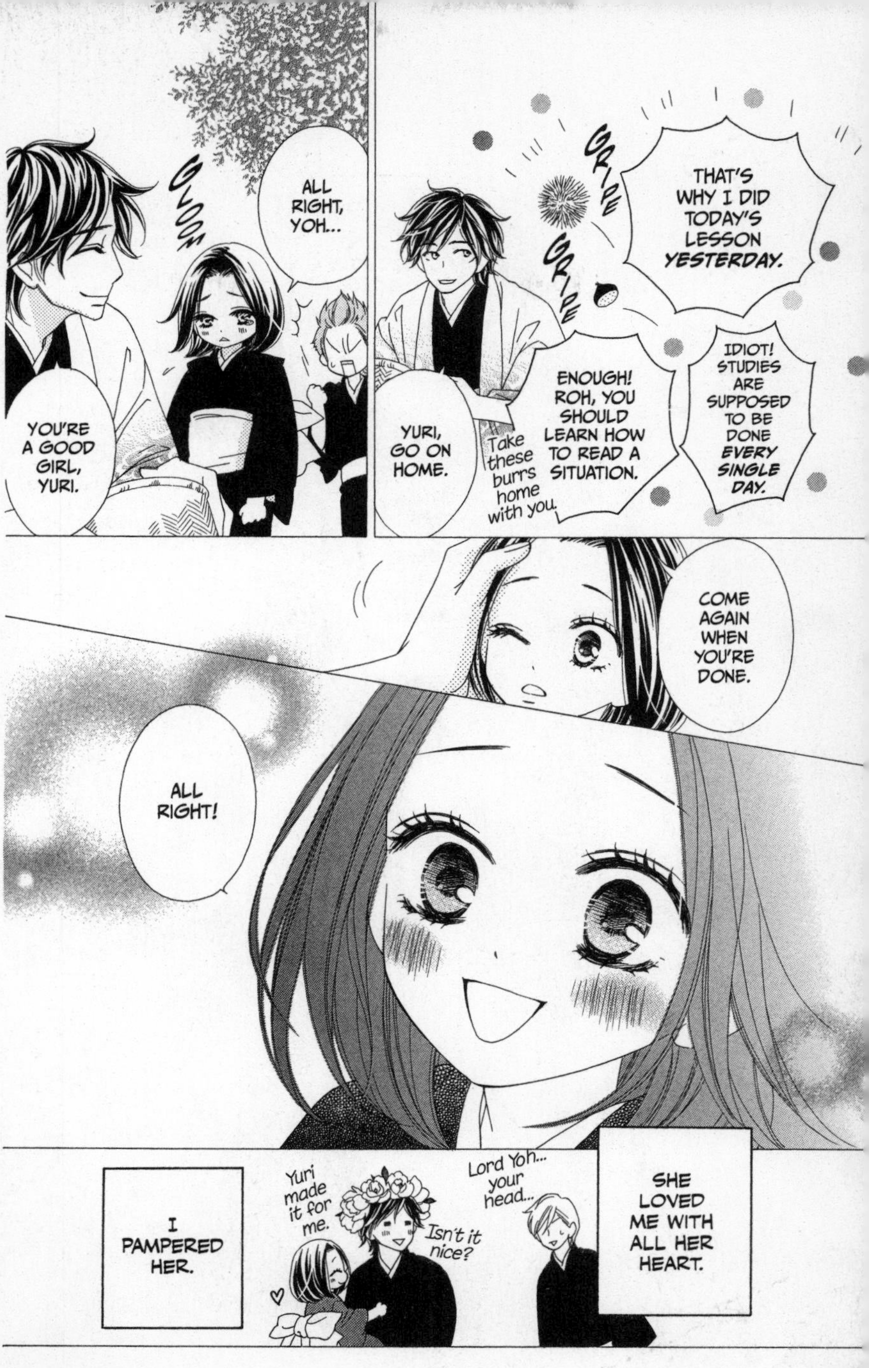
THAT'S WHY I DID TODAY'S LESSON YESTERDAY.
IDIOT! STUDIES ARE SUPPOSED TO BE DONE EVERY SINGLE DAY.
GRIPE GRIPE
ENOUGH! ROH, YOU SHOULD LEARN HOW TO READ A SITUATION.
Take these burrs home with you.
YURI, GO ON HOME.
ALL RIGHT, YOH...
GLOOM
YOU'RE A GOOD GIRL, YURI.
COME AGAIN WHEN YOU'RE DONE.
ALL RIGHT!
SHE LOVED ME WITH ALL HER HEART.
Lord Yoh... your head...
Isn't it nice?
Yuri made it for me.
I PAMPERED HER.

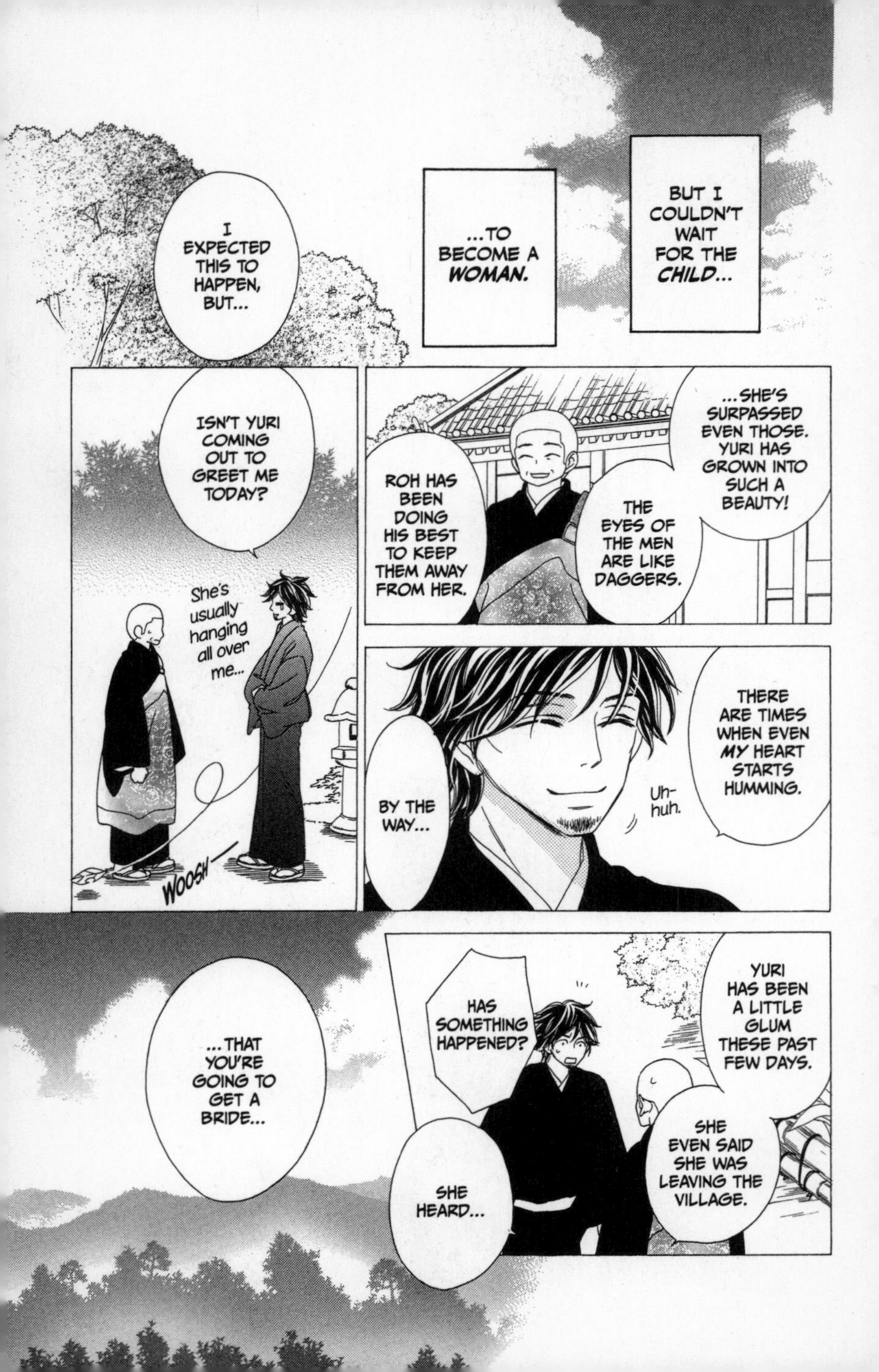
BUT I COULDN'T WAIT FOR THE *CHILD*...
...TO BECOME A *WOMAN.*
I EXPECTED THIS TO HAPPEN, BUT...
...SHE'S SURPASSED EVEN THOSE. YURI HAS GROWN INTO SUCH A BEAUTY!
THE EYES OF THE MEN ARE LIKE DAGGERS.
ROH HAS BEEN DOING HIS BEST TO KEEP THEM AWAY FROM HER.
THERE ARE TIMES WHEN EVEN *MY* HEART STARTS HUMMING.
Uh-huh.
BY THE WAY...
ISN'T YURI COMING OUT TO GREET ME TODAY?
She's usually hanging all over me...
WOOSH
YURI HAS BEEN A LITTLE GLUM THESE PAST FEW DAYS.
HAS SOMETHING HAPPENED?
SHE EVEN SAID SHE WAS LEAVING THE VILLAGE.
SHE HEARD...
...THAT YOU'RE GOING TO GET A BRIDE...

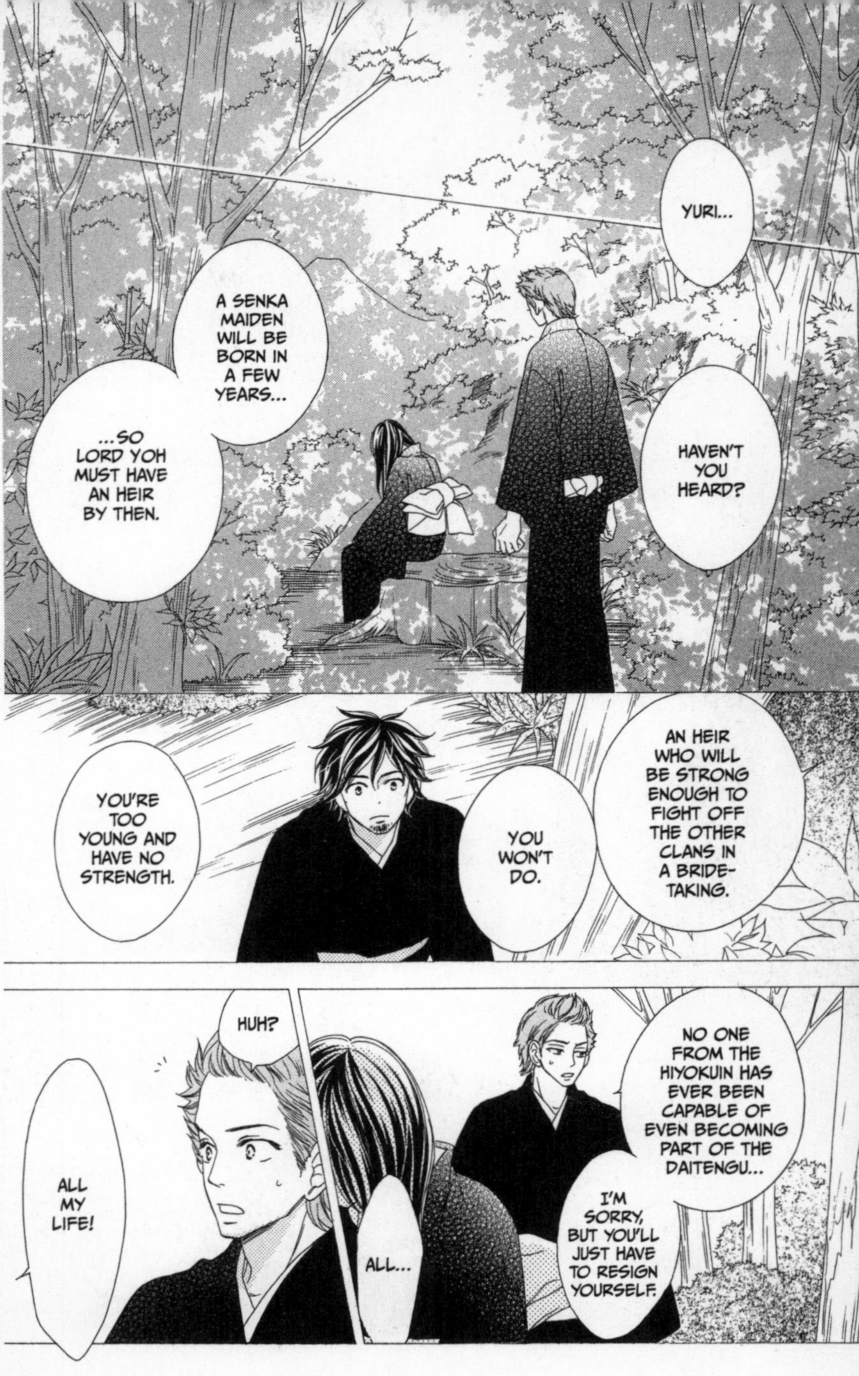
YURI...
HAVEN'T YOU HEARD?
A SENKA MAIDEN WILL BE BORN IN A FEW YEARS...
...SO LORD YOH MUST HAVE AN HEIR BY THEN.
AN HEIR WHO WILL BE STRONG ENOUGH TO FIGHT OFF THE OTHER CLANS IN A BRIDE-TAKING.
YOU WON'T DO.
YOU'RE TOO YOUNG AND HAVE NO STRENGTH.
NO ONE FROM THE HIYOKUIN HAS EVER BEEN CAPABLE OF EVEN BECOMING PART OF THE DAITENGU...
I'M SORRY, BUT YOU'LL JUST HAVE TO RESIGN YOURSELF.
ALL...
HUH?
ALL MY LIFE!

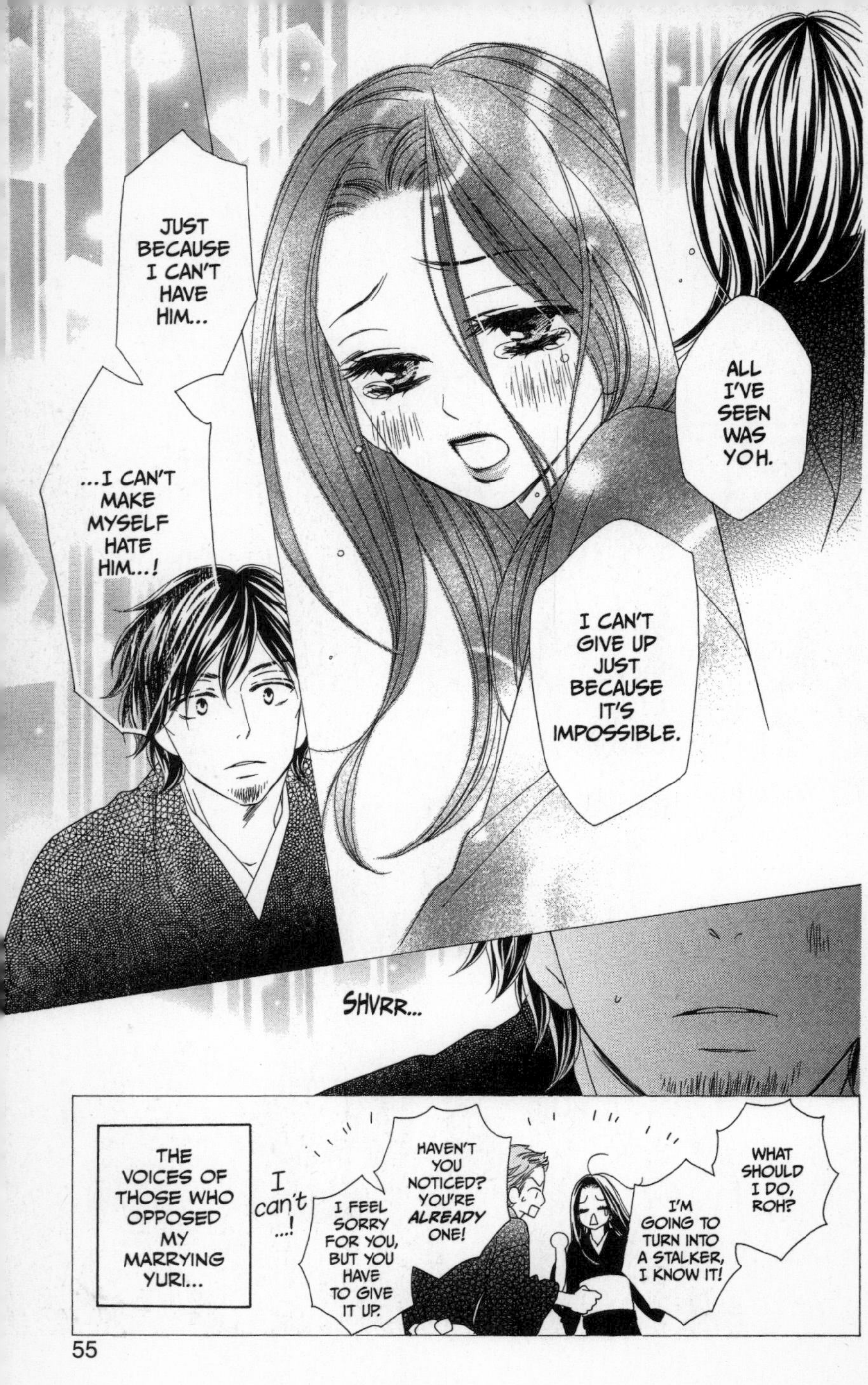
ALL I'VE SEEN WAS YOH.
I CAN'T GIVE UP JUST BECAUSE IT'S IMPOSSIBLE.
JUST BECAUSE I CAN'T HAVE HIM...
...I CAN'T MAKE MYSELF HATE HIM...!
SHVRR...
WHAT SHOULD I DO, ROH?
I'M GOING TO TURN INTO A STALKER, I KNOW IT!
HAVEN'T YOU NOTICED? YOU'RE *ALREADY* ONE!
I FEEL SORRY FOR YOU, BUT YOU HAVE TO GIVE IT UP.
I can't ...!
THE VOICES OF THOSE WHO OPPOSED MY MARRYING YURI...

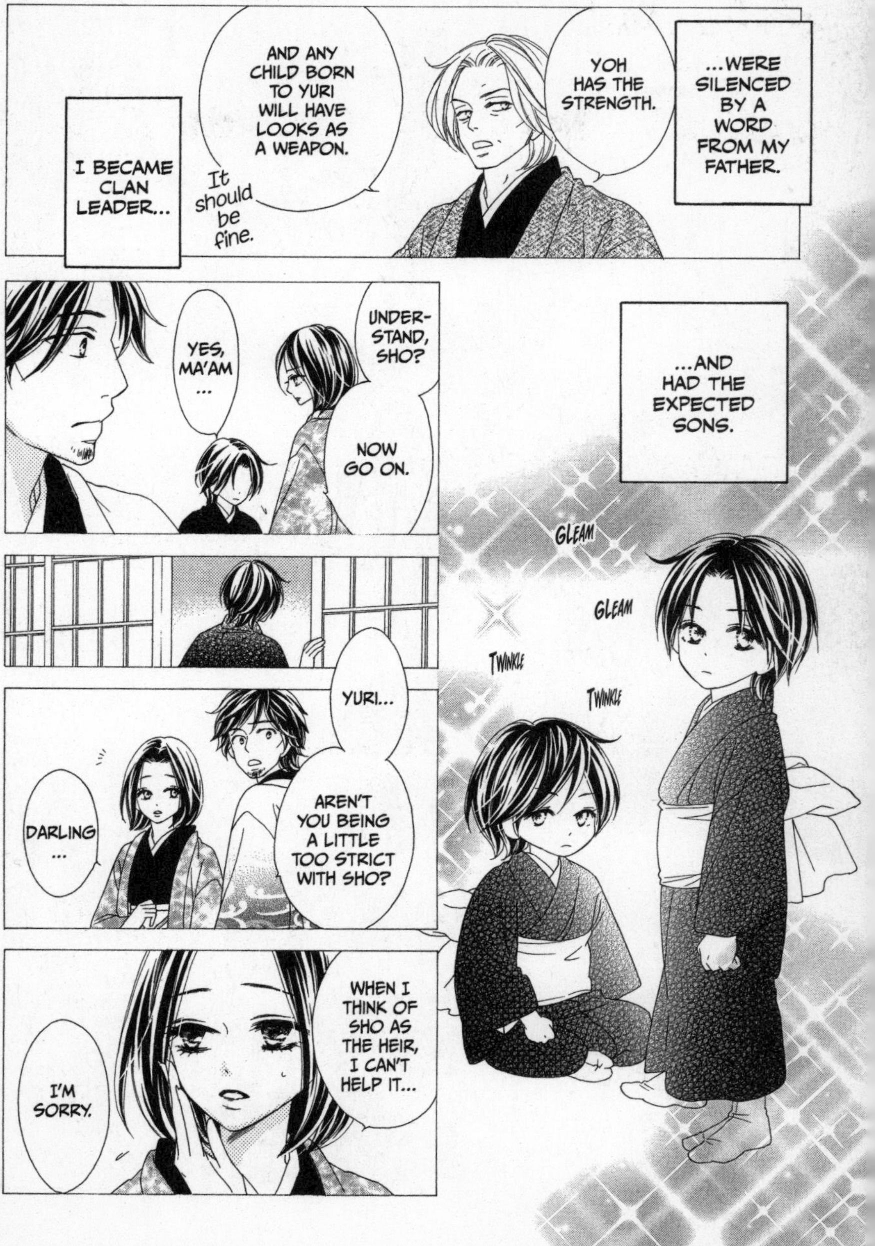
...WERE SILENCED BY A WORD FROM MY FATHER.
YOH HAS THE STRENGTH.
AND ANY CHILD BORN TO YURI WILL HAVE LOOKS AS A WEAPON.
It should be fine.
I BECAME CLAN LEADER...
...AND HAD THE EXPECTED SONS.
GLEAM
GLEAM
TWINKLE
TWINKLE
UNDER-STAND, SHO?
NOW GO ON.
YES, MA'AM...
YURI...
AREN'T YOU BEING A LITTLE TOO STRICT WITH SHO?
DARLING...
WHEN I THINK OF SHO AS THE HEIR, I CAN'T HELP IT...
I'M SORRY.

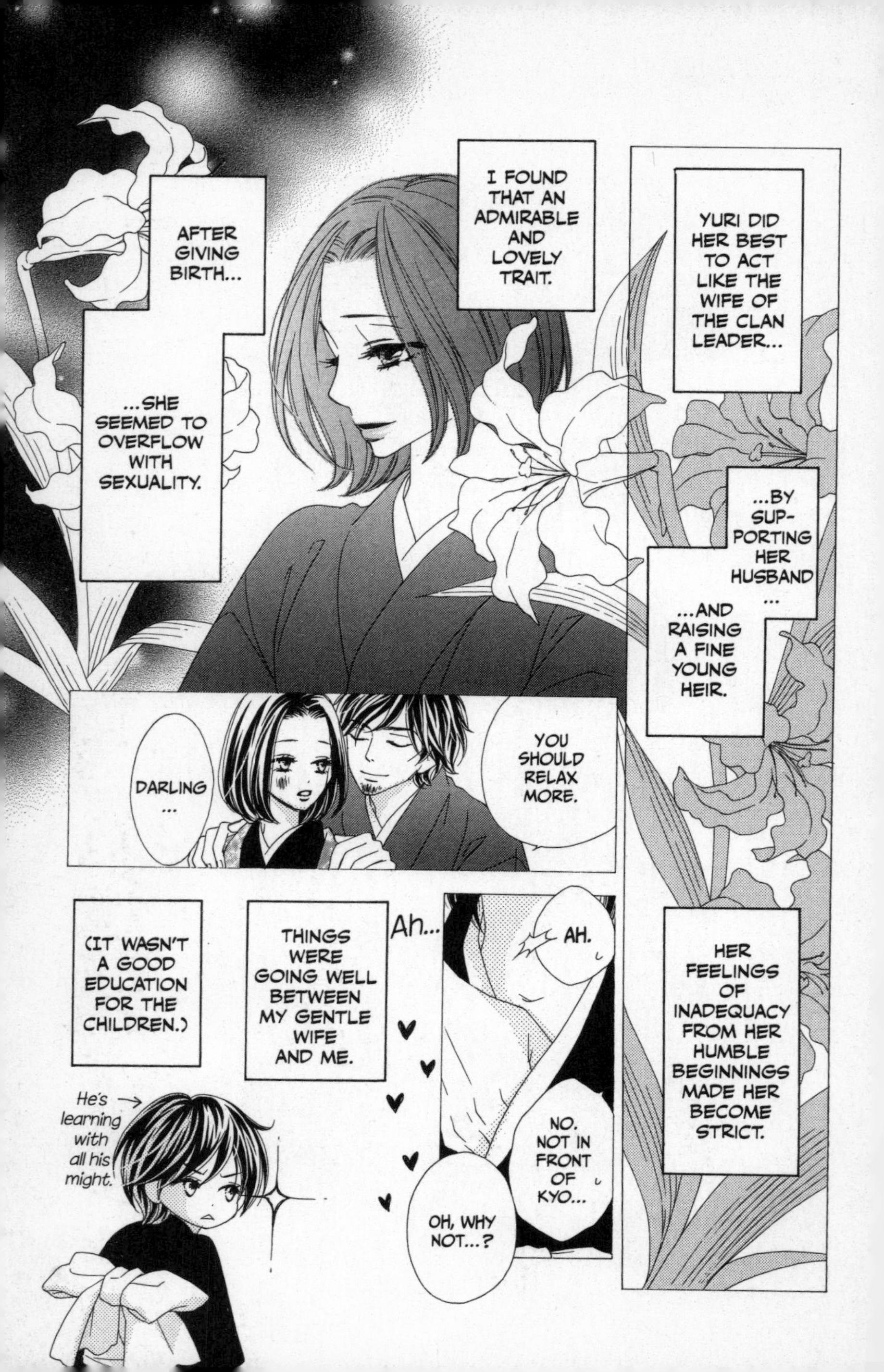
YURI DID HER BEST TO ACT LIKE THE WIFE OF THE CLAN LEADER...
...BY SUPPORTING HER HUSBAND...
...AND RAISING A FINE YOUNG HEIR.
HER FEELINGS OF INADEQUACY FROM HER HUMBLE BEGINNINGS MADE HER BECOME STRICT.
I FOUND THAT AN ADMIRABLE AND LOVELY TRAIT.
AFTER GIVING BIRTH...
...SHE SEEMED TO OVERFLOW WITH SEXUALITY.
YOU SHOULD RELAX MORE.
DARLING...
AH.
NO. NOT IN FRONT OF KYO...
OH, WHY NOT...?
Ah...
THINGS WERE GOING WELL BETWEEN MY GENTLE WIFE AND ME.
(IT WASN'T A GOOD EDUCATION FOR THE CHILDREN.)
He's learning with all his might.

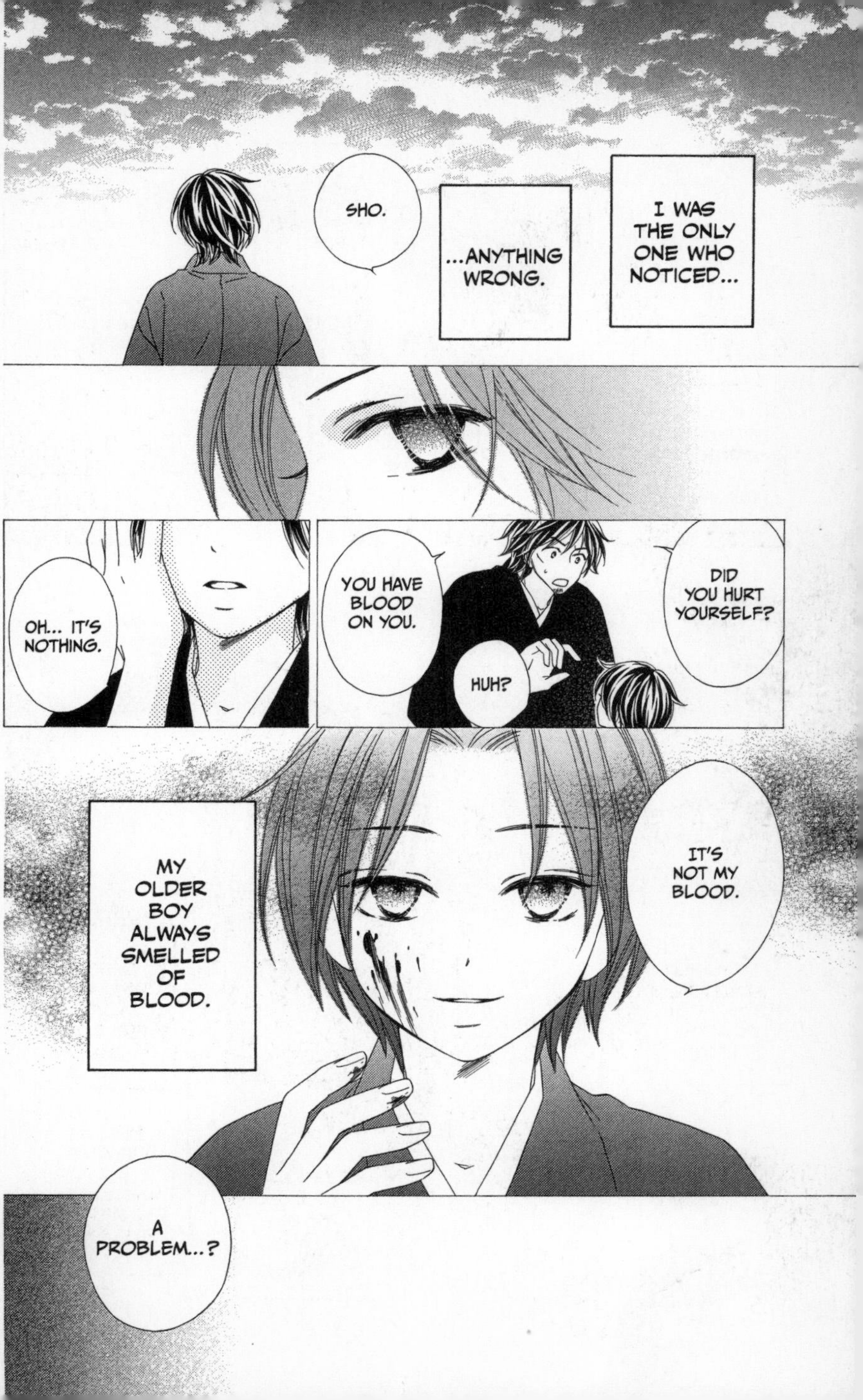
I WAS THE ONLY ONE WHO NOTICED...
...ANYTHING WRONG.
SHO.
DID YOU HURT YOURSELF?
YOU HAVE BLOOD ON YOU.
HUH?
OH... IT'S NOTHING.
IT'S NOT MY BLOOD.
MY OLDER BOY ALWAYS SMELLED OF BLOOD.
A PROBLEM...?

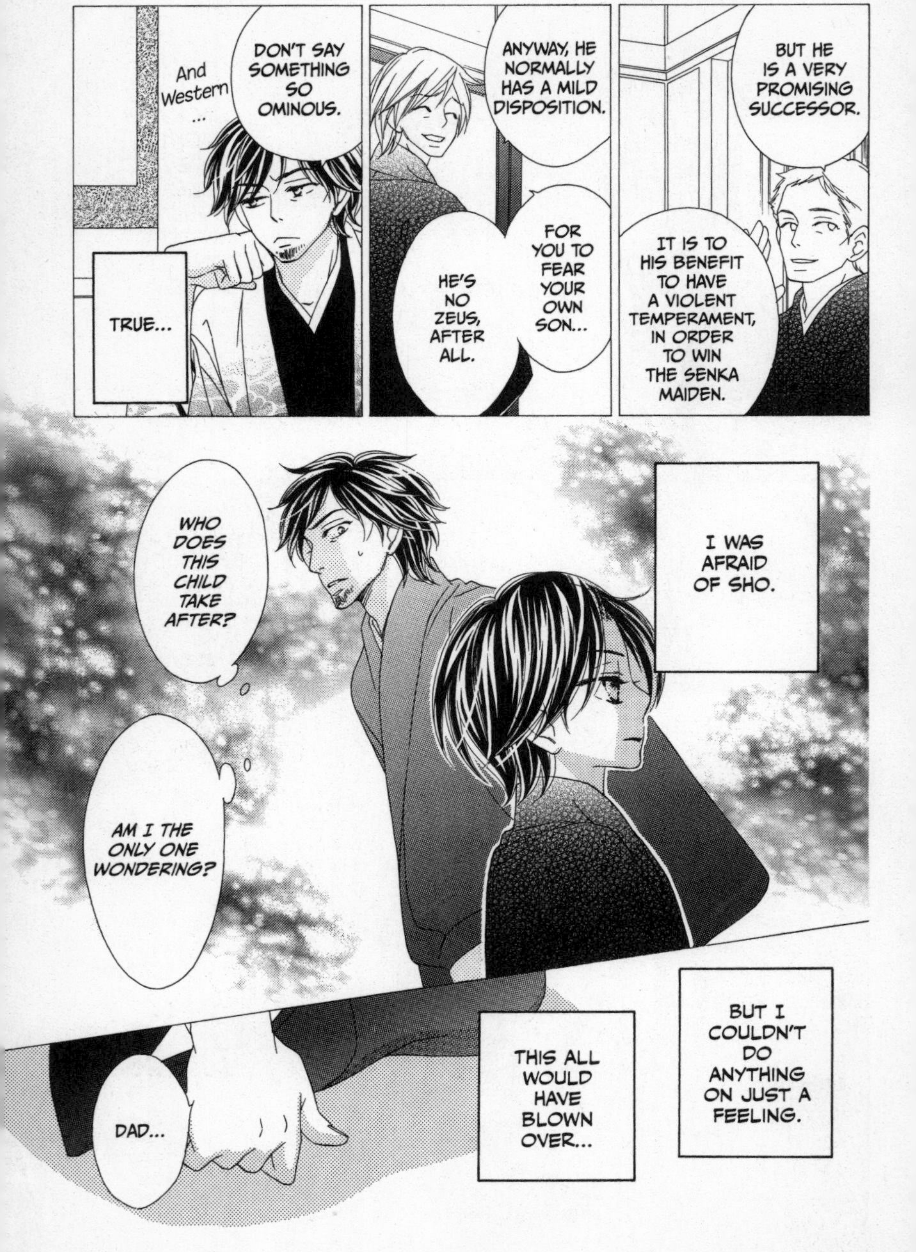
BUT HE IS A VERY PROMISING SUCCESSOR.
IT IS TO HIS BENEFIT TO HAVE A VIOLENT TEMPERAMENT, IN ORDER TO WIN THE SENKA MAIDEN.
ANYWAY, HE NORMALLY HAS A MILD DISPOSITION.
FOR YOU TO FEAR YOUR OWN SON...
HE'S NO ZEUS, AFTER ALL.
DON'T SAY SOMETHING SO OMINOUS.
And Western ...
TRUE...
I WAS AFRAID OF SHO.
WHO DOES THIS CHILD TAKE AFTER?
AM I THE ONLY ONE WONDERING?
BUT I COULDN'T DO ANYTHING ON JUST A FEELING.
THIS ALL WOULD HAVE BLOWN OVER...
DAD...

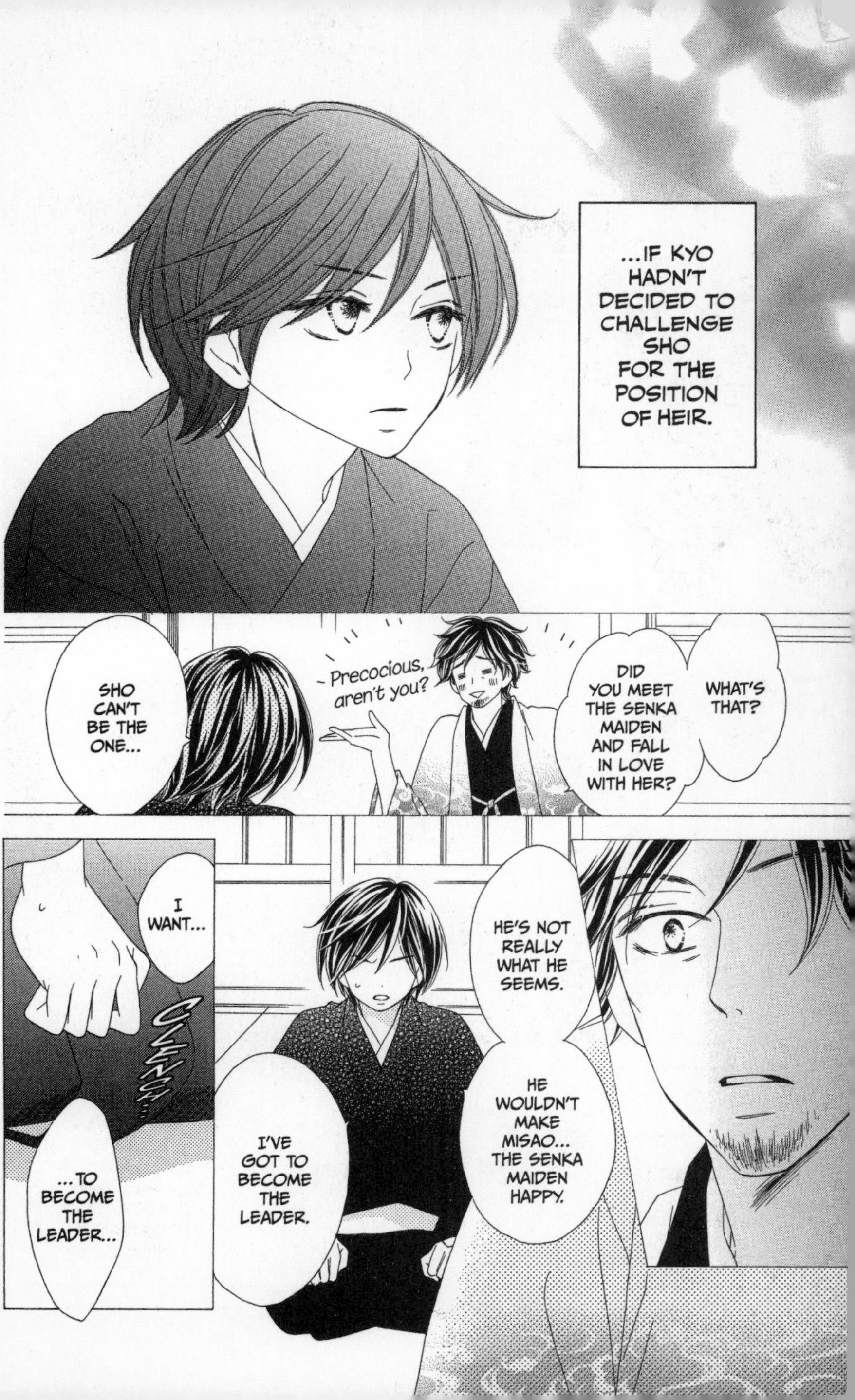
...IF KYO HADN'T DECIDED TO CHALLENGE SHO FOR THE POSITION OF HEIR.
WHAT'S THAT?
DID YOU MEET THE SENKA MAIDEN AND FALL IN LOVE WITH HER?
Precocious, aren't you?
SHO CAN'T BE THE ONE...
HE'S NOT REALLY WHAT HE SEEMS.
HE WOULDN'T MAKE MISAO... THE SENKA MAIDEN HAPPY.
I'VE GOT TO BECOME THE LEADER.
I WANT...
CLENCH...
...TO BECOME THE LEADER...

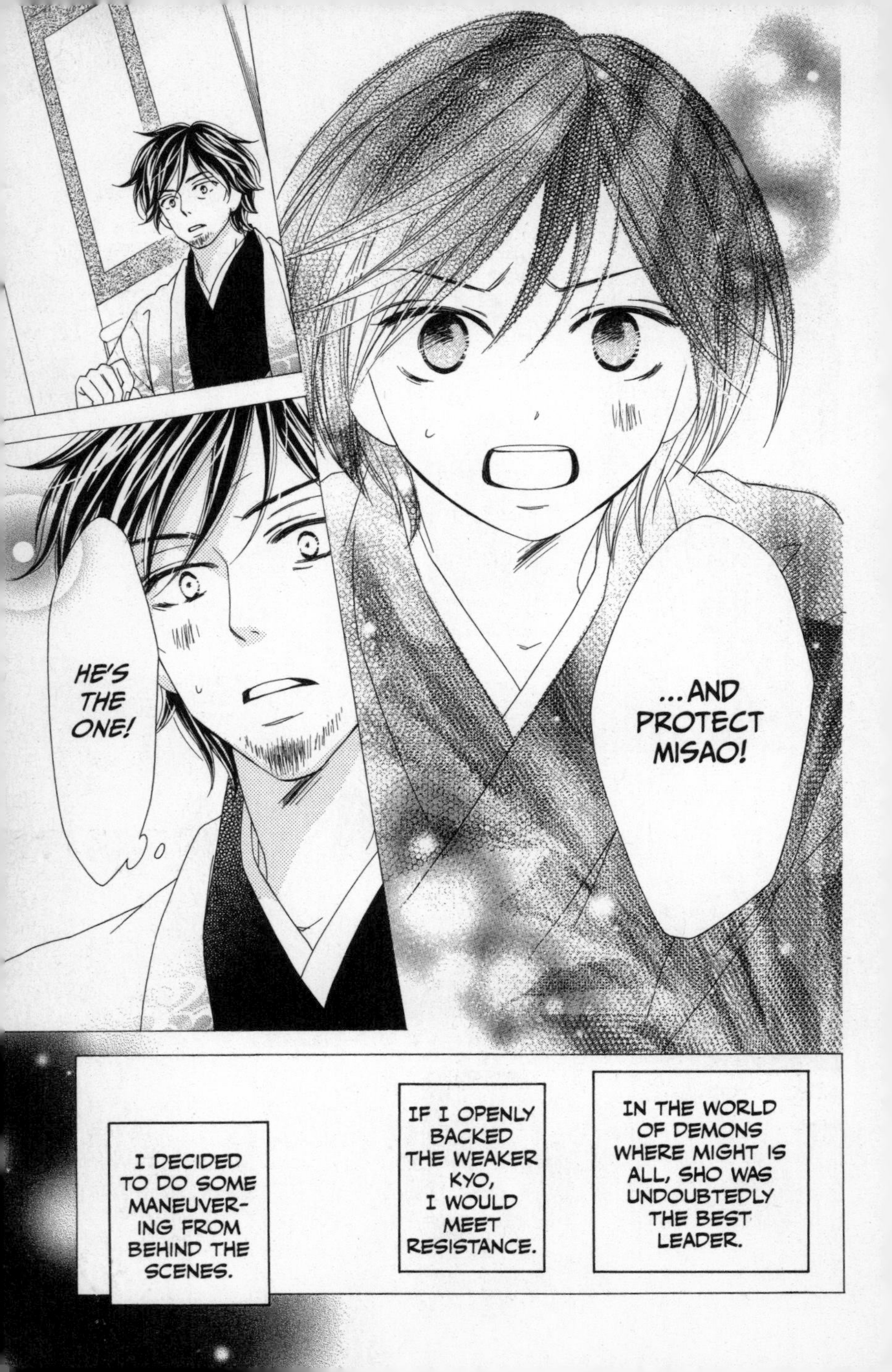
...AND PROTECT MISAO!
HE'S THE ONE!
IN THE WORLD OF DEMONS WHERE MIGHT IS ALL, SHO WAS UNDOUBTEDLY THE BEST LEADER.
IF I OPENLY BACKED THE WEAKER KYO, I WOULD MEET RESISTANCE.
I DECIDED TO DO SOME MANEUVER-ING FROM BEHIND THE SCENES.

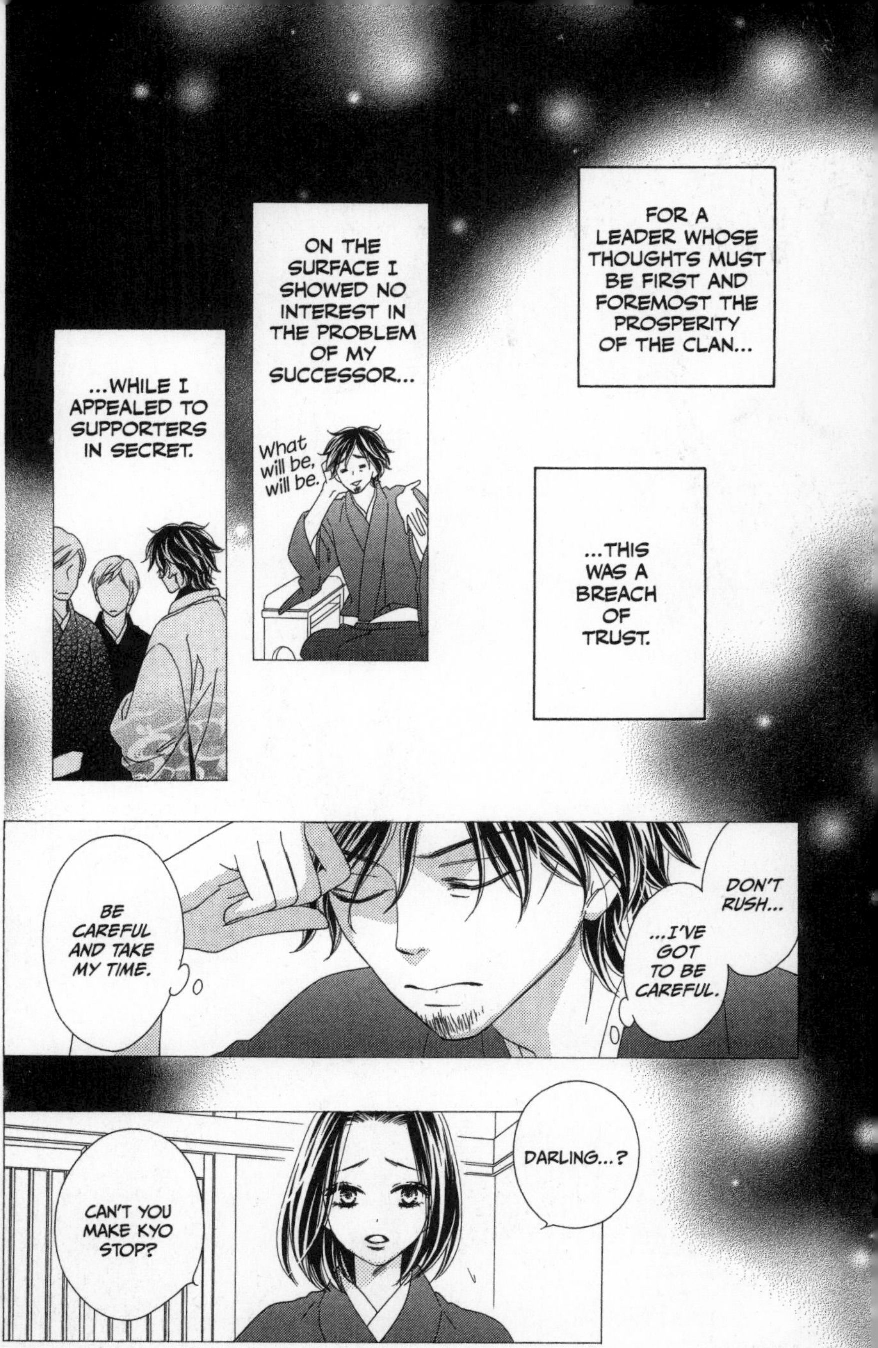
FOR A LEADER WHOSE THOUGHTS MUST BE FIRST AND FOREMOST THE PROSPERITY OF THE CLAN...
...THIS WAS A BREACH OF TRUST.
ON THE SURFACE I SHOWED NO INTEREST IN THE PROBLEM OF MY SUCCESSOR...
What will be, will be.
...WHILE I APPEALED TO SUPPORTERS IN SECRET.
DON'T RUSH...
...I'VE GOT TO BE CAREFUL.
BE CAREFUL AND TAKE MY TIME.
DARLING...?
CAN'T YOU MAKE KYO STOP?

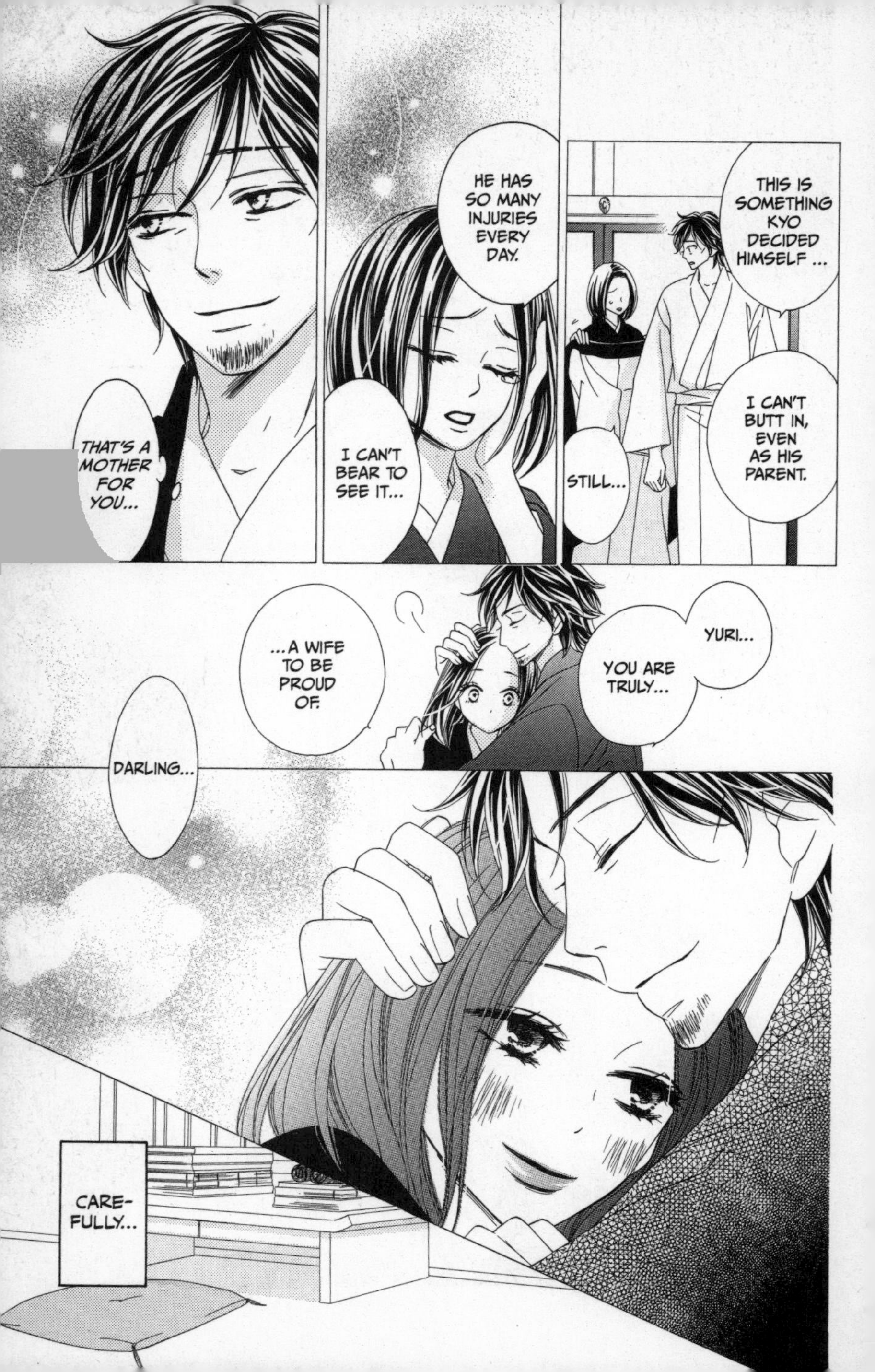
THIS IS SOMETHING KYO DECIDED HIMSELF ...
I CAN'T BUTT IN, EVEN AS HIS PARENT.
STILL...
HE HAS SO MANY INJURIES EVERY DAY.
I CAN'T BEAR TO SEE IT...
THAT'S A MOTHER FOR YOU...
YURI...
YOU ARE TRULY...
...A WIFE TO BE PROUD OF.
DARLING...
CARE-FULLY...

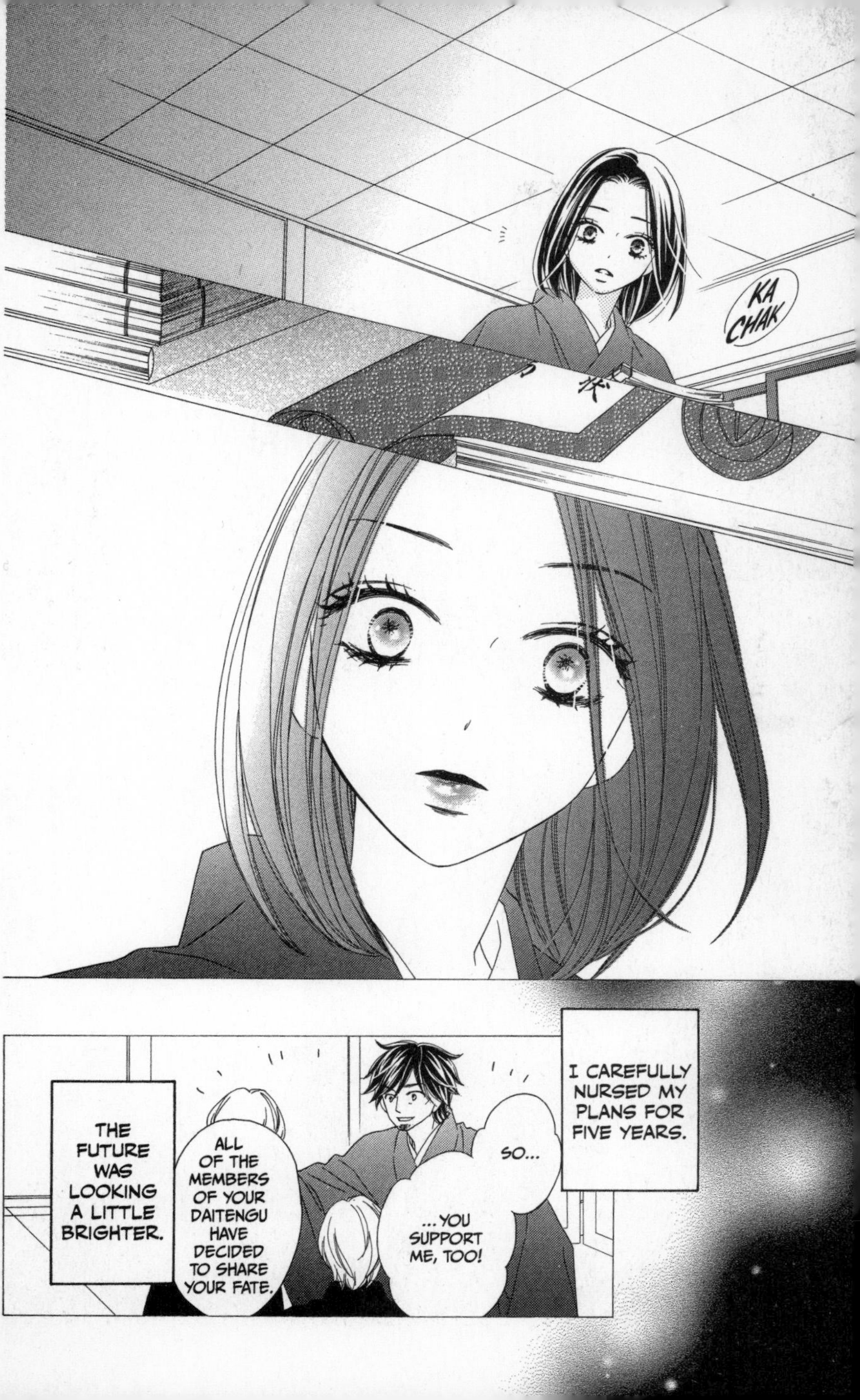
KA CHAK
I CAREFULLY NURSED MY PLANS FOR FIVE YEARS.
SO...
...YOU SUPPORT ME, TOO!
ALL OF THE MEMBERS OF YOUR DAITENGU HAVE DECIDED TO SHARE YOUR FATE.
THE FUTURE WAS LOOKING A LITTLE BRIGHTER.

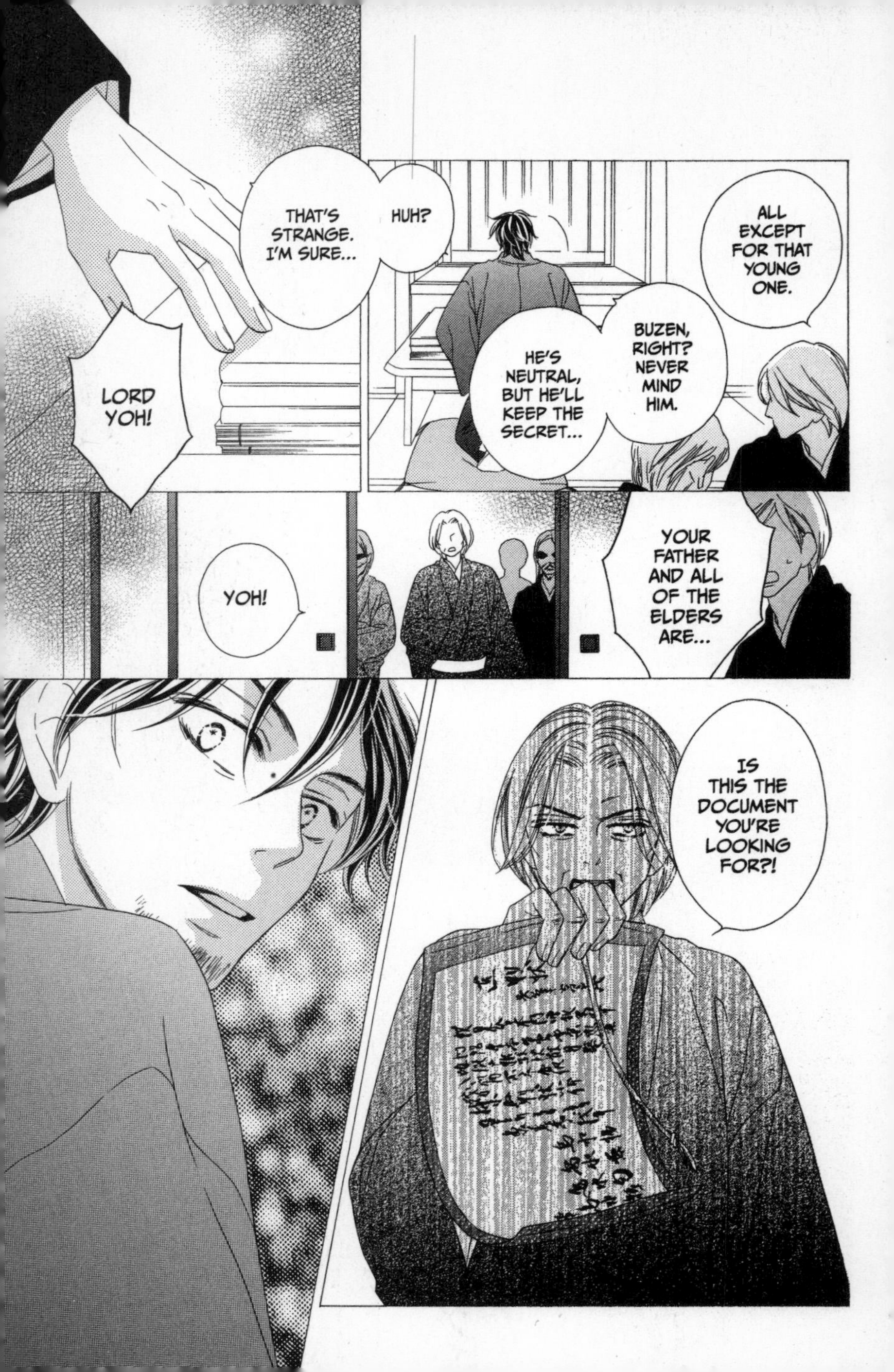
ALL EXCEPT FOR THAT YOUNG ONE.
BUZEN, RIGHT? NEVER MIND HIM.
HE'S NEUTRAL, BUT HE'LL KEEP THE SECRET...
HUH?
THAT'S STRANGE. I'M SURE...
LORD YOH!
YOUR FATHER AND ALL OF THE ELDERS ARE...
YOH!
IS THIS THE DOCUMENT YOU'RE LOOKING FOR?!

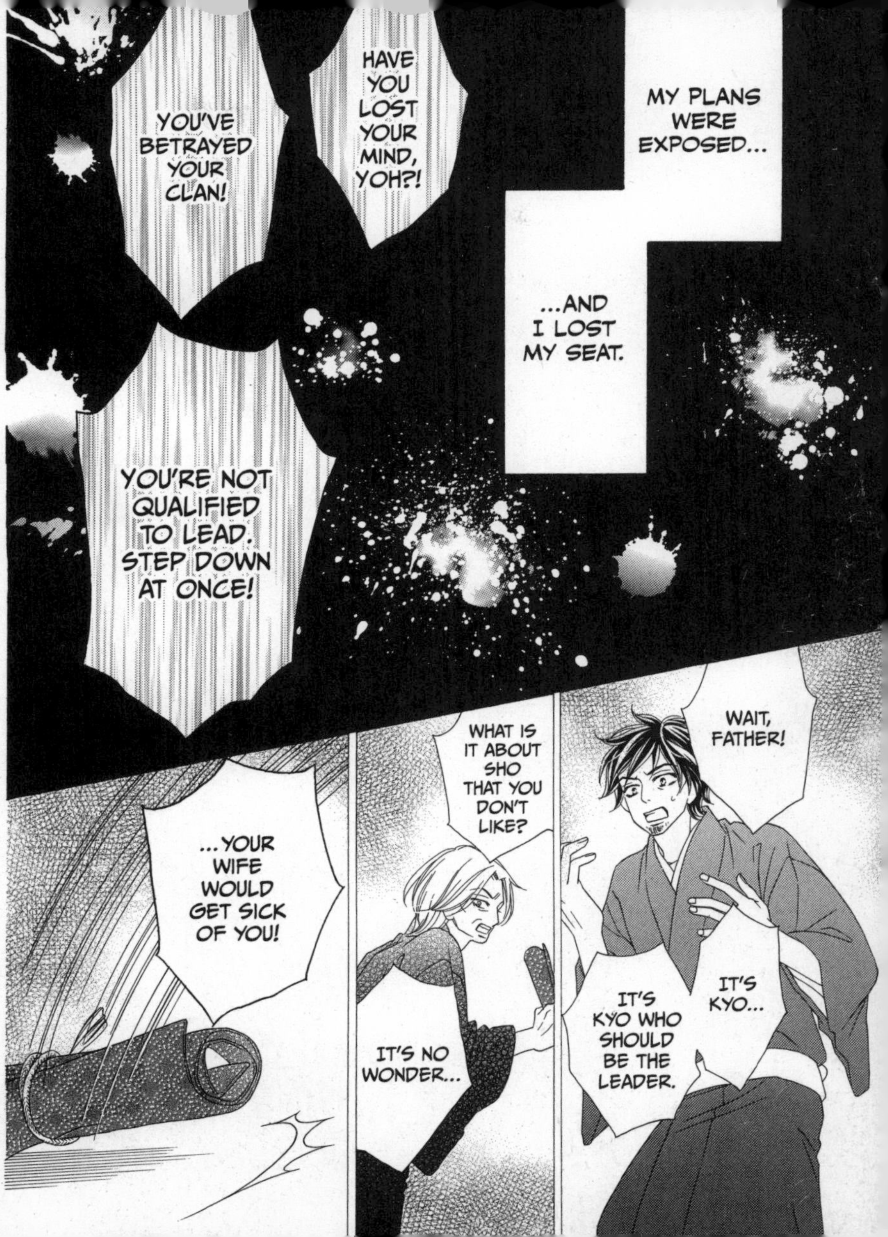
MY PLANS WERE EXPOSED...
...AND I LOST MY SEAT.
HAVE YOU LOST YOUR MIND, YOH?!
YOU'VE BETRAYED YOUR CLAN!
YOU'RE NOT QUALIFIED TO LEAD. STEP DOWN AT ONCE!
WAIT, FATHER!
IT'S KYO...
IT'S KYO WHO SHOULD BE THE LEADER.
WHAT IS IT ABOUT SHO THAT YOU DON'T LIKE?
IT'S NO WONDER...
...YOUR WIFE WOULD GET SICK OF YOU!

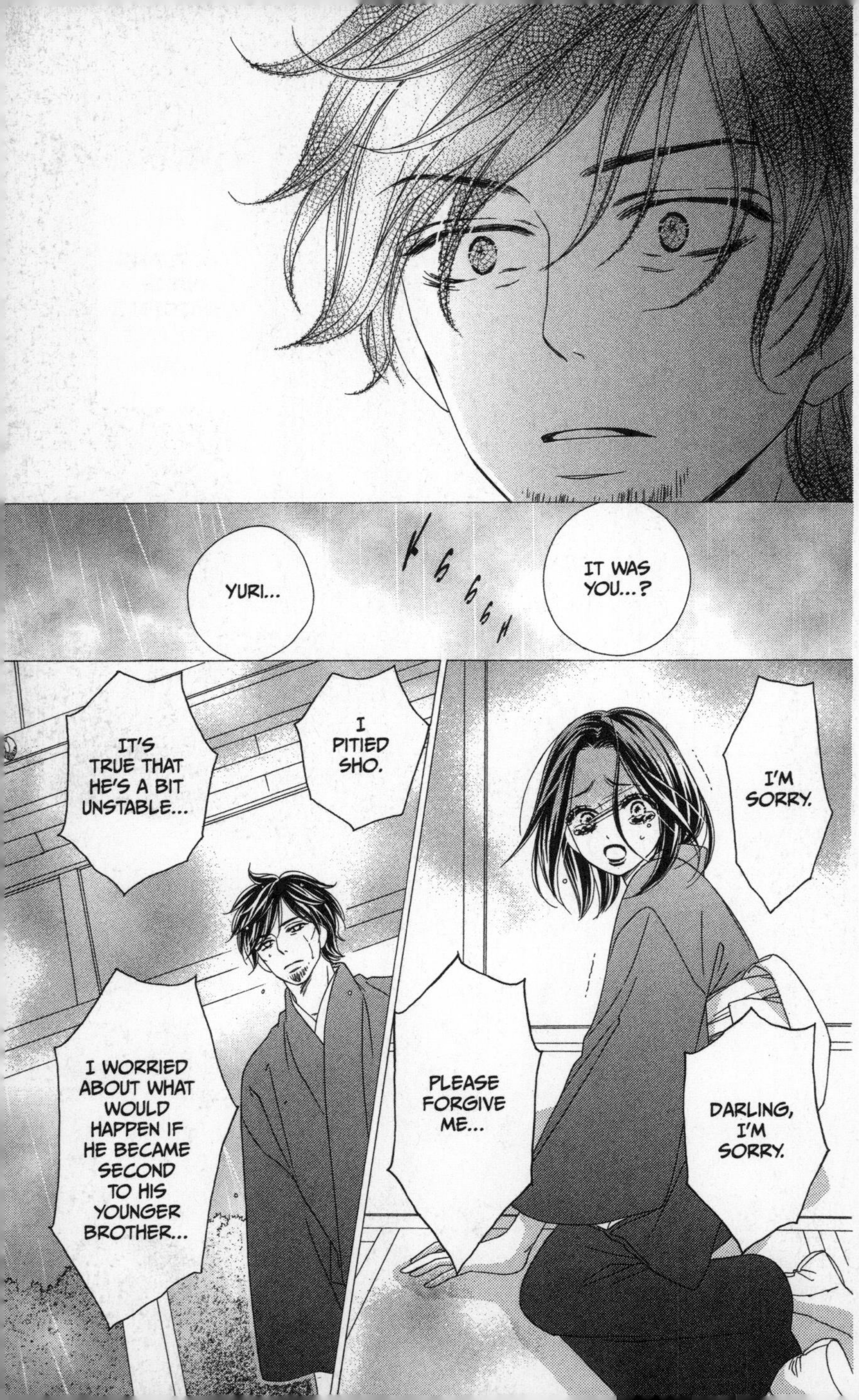
IT WAS YOU...?
YURI...
I'M SORRY.
DARLING, I'M SORRY.
PLEASE FORGIVE ME...
I PITIED SHO.
IT'S TRUE THAT HE'S A BIT UNSTABLE...
I WORRIED ABOUT WHAT WOULD HAPPEN IF HE BECAME SECOND TO HIS YOUNGER BROTHER...

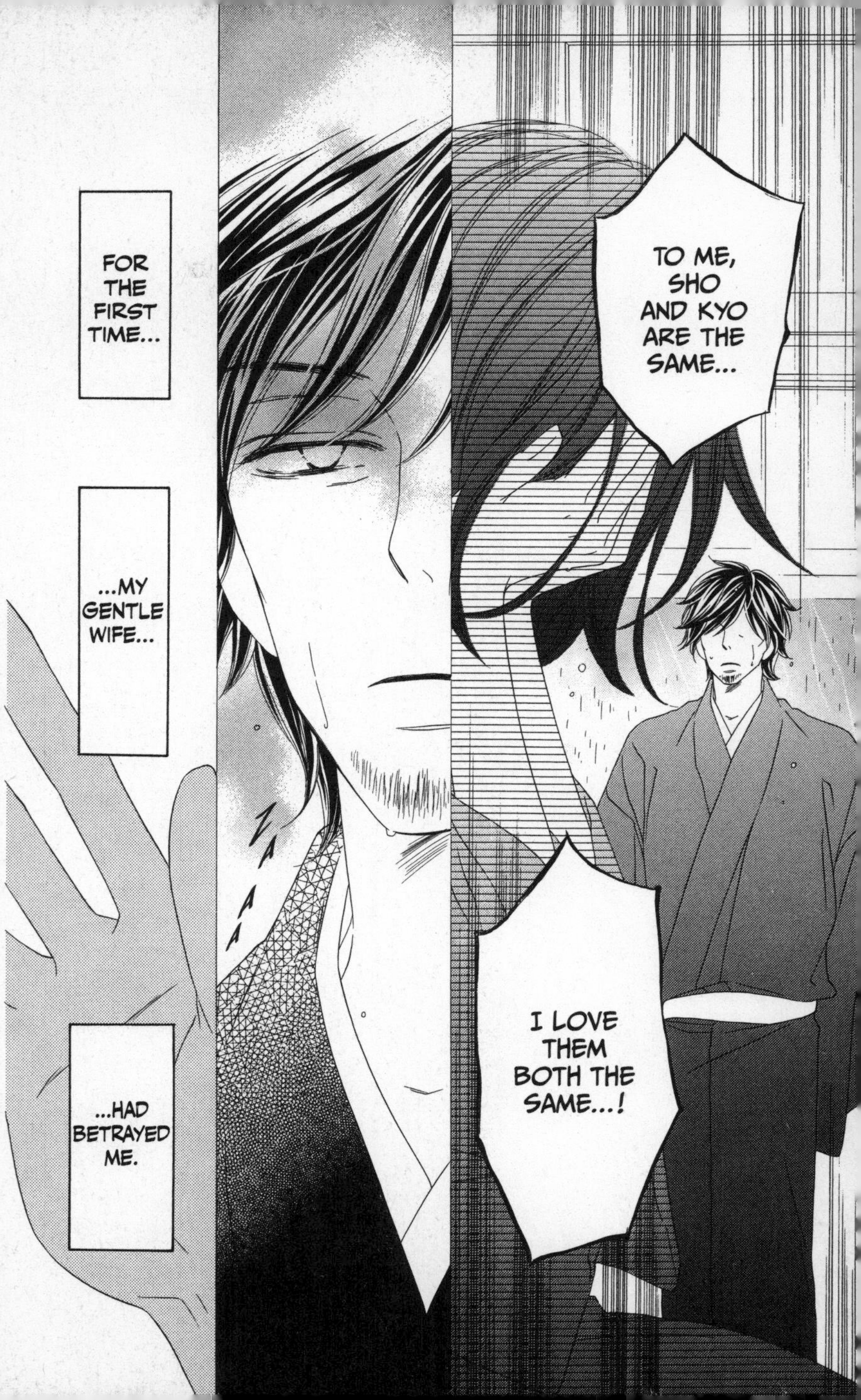
TO ME, SHO AND KYO ARE THE SAME...
I LOVE THEM BOTH THE SAME...!
ZAAAA
FOR THE FIRST TIME...
...MY GENTLE WIFE...
...HAD BETRAYED ME.

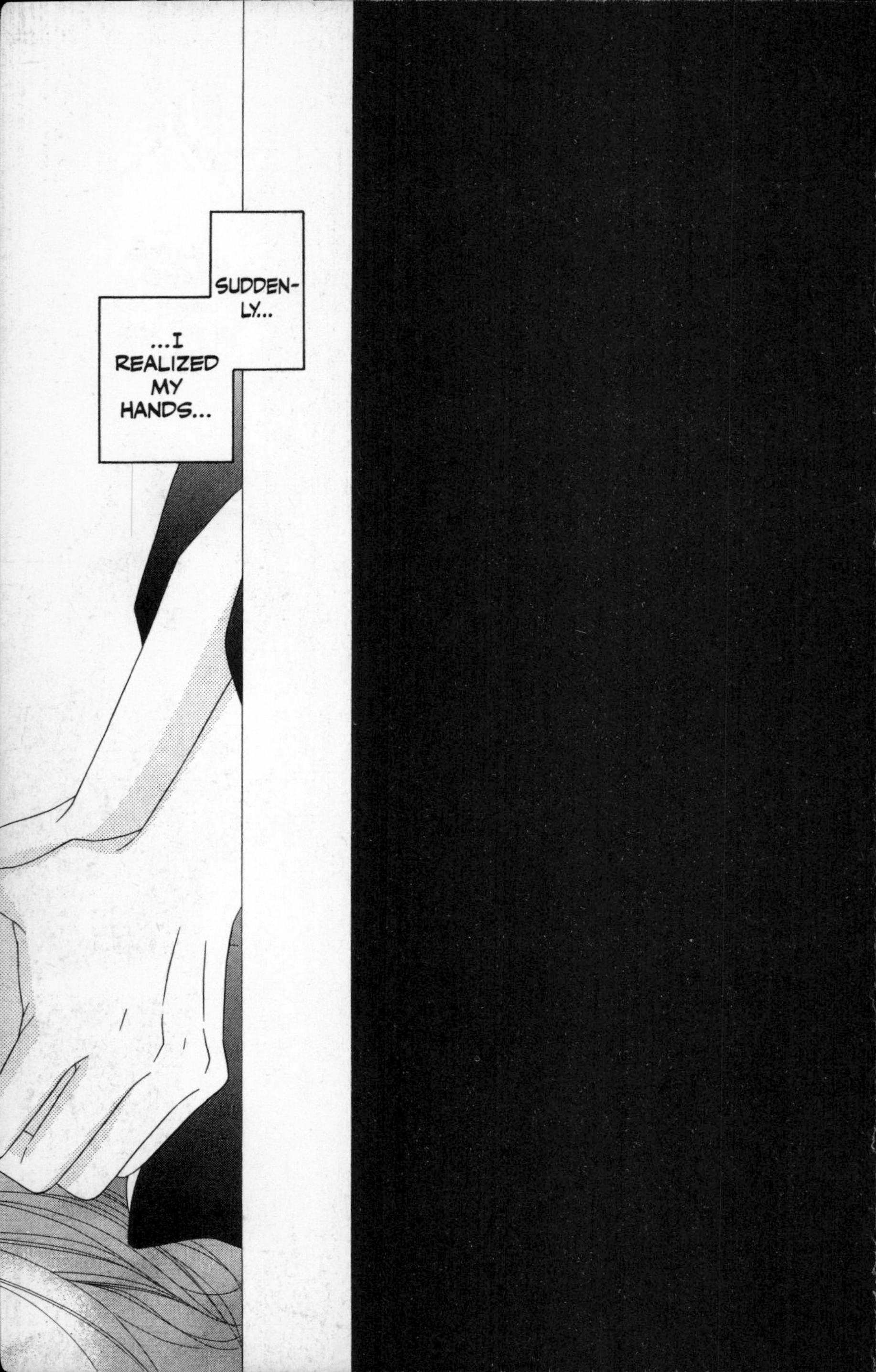
SUDDEN-LY...
...I REALIZED MY HANDS...

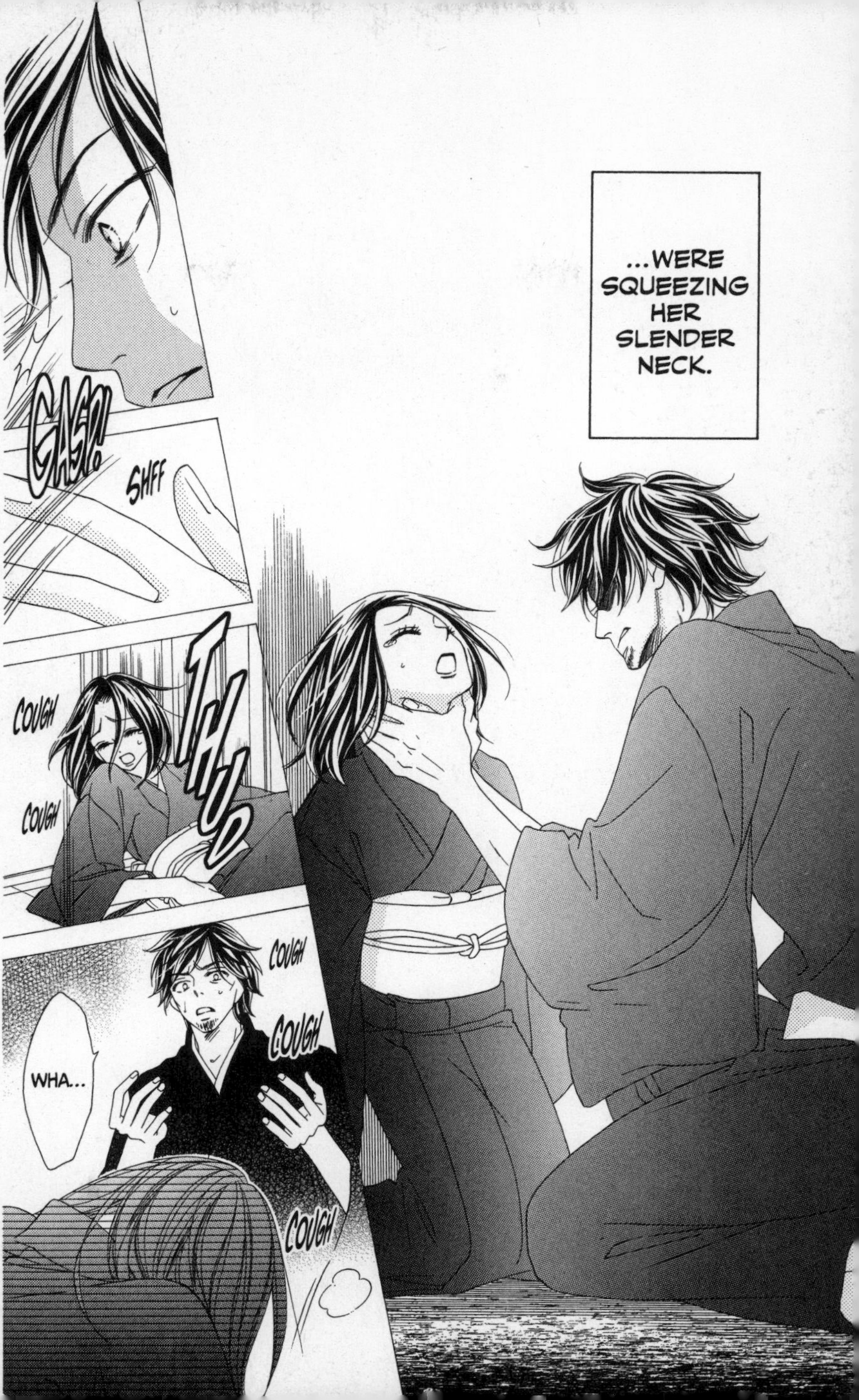
...WERE SQUEEZING HER SLENDER NECK.
GASP!
SHFF
THUD
COUGH
COUGH
COUGH
COUGH
WHA...
COUGH

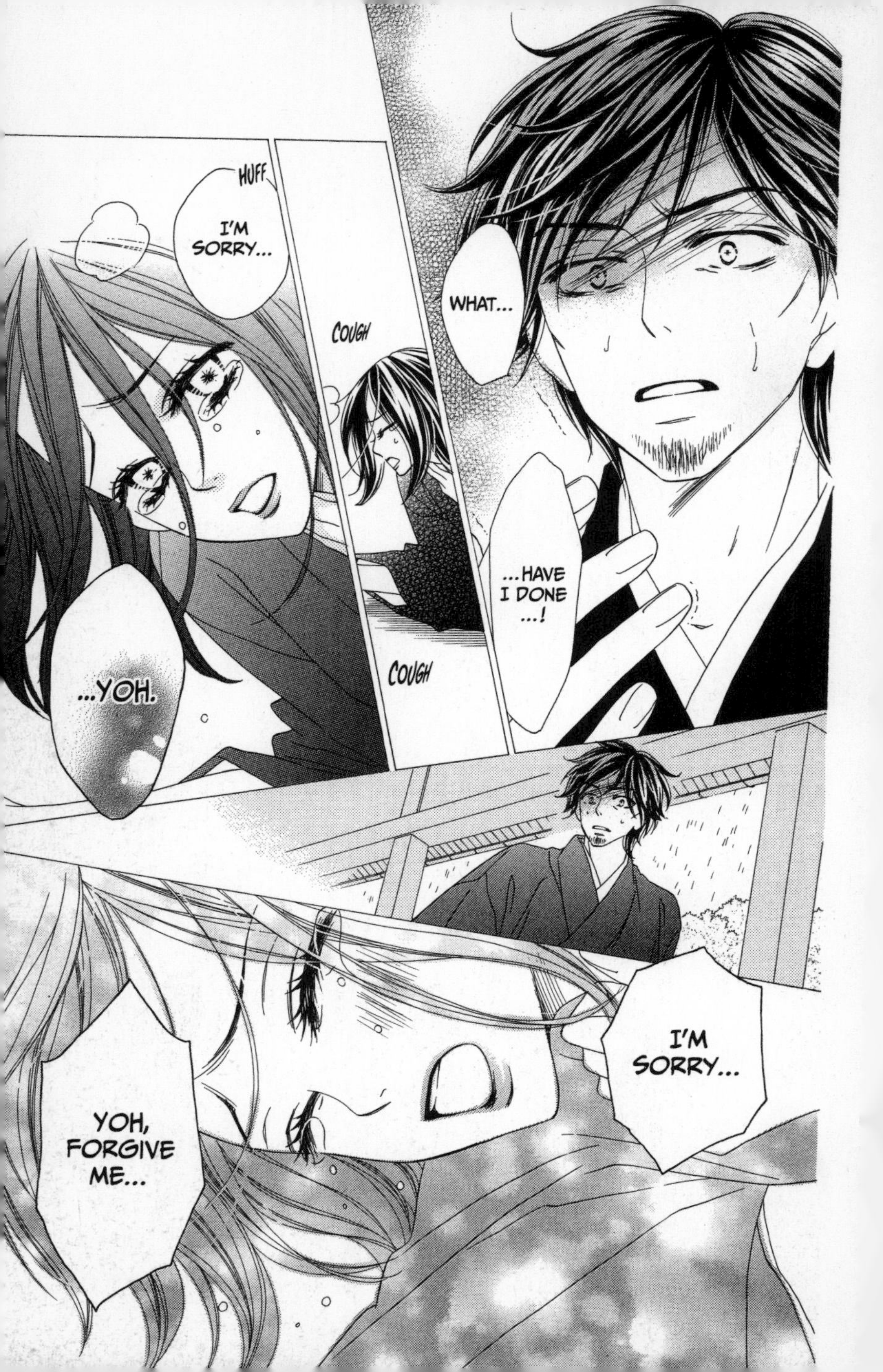
WHAT...
...HAVE I DONE ...!
COUGH
COUGH
HUFF
I'M SORRY...
...YOH.
I'M SORRY...
YOH, FORGIVE ME...

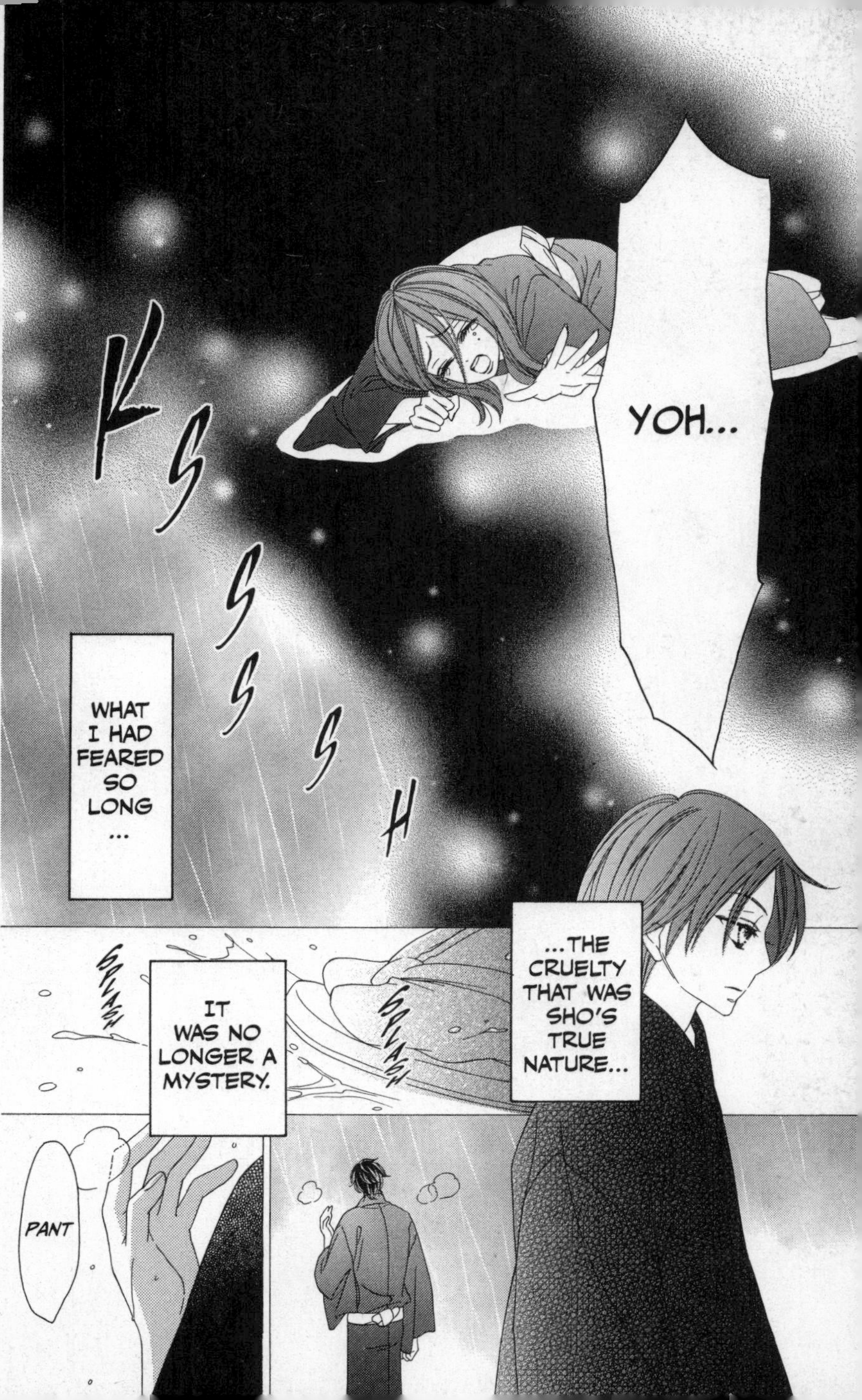
YOH...
KSSSSH
WHAT I HAD FEARED SO LONG ...
...THE CRUELTY THAT WAS SHO'S TRUE NATURE...
SPLASH
SPLASH
IT WAS NO LONGER A MYSTERY.
PANT

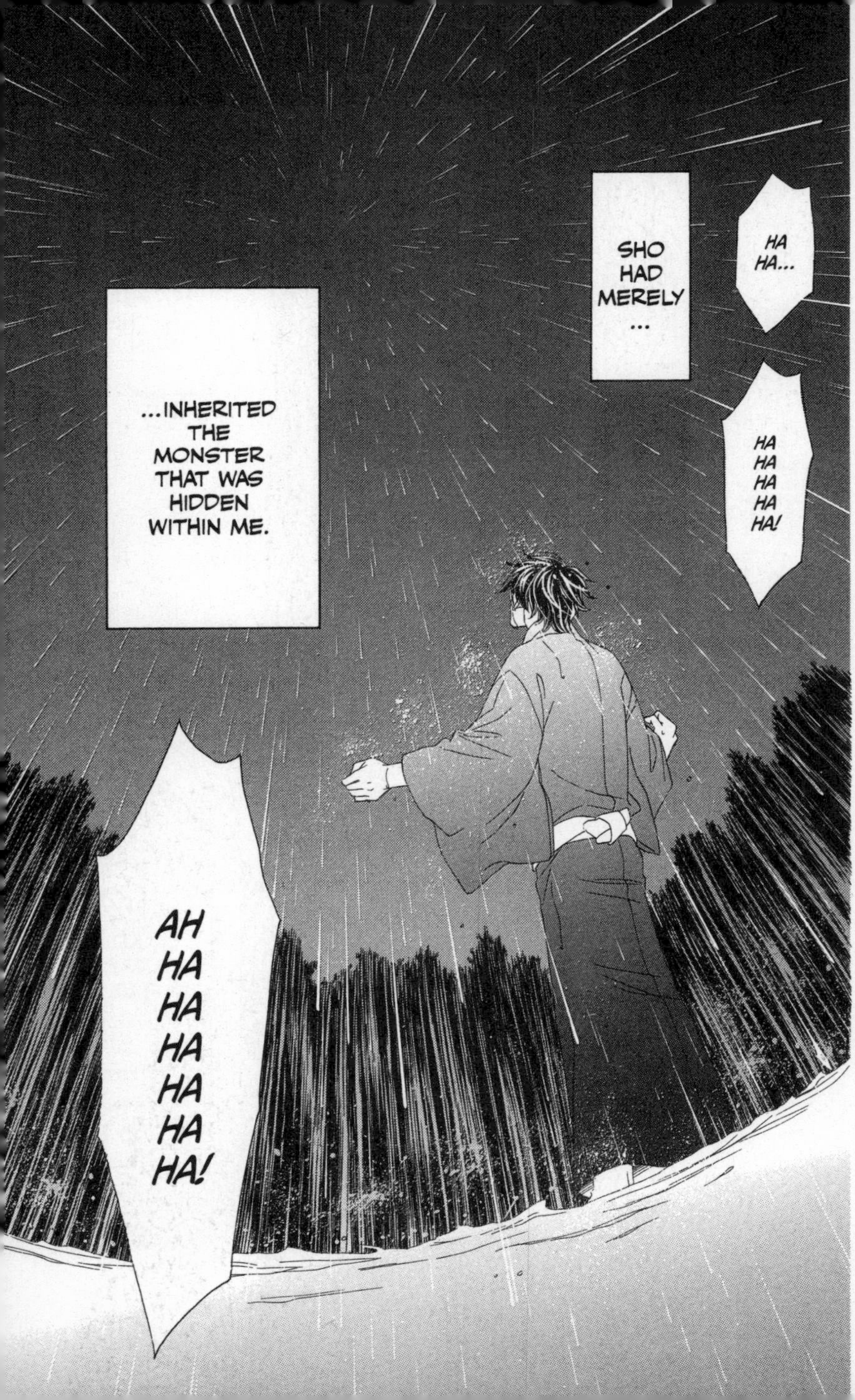
HA HA...
SHO HAD MERELY...
HA HA HA HA HA!
...INHERITED THE MONSTER THAT WAS HIDDEN WITHIN ME.
AH HA HA HA HA HA HA!

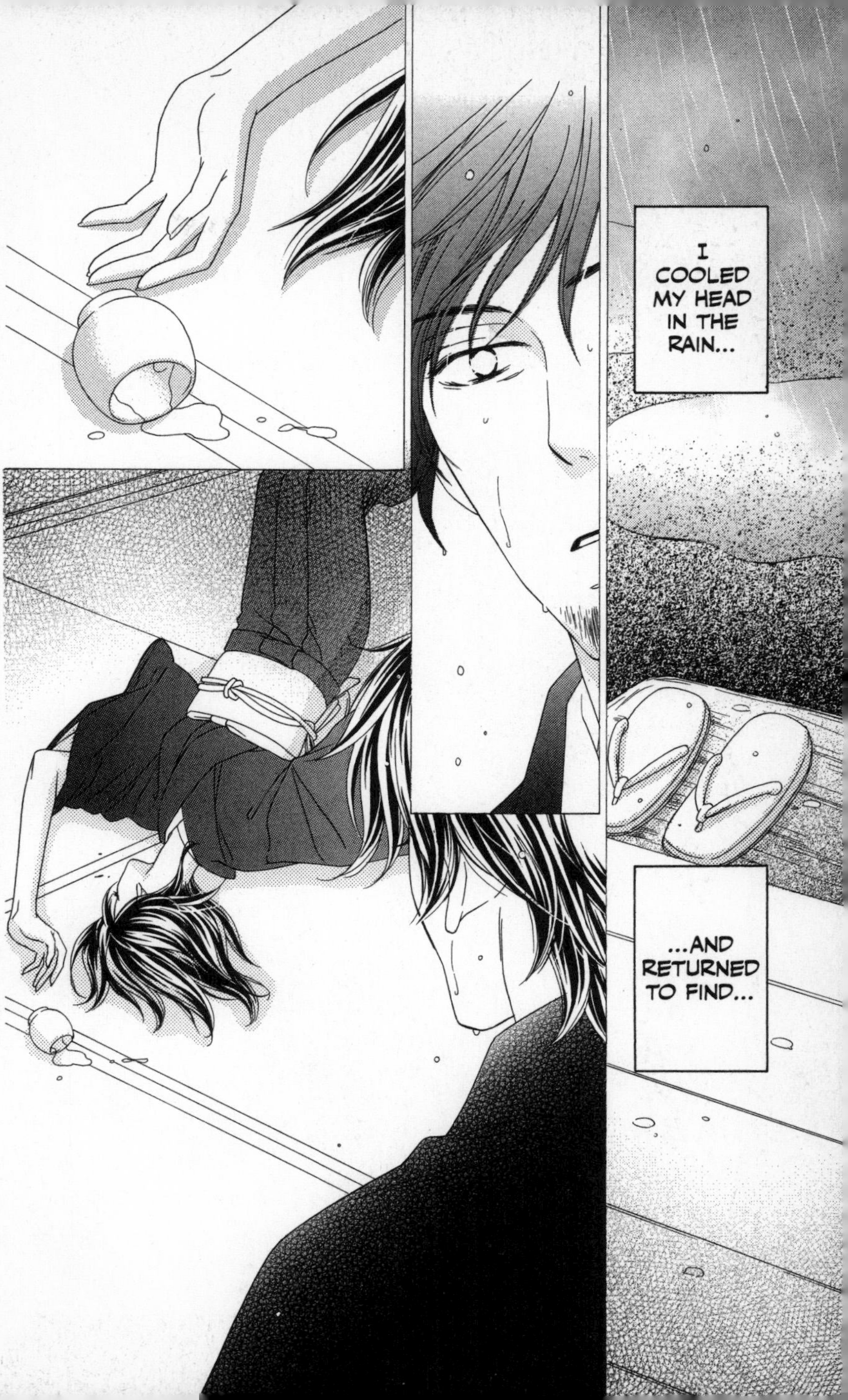
I COOLED MY HEAD IN THE RAIN...
...AND RETURNED TO FIND...

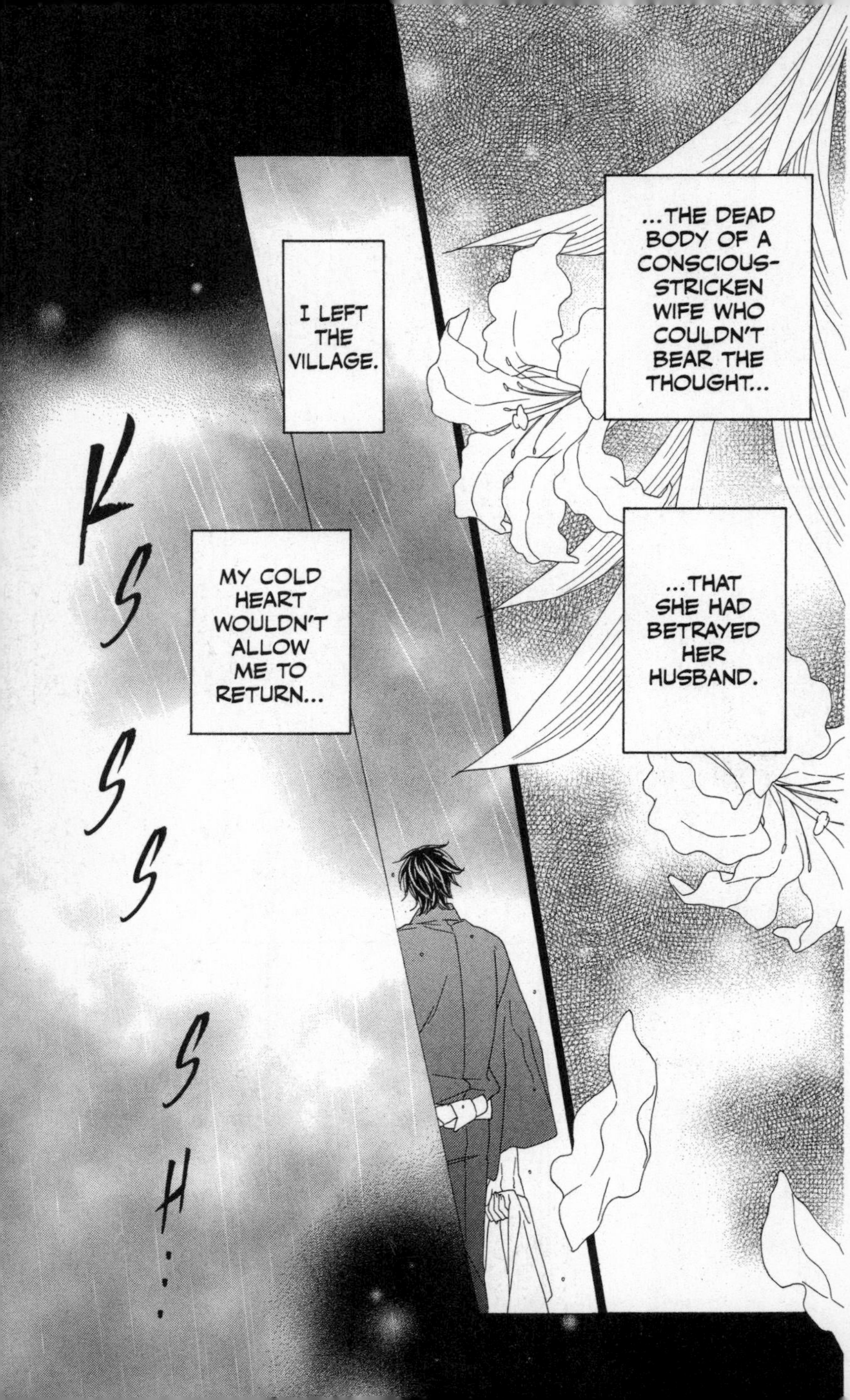
...THE DEAD BODY OF A CONSCIOUS-STRICKEN WIFE WHO COULDN'T BEAR THE THOUGHT...
...THAT SHE HAD BETRAYED HER HUSBAND.
I LEFT THE VILLAGE.
MY COLD HEART WOULDN'T ALLOW ME TO RETURN...
KSSSSH...

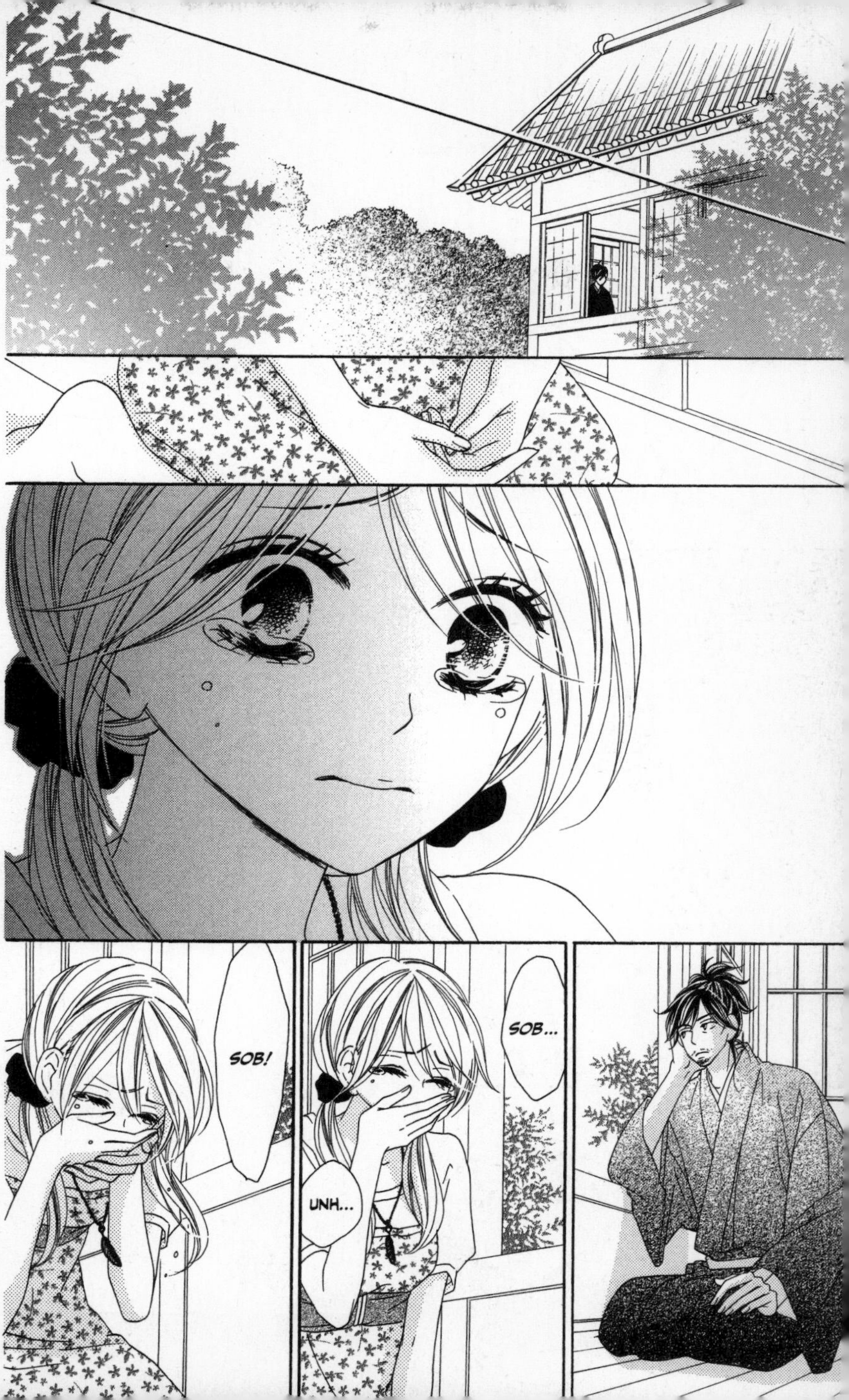
SOB...
UNH...
SOB!

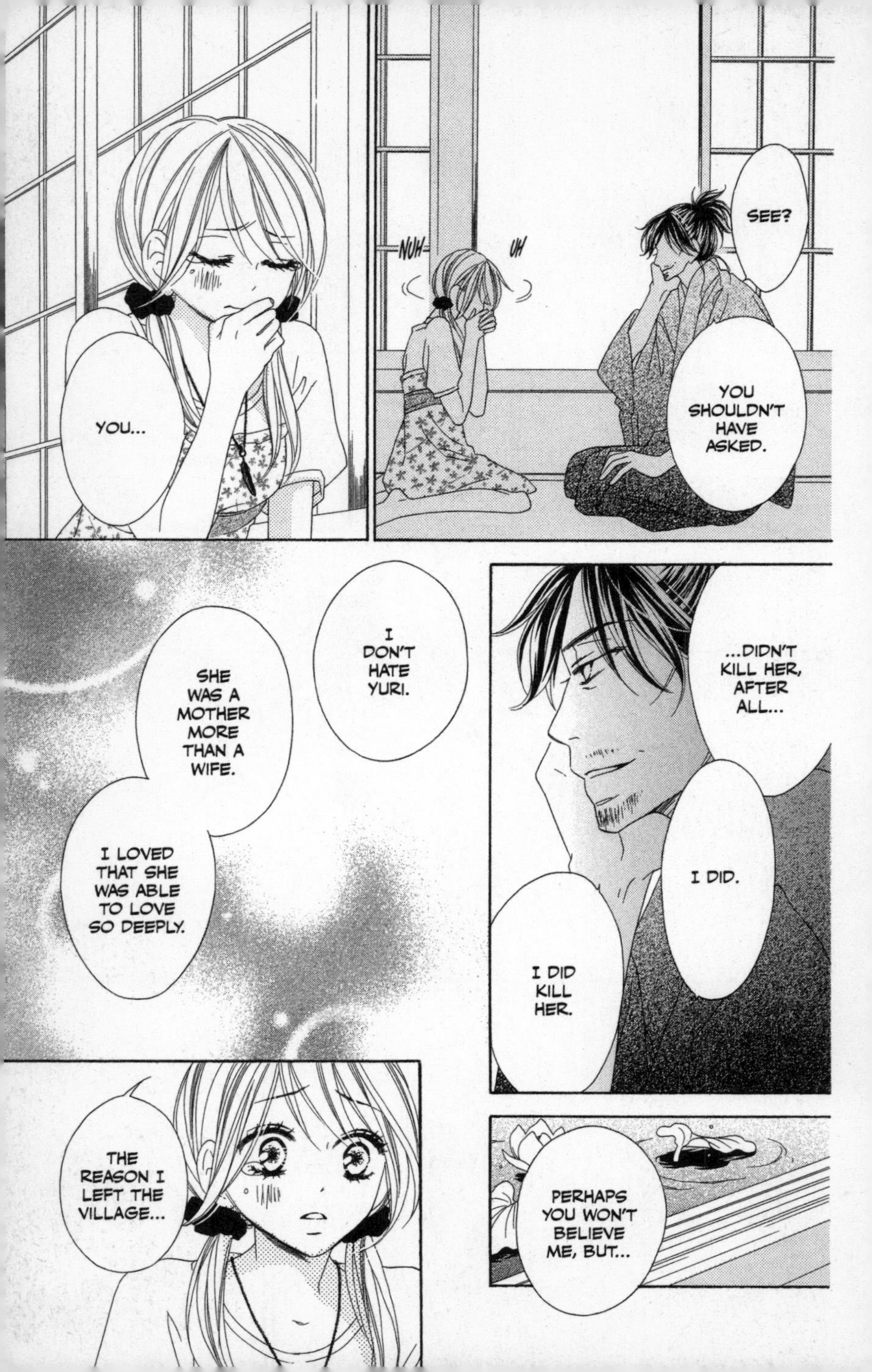
SEE?
NUH UH
YOU SHOULDN'T HAVE ASKED.
YOU...
...DIDN'T KILL HER, AFTER ALL...
I DID.
I DID KILL HER.
I DON'T HATE YURI.
SHE WAS A MOTHER MORE THAN A WIFE.
I LOVED THAT SHE WAS ABLE TO LOVE SO DEEPLY.
PERHAPS YOU WON'T BELIEVE ME, BUT...
THE REASON I LEFT THE VILLAGE...

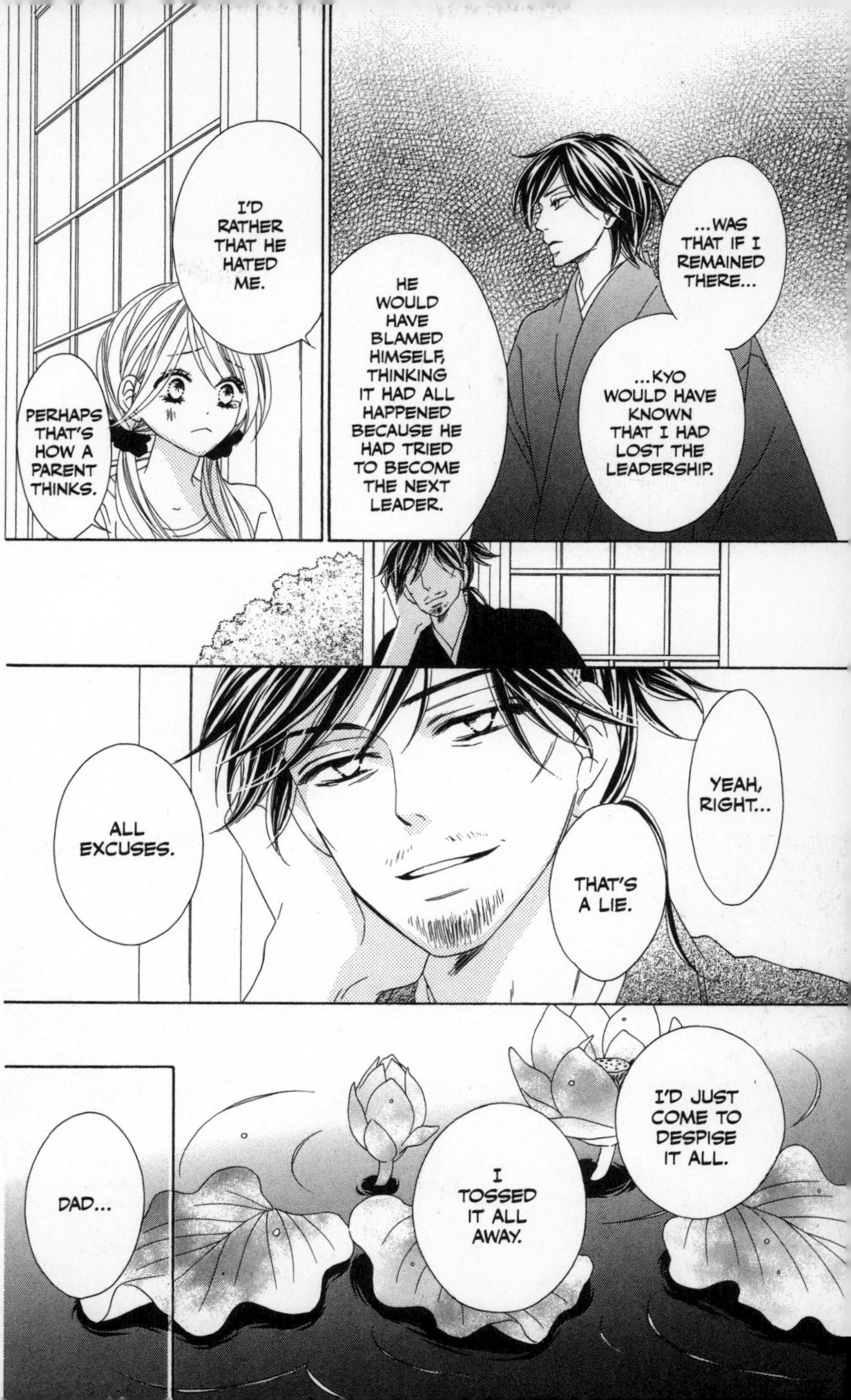
...WAS THAT IF I REMAINED THERE...
...KYO WOULD HAVE KNOWN THAT I HAD LOST THE LEADERSHIP.
HE WOULD HAVE BLAMED HIMSELF, THINKING IT HAD ALL HAPPENED BECAUSE HE HAD TRIED TO BECOME THE NEXT LEADER.
I'D RATHER THAT HE HATED ME.
PERHAPS THAT'S HOW A PARENT THINKS.
YEAH, RIGHT...
THAT'S A LIE.
ALL EXCUSES.
I'D JUST COME TO DESPISE IT ALL.
I TOSSED IT ALL AWAY.
DAD...

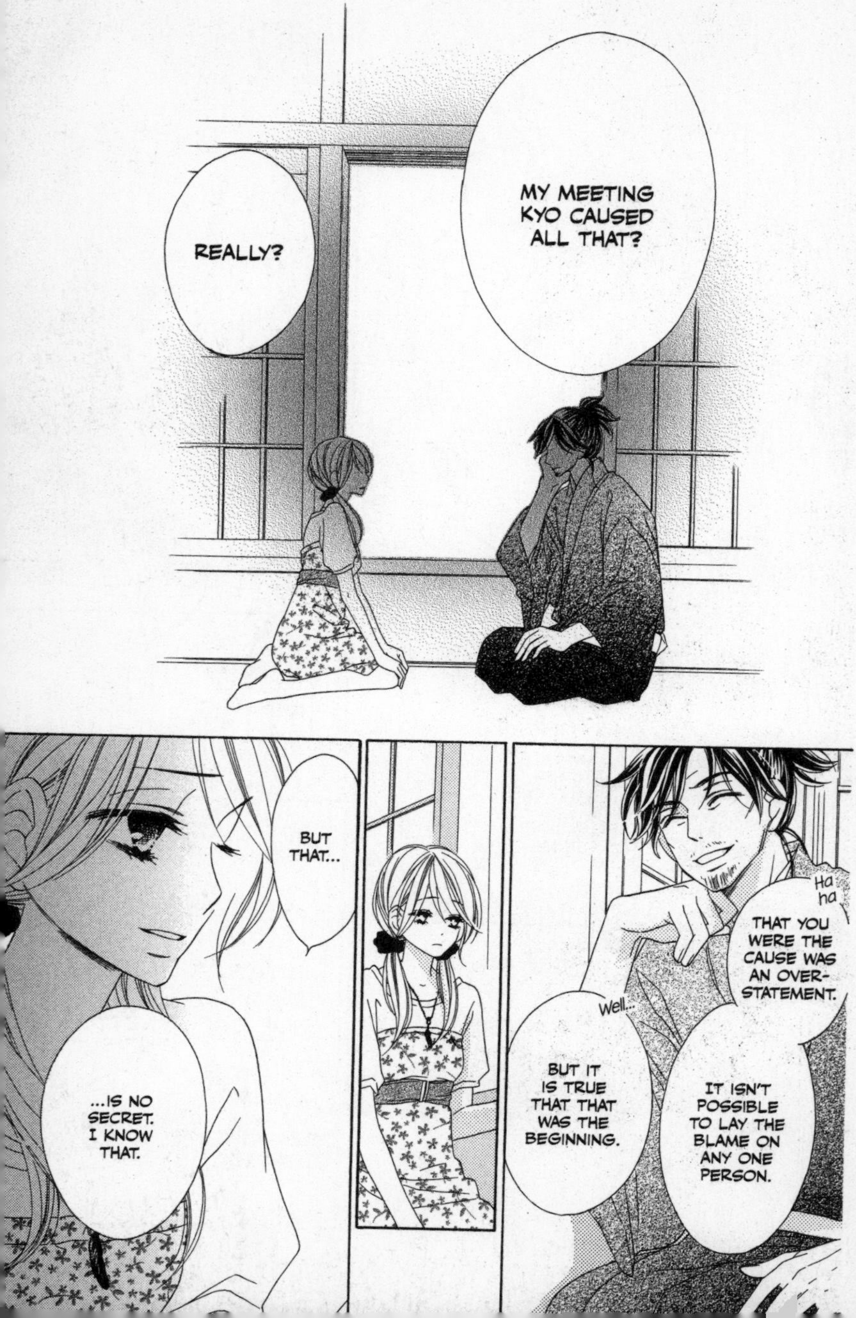

MY MEETING KYO CAUSED ALL THAT?
REALLY?
Ha ha
THAT YOU WERE THE CAUSE WAS AN OVER-STATEMENT.
IT ISN'T POSSIBLE TO LAY THE BLAME ON ANY ONE PERSON.
Well...
BUT IT IS TRUE THAT THAT WAS THE BEGINNING.
BUT THAT...
...IS NO SECRET. I KNOW THAT.

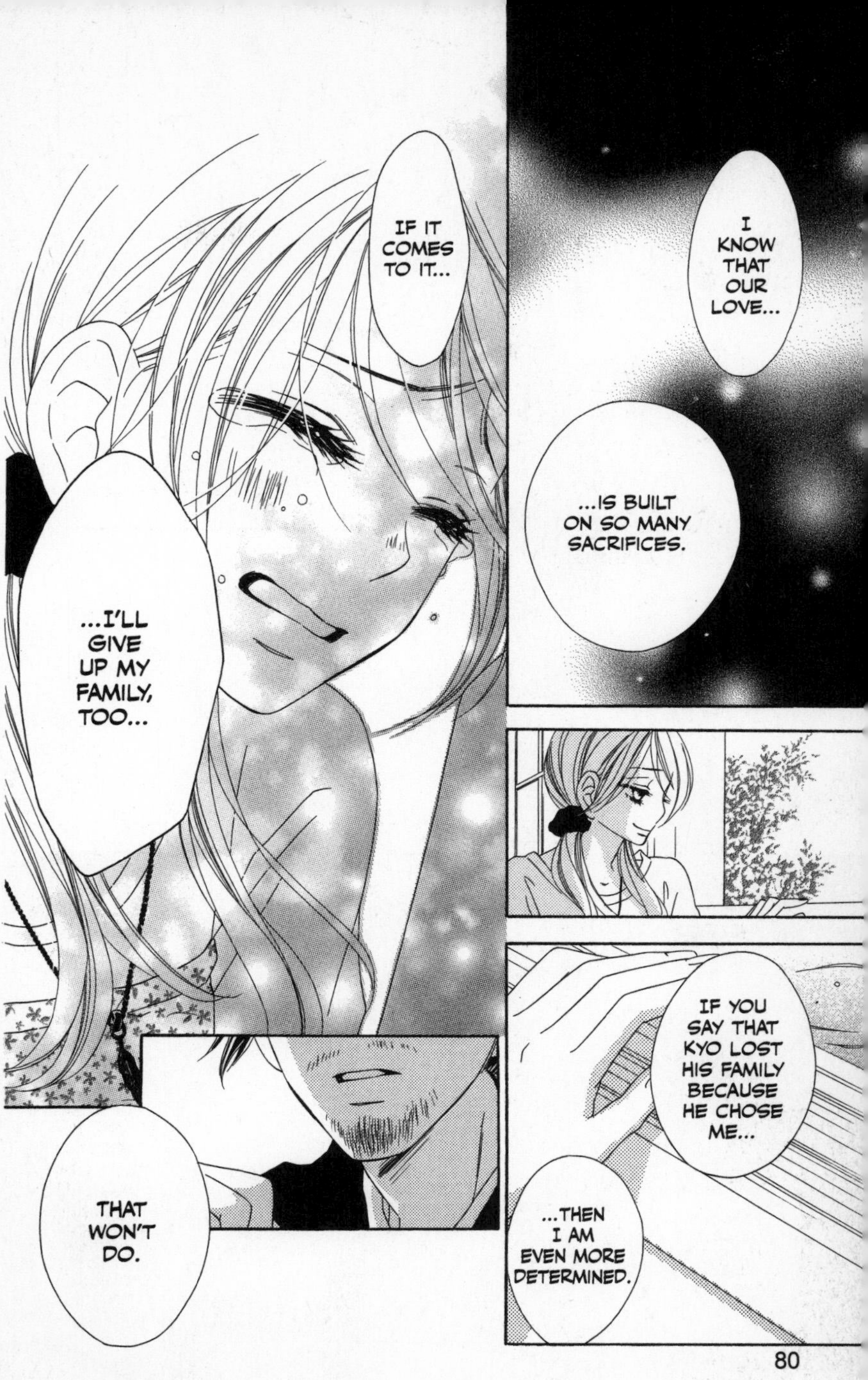
I KNOW THAT OUR LOVE...
...IS BUILT ON SO MANY SACRIFICES.
IF IT COMES TO IT...
...I'LL GIVE UP MY FAMILY, TOO...
THAT WON'T DO.
IF YOU SAY THAT KYO LOST HIS FAMILY BECAUSE HE CHOSE ME...
...THEN I AM EVEN MORE DETERMINED.

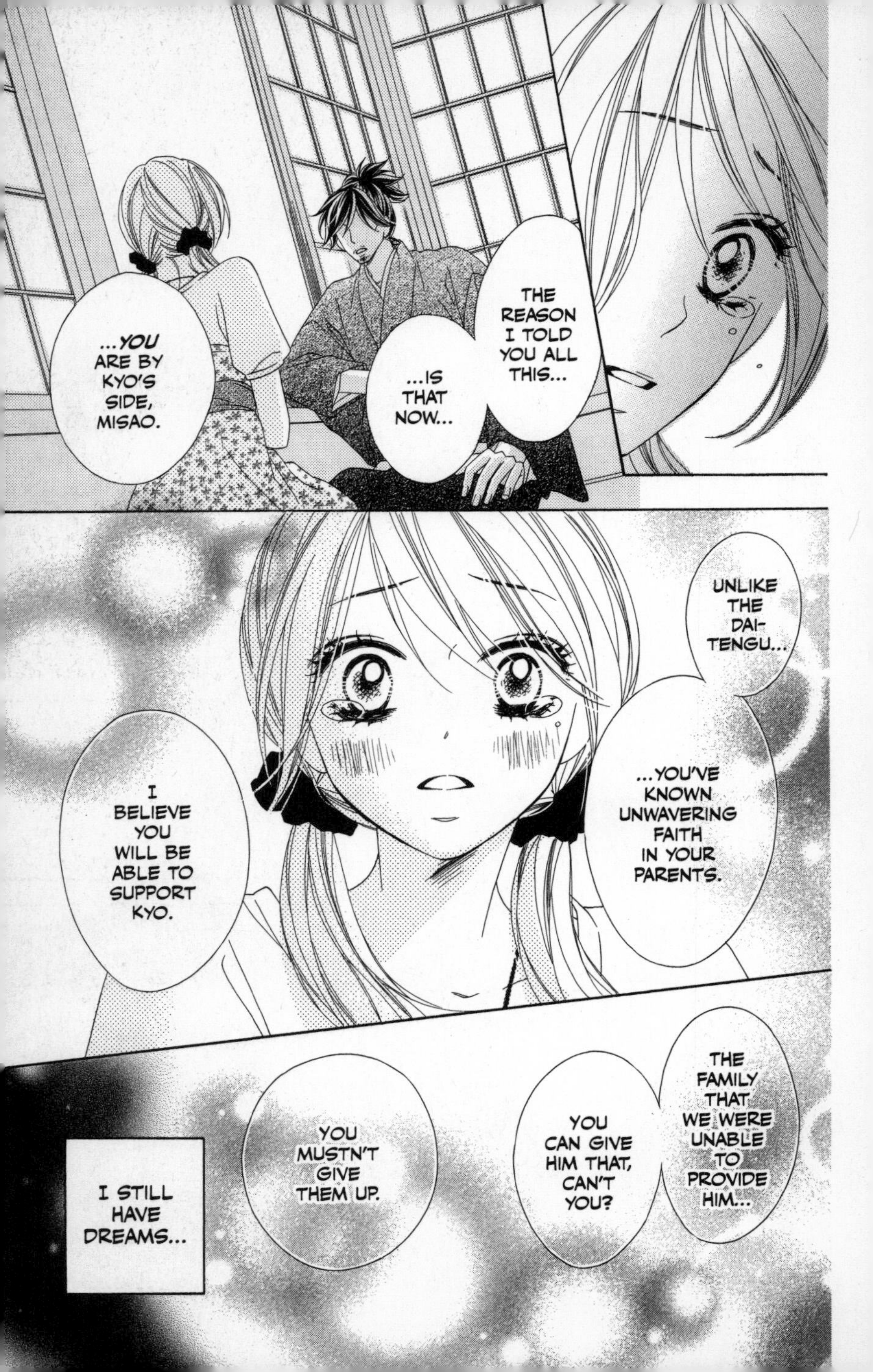
THE REASON I TOLD YOU ALL THIS...
...IS THAT NOW...
...*YOU* ARE BY KYO'S SIDE, MISAO.
UNLIKE THE DAI-TENGU...
...YOU'VE KNOWN UNWAVERING FAITH IN YOUR PARENTS.
I BELIEVE YOU WILL BE ABLE TO SUPPORT KYO.
THE FAMILY THAT WE WERE UNABLE TO PROVIDE HIM...
YOU CAN GIVE HIM THAT, CAN'T YOU?
YOU MUSTN'T GIVE THEM UP.
I STILL HAVE DREAMS...

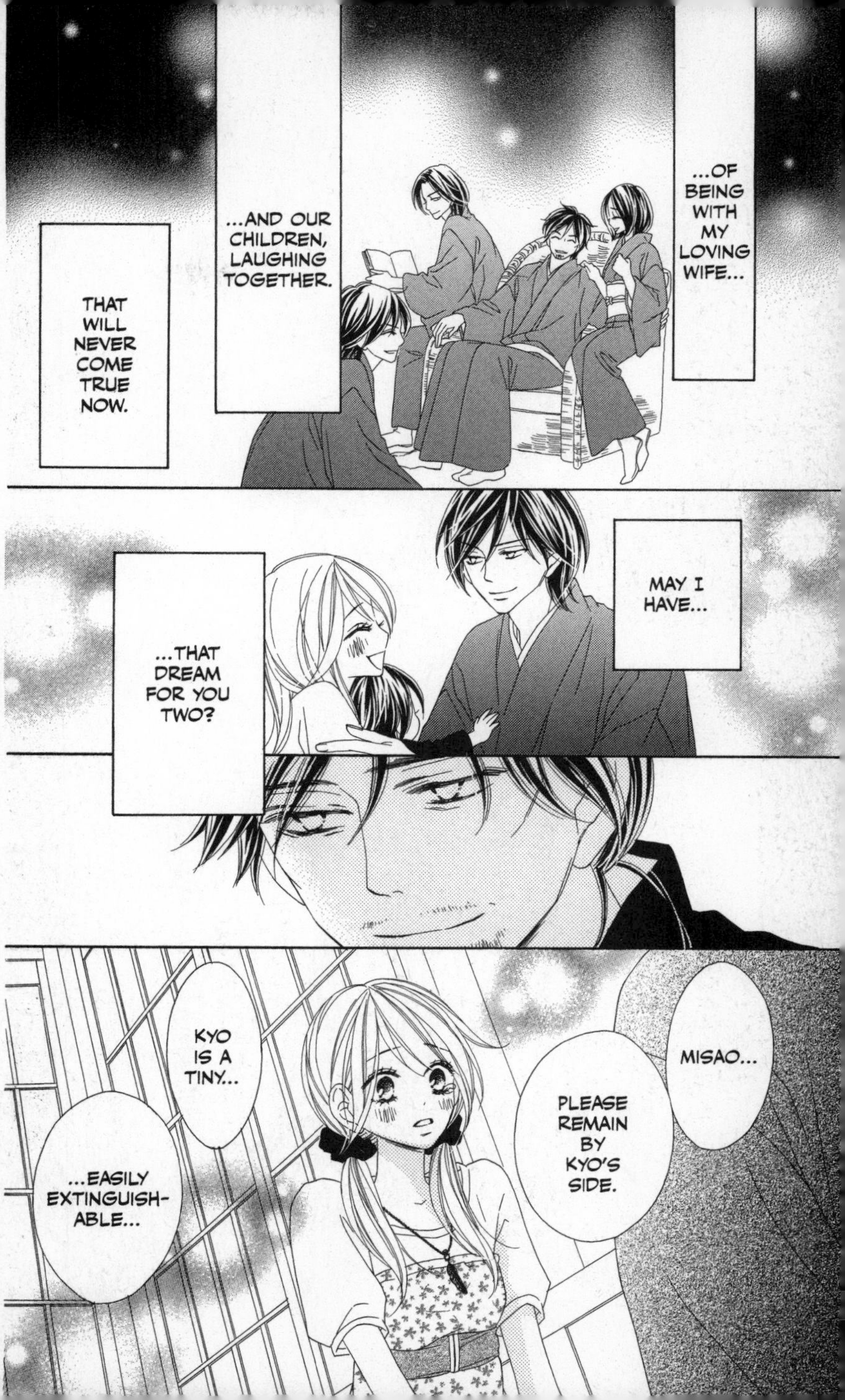
...OF BEING WITH MY LOVING WIFE...
...AND OUR CHILDREN, LAUGHING TOGETHER.
THAT WILL NEVER COME TRUE NOW.
MAY I HAVE...
...THAT DREAM FOR YOU TWO?
MISAO...
PLEASE REMAIN BY KYO'S SIDE.
KYO IS A TINY...
...EASILY EXTINGUISH-ABLE...

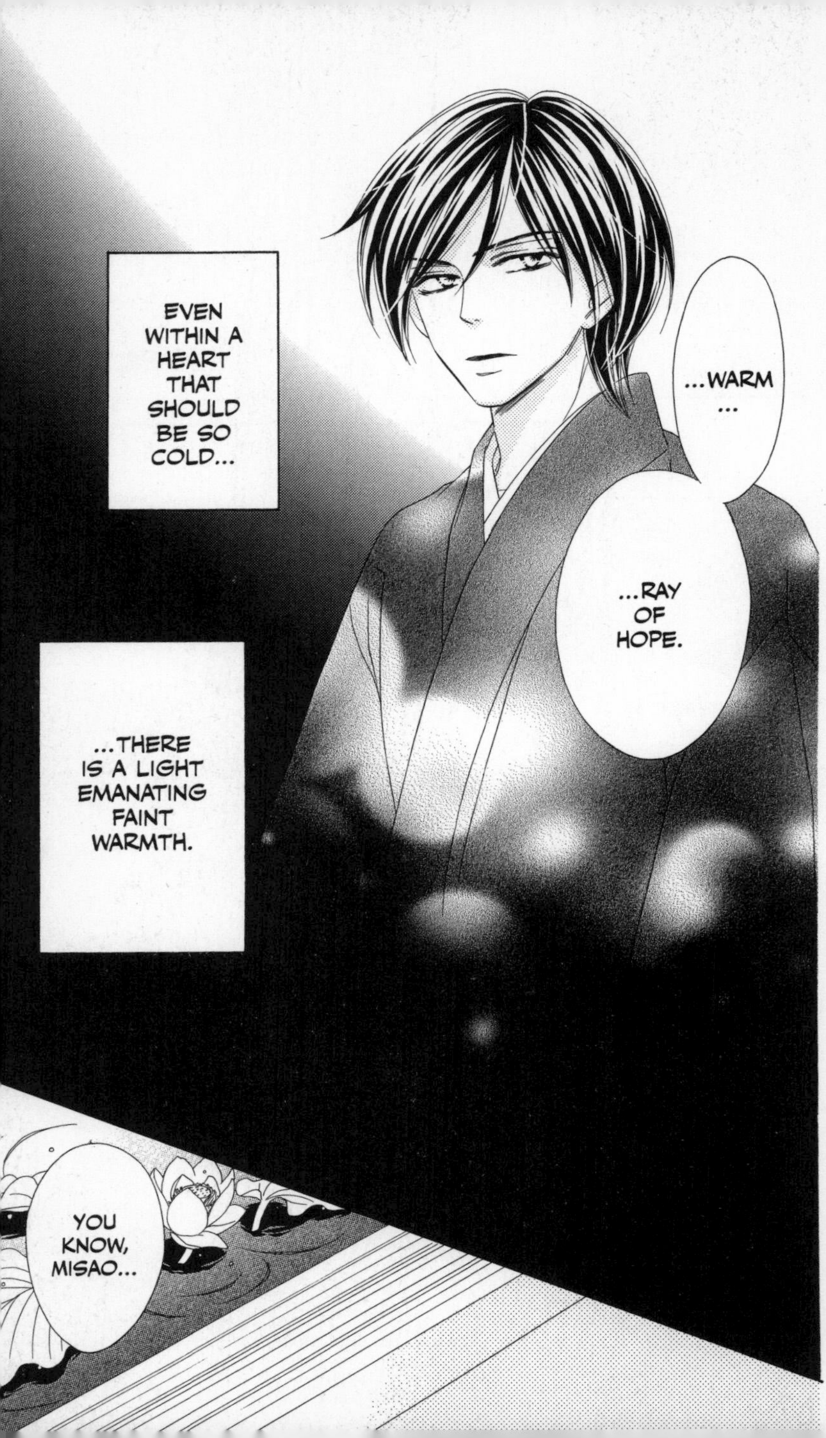
...WARM ...
...RAY OF HOPE.
EVEN WITHIN A HEART THAT SHOULD BE SO COLD...
...THERE IS A LIGHT EMANATING FAINT WARMTH.
YOU KNOW, MISAO...

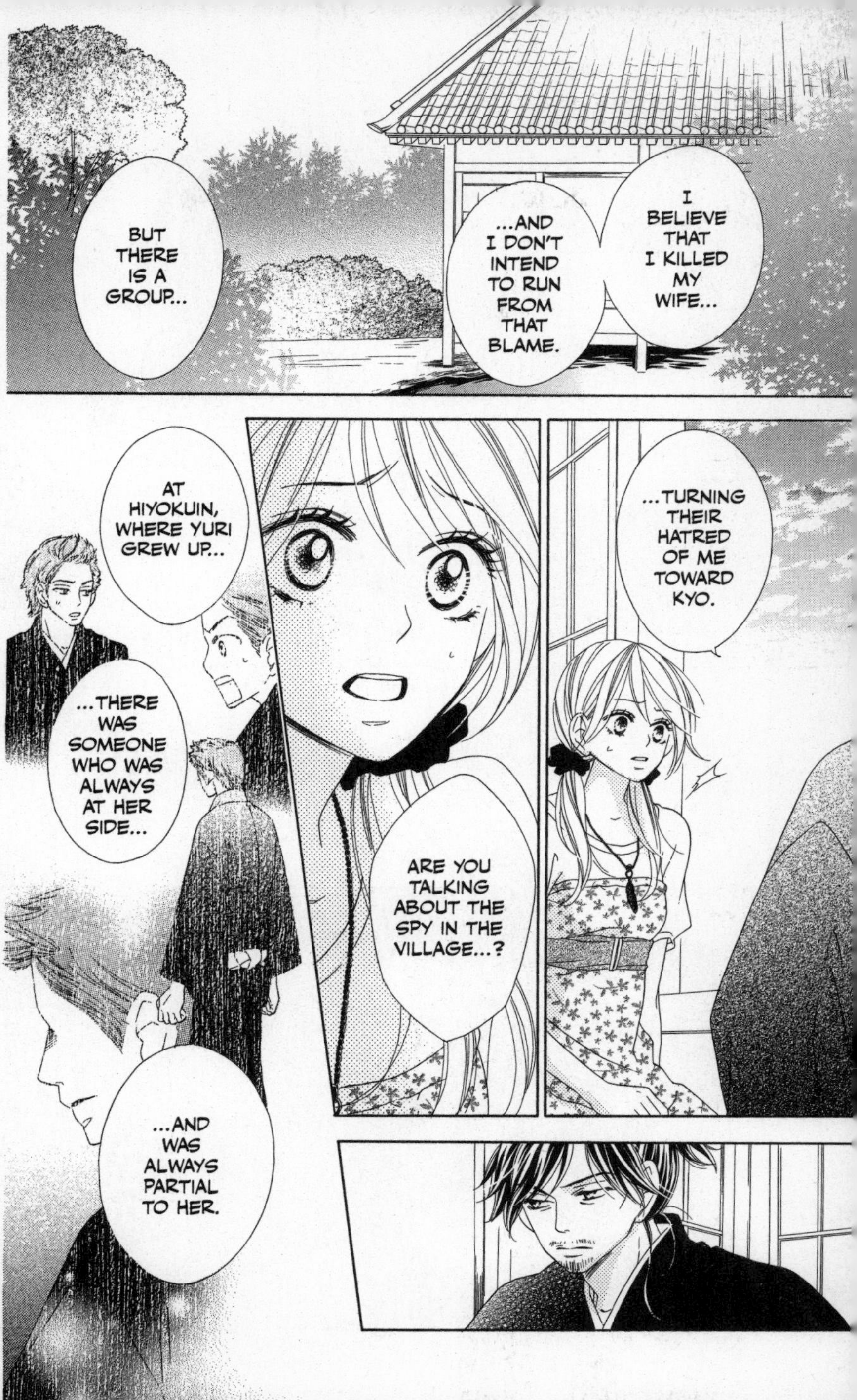
I BELIEVE THAT I KILLED MY WIFE...
...AND I DON'T INTEND TO RUN FROM THAT BLAME.
BUT THERE IS A GROUP...
...TURNING THEIR HATRED OF ME TOWARD KYO.
ARE YOU TALKING ABOUT THE SPY IN THE VILLAGE...?
AT HIYOKUIN, WHERE YURI GREW UP...
...THERE WAS SOMEONE WHO WAS ALWAYS AT HER SIDE...
...AND WAS ALWAYS PARTIAL TO HER.

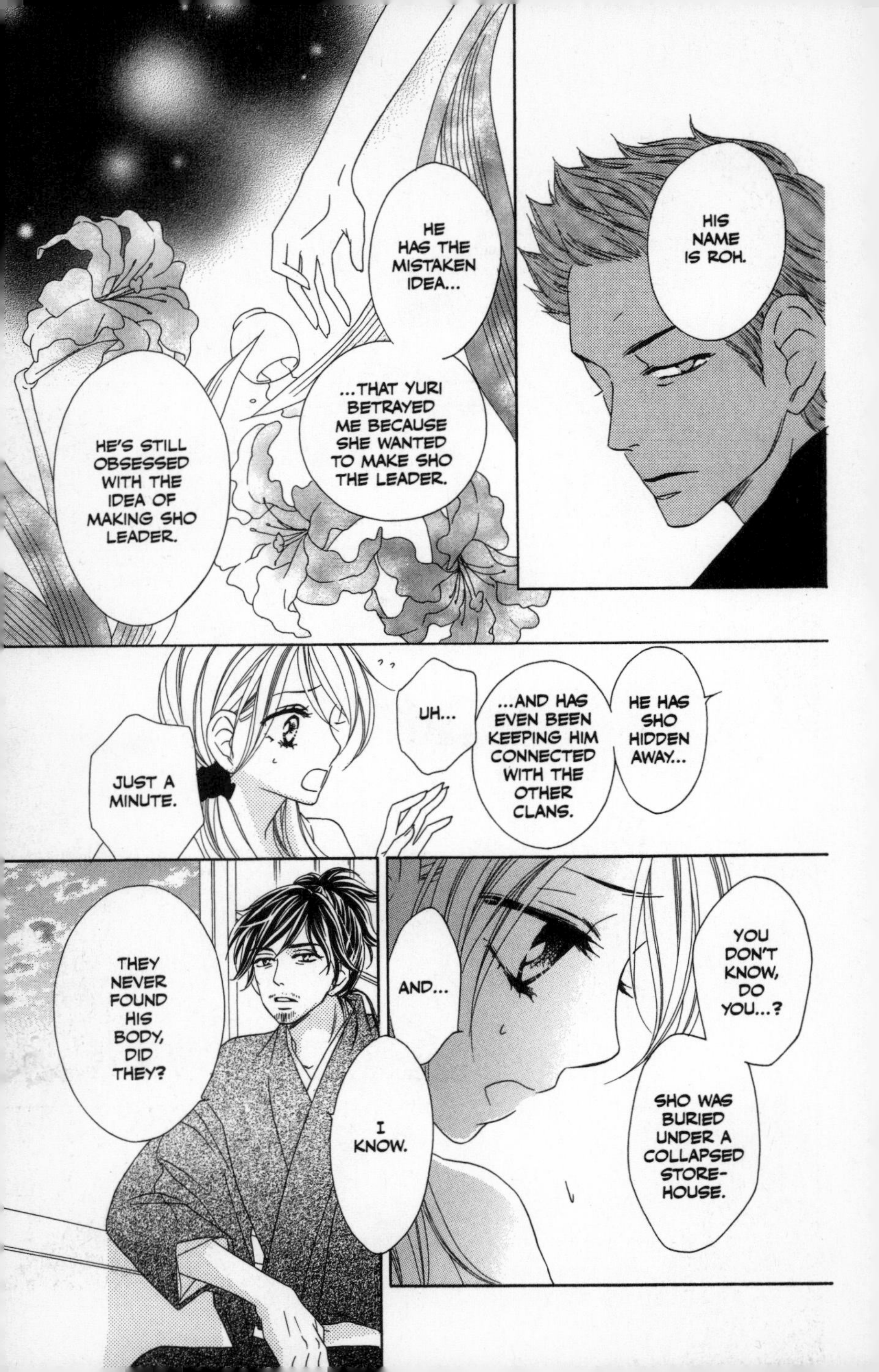
HIS NAME IS ROH.
HE HAS THE MISTAKEN IDEA...
...THAT YURI BETRAYED ME BECAUSE SHE WANTED TO MAKE SHO THE LEADER.
HE'S STILL OBSESSED WITH THE IDEA OF MAKING SHO LEADER.
HE HAS SHO HIDDEN AWAY...
...AND HAS EVEN BEEN KEEPING HIM CONNECTED WITH THE OTHER CLANS.
UH...
JUST A MINUTE.
YOU DON'T KNOW, DO YOU...?
SHO WAS BURIED UNDER A COLLAPSED STORE-HOUSE.
AND...
I KNOW.
THEY NEVER FOUND HIS BODY, DID THEY?

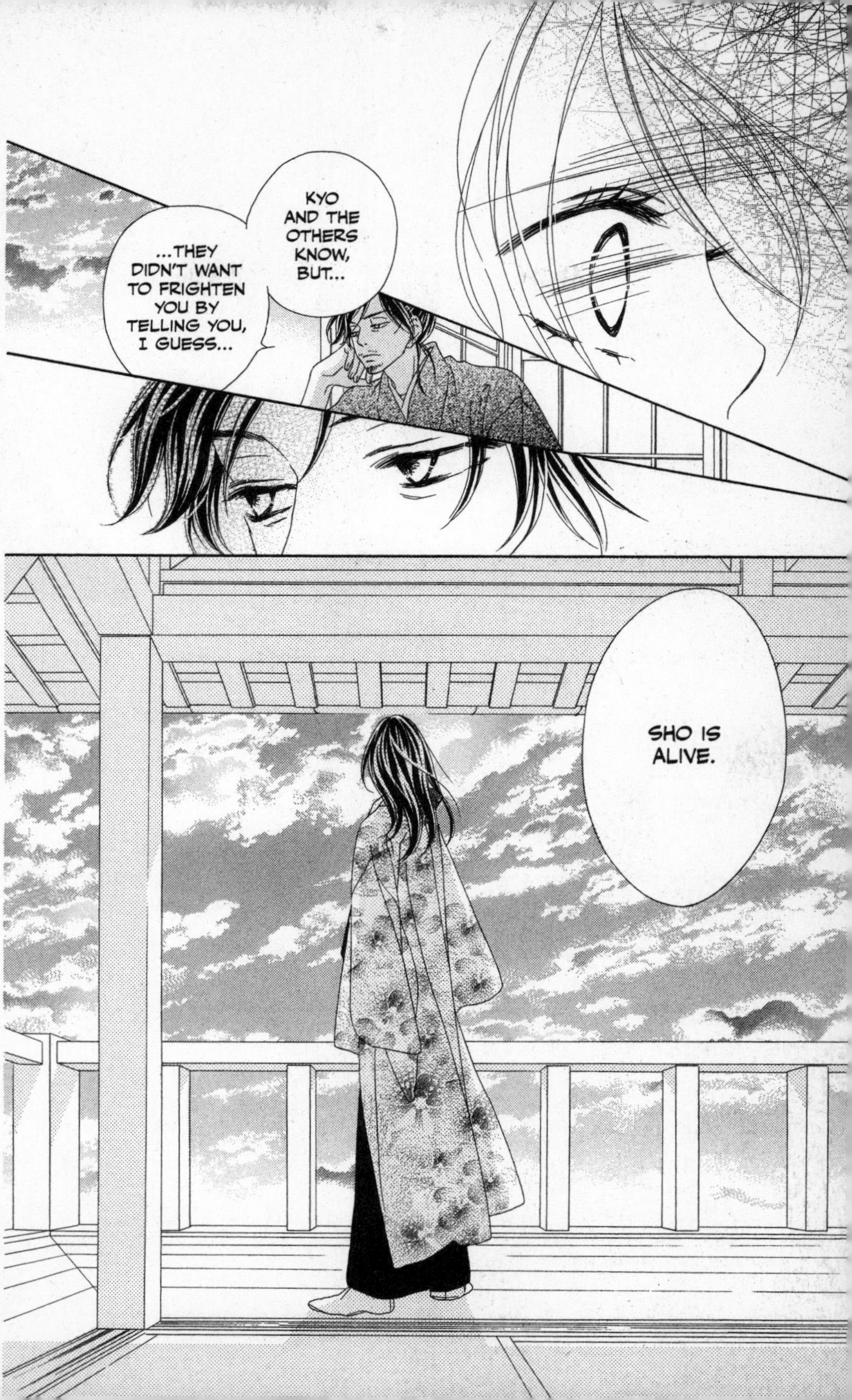
KYO AND THE OTHERS KNOW, BUT...
...THEY DIDN'T WANT TO FRIGHTEN YOU BY TELLING YOU, I GUESS...
SHO IS ALIVE.

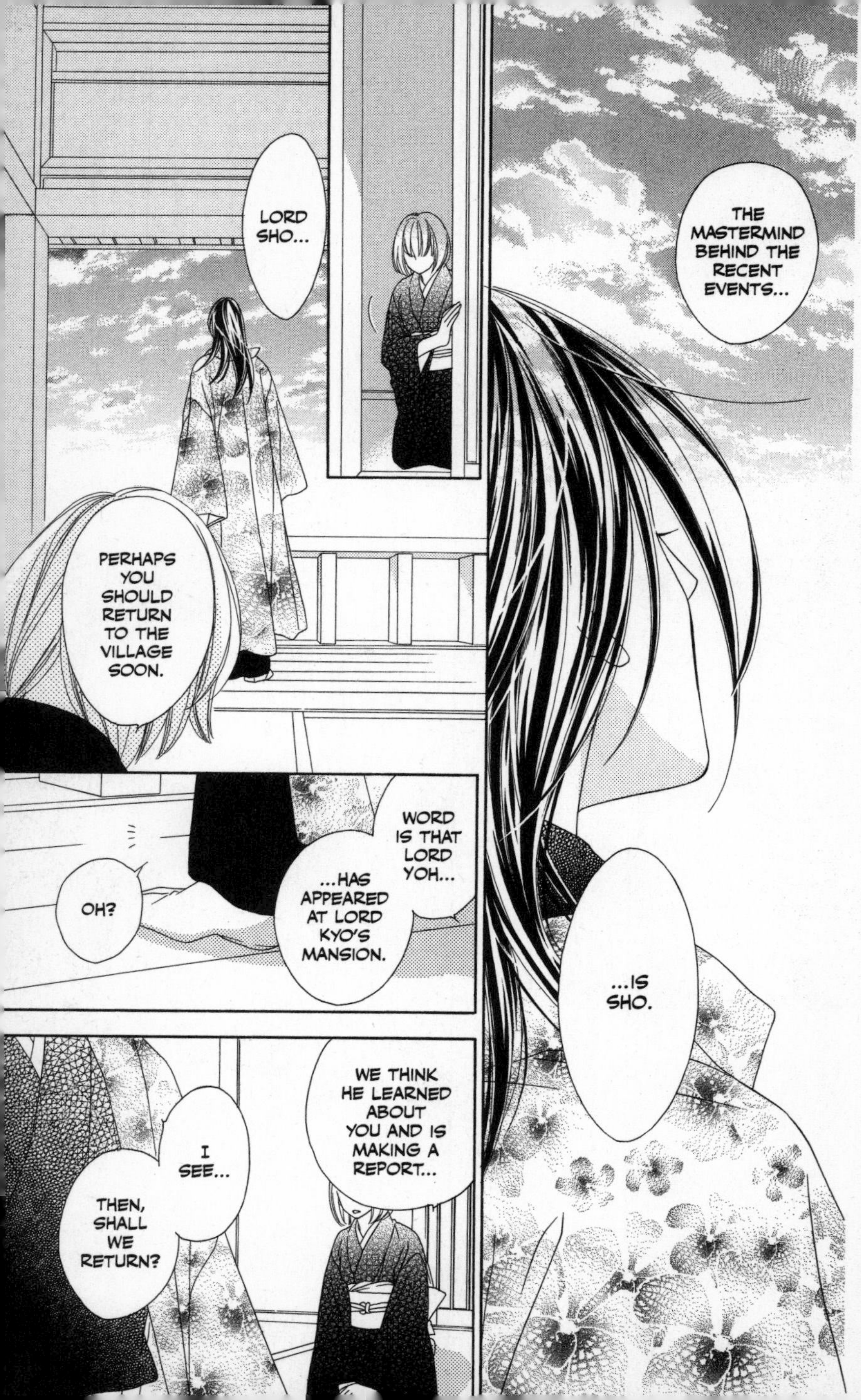
THE MASTERMIND BEHIND THE RECENT EVENTS...
...IS SHO.
LORD SHO...
PERHAPS YOU SHOULD RETURN TO THE VILLAGE SOON.
WORD IS THAT LORD YOH...
...HAS APPEARED AT LORD KYO'S MANSION.
OH?
WE THINK HE LEARNED ABOUT YOU AND IS MAKING A REPORT...
I SEE...
THEN, SHALL WE RETURN?

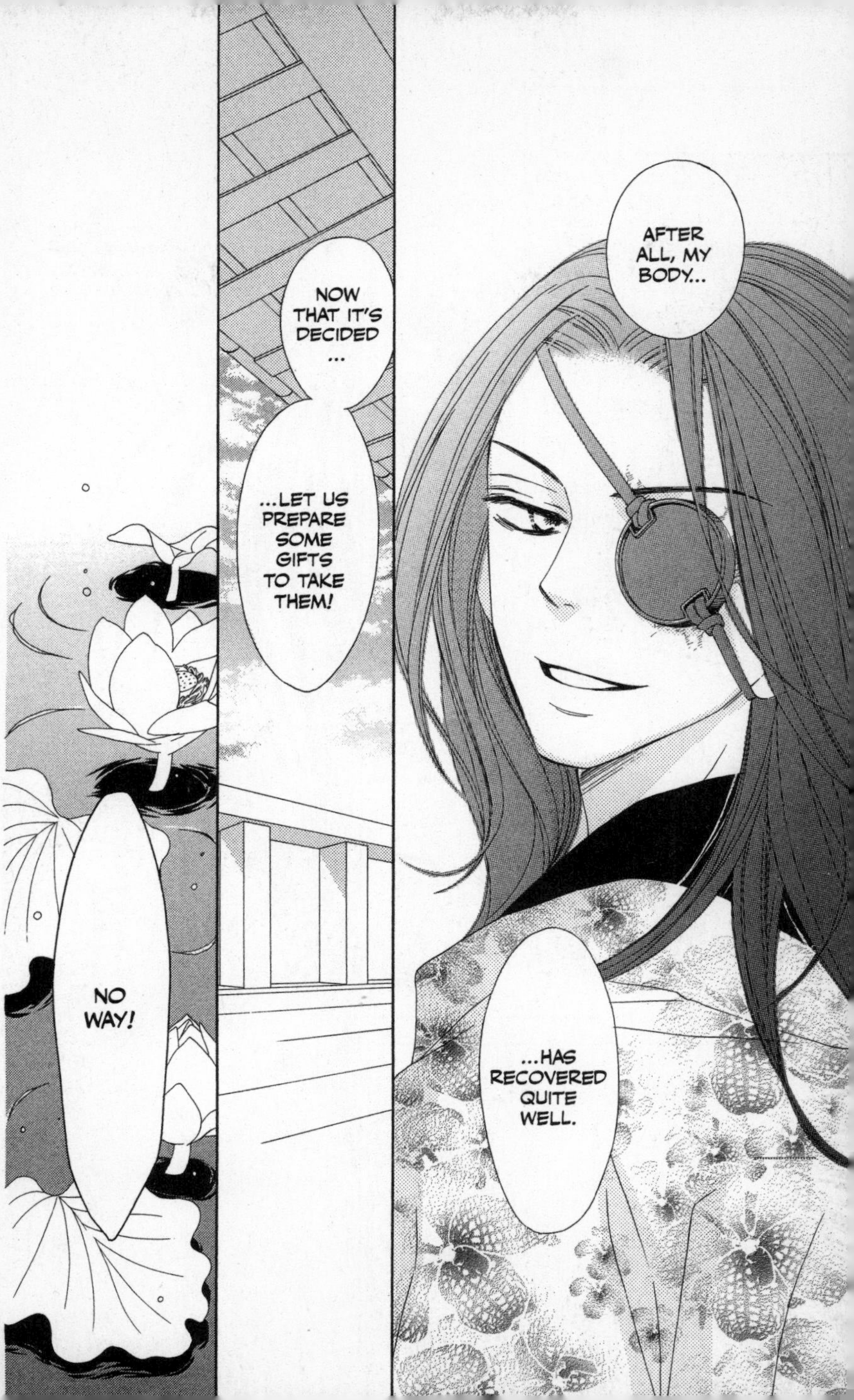
AFTER ALL, MY BODY...
...HAS RECOVERED QUITE WELL.
NOW THAT IT'S DECIDED ...
...LET US PREPARE SOME GIFTS TO TAKE THEM!
NO WAY!

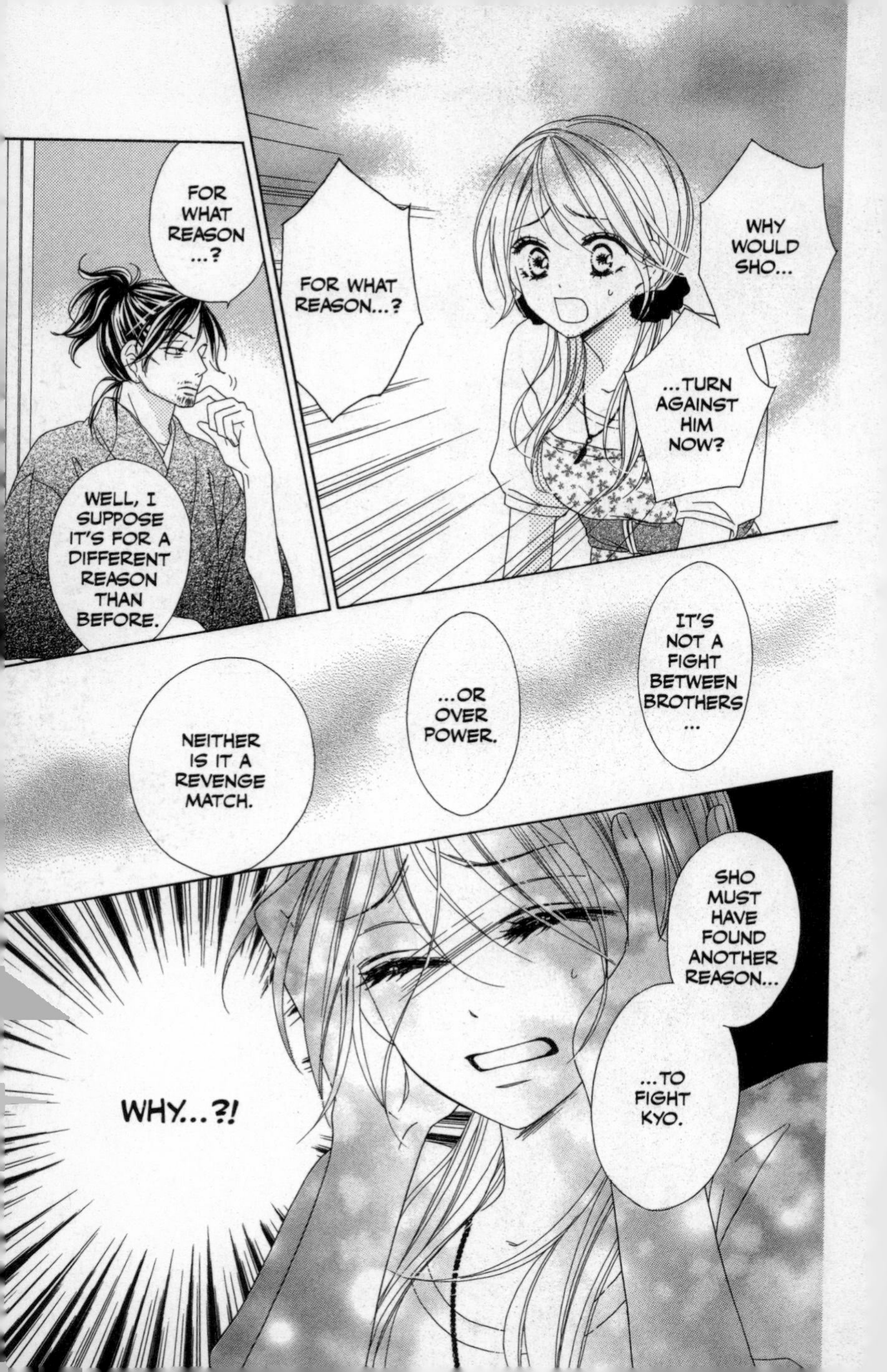
WHY WOULD SHO...
...TURN AGAINST HIM NOW?
FOR WHAT REASON...?
FOR WHAT REASON ...?
WELL, I SUPPOSE IT'S FOR A DIFFERENT REASON THAN BEFORE.
IT'S NOT A FIGHT BETWEEN BROTHERS...
...OR OVER POWER.
NEITHER IS IT A REVENGE MATCH.
SHO MUST HAVE FOUND ANOTHER REASON...
...TO FIGHT KYO.
WHY...?!

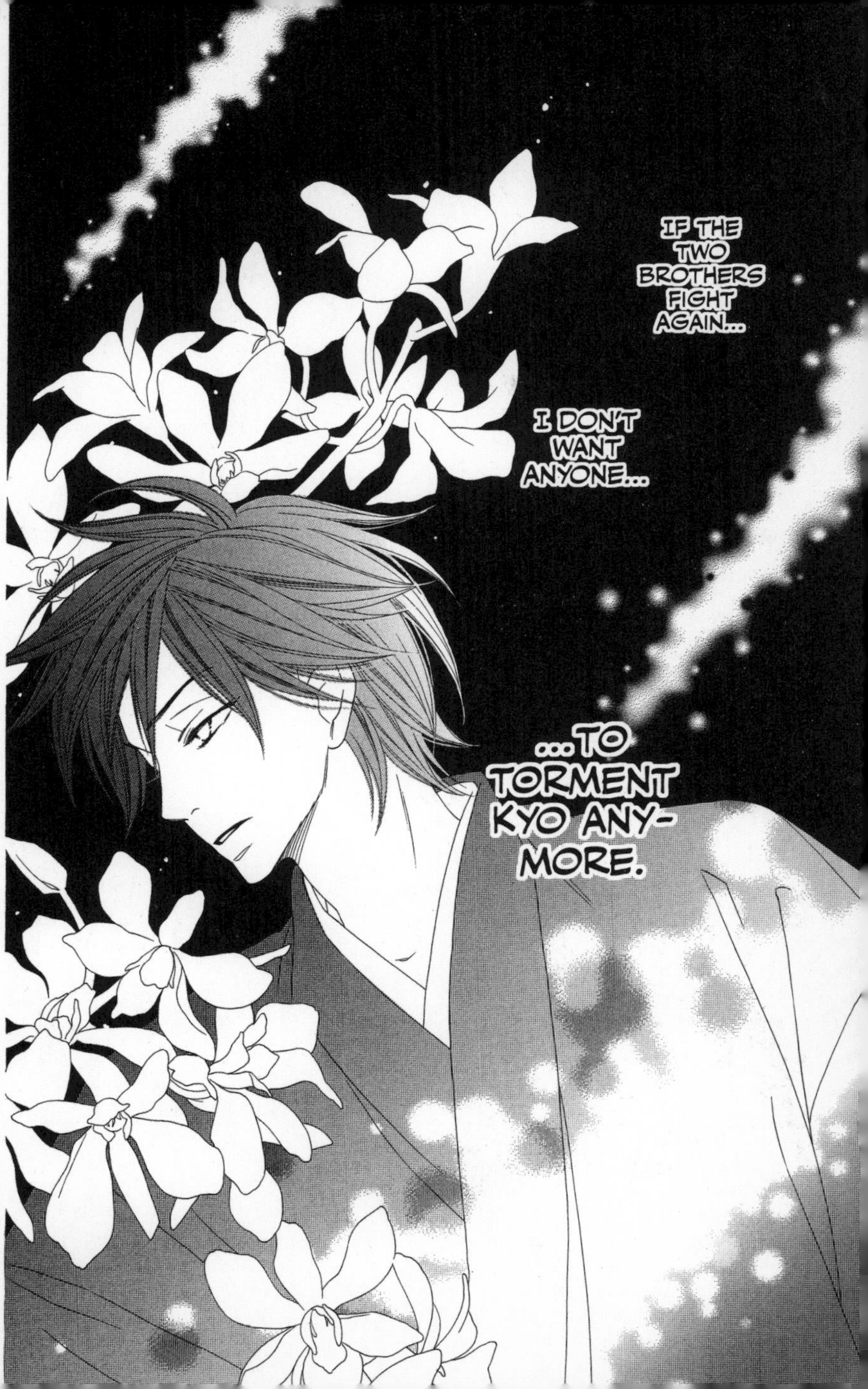
IF THE TWO BROTHERS FIGHT AGAIN...
I DON'T WANT ANYONE...
...TO TORMENT KYO ANY-MORE.

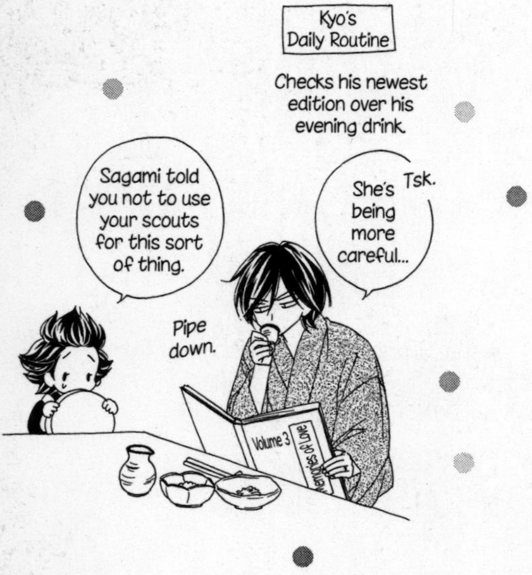
Kyo's Daily Routine
Checks his newest edition over his evening drink.
She's being more careful...
Tsk.
Sagami told you not to use your scouts for this sort of thing.
Pipe down.
Volume 3
Memories of Love

Illustration Request Number 12

"Little Kyo with Misao Today"

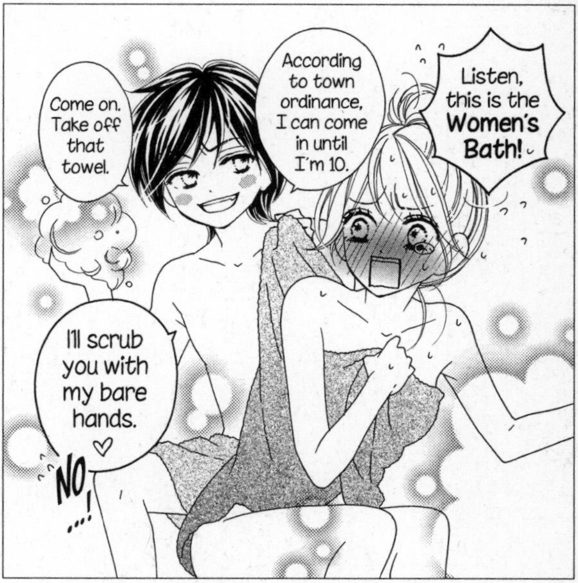
Listen, this is the Women's Bath!
According to town ordinance, I can come in until I'm 10.
Come on. Take off that towel.
I'll scrub you with my bare hands. ♡
NO...!

It's the opposite of the 4-panel cartoon I did in Volume 3. Seems this is the only way things can go...

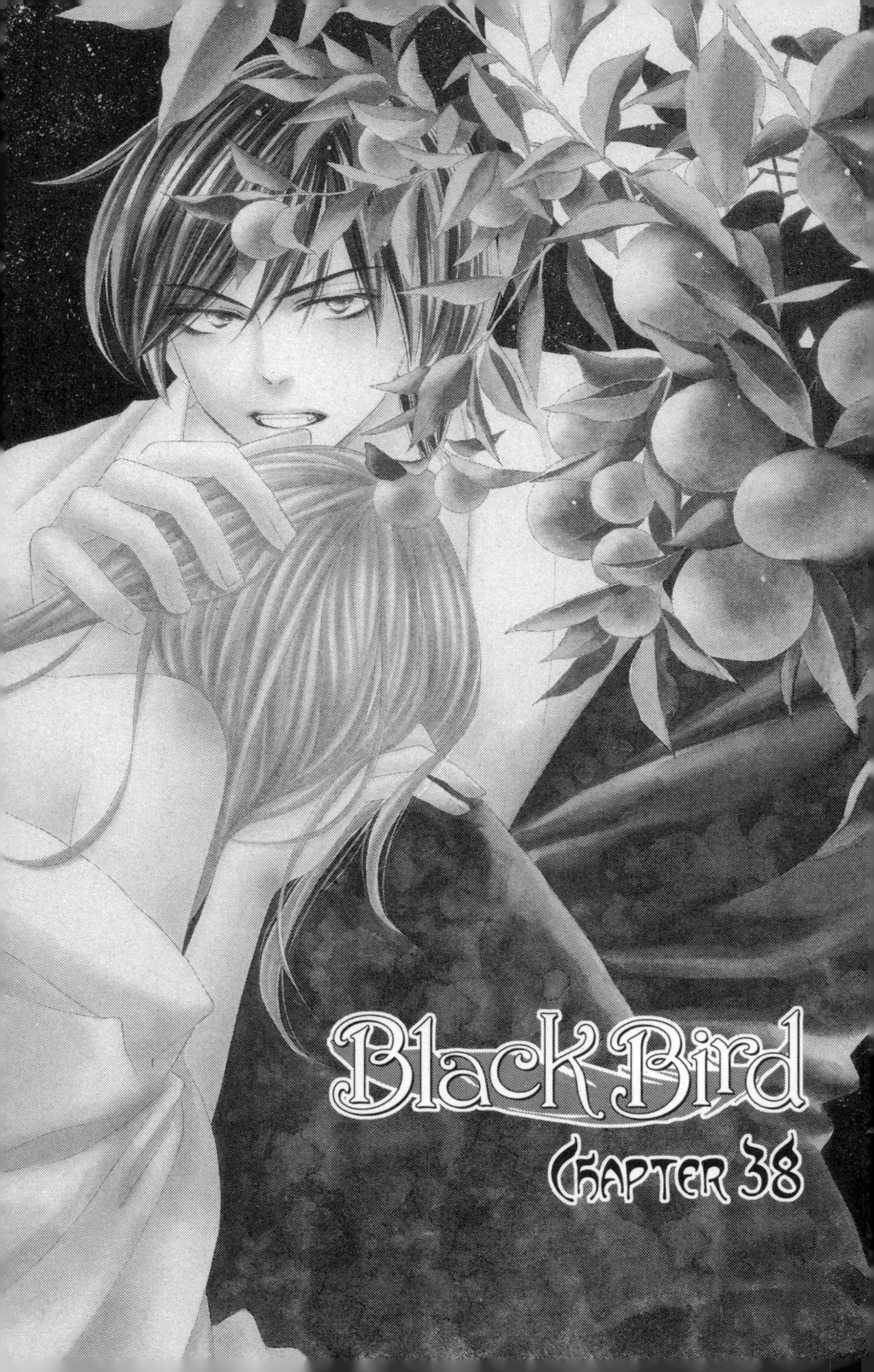
Black Bird
Chapter 38

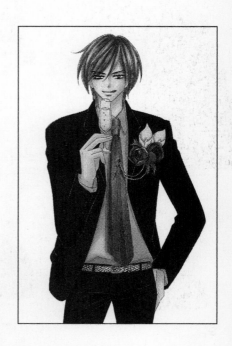

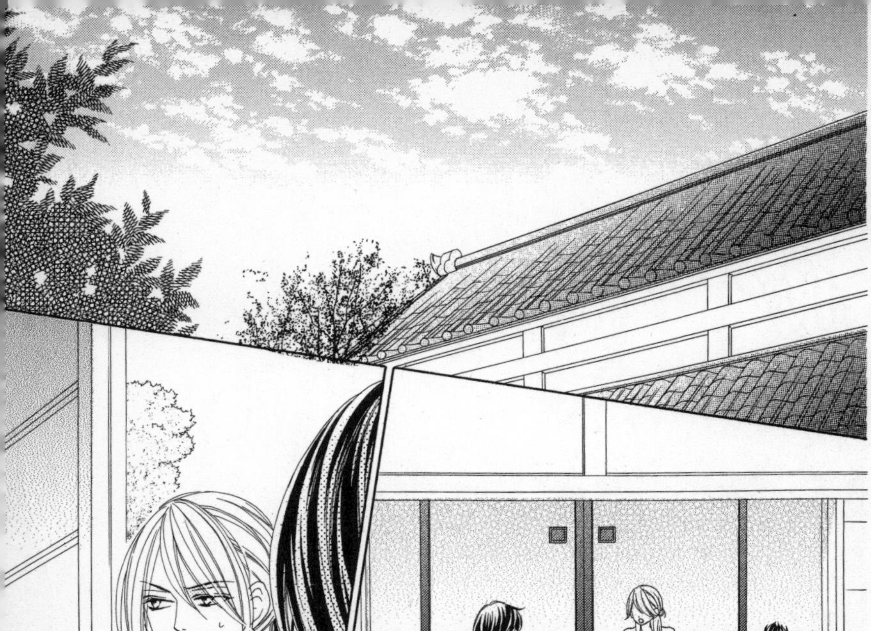

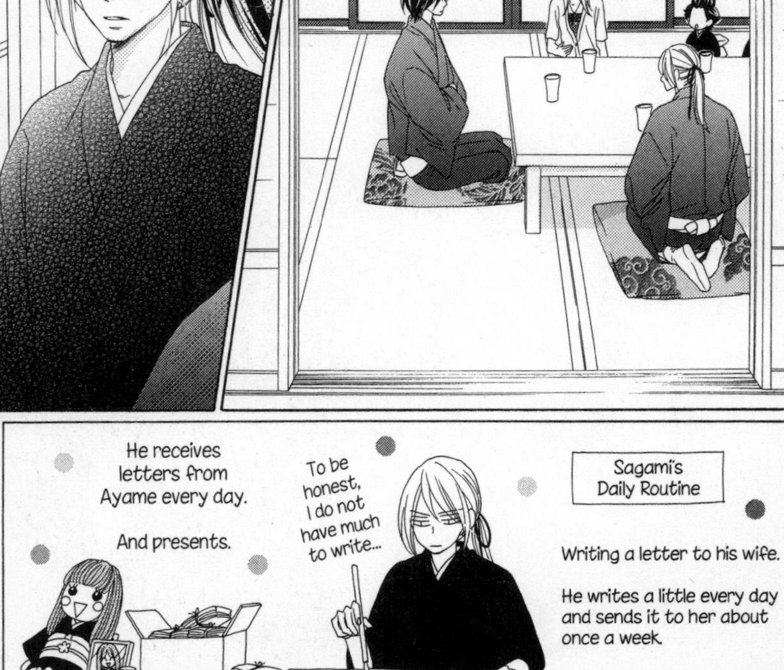

Sagami's Daily Routine
Writing a letter to his wife.
He writes a little every day and sends it to her about once a week.
To be honest, I do not have much to write...
He receives letters from Ayame every day.
And presents.

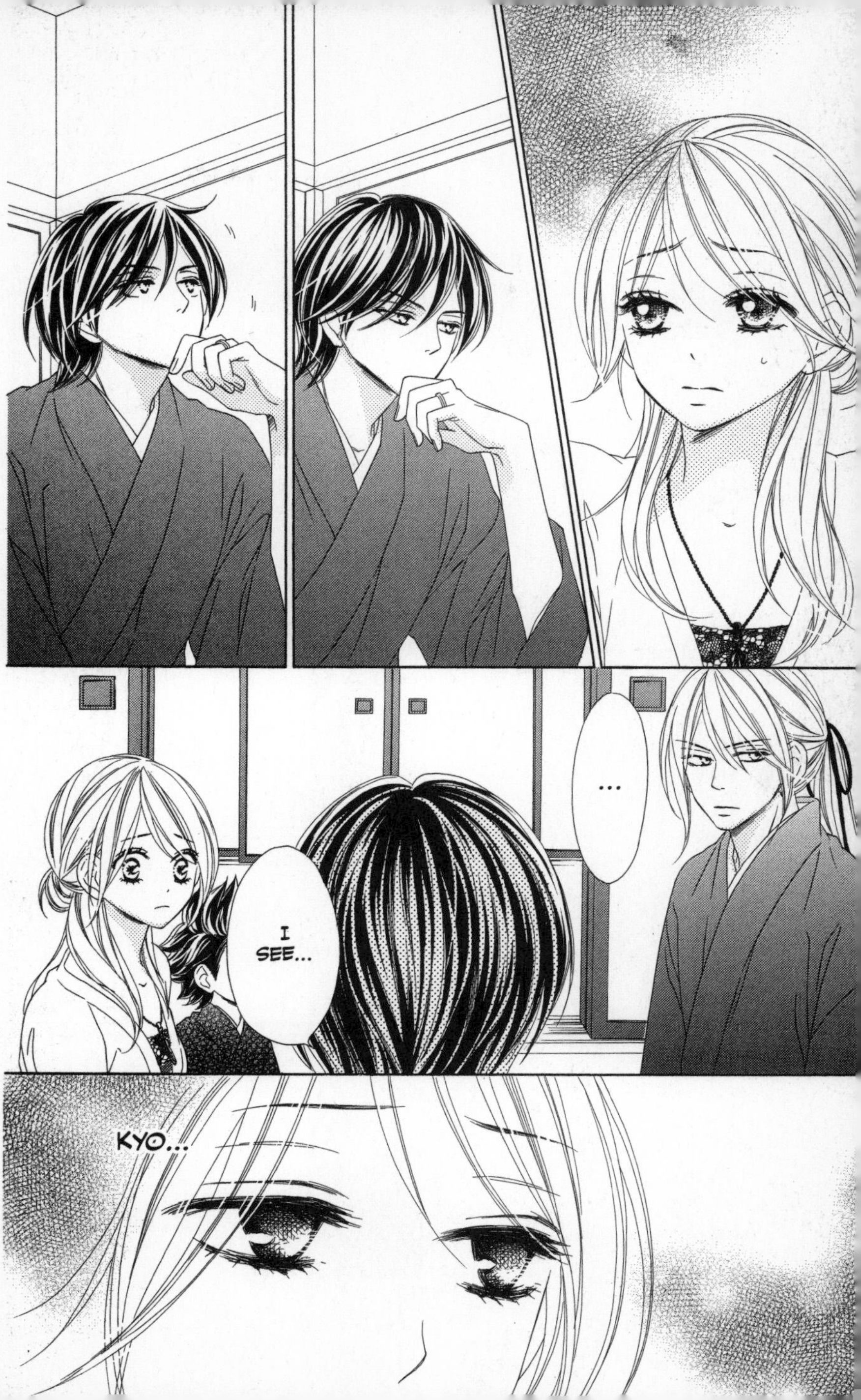
...
I SEE...
KYO...

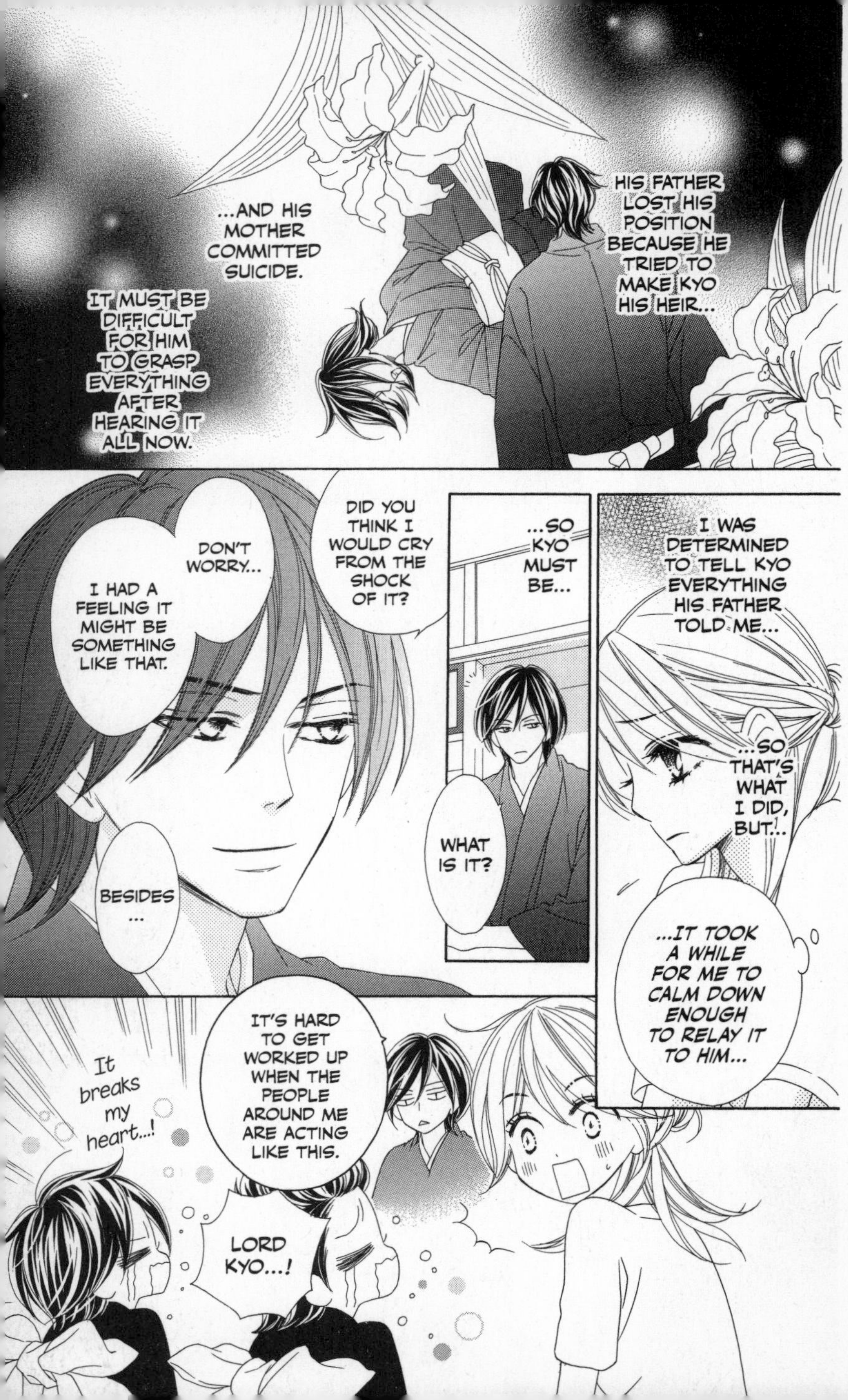
HIS FATHER LOST HIS POSITION BECAUSE HE TRIED TO MAKE KYO HIS HEIR...
...AND HIS MOTHER COMMITTED SUICIDE.
IT MUST BE DIFFICULT FOR HIM TO GRASP EVERYTHING AFTER HEARING IT ALL NOW.
I WAS DETERMINED TO TELL KYO EVERYTHING HIS FATHER TOLD ME...
...SO THAT'S WHAT I DID, BUT...
...IT TOOK A WHILE FOR ME TO CALM DOWN ENOUGH TO RELAY IT TO HIM...
...SO KYO MUST BE...
WHAT IS IT?
DID YOU THINK I WOULD CRY FROM THE SHOCK OF IT?
DON'T WORRY...
I HAD A FEELING IT MIGHT BE SOMETHING LIKE THAT.
BESIDES...
IT'S HARD TO GET WORKED UP WHEN THE PEOPLE AROUND ME ARE ACTING LIKE THIS.
It breaks my heart...!
LORD KYO...!

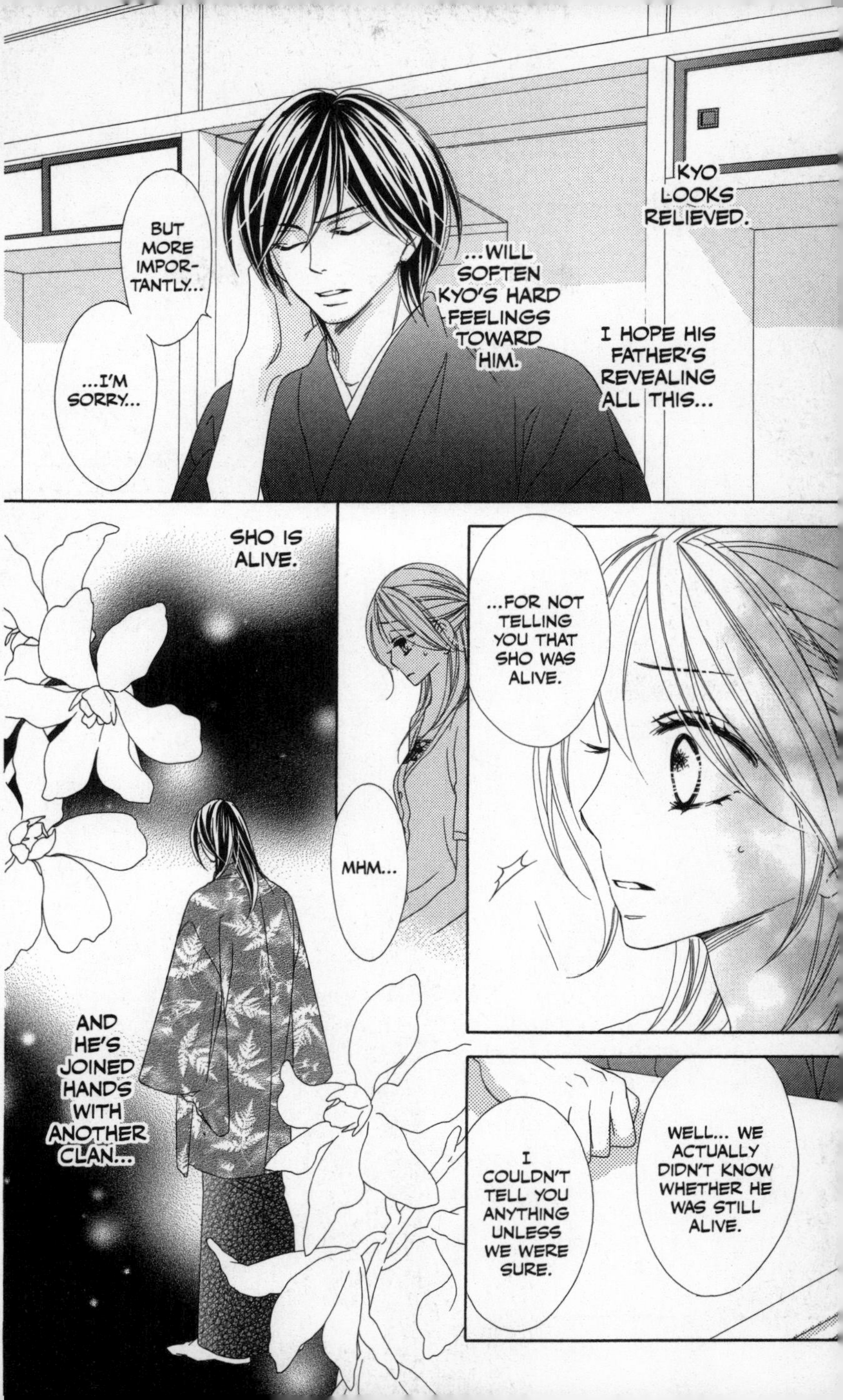
KYO LOOKS RELIEVED.
I HOPE HIS FATHER'S REVEALING ALL THIS...
...WILL SOFTEN KYO'S HARD FEELINGS TOWARD HIM.
BUT MORE IMPORTANTLY...
...I'M SORRY...
...FOR NOT TELLING YOU THAT SHO WAS ALIVE.
MHM...
WELL... WE ACTUALLY DIDN'T KNOW WHETHER HE WAS STILL ALIVE.
I COULDN'T TELL YOU ANYTHING UNLESS WE WERE SURE.
SHO IS ALIVE.
AND HE'S JOINED HANDS WITH ANOTHER CLAN...

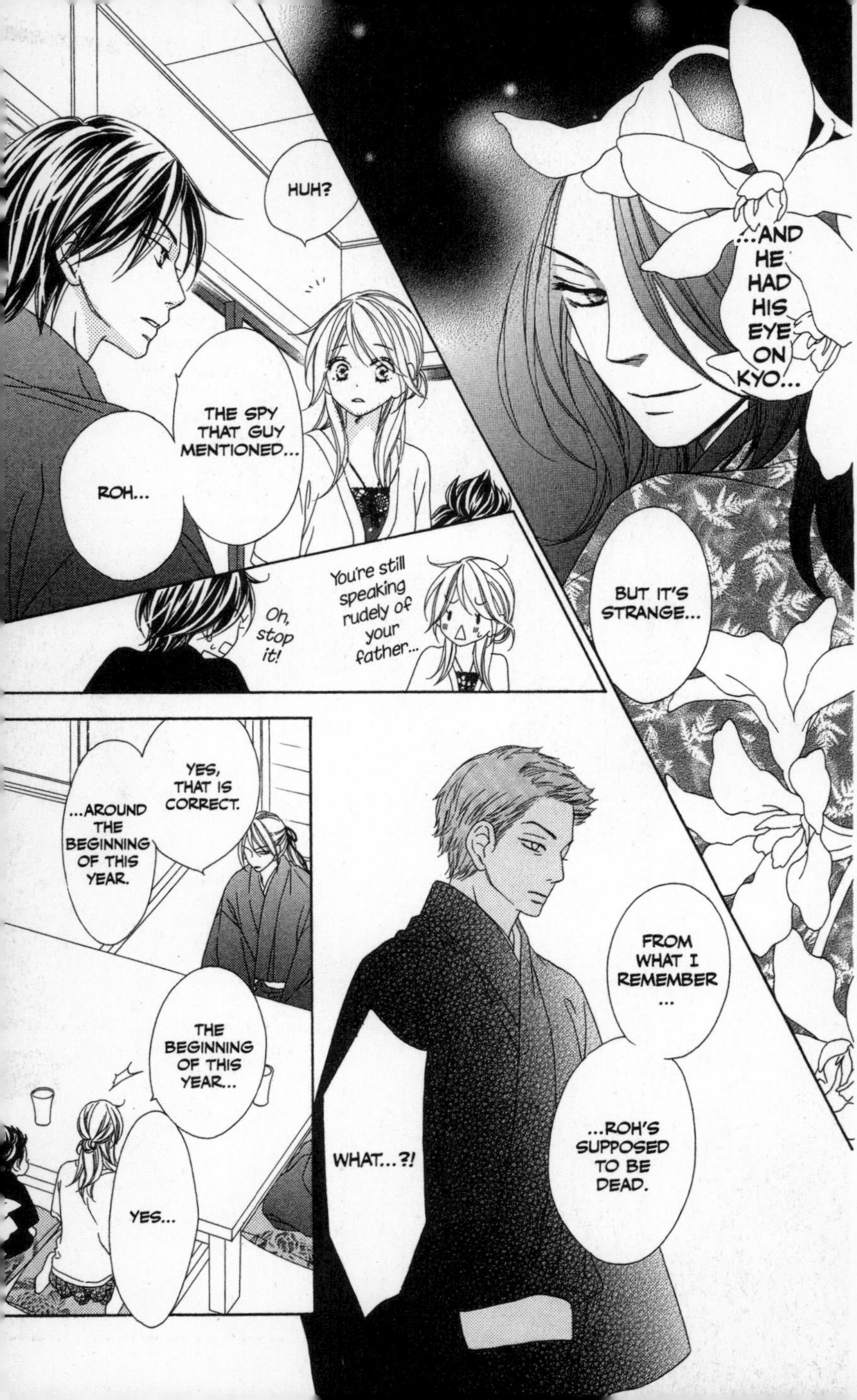
...AND HE HAD HIS EYE ON KYO...
BUT IT'S STRANGE...
HUH?
THE SPY THAT GUY MENTIONED...
ROH...
You're still speaking rudely of your father...
Oh, stop it!
FROM WHAT I REMEMBER ...
...ROH'S SUPPOSED TO BE DEAD.
WHAT...?!
YES, THAT IS CORRECT.
...AROUND THE BEGINNING OF THIS YEAR.
THE BEGINNING OF THIS YEAR...
YES...

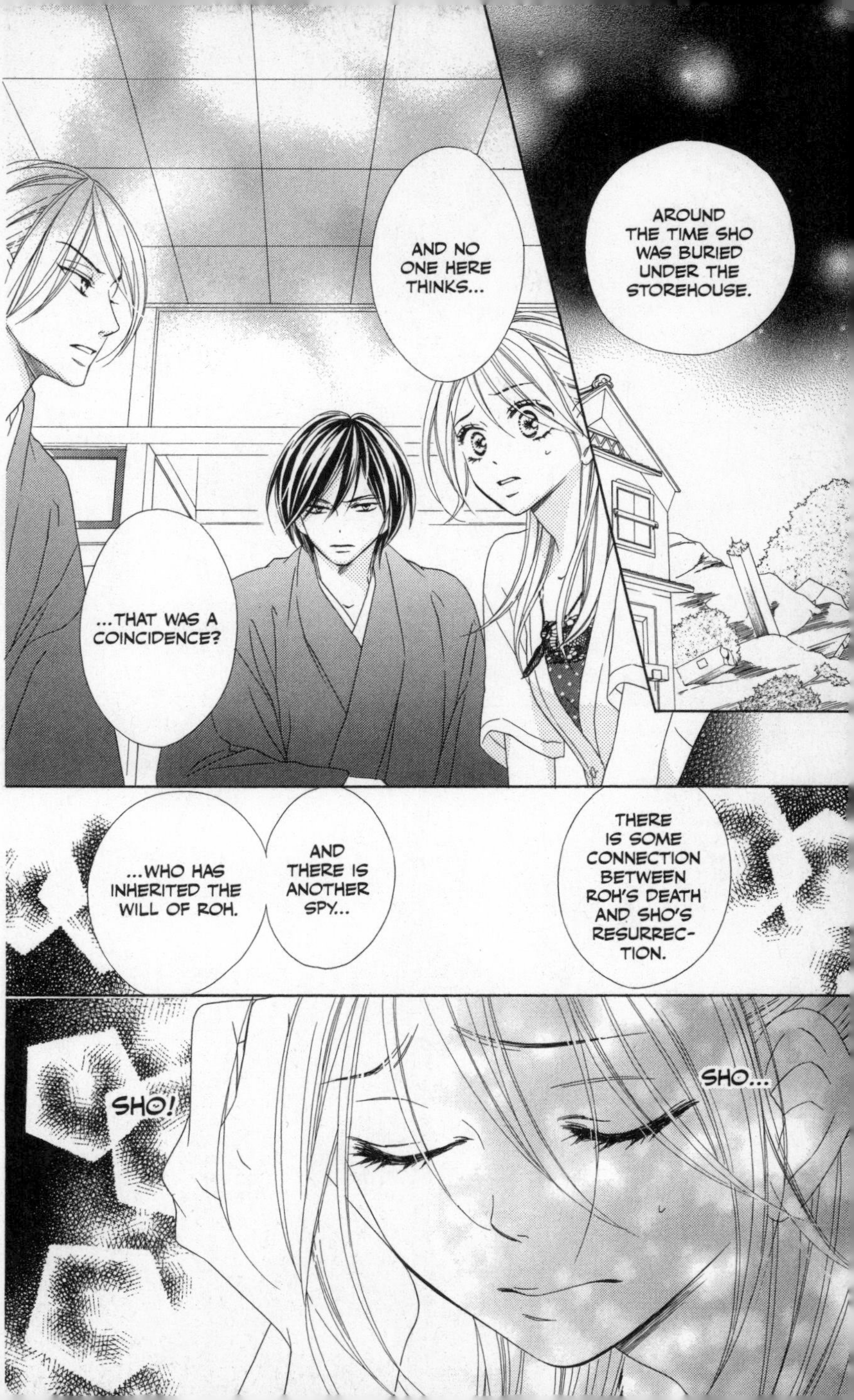
AROUND THE TIME SHO WAS BURIED UNDER THE STOREHOUSE.
AND NO ONE HERE THINKS...
...THAT WAS A COINCIDENCE?
THERE IS SOME CONNECTION BETWEEN ROH'S DEATH AND SHO'S RESURREC-TION.
AND THERE IS ANOTHER SPY...
...WHO HAS INHERITED THE WILL OF ROH.
SHO...
SHO!

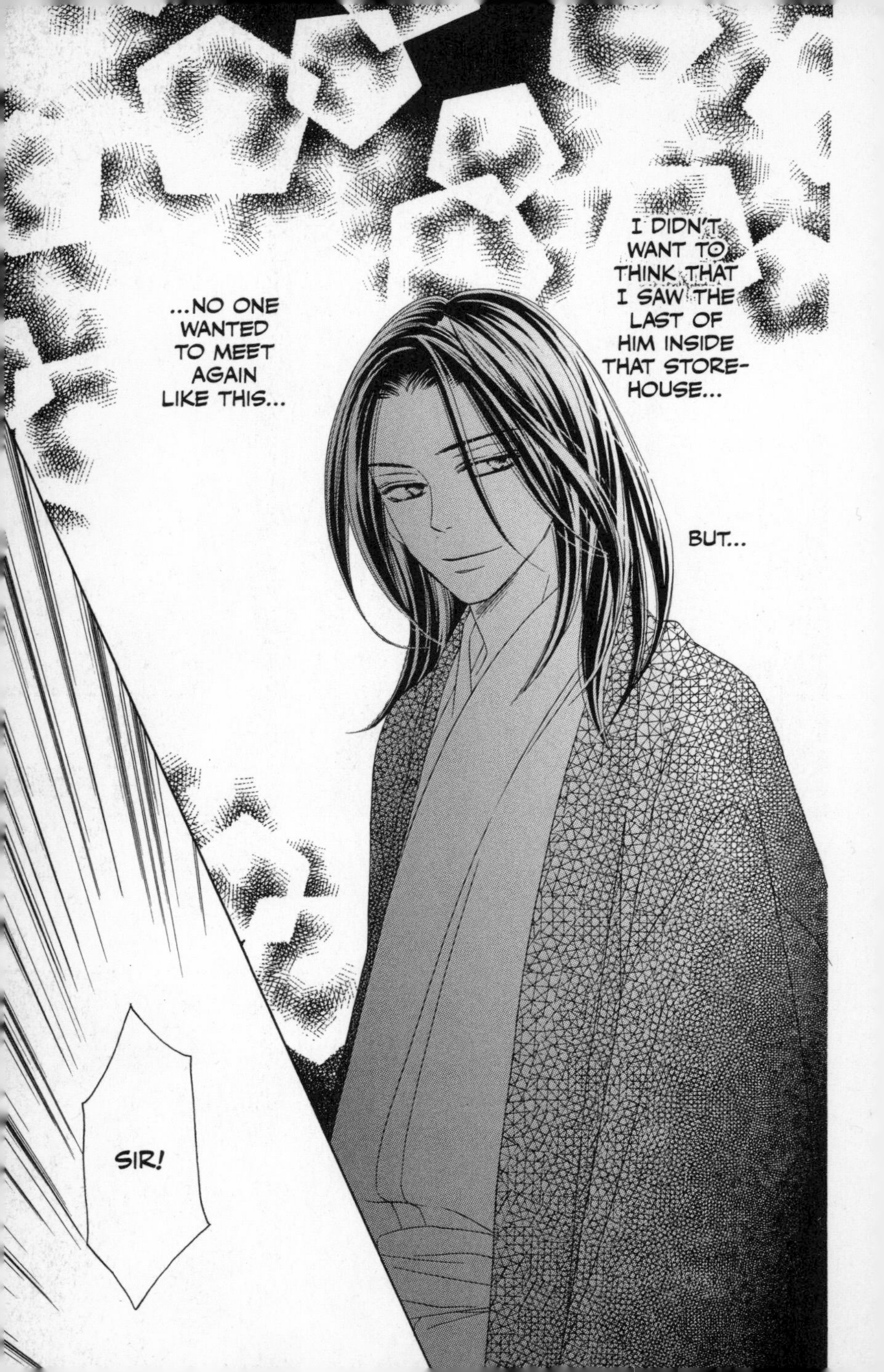
I DIDN'T WANT TO THINK THAT I SAW THE LAST OF HIM INSIDE THAT STORE-HOUSE...
...NO ONE WANTED TO MEET AGAIN LIKE THIS...
BUT...
SIR!

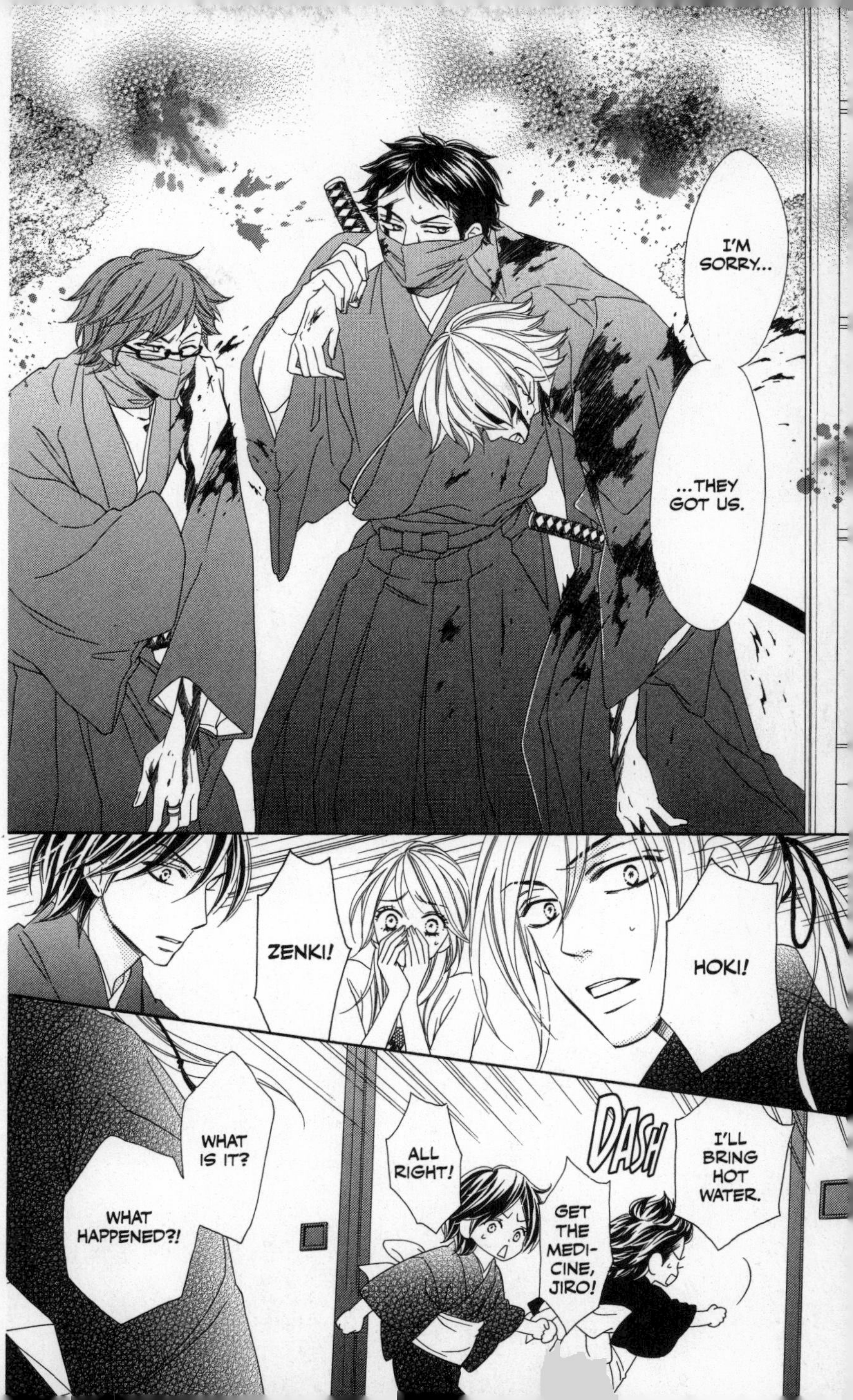
I'M SORRY...
...THEY GOT US.
HOKI!
ZENKI!
I'LL BRING HOT WATER.
DASH
GET THE MEDICINE, JIRO!
ALL RIGHT!
WHAT IS IT?
WHAT HAPPENED?!

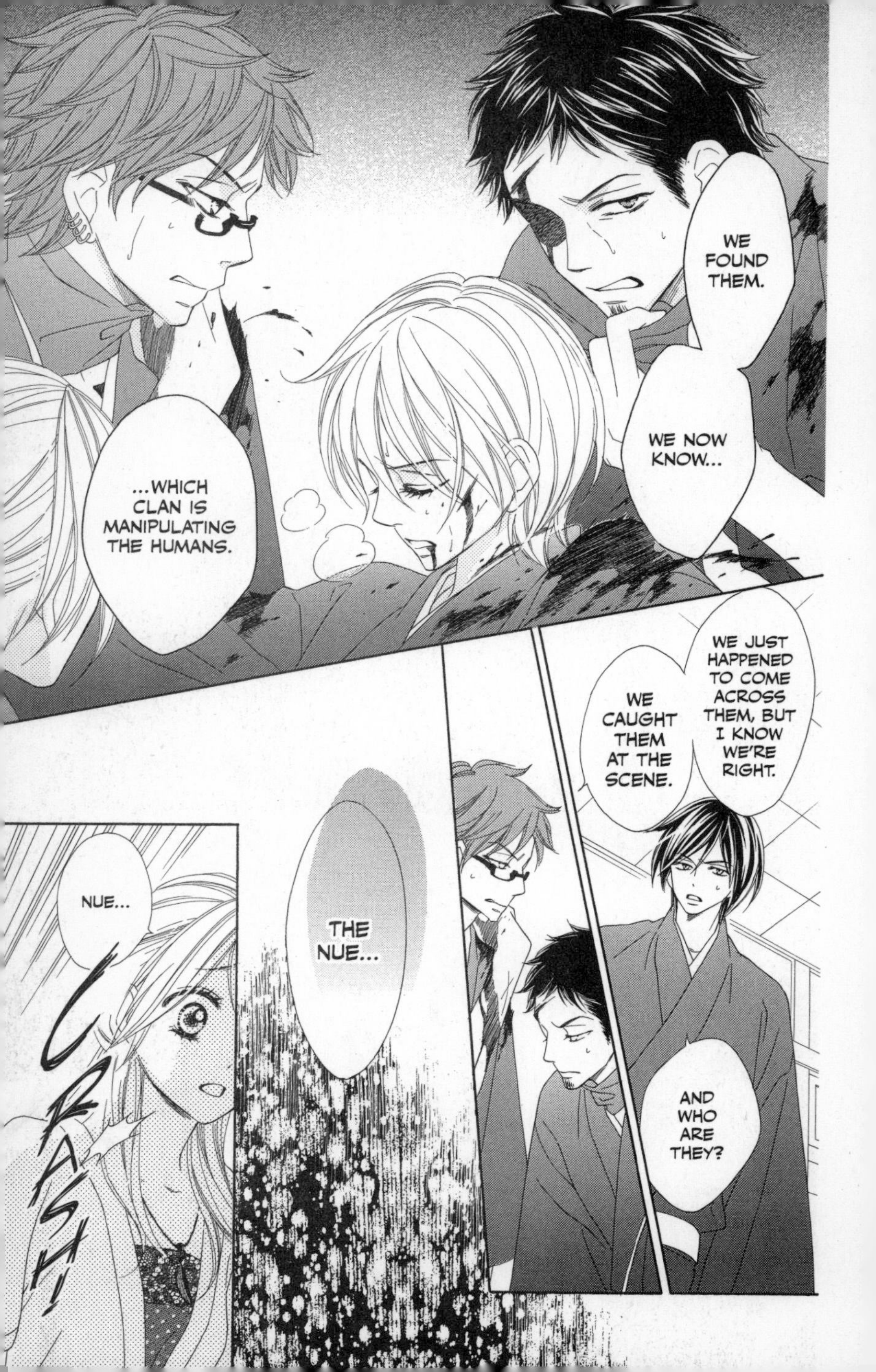
WE FOUND THEM.
WE NOW KNOW...
...WHICH CLAN IS MANIPULATING THE HUMANS.
WE JUST HAPPENED TO COME ACROSS THEM, BUT I KNOW WE'RE RIGHT.
WE CAUGHT THEM AT THE SCENE.
AND WHO ARE THEY?
THE NUE...
NUE...
CRASH!

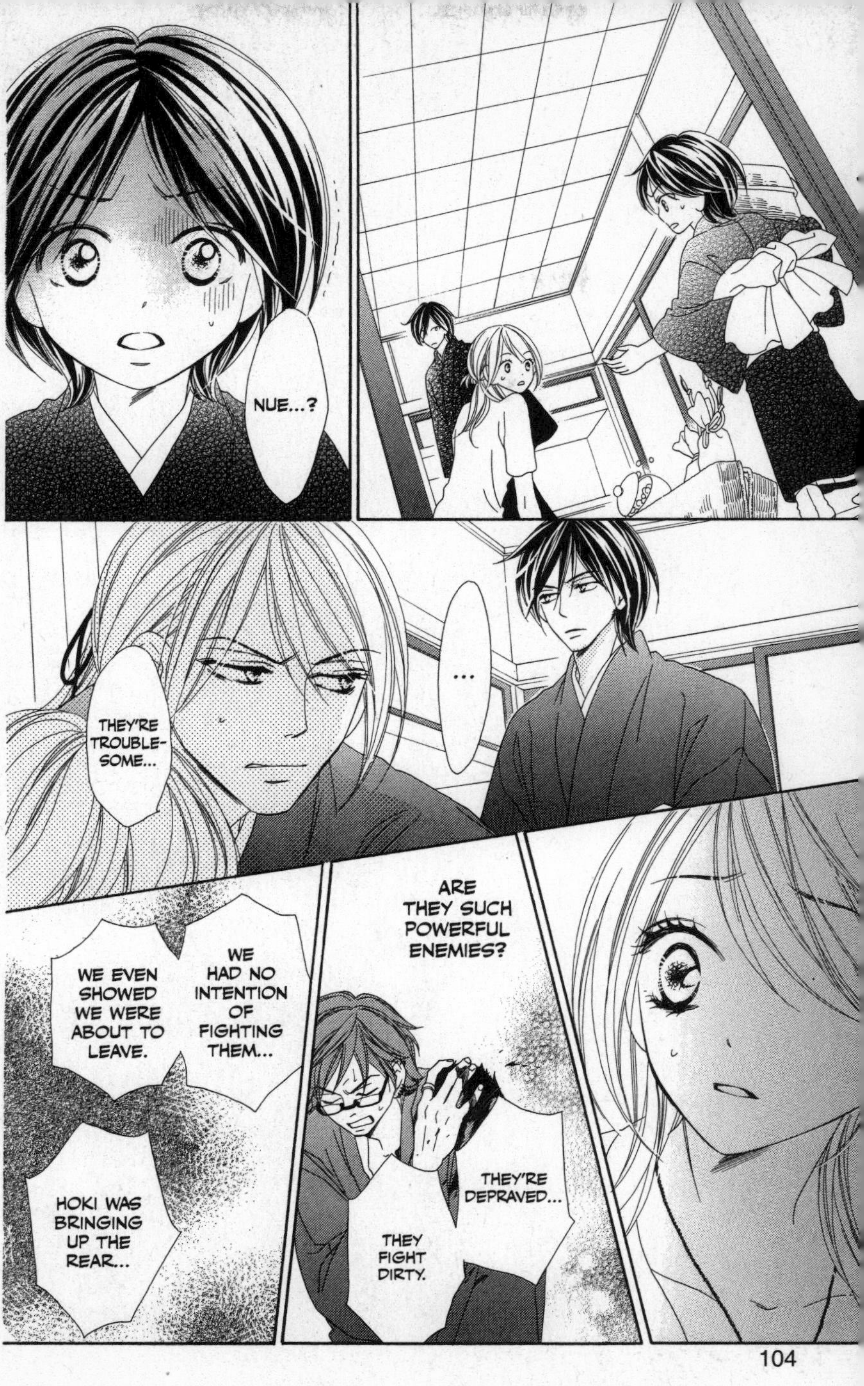
NUE...?
...
THEY'RE TROUBLE-SOME...
ARE THEY SUCH POWERFUL ENEMIES?
THEY'RE DEPRAVED...
THEY FIGHT DIRTY.
WE HAD NO INTENTION OF FIGHTING THEM...
WE EVEN SHOWED WE WERE ABOUT TO LEAVE.
HOKI WAS BRINGING UP THE REAR...

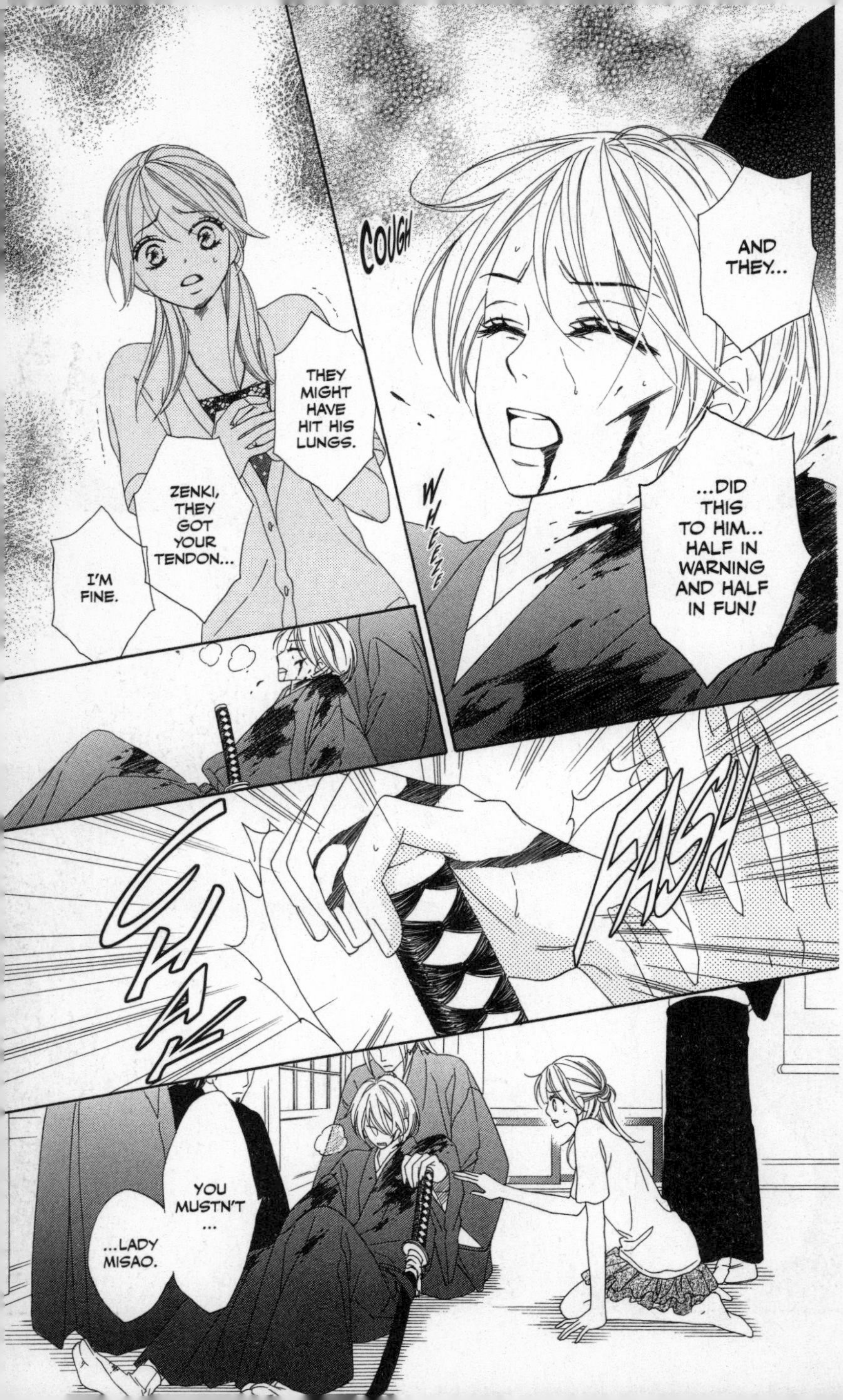
AND THEY...
COUGH
WHEEZE
...DID THIS TO HIM... HALF IN WARNING AND HALF IN FUN!
THEY MIGHT HAVE HIT HIS LUNGS.
ZENKI, THEY GOT YOUR TENDON...
I'M FINE.
FASH
WHAP
YOU MUSTN'T ...
...LADY MISAO.

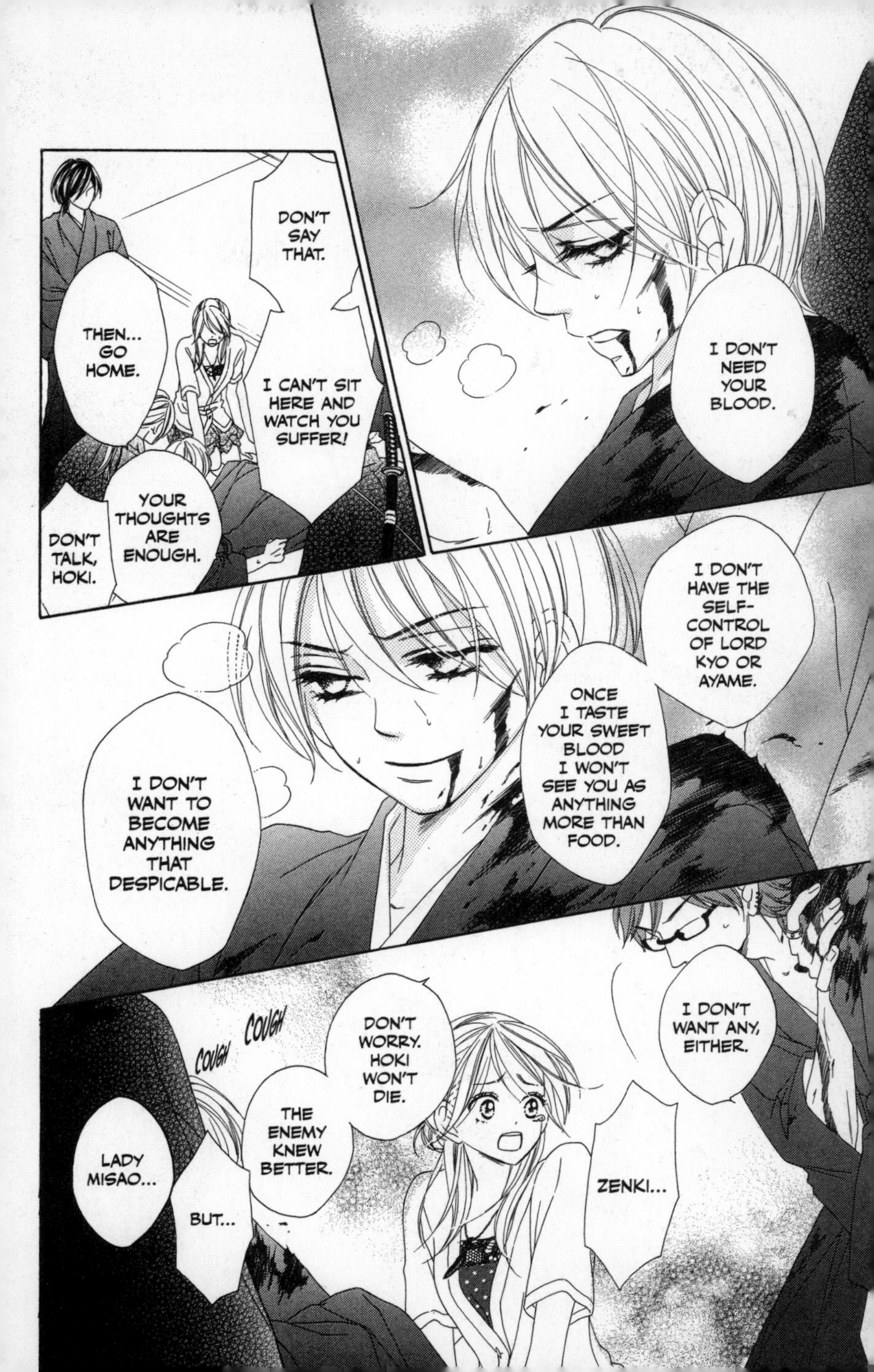
I DON'T NEED YOUR BLOOD.
DON'T SAY THAT.
I CAN'T SIT HERE AND WATCH YOU SUFFER!
THEN... GO HOME.
YOUR THOUGHTS ARE ENOUGH.
DON'T TALK, HOKI.
I DON'T HAVE THE SELF-CONTROL OF LORD KYO OR AYAME.
ONCE I TASTE YOUR SWEET BLOOD I WON'T SEE YOU AS ANYTHING MORE THAN FOOD.
I DON'T WANT TO BECOME ANYTHING THAT DESPICABLE.
I DON'T WANT ANY, EITHER.
ZENKI...
DON'T WORRY. HOKI WON'T DIE.
COUGH COUGH
THE ENEMY KNEW BETTER.
BUT...
LADY MISAO...

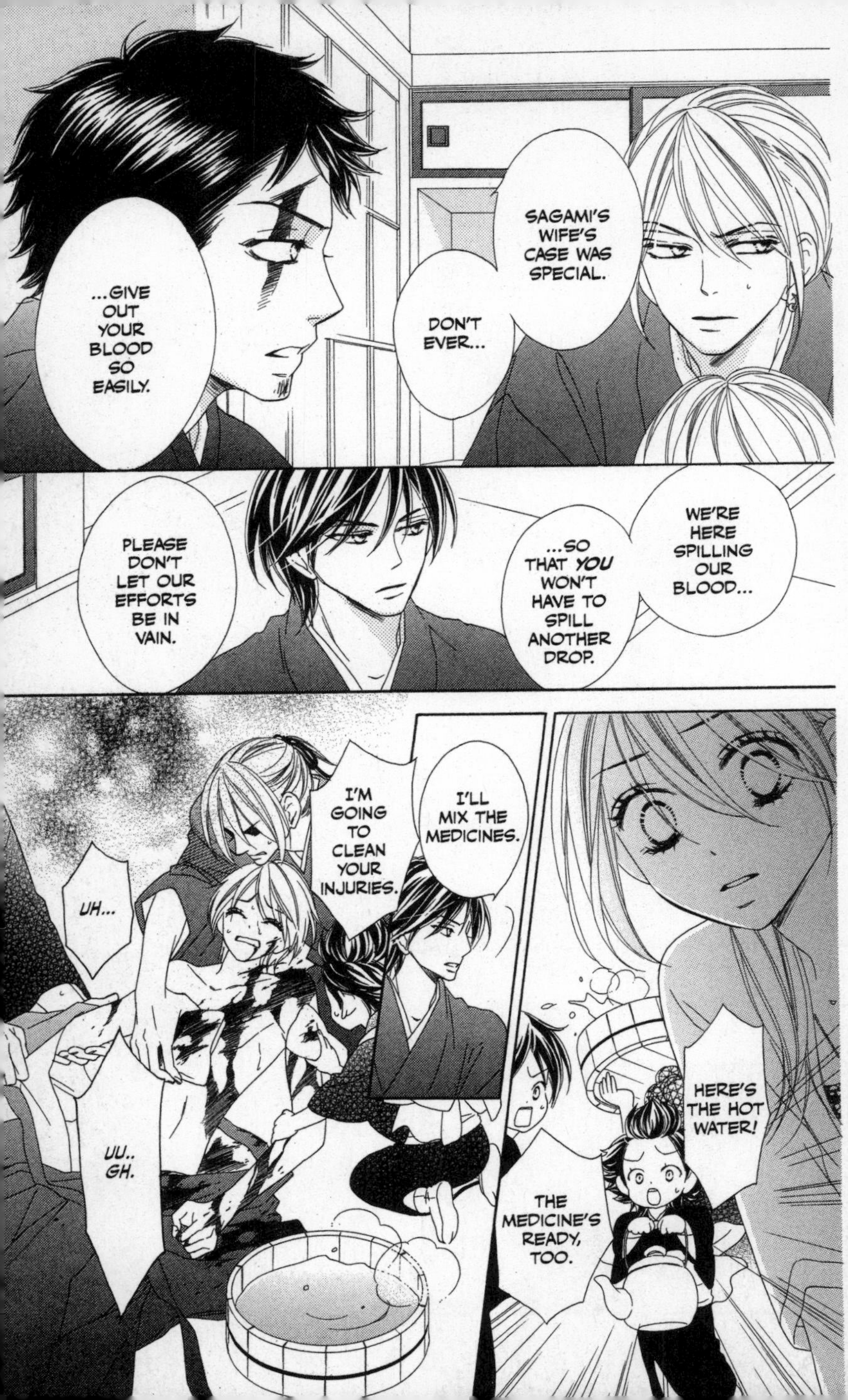
SAGAMI'S WIFE'S CASE WAS SPECIAL.
DON'T EVER...
...GIVE OUT YOUR BLOOD SO EASILY.
WE'RE HERE SPILLING OUR BLOOD...
...SO THAT *YOU* WON'T HAVE TO SPILL ANOTHER DROP.
PLEASE DON'T LET OUR EFFORTS BE IN VAIN.
HERE'S THE HOT WATER!
THE MEDICINE'S READY, TOO.
I'LL MIX THE MEDICINES.
I'M GOING TO CLEAN YOUR INJURIES.
UH...
UU.. GH.

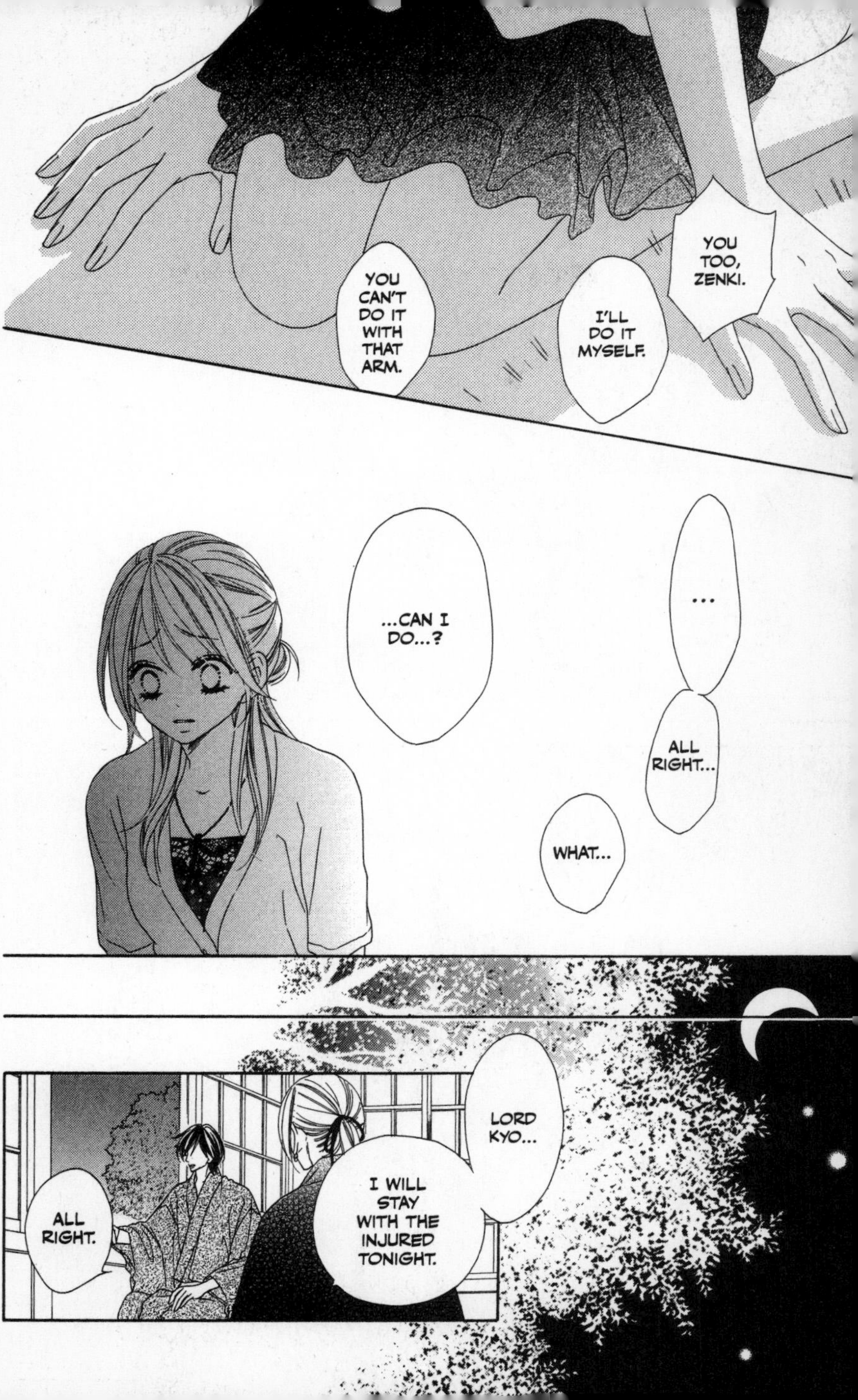
YOU TOO, ZENKI.
I'LL DO IT MYSELF.
YOU CAN'T DO IT WITH THAT ARM.
...
ALL RIGHT...
WHAT...
...CAN I DO...?
LORD KYO...
I WILL STAY WITH THE INJURED TONIGHT.
ALL RIGHT.

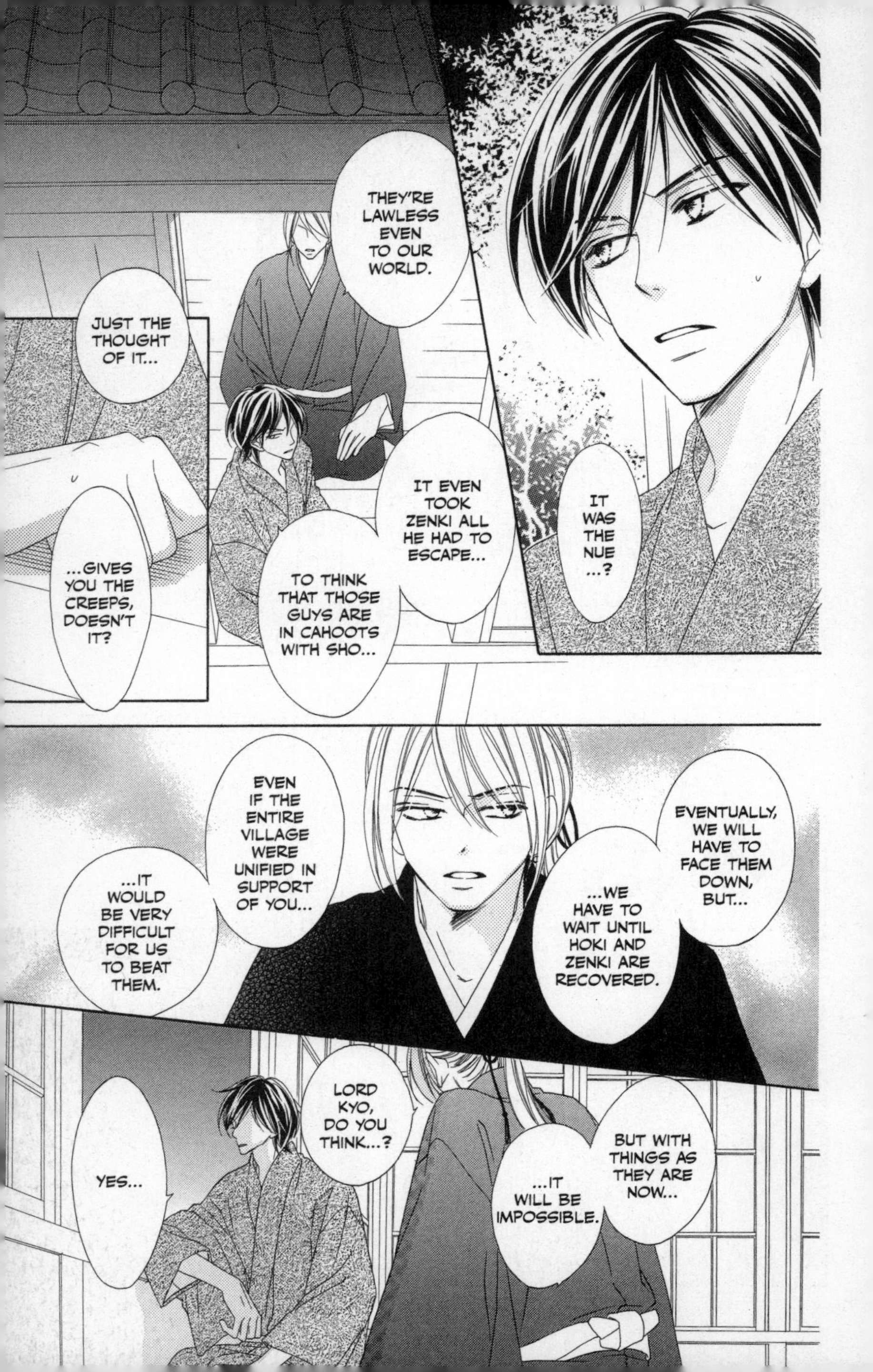
IT WAS THE NUE ...?
THEY'RE LAWLESS EVEN TO OUR WORLD.
IT EVEN TOOK ZENKI ALL HE HAD TO ESCAPE...
TO THINK THAT THOSE GUYS ARE IN CAHOOTS WITH SHO...
JUST THE THOUGHT OF IT...
...GIVES YOU THE CREEPS, DOESN'T IT?
EVENTUALLY, WE WILL HAVE TO FACE THEM DOWN, BUT...
...WE HAVE TO WAIT UNTIL HOKI AND ZENKI ARE RECOVERED.
EVEN IF THE ENTIRE VILLAGE WERE UNIFIED IN SUPPORT OF YOU...
...IT WOULD BE VERY DIFFICULT FOR US TO BEAT THEM.
BUT WITH THINGS AS THEY ARE NOW...
...IT WILL BE IMPOSSIBLE.
LORD KYO, DO YOU THINK...?
YES...

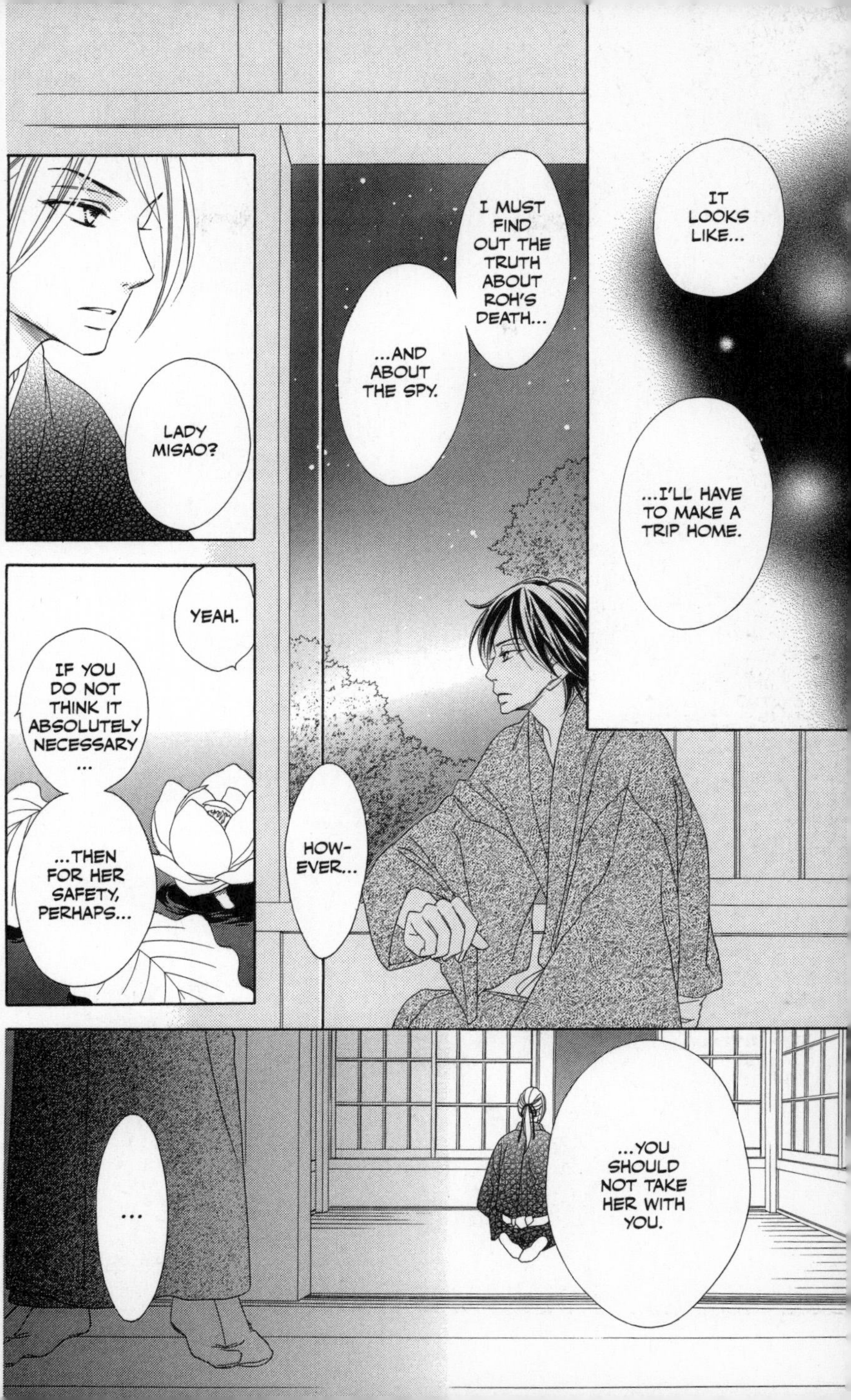
IT LOOKS LIKE...
...I'LL HAVE TO MAKE A TRIP HOME.
I MUST FIND OUT THE TRUTH ABOUT ROH'S DEATH...
...AND ABOUT THE SPY.
HOW-EVER...
LADY MISAO?
YEAH.
IF YOU DO NOT THINK IT ABSOLUTELY NECESSARY ...
...THEN FOR HER SAFETY, PERHAPS...
...YOU SHOULD NOT TAKE HER WITH YOU.
...

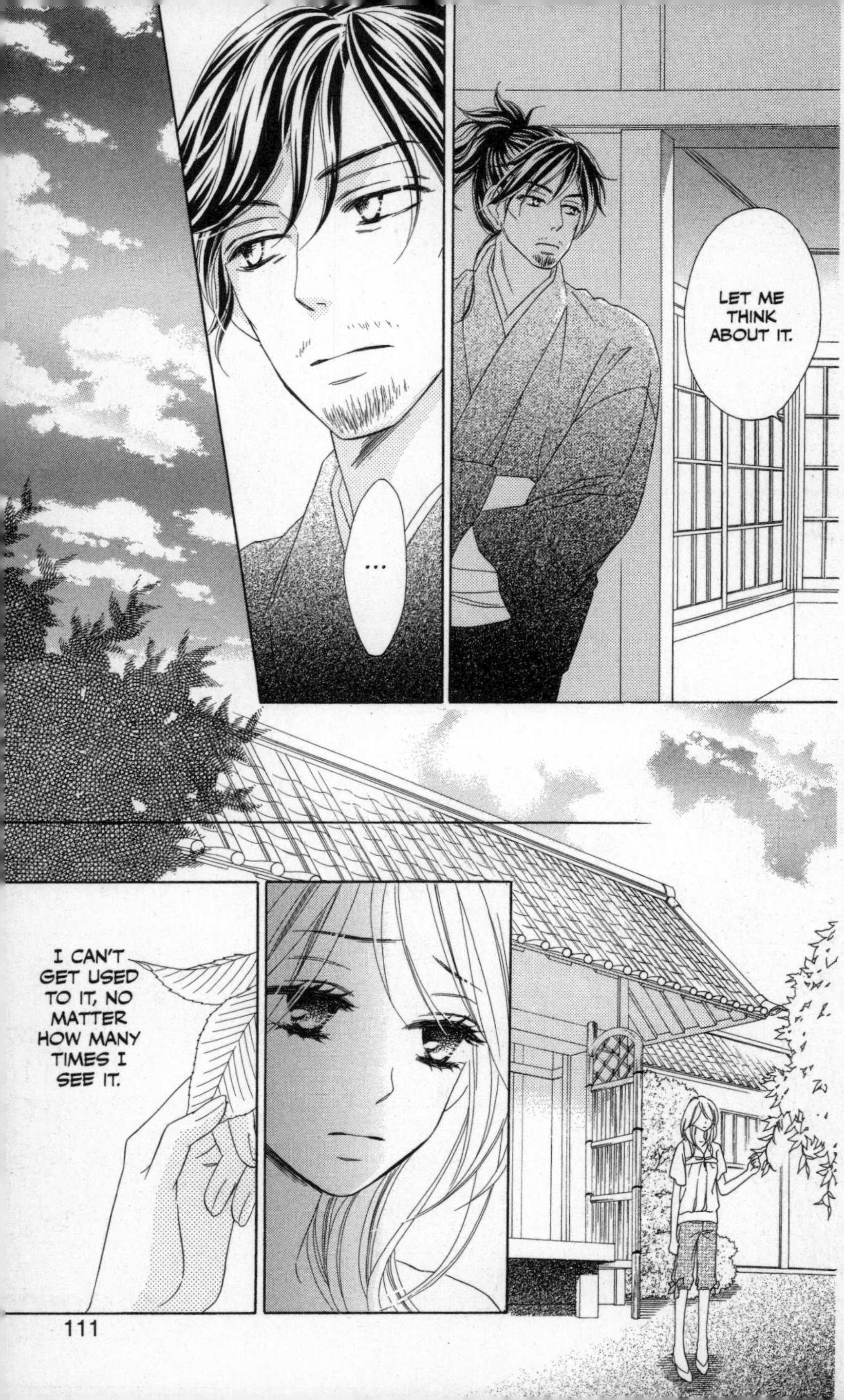
LET ME THINK ABOUT IT.
...
I CAN'T GET USED TO IT, NO MATTER HOW MANY TIMES I SEE IT.

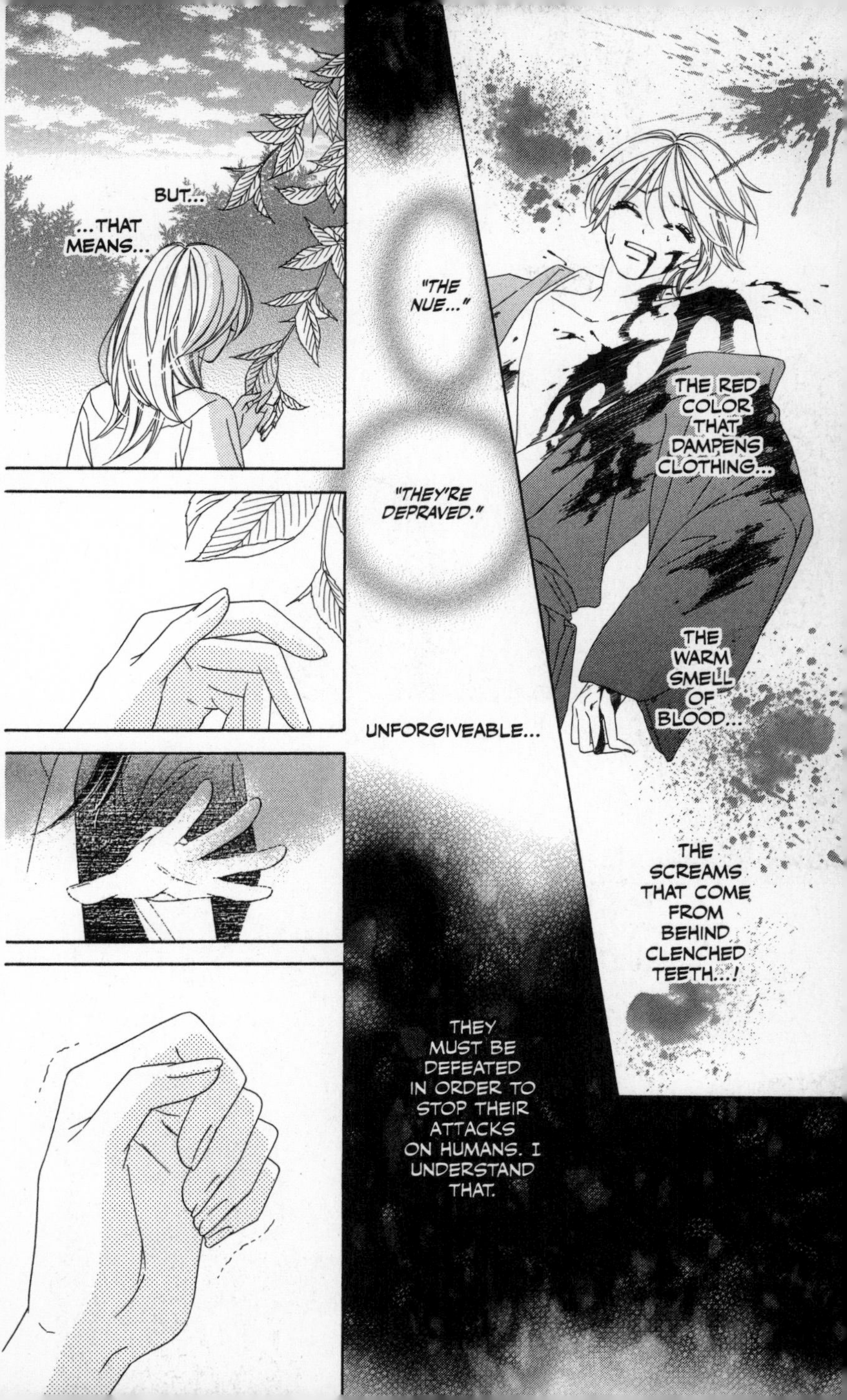
THE RED COLOR THAT DAMPENS CLOTHING...
THE WARM SMELL OF BLOOD...
THE SCREAMS THAT COME FROM BEHIND CLENCHED TEETH...!
"THE NUE..."
"THEY'RE DEPRAVED."
UNFORGIVEABLE...
THEY MUST BE DEFEATED IN ORDER TO STOP THEIR ATTACKS ON HUMANS. I UNDERSTAND THAT.
BUT...
...THAT MEANS...

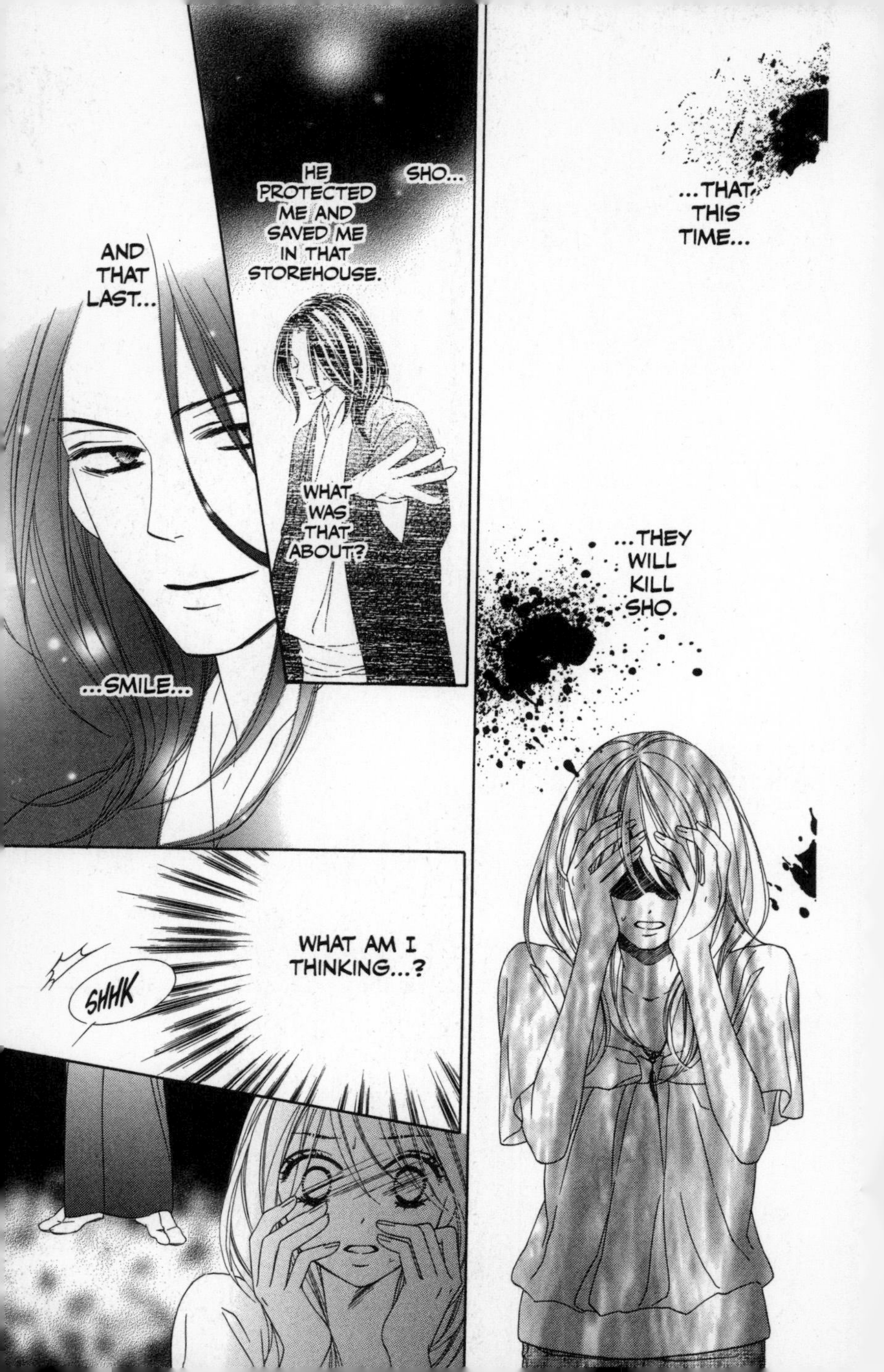
...THAT THIS TIME...
...THEY WILL KILL SHO.
SHO...
HE PROTECTED ME AND SAVED ME IN THAT STOREHOUSE.
WHAT WAS THAT ABOUT?
AND THAT LAST...
...SMILE...
WHAT AM I THINKING...?
SHHK

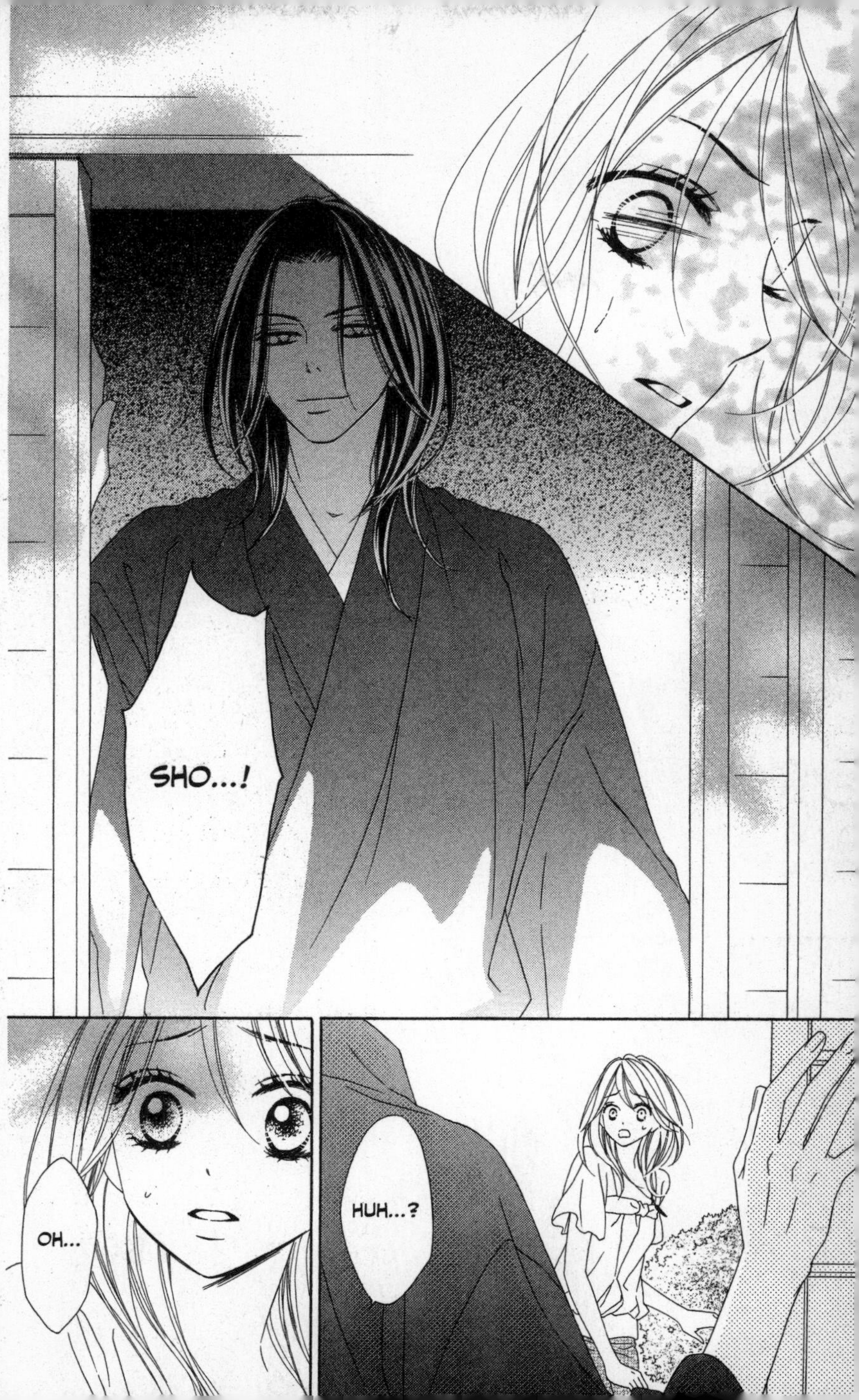
SHO...!
HUH...?
OH...

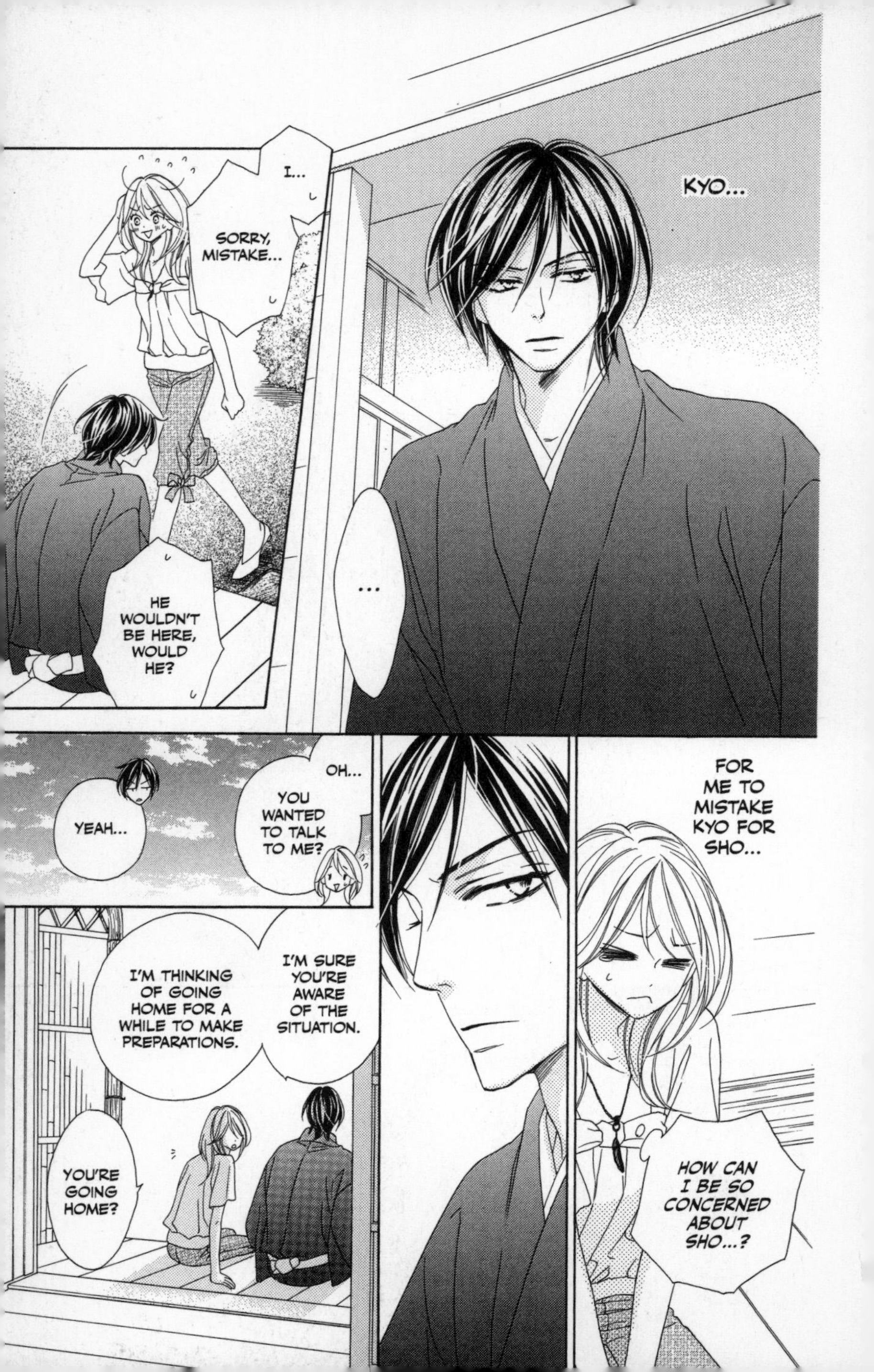
KYO...
...
I...
SORRY, MISTAKE...
HE WOULDN'T BE HERE, WOULD HE?
FOR ME TO MISTAKE KYO FOR SHO...
HOW CAN I BE SO CONCERNED ABOUT SHO...?
OH... YOU WANTED TO TALK TO ME?
YEAH...
I'M SURE YOU'RE AWARE OF THE SITUATION.
I'M THINKING OF GOING HOME FOR A WHILE TO MAKE PREPARATIONS.
YOU'RE GOING HOME?

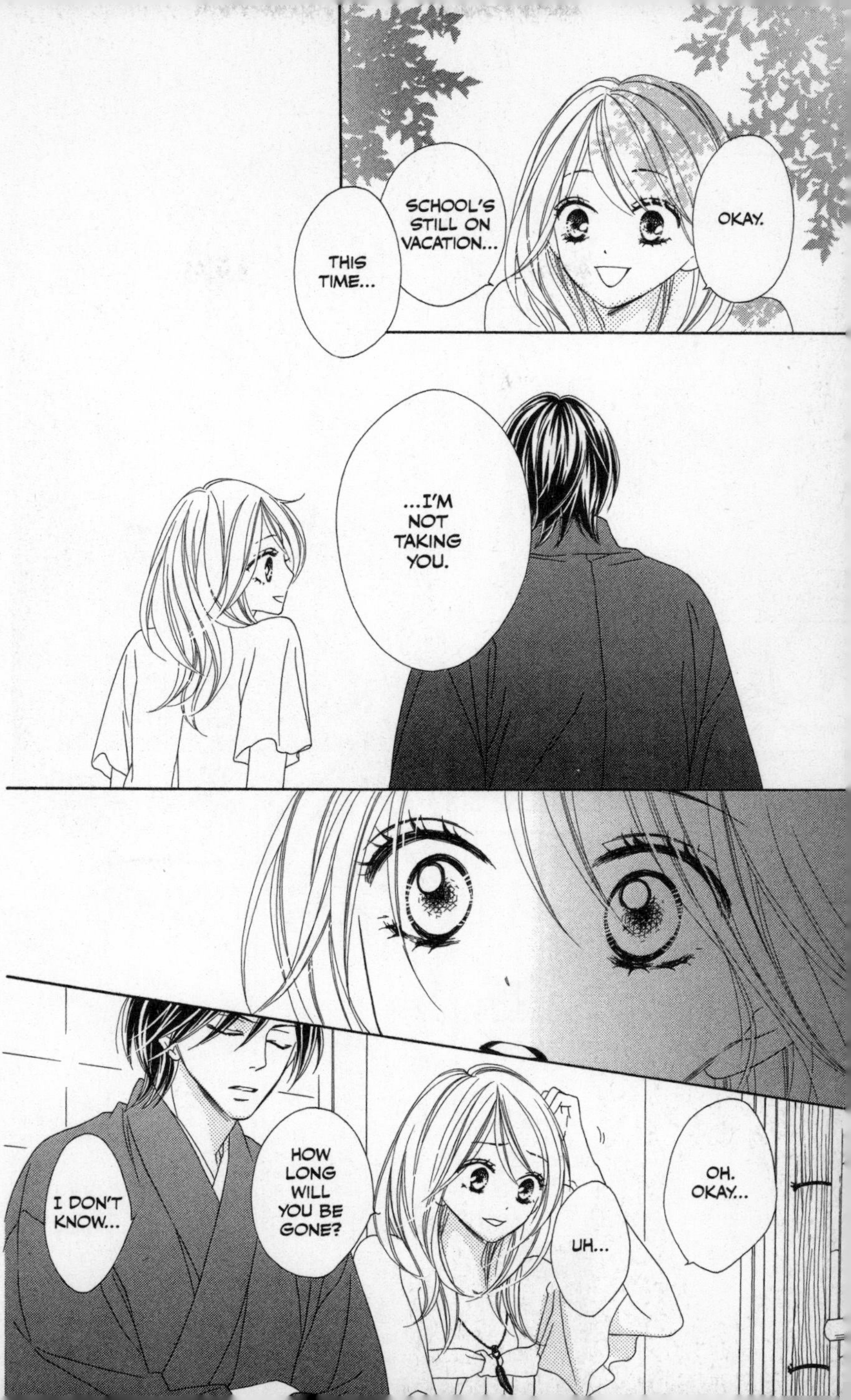
OKAY.
SCHOOL'S STILL ON VACATION...
THIS TIME...
...I'M NOT TAKING YOU.
OH. OKAY...
UH...
HOW LONG WILL YOU BE GONE?
I DON'T KNOW...

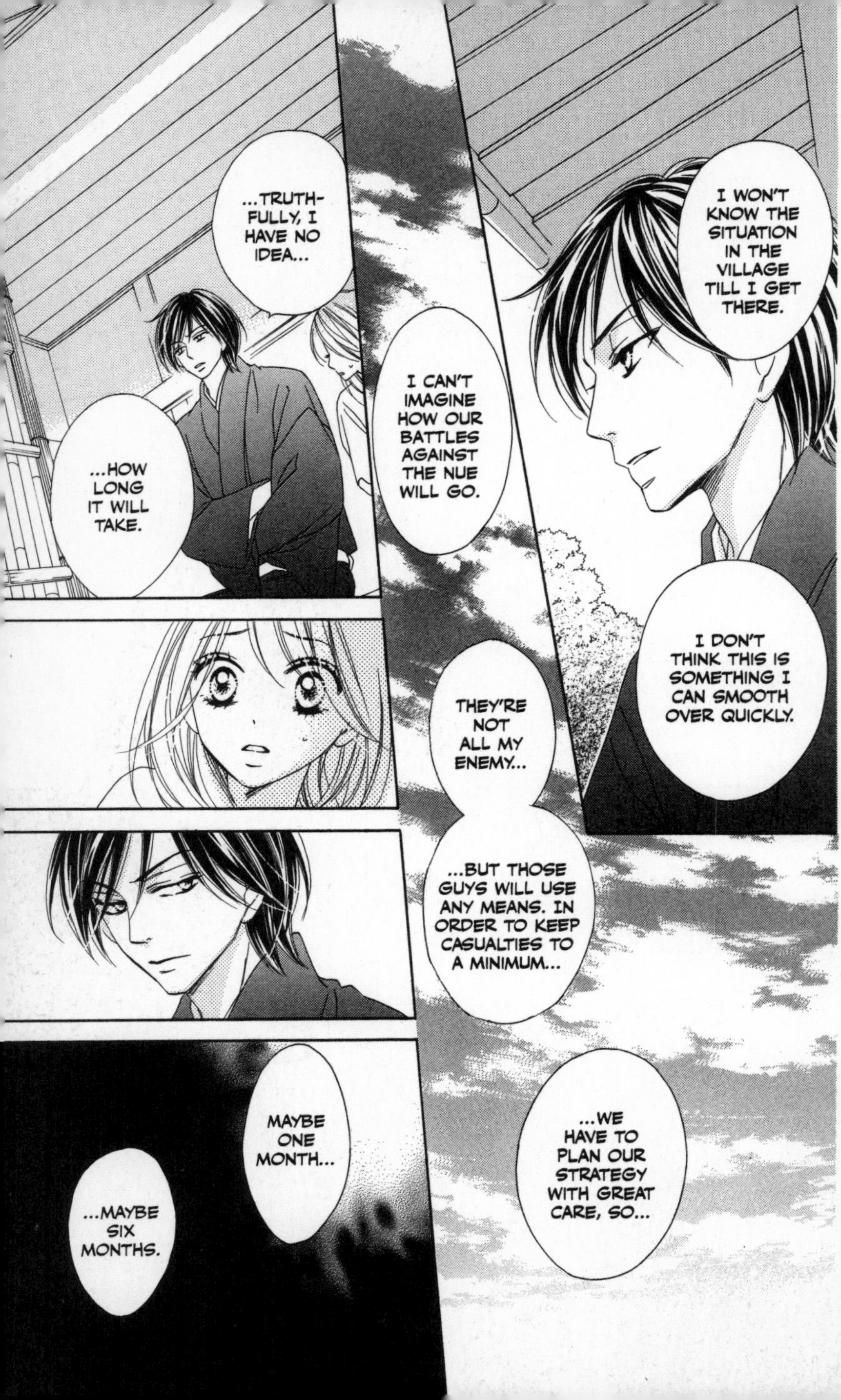
I WON'T KNOW THE SITUATION IN THE VILLAGE TILL I GET THERE.
I DON'T THINK THIS IS SOMETHING I CAN SMOOTH OVER QUICKLY.
I CAN'T IMAGINE HOW OUR BATTLES AGAINST THE NUE WILL GO.
THEY'RE NOT ALL MY ENEMY...
...BUT THOSE GUYS WILL USE ANY MEANS. IN ORDER TO KEEP CASUALTIES TO A MINIMUM...
...WE HAVE TO PLAN OUR STRATEGY WITH GREAT CARE, SO...
...TRUTH-FULLY, I HAVE NO IDEA...
...HOW LONG IT WILL TAKE.
MAYBE ONE MONTH...
...MAYBE SIX MONTHS.

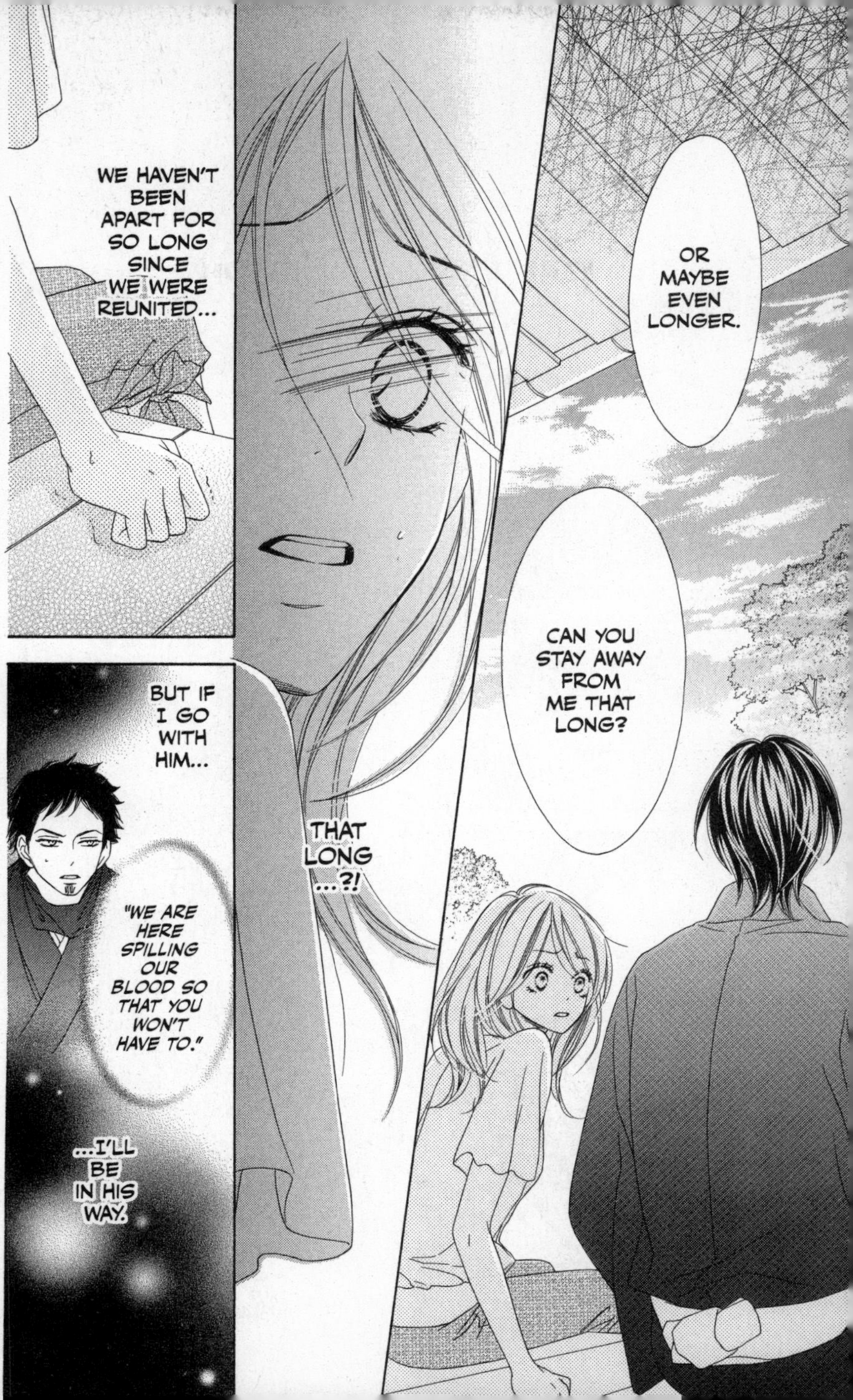
OR MAYBE EVEN LONGER.
CAN YOU STAY AWAY FROM ME THAT LONG?
THAT LONG ...?!
WE HAVEN'T BEEN APART FOR SO LONG SINCE WE WERE REUNITED...
BUT IF I GO WITH HIM...
"WE ARE HERE SPILLING OUR BLOOD SO THAT YOU WON'T HAVE TO."
...I'LL BE IN HIS WAY.

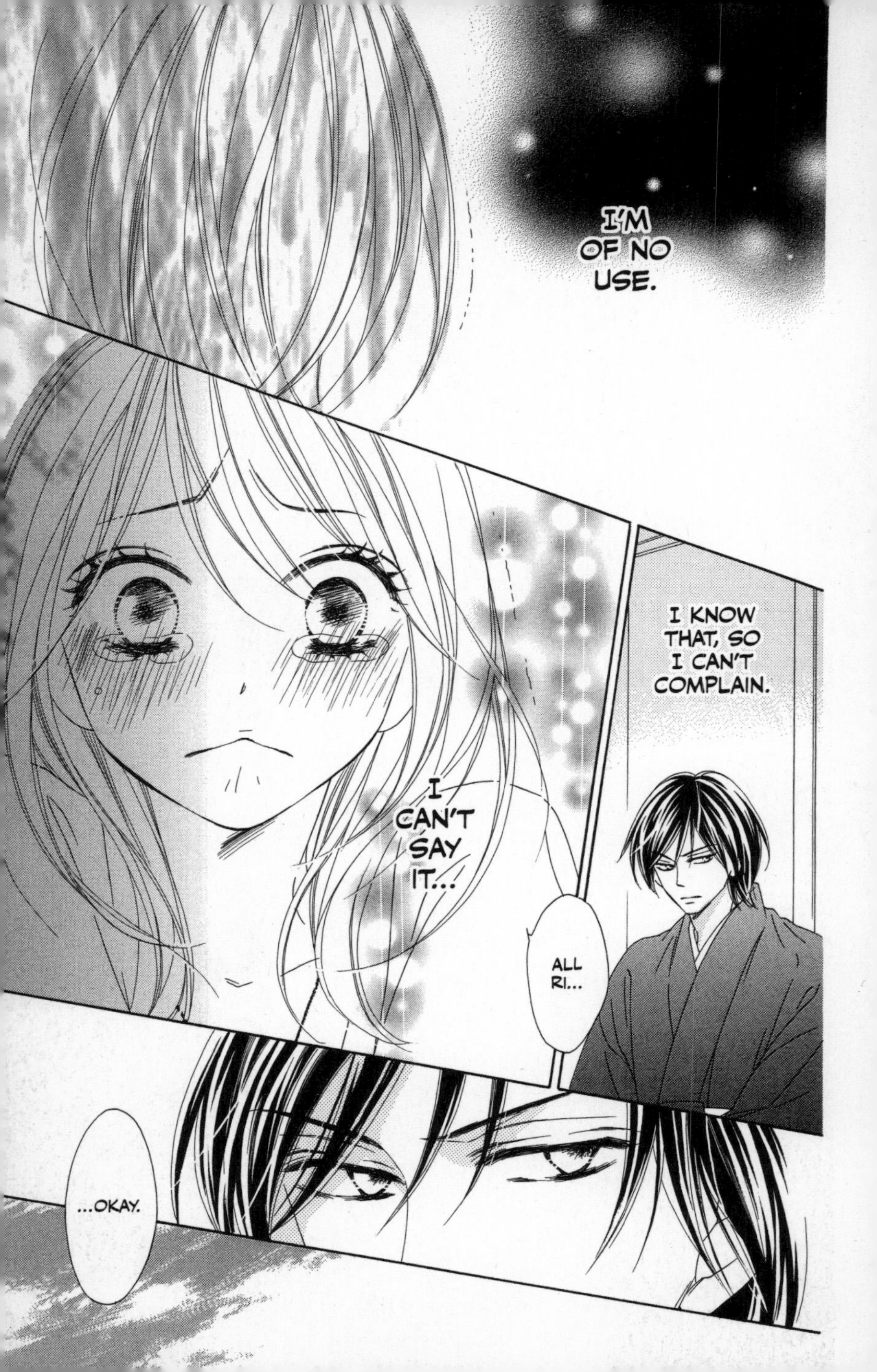
I'M OF NO USE.
I KNOW THAT, SO I CAN'T COMPLAIN.
I CAN'T SAY IT...
ALL RI...
...OKAY.

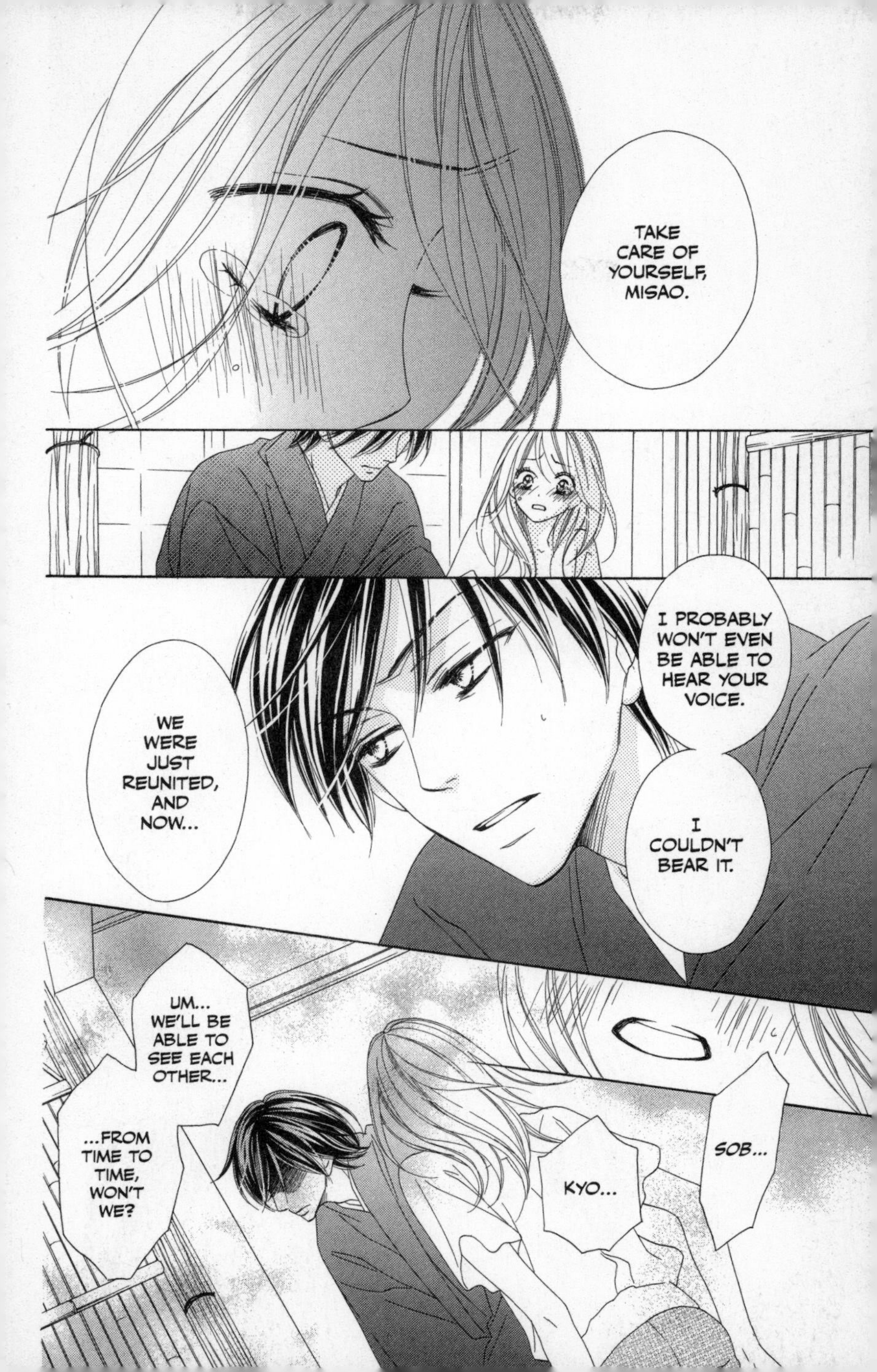
TAKE CARE OF YOURSELF, MISAO.
I PROBABLY WON'T EVEN BE ABLE TO HEAR YOUR VOICE.
WE WERE JUST REUNITED, AND NOW...
I COULDN'T BEAR IT.
SOB...
KYO...
UM... WE'LL BE ABLE TO SEE EACH OTHER...
...FROM TIME TO TIME, WON'T WE?

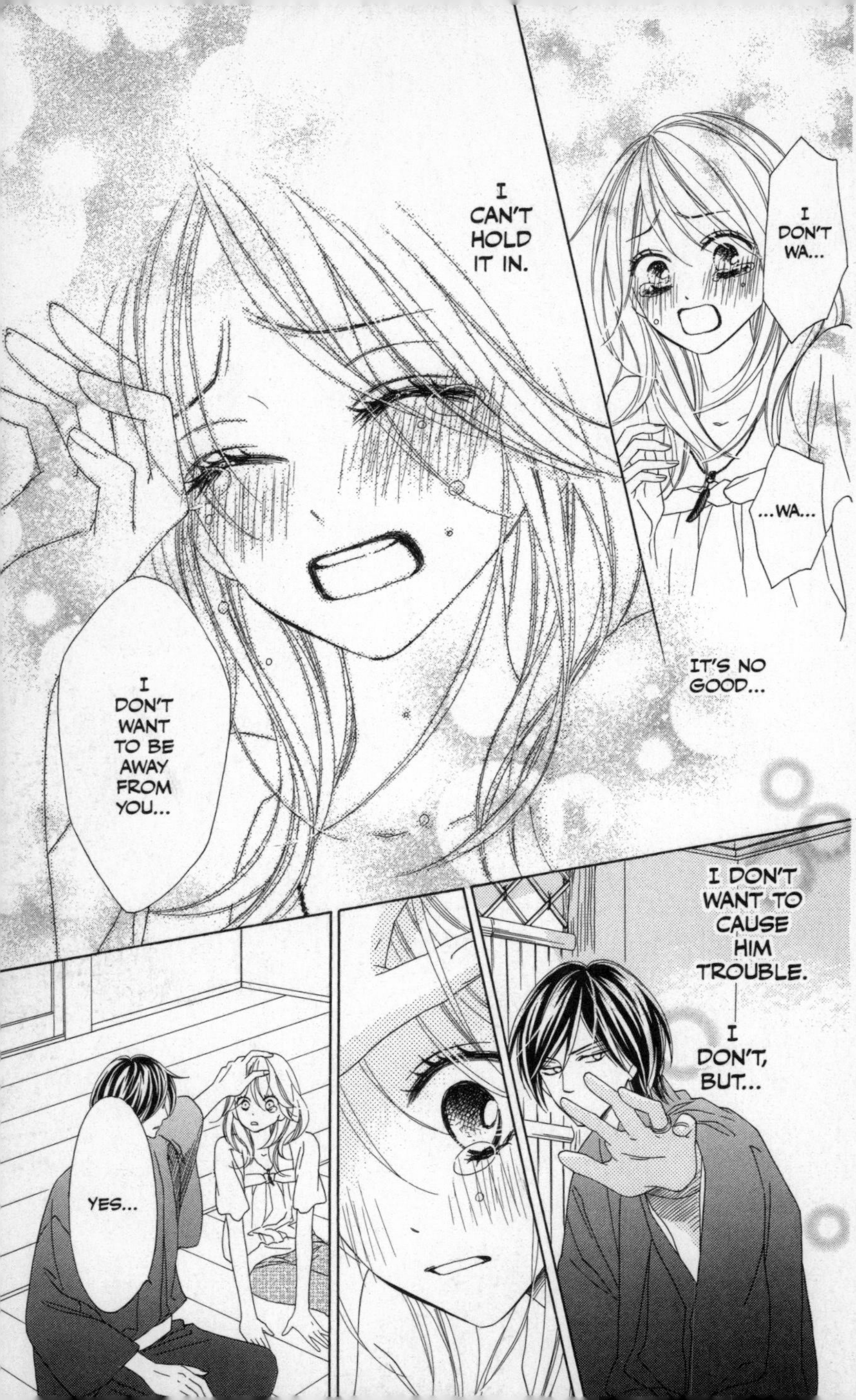
I DON'T WA...
...WA...
IT'S NO GOOD...
I CAN'T HOLD IT IN.
I DON'T WANT TO BE AWAY FROM YOU...
I DON'T WANT TO CAUSE HIM TROUBLE.
I DON'T, BUT...
YES...

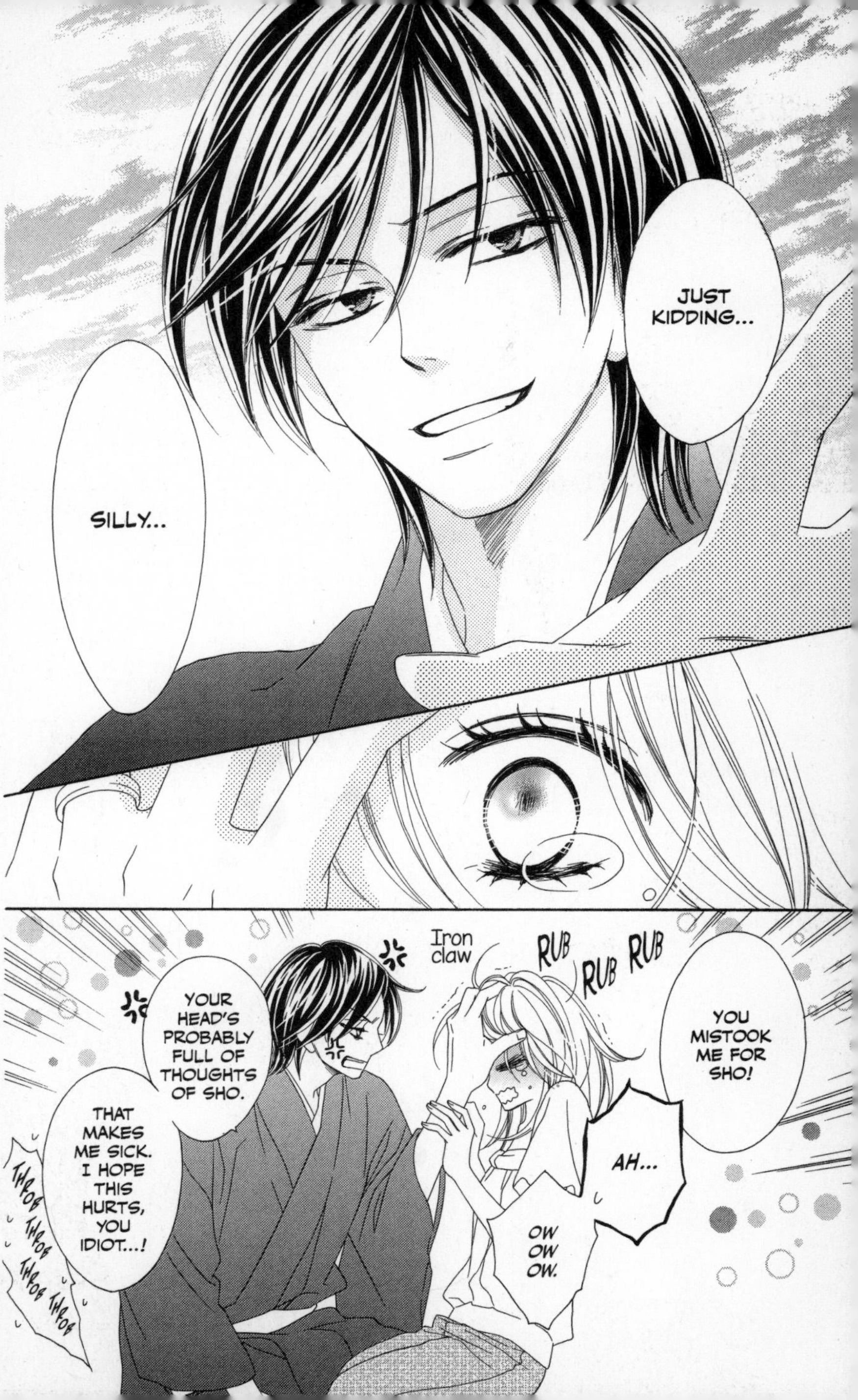
JUST KIDDING...
SILLY...
YOU MISTOOK ME FOR SHO!
RUB RUB RUB
AH...
OW OW OW.
Iron claw
YOUR HEAD'S PROBABLY FULL OF THOUGHTS OF SHO.
THAT MAKES ME SICK. I HOPE THIS HURTS, YOU IDIOT...!
THROB THROB THROB THROB

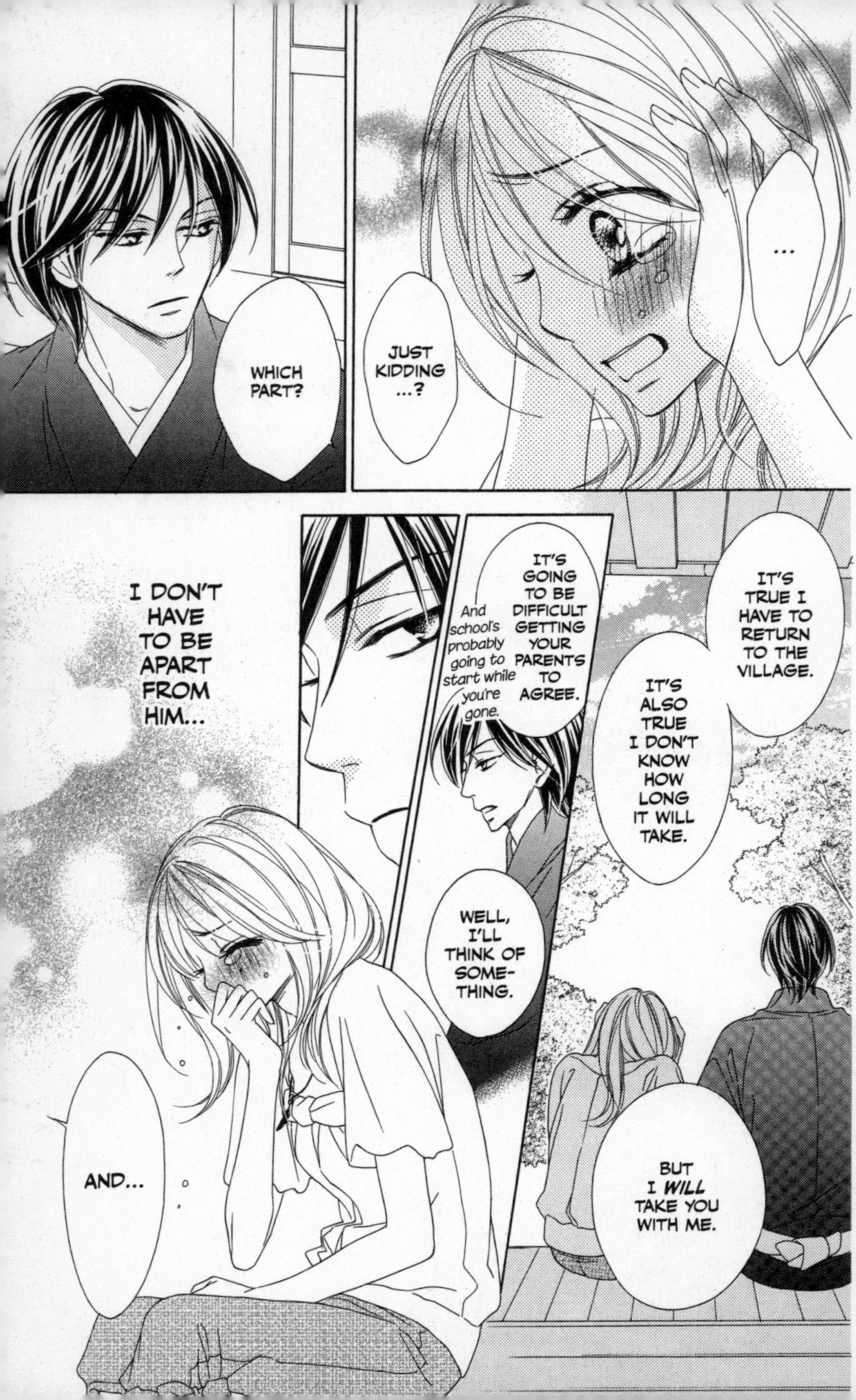
...
JUST KIDDING ...?
WHICH PART?
IT'S TRUE I HAVE TO RETURN TO THE VILLAGE.
IT'S ALSO TRUE I DON'T KNOW HOW LONG IT WILL TAKE.
IT'S GOING TO BE DIFFICULT GETTING YOUR PARENTS TO AGREE.
And school's probably going to start while you're gone.
WELL, I'LL THINK OF SOME-THING.
BUT I *WILL* TAKE YOU WITH ME.
I DON'T HAVE TO BE APART FROM HIM...
AND...

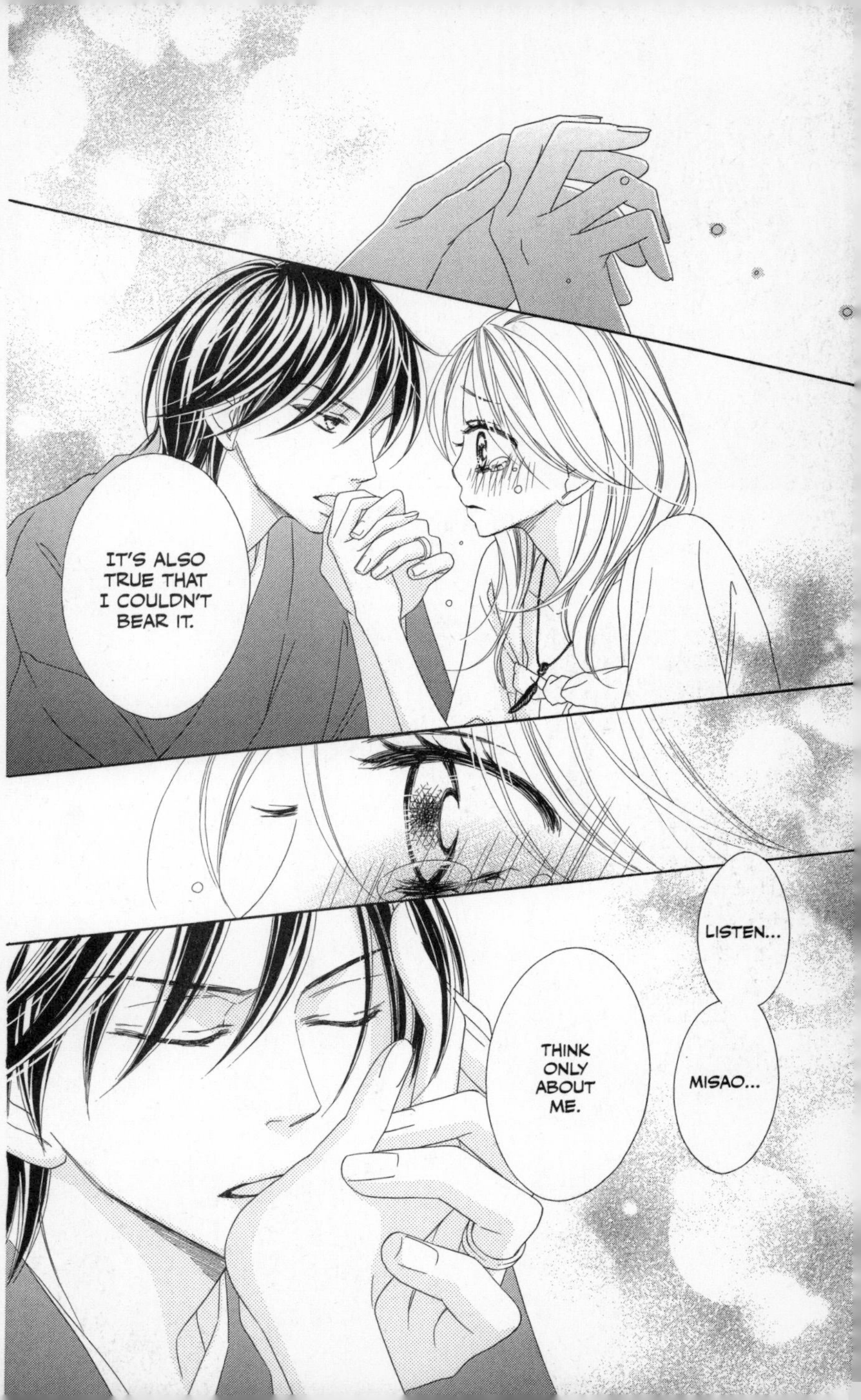
IT'S ALSO TRUE THAT I COULDN'T BEAR IT.
LISTEN...
MISAO...
THINK ONLY ABOUT ME.

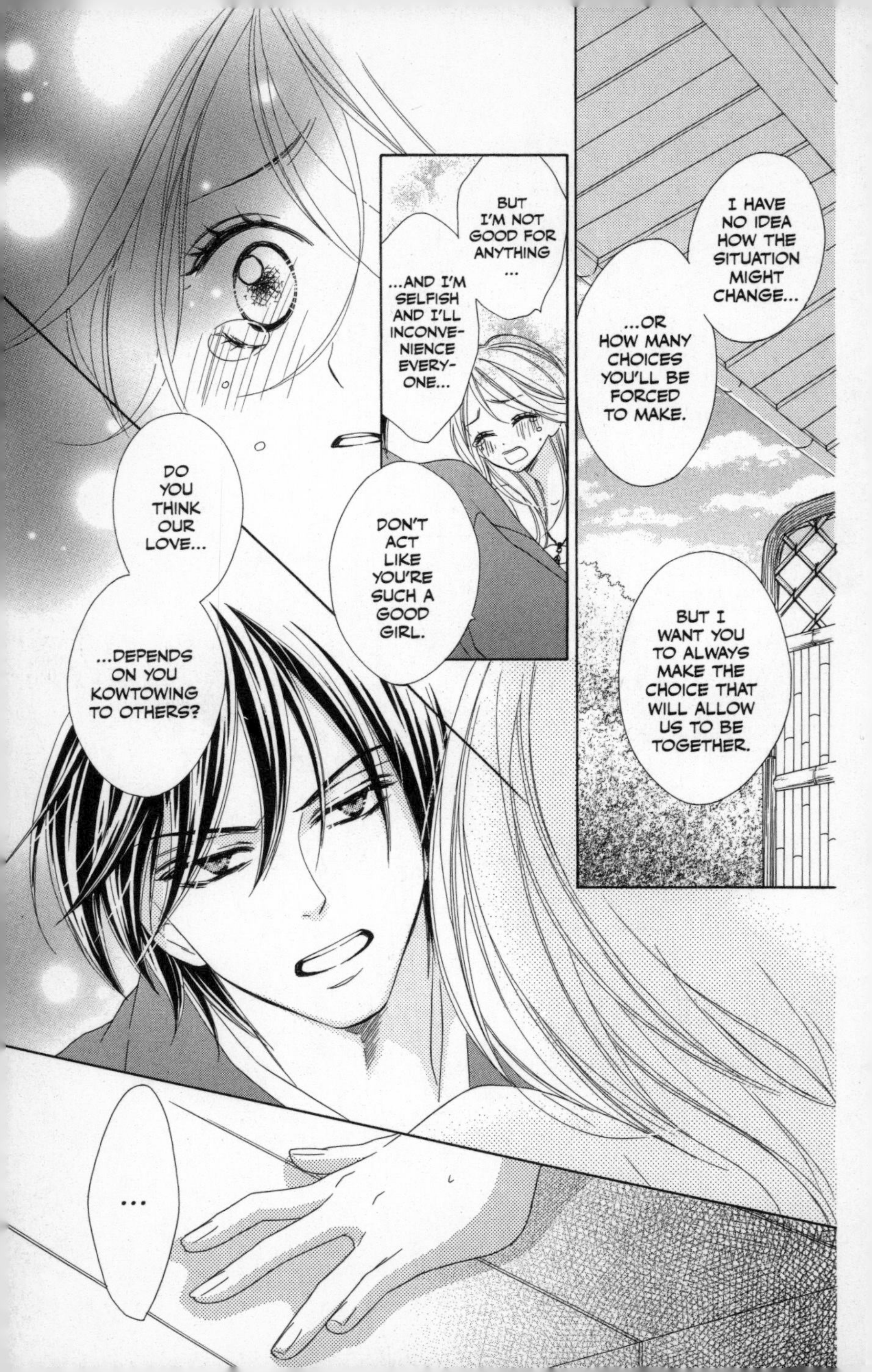
I HAVE NO IDEA HOW THE SITUATION MIGHT CHANGE...
...OR HOW MANY CHOICES YOU'LL BE FORCED TO MAKE.
BUT I WANT YOU TO ALWAYS MAKE THE CHOICE THAT WILL ALLOW US TO BE TOGETHER.
BUT I'M NOT GOOD FOR ANYTHING...
...AND I'M SELFISH AND I'LL INCONVENIENCE EVERYONE...
DON'T ACT LIKE YOU'RE SUCH A GOOD GIRL.
DO YOU THINK OUR LOVE...
...DEPENDS ON YOU KOWTOWING TO OTHERS?
...

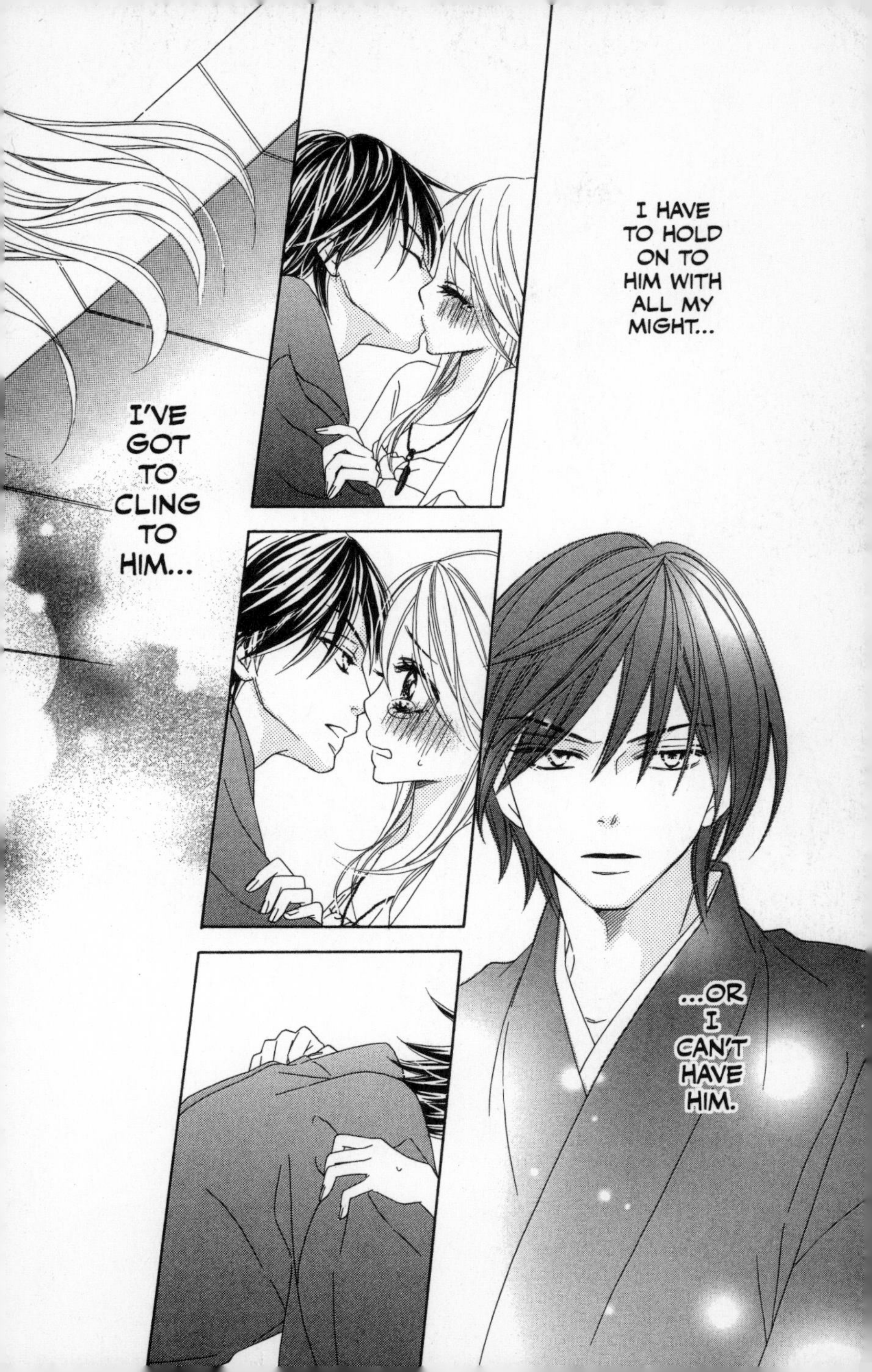
I HAVE TO HOLD ON TO HIM WITH ALL MY MIGHT...
I'VE GOT TO CLING TO HIM...
...OR I CAN'T HAVE HIM.

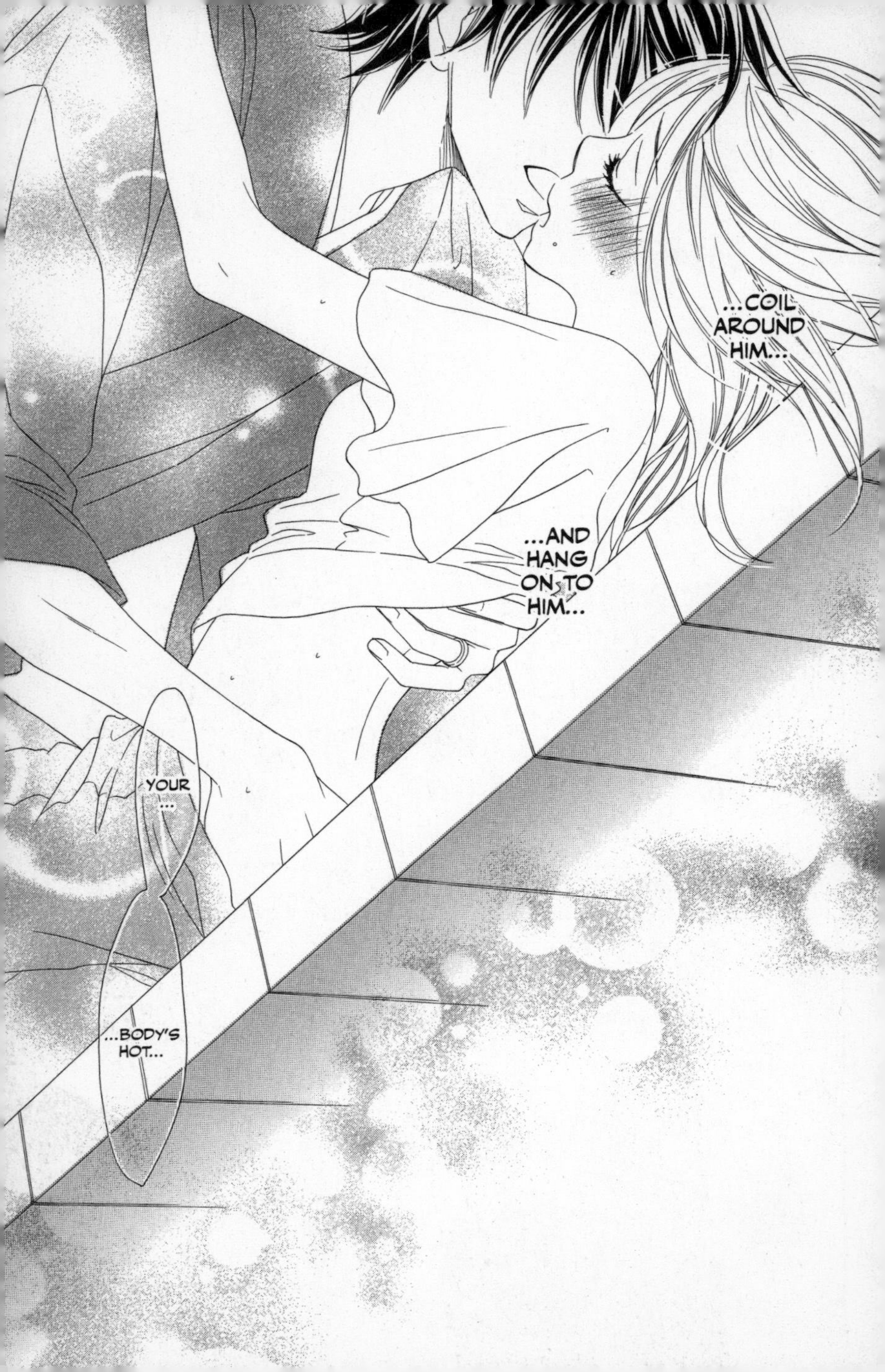
...COIL AROUND HIM...
...AND HANG ON TO HIM...
YOUR ...
...BODY'S HOT...

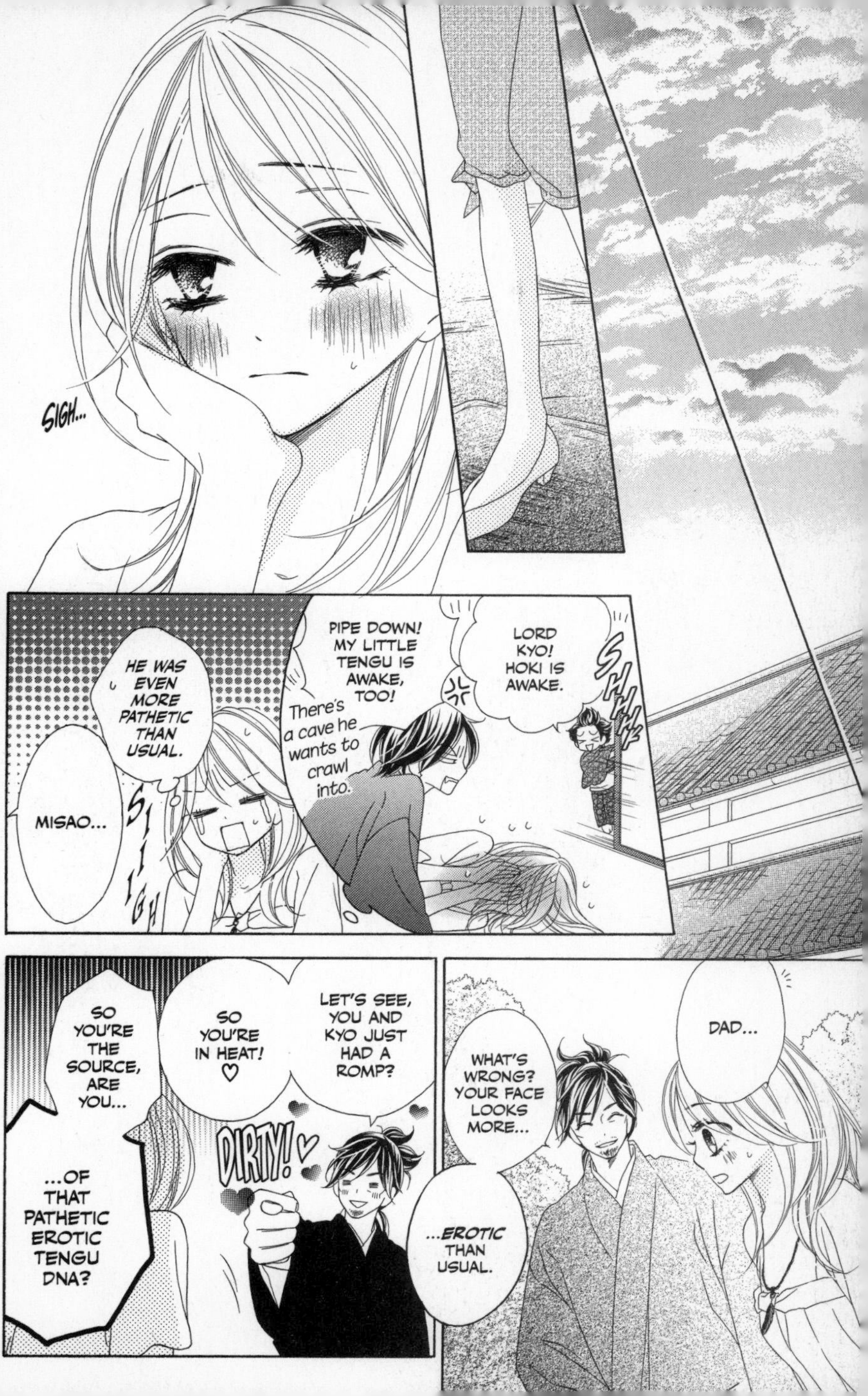
SIGH...
SHHH
LORD KYO! HOKI IS AWAKE.
PIPE DOWN! MY LITTLE TENGU IS AWAKE, TOO!
There's a cave he wants to crawl into.
HE WAS EVEN MORE PATHETIC THAN USUAL.
MISAO...
SIIIGH
DAD...
WHAT'S WRONG? YOUR FACE LOOKS MORE...
...EROTIC THAN USUAL.
LET'S SEE, YOU AND KYO JUST HAD A ROMP?
SO YOU'RE IN HEAT! ♡
DIRTY! ♡
SO YOU'RE THE SOURCE, ARE YOU...
...OF THAT PATHETIC EROTIC TENGU DNA?

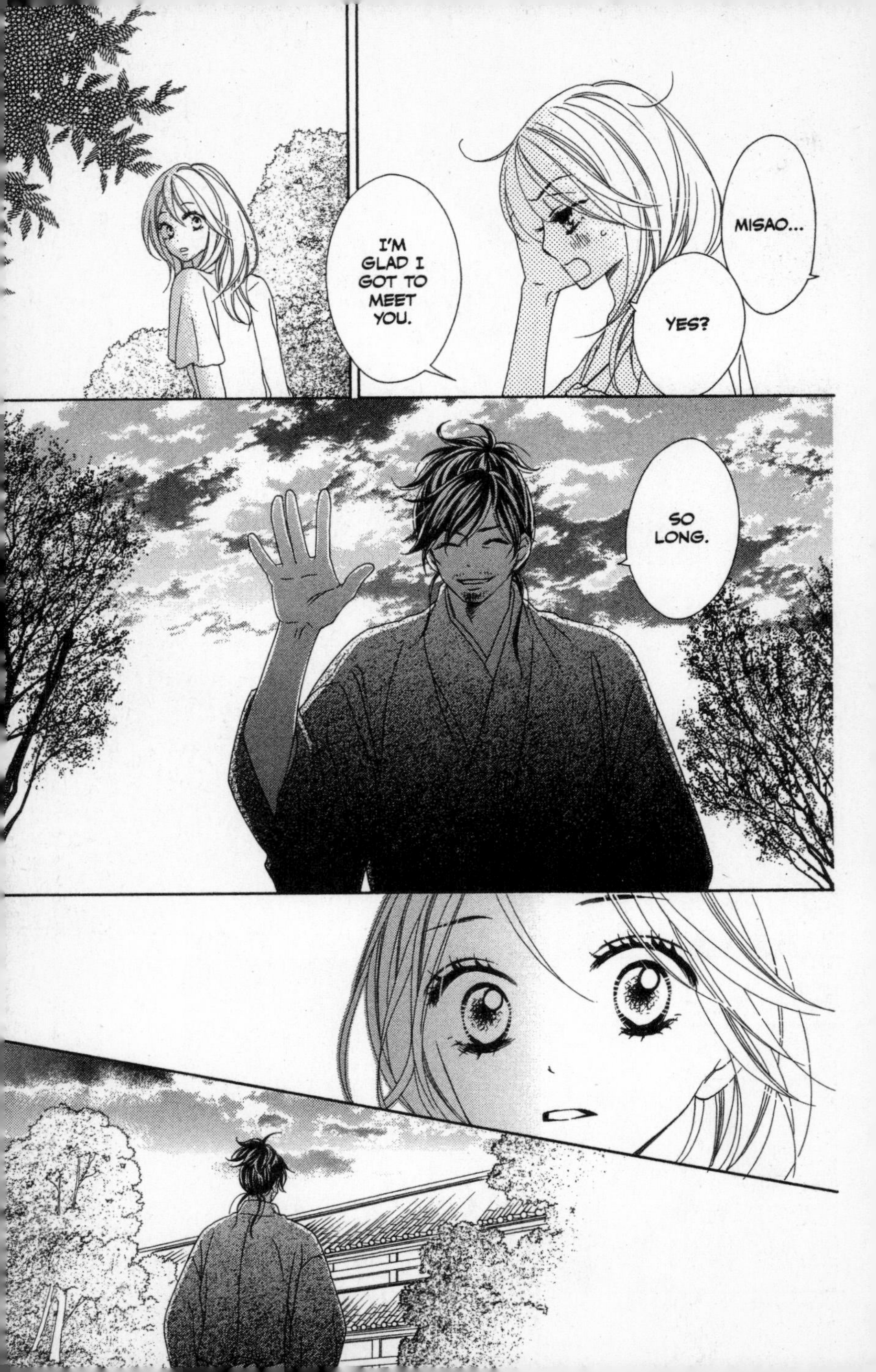
MISAO...
YES?
I'M GLAD I GOT TO MEET YOU.
SO LONG.

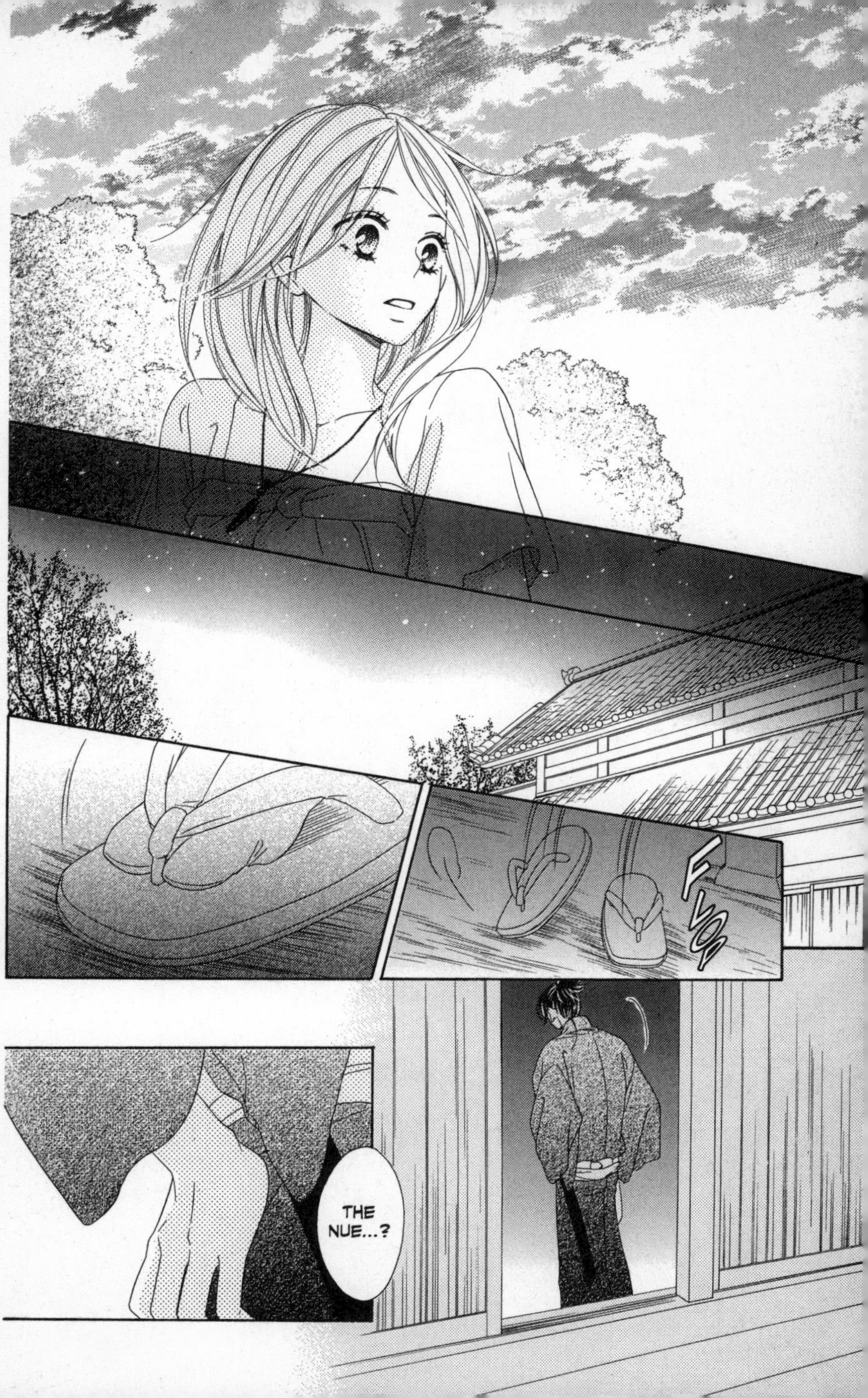
FLOP
THE NUE...?

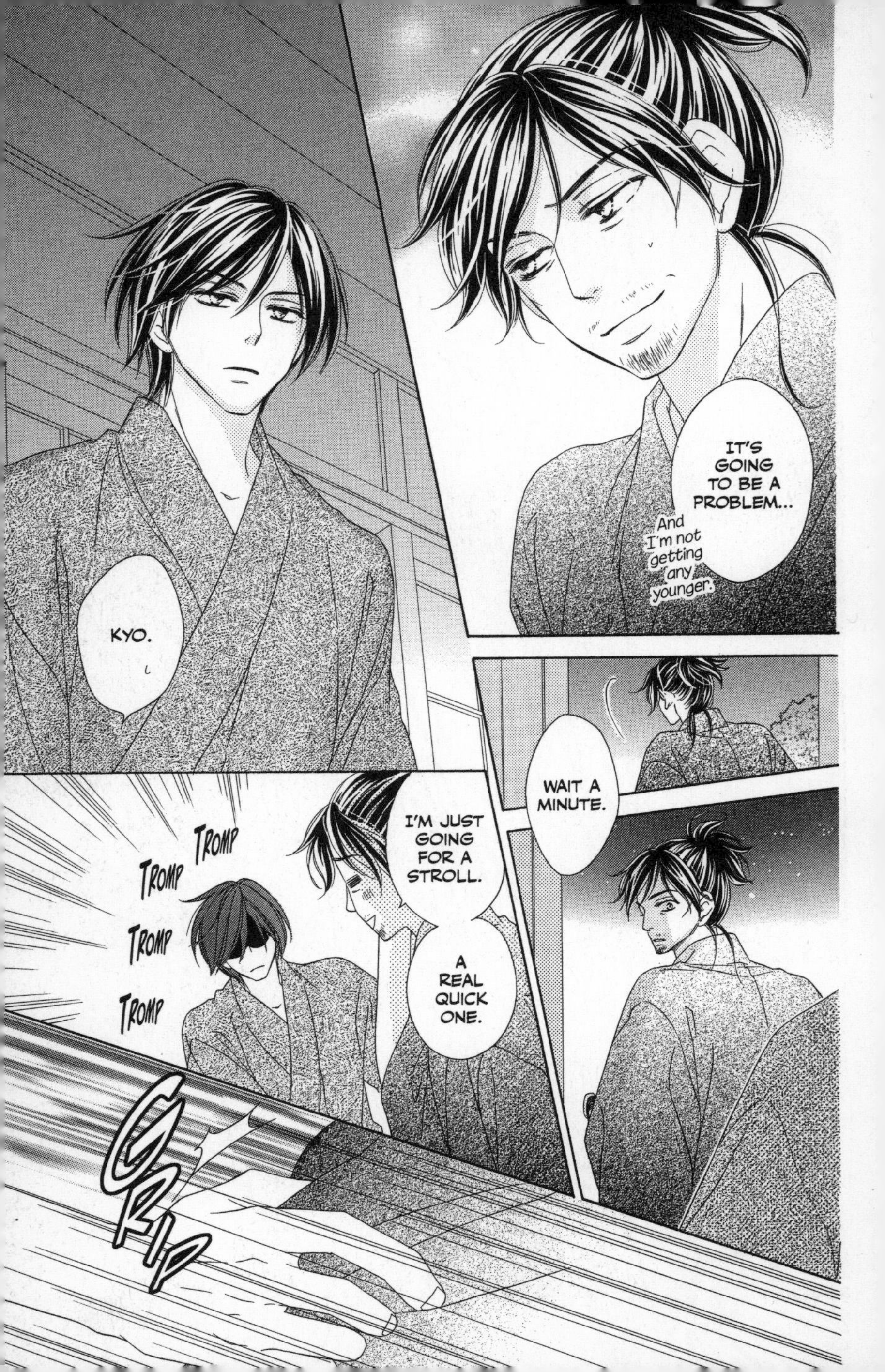
IT'S GOING TO BE A PROBLEM...
And I'm not getting any younger.
KYO.
WAIT A MINUTE.
I'M JUST GOING FOR A STROLL.
A REAL QUICK ONE.
TROMP
TROMP
TROMP
TROMP
GRIP

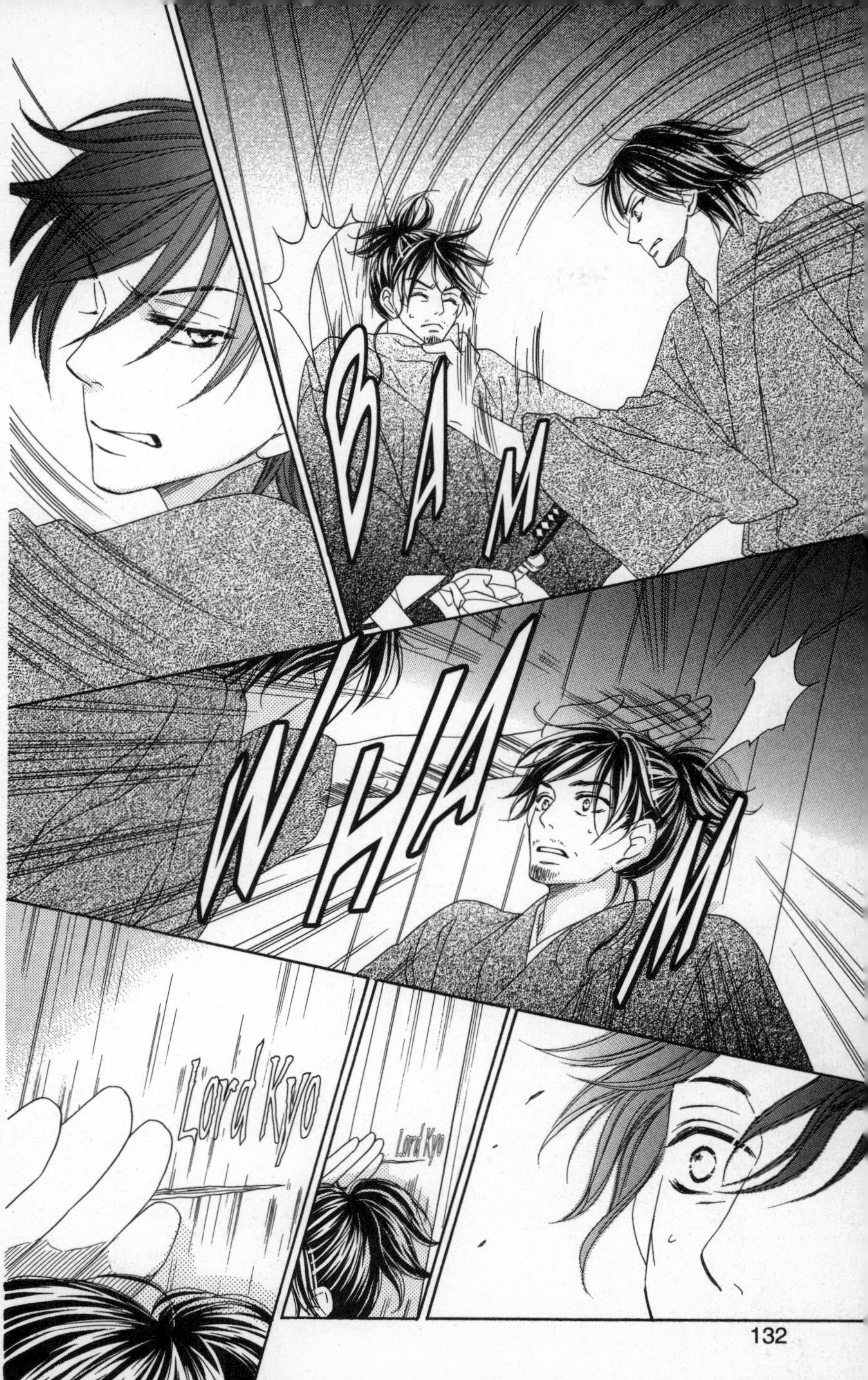
SAM
WHAM
Lord Kyo
Lord Kyo

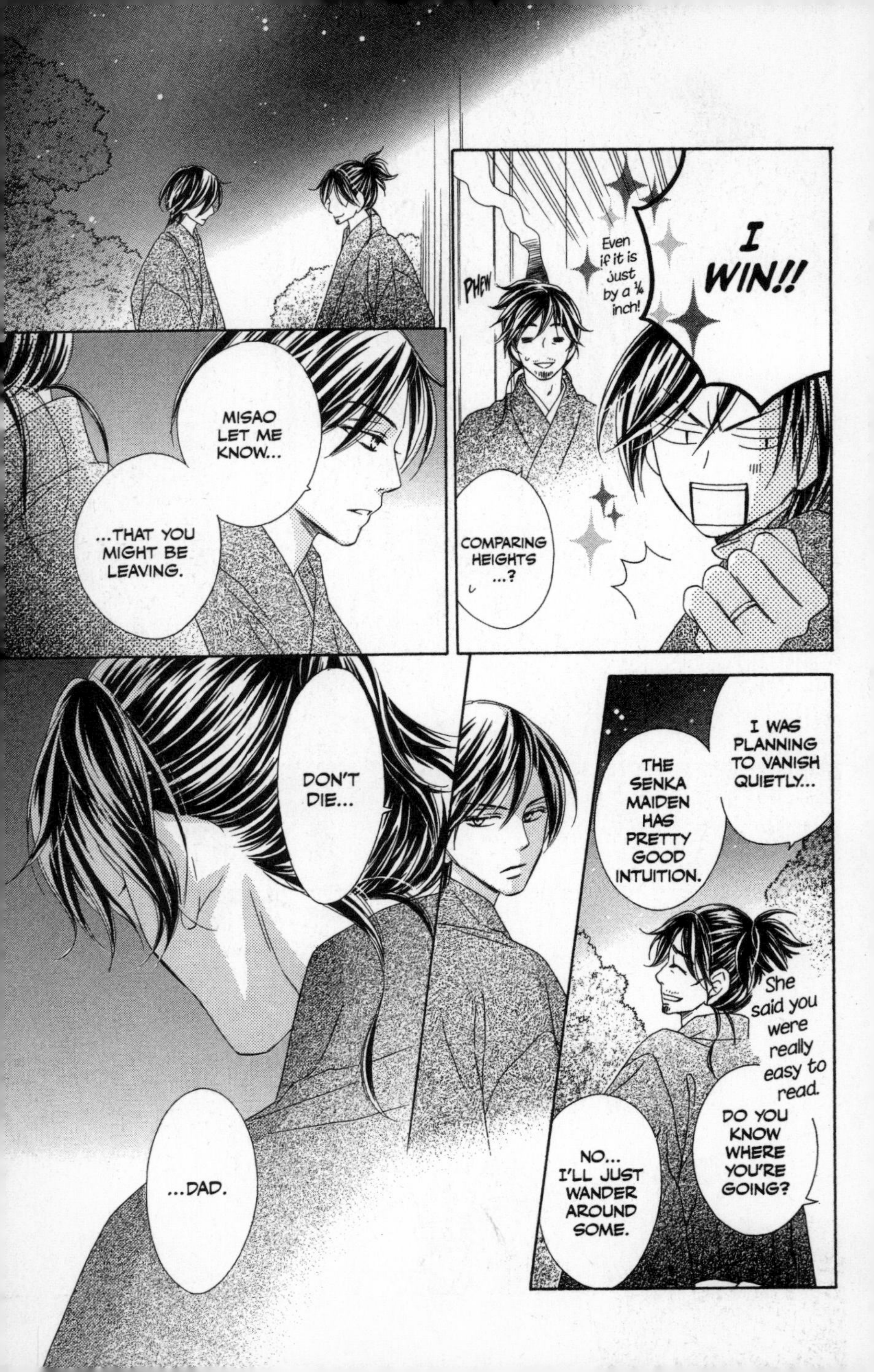
I WIN!!
Even if it is just by a 1/4 inch!
PHEW
COMPARING HEIGHTS ...?
MISAO LET ME KNOW...
...THAT YOU MIGHT BE LEAVING.
I WAS PLANNING TO VANISH QUIETLY...
THE SENKA MAIDEN HAS PRETTY GOOD INTUITION.
She said you were really easy to read.
DO YOU KNOW WHERE YOU'RE GOING?
NO... I'LL JUST WANDER AROUND SOME.
DON'T DIE...
...DAD.

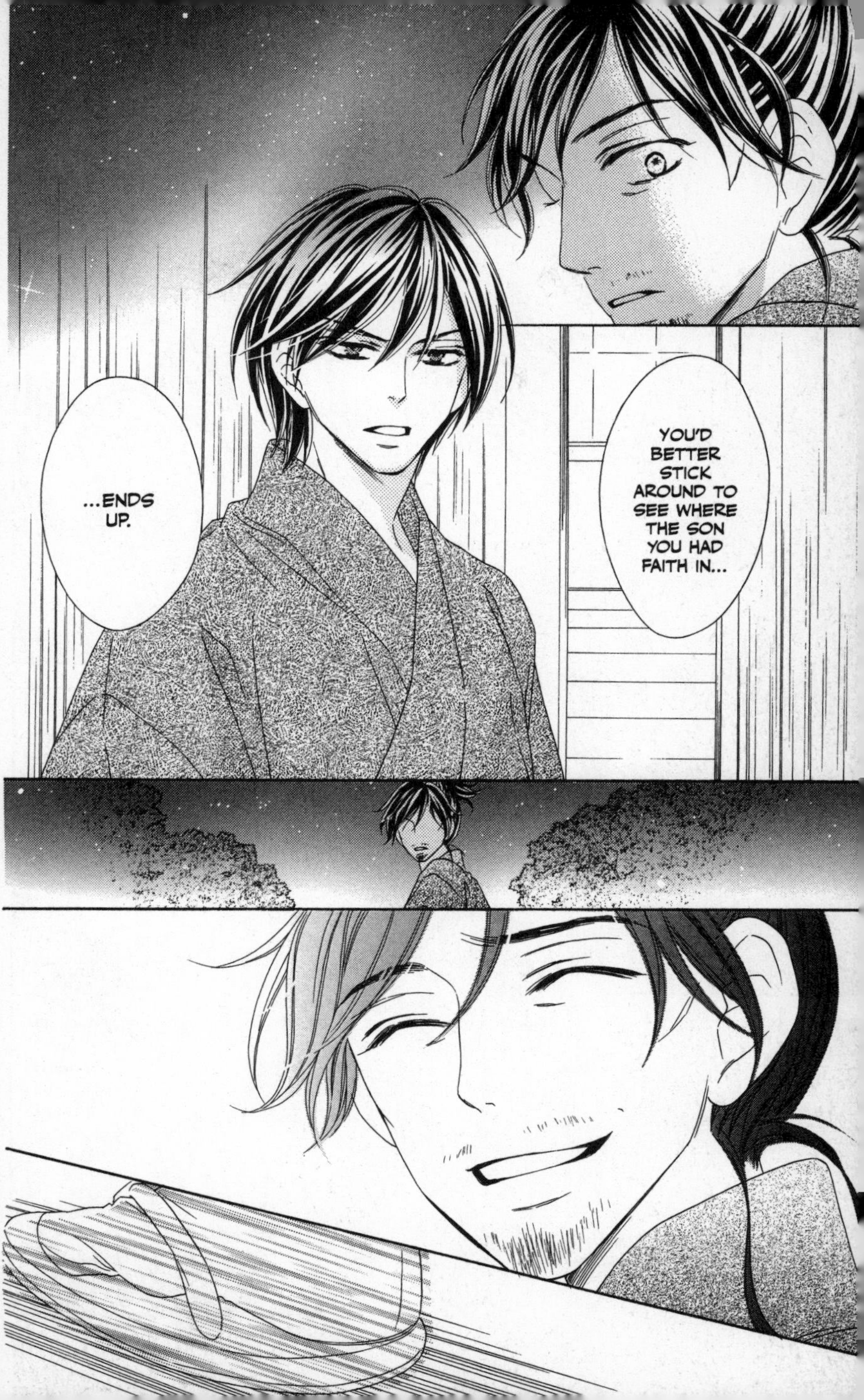
YOU'D BETTER STICK AROUND TO SEE WHERE THE SON YOU HAD FAITH IN...
...ENDS UP.

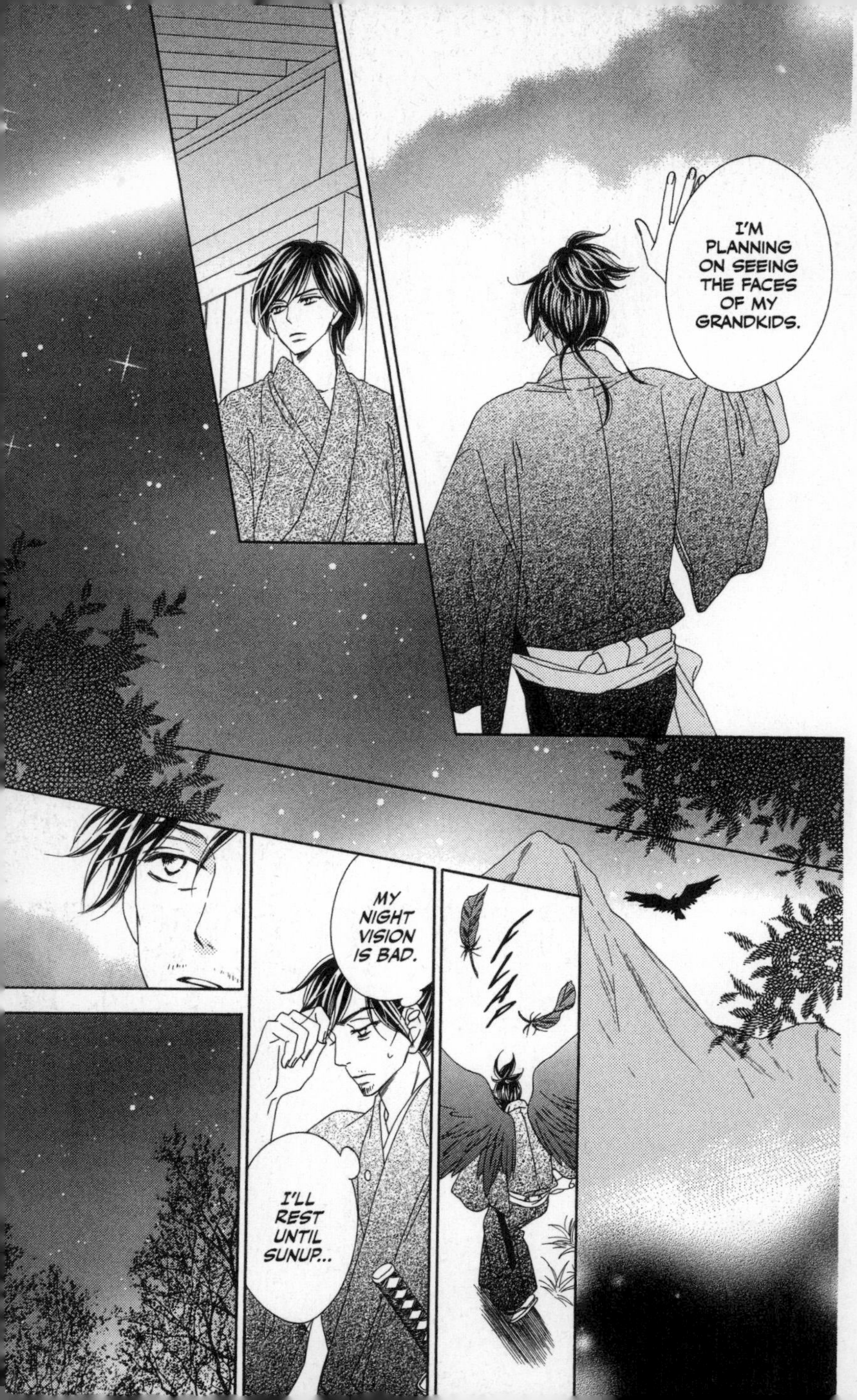
I'M PLANNING ON SEEING THE FACES OF MY GRANDKIDS.
FLAP
MY NIGHT VISION IS BAD.
I'LL REST UNTIL SUNUP...

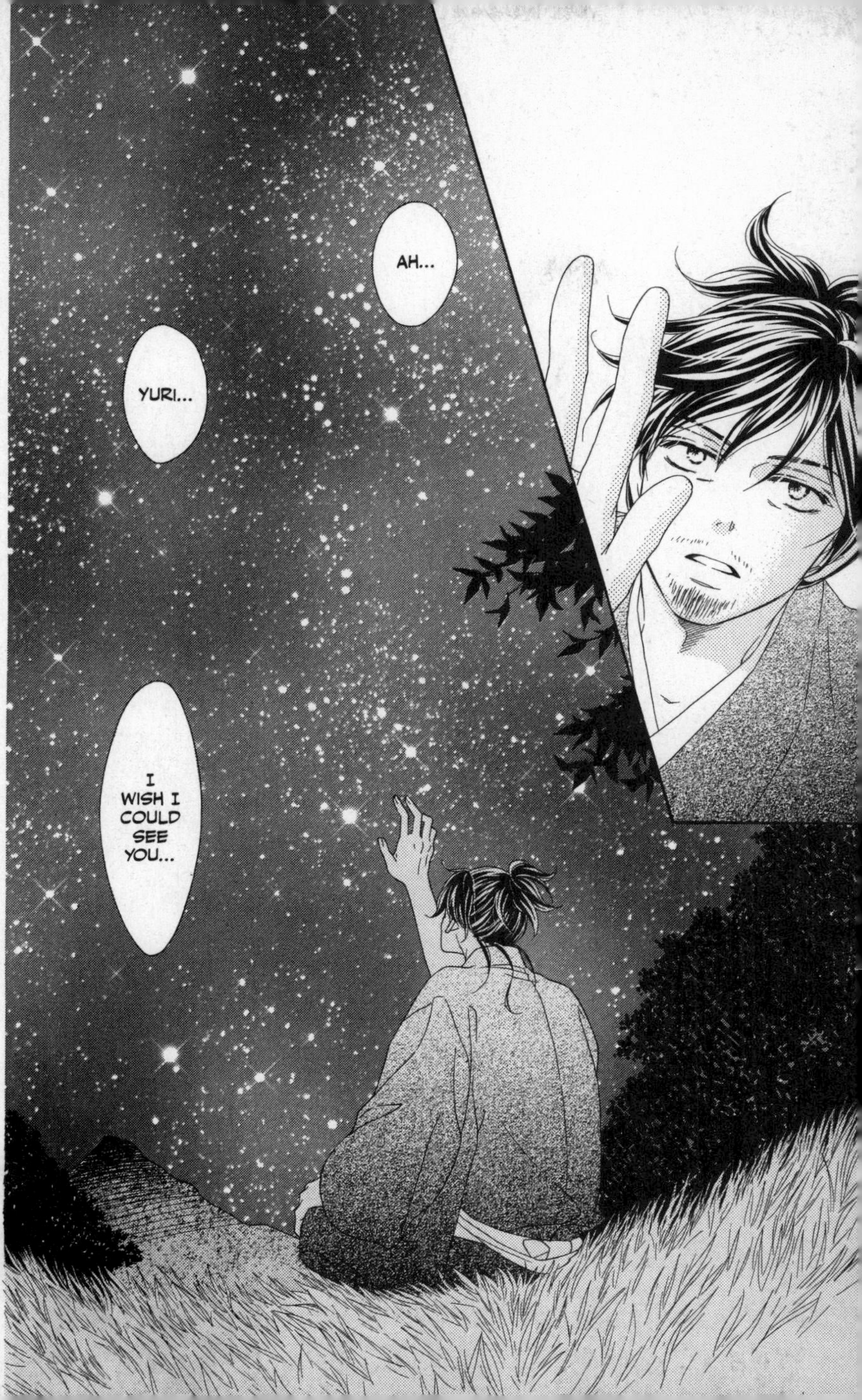
AH...
YURI...
I WISH I COULD SEE YOU...

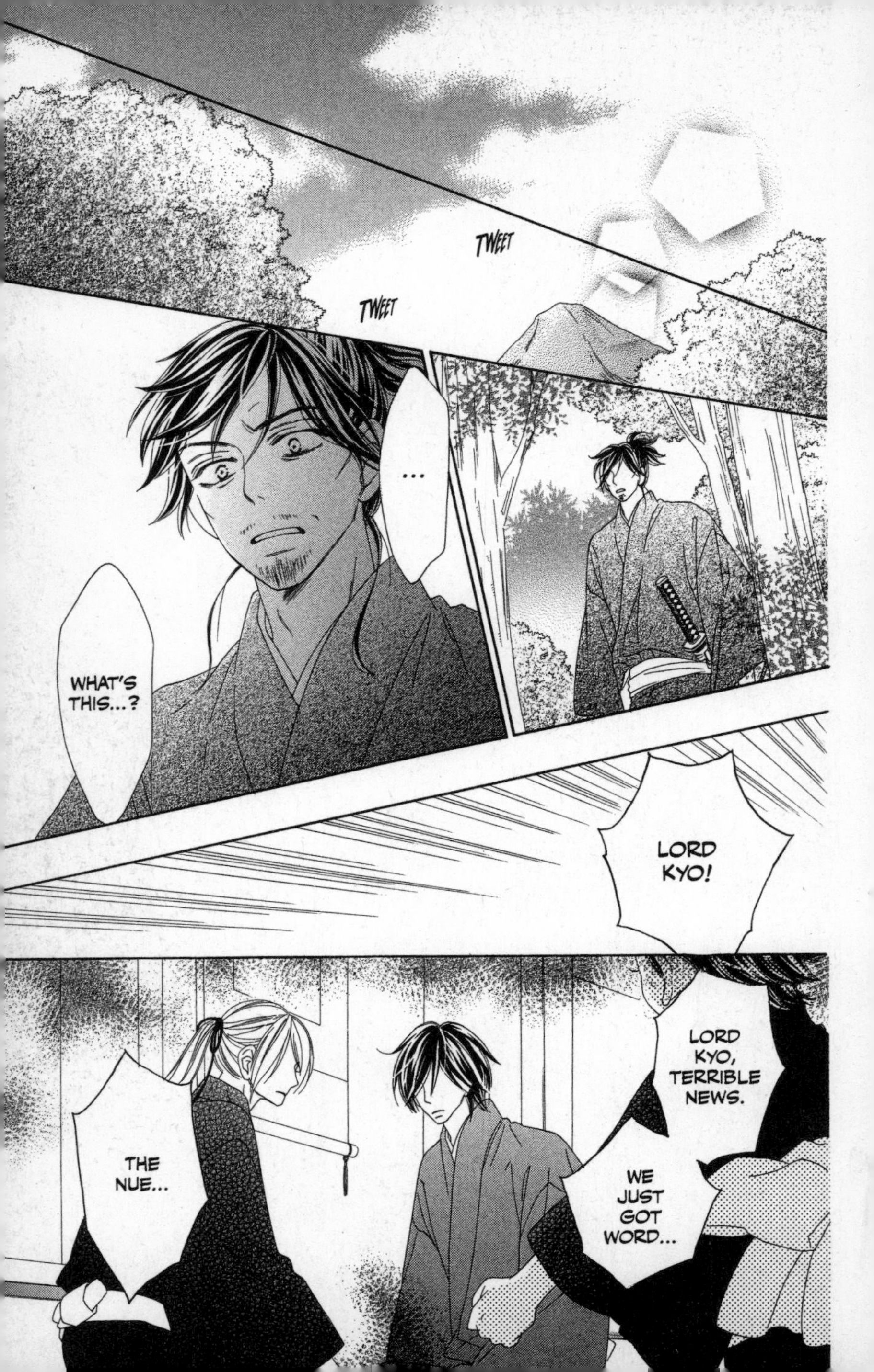
TWEET
TWEET
...
WHAT'S THIS...?
LORD KYO!
LORD KYO, TERRIBLE NEWS.
WE JUST GOT WORD...
THE NUE...

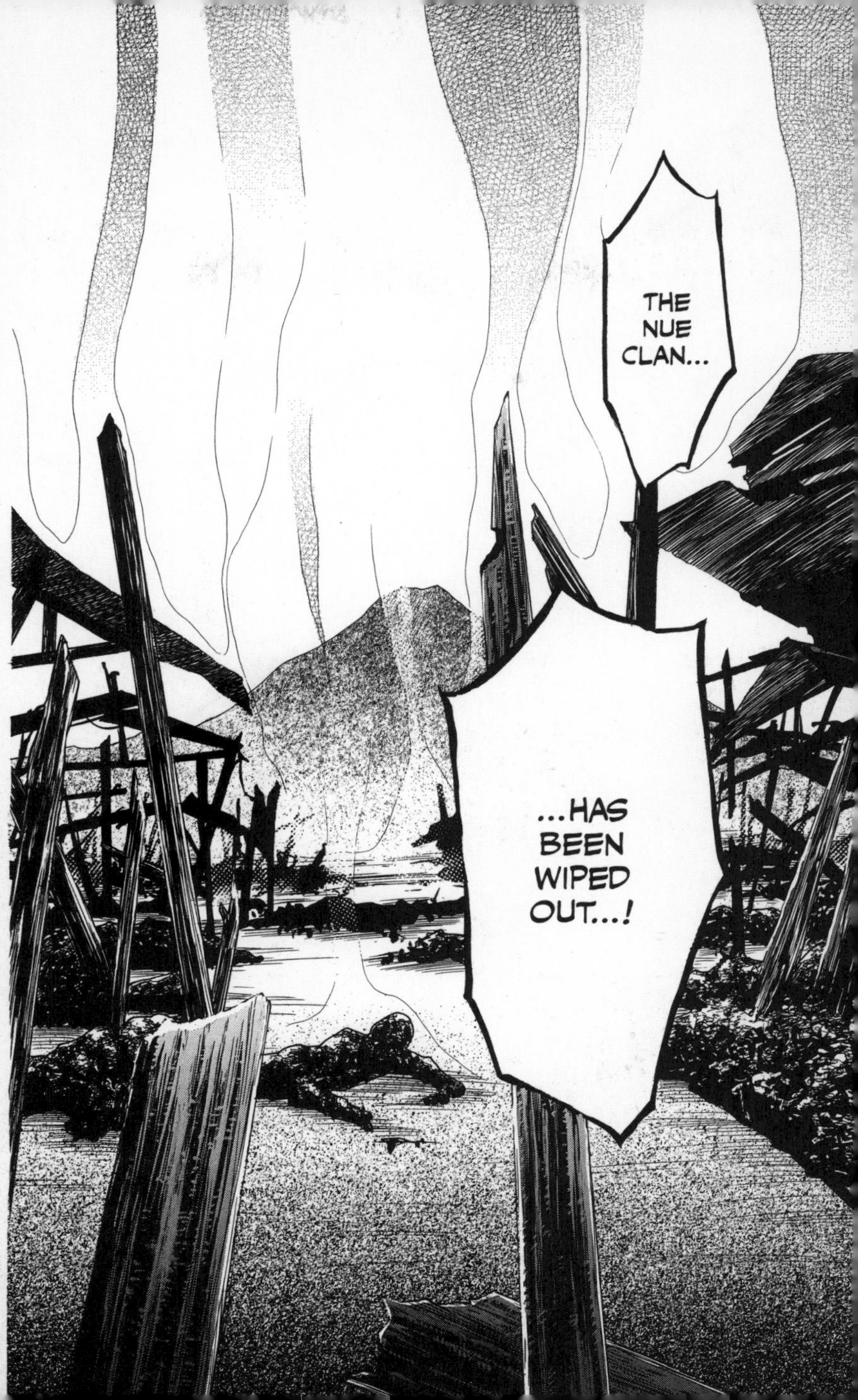
THE NUE CLAN...
...HAS BEEN WIPED OUT...!

Black Bird Chapter 39

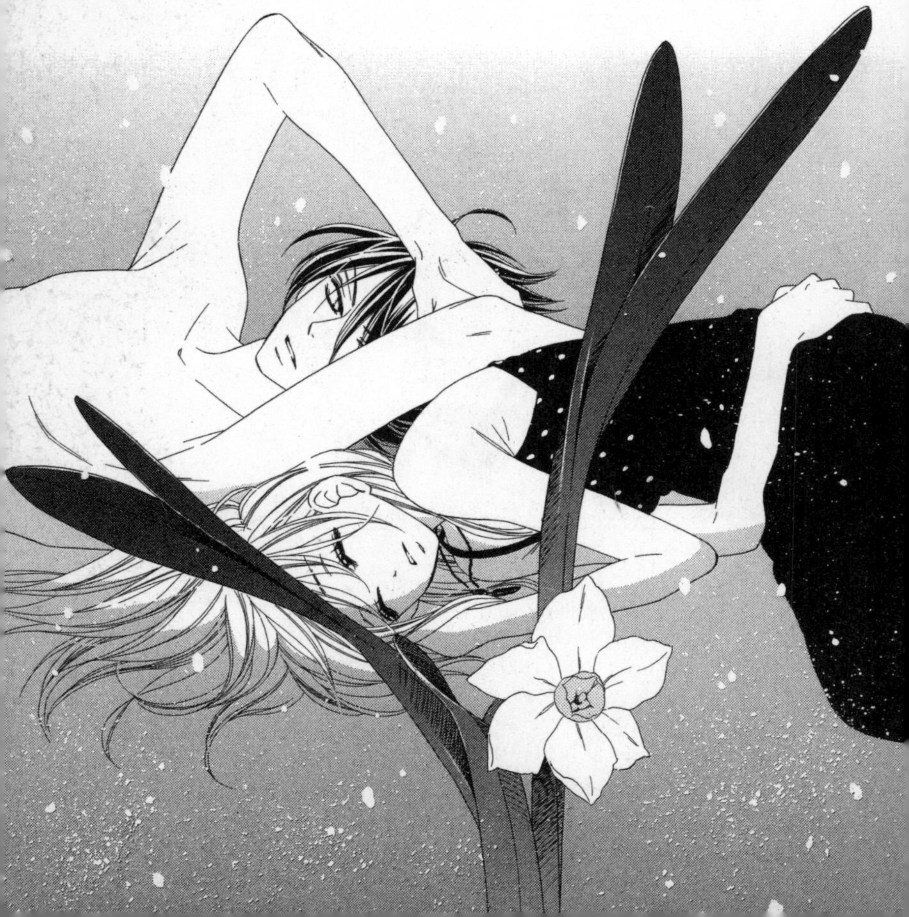

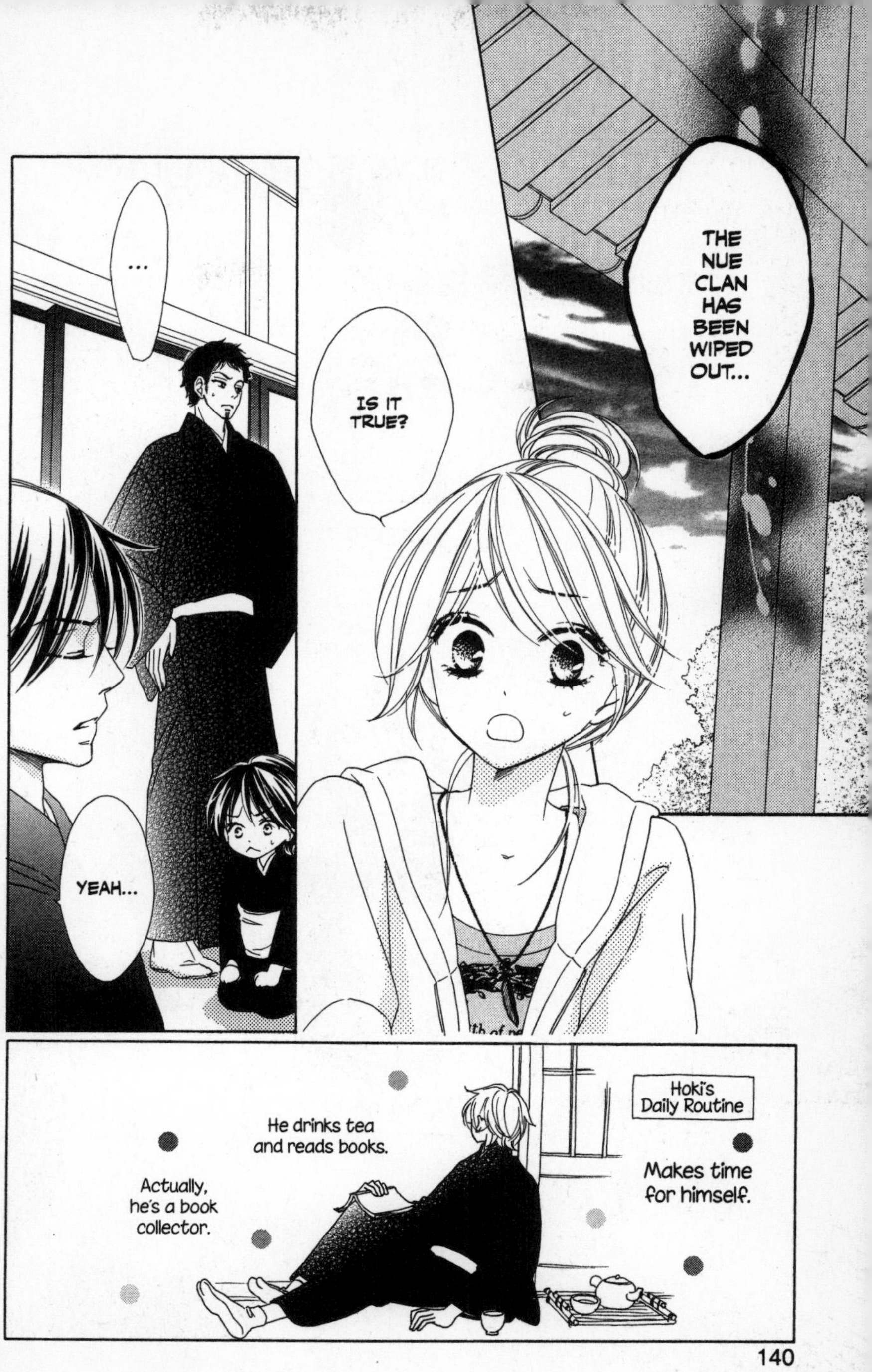
THE NUE CLAN HAS BEEN WIPED OUT...
IS IT TRUE?
...
YEAH...
Hoki's Daily Routine
Makes time for himself.
He drinks tea and reads books.
Actually, he's a book collector.

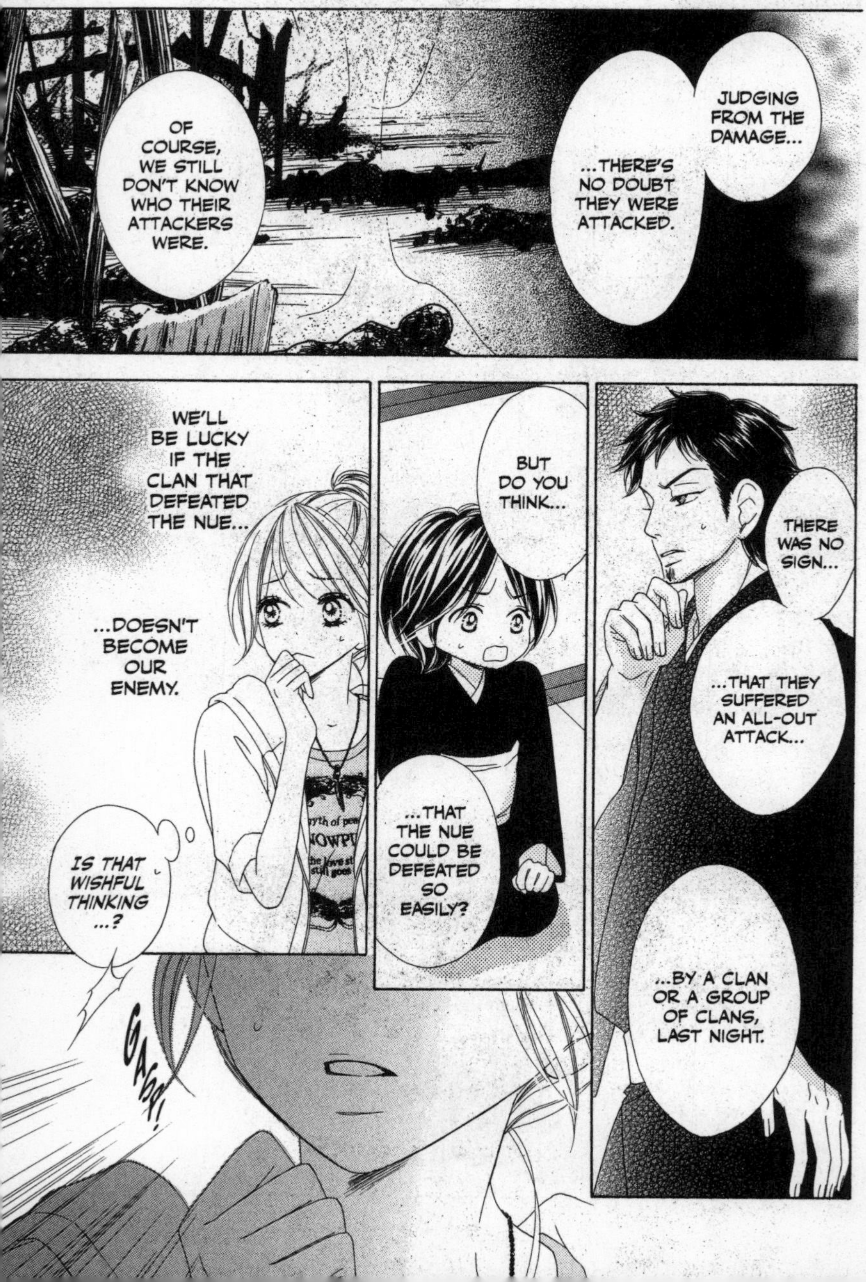
JUDGING FROM THE DAMAGE...
...THERE'S NO DOUBT THEY WERE ATTACKED.
OF COURSE, WE STILL DON'T KNOW WHO THEIR ATTACKERS WERE.
THERE WAS NO SIGN...
...THAT THEY SUFFERED AN ALL-OUT ATTACK...
...BY A CLAN OR A GROUP OF CLANS, LAST NIGHT.
BUT DO YOU THINK...
...THAT THE NUE COULD BE DEFEATED SO EASILY?
WE'LL BE LUCKY IF THE CLAN THAT DEFEATED THE NUE...
...DOESN'T BECOME OUR ENEMY.
IS THAT WISHFUL THINKING ...?
GASP!

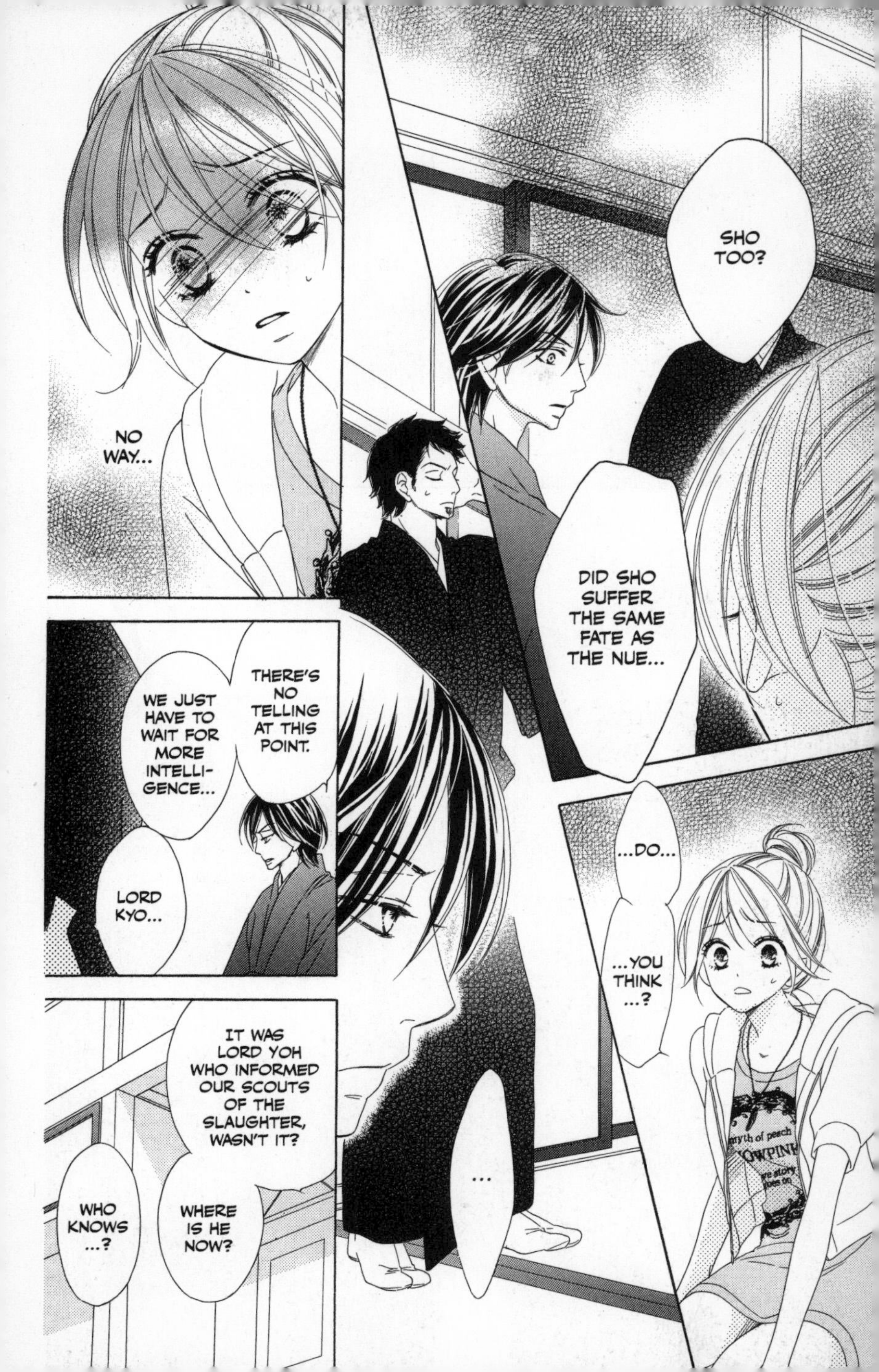
SHO TOO?
DID SHO SUFFER THE SAME FATE AS THE NUE...
NO WAY...
...DO...
...YOU THINK ...?
...
THERE'S NO TELLING AT THIS POINT.
WE JUST HAVE TO WAIT FOR MORE INTELLI-GENCE...
LORD KYO...
IT WAS LORD YOH WHO INFORMED OUR SCOUTS OF THE SLAUGHTER, WASN'T IT?
WHERE IS HE NOW?
WHO KNOWS ...?

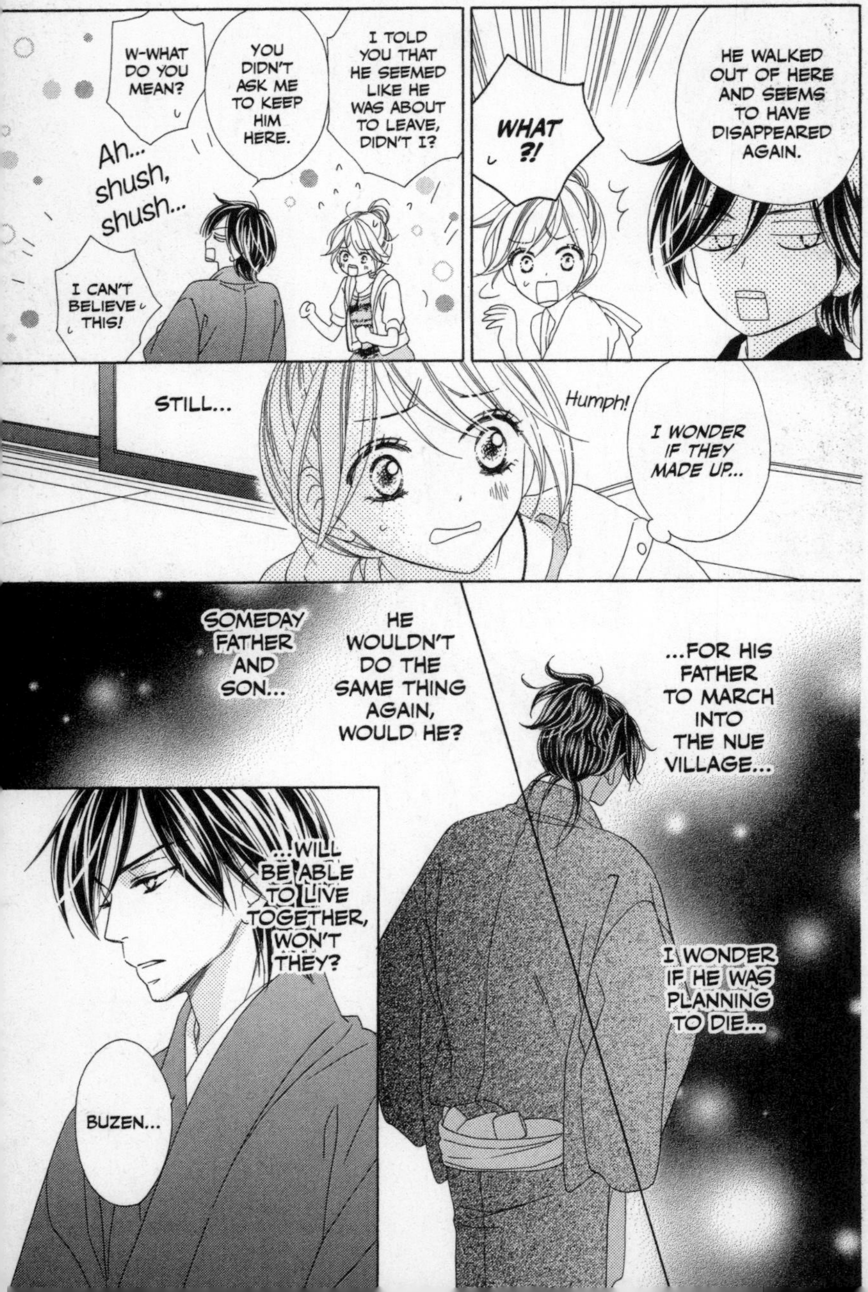
HE WALKED OUT OF HERE AND SEEMS TO HAVE DISAPPEARED AGAIN.
WHAT ?!
I TOLD YOU THAT HE SEEMED LIKE HE WAS ABOUT TO LEAVE, DIDN'T I?
YOU DIDN'T ASK ME TO KEEP HIM HERE.
W-WHAT DO YOU MEAN?
Ah... shush, shush...
I CAN'T BELIEVE THIS!
I WONDER IF THEY MADE UP...
Humph!
STILL...
...FOR HIS FATHER TO MARCH INTO THE NUE VILLAGE...
I WONDER IF HE WAS PLANNING TO DIE...
HE WOULDN'T DO THE SAME THING AGAIN, WOULD HE?
SOMEDAY FATHER AND SON...
...WILL BE ABLE TO LIVE TOGETHER, WON'T THEY?
BUZEN...

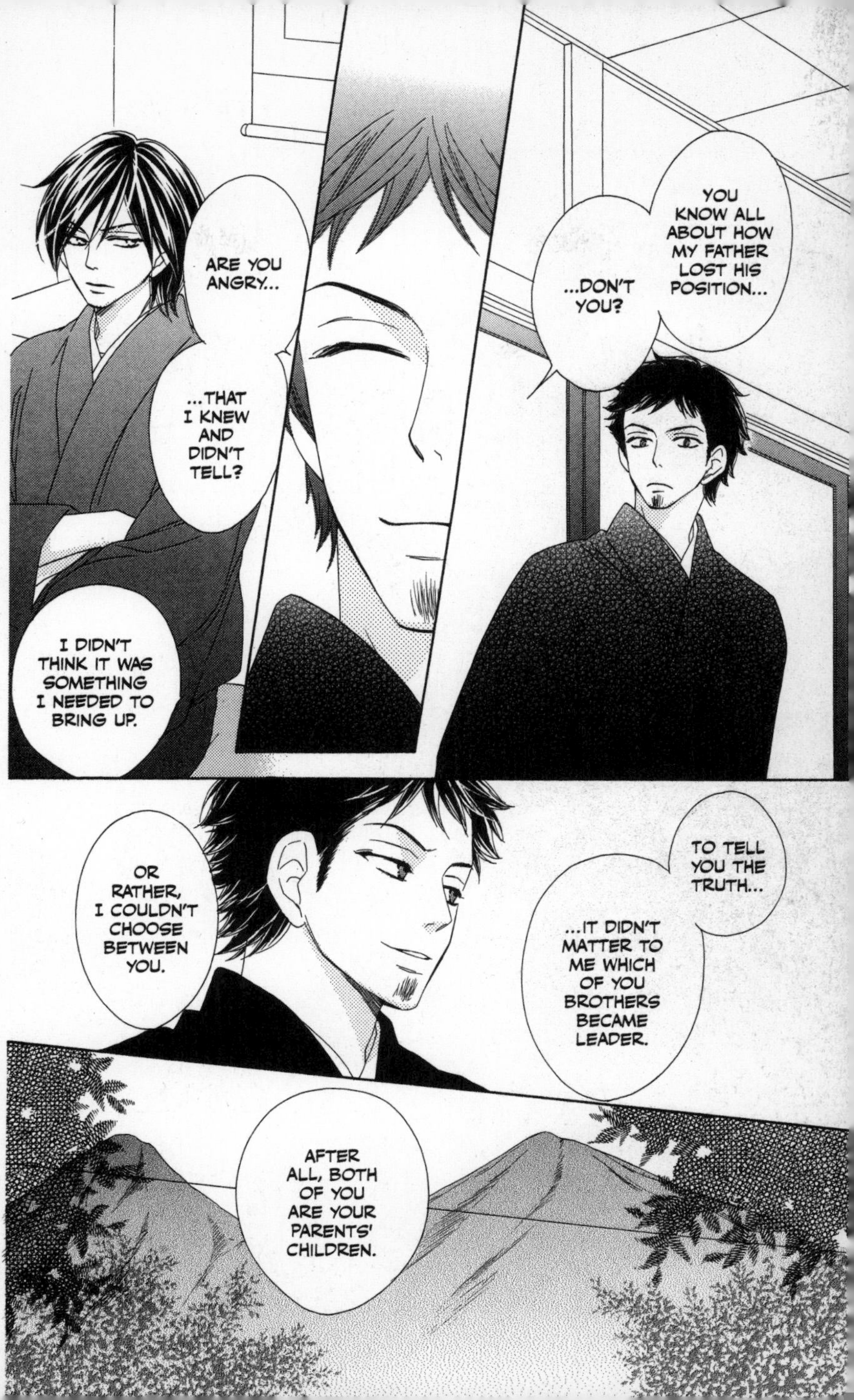
YOU KNOW ALL ABOUT HOW MY FATHER LOST HIS POSITION...
...DON'T YOU?
ARE YOU ANGRY...
...THAT I KNEW AND DIDN'T TELL?
I DIDN'T THINK IT WAS SOMETHING I NEEDED TO BRING UP.
TO TELL YOU THE TRUTH...
...IT DIDN'T MATTER TO ME WHICH OF YOU BROTHERS BECAME LEADER.
OR RATHER, I COULDN'T CHOOSE BETWEEN YOU.
AFTER ALL, BOTH OF YOU ARE YOUR PARENTS' CHILDREN.

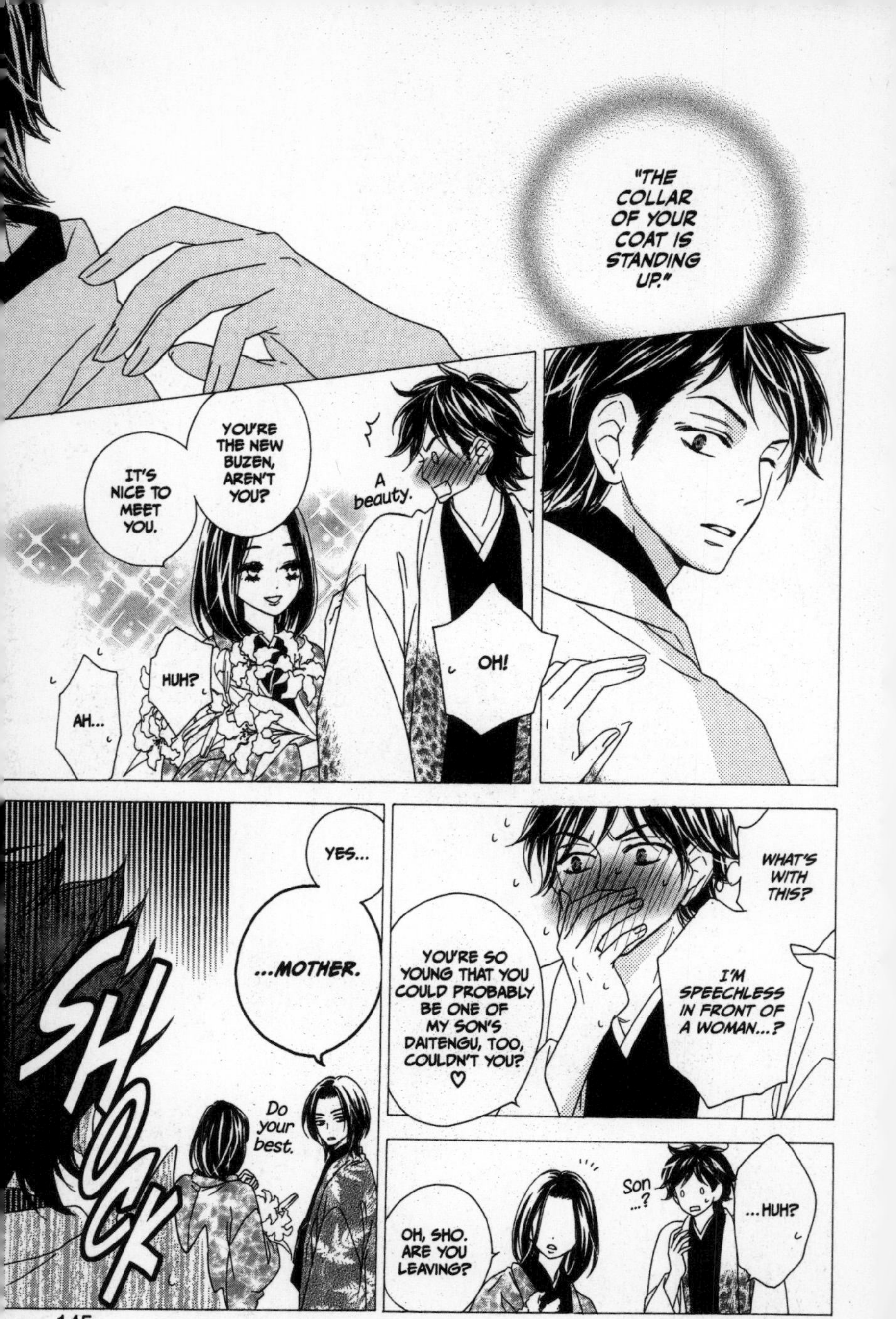
"THE COLLAR OF YOUR COAT IS STANDING UP."
A beauty.
OH!
YOU'RE THE NEW BUZEN, AREN'T YOU?
IT'S NICE TO MEET YOU.
HUH?
AH...
WHAT'S WITH THIS?
I'M SPEECHLESS IN FRONT OF A WOMAN...?
YOU'RE SO YOUNG THAT YOU COULD PROBABLY BE ONE OF MY SON'S DAITENGU, TOO, COULDN'T YOU? ♡
...HUH?
Son ...?
OH, SHO. ARE YOU LEAVING?
YES...
...MOTHER.
Do your best.
SHOCK

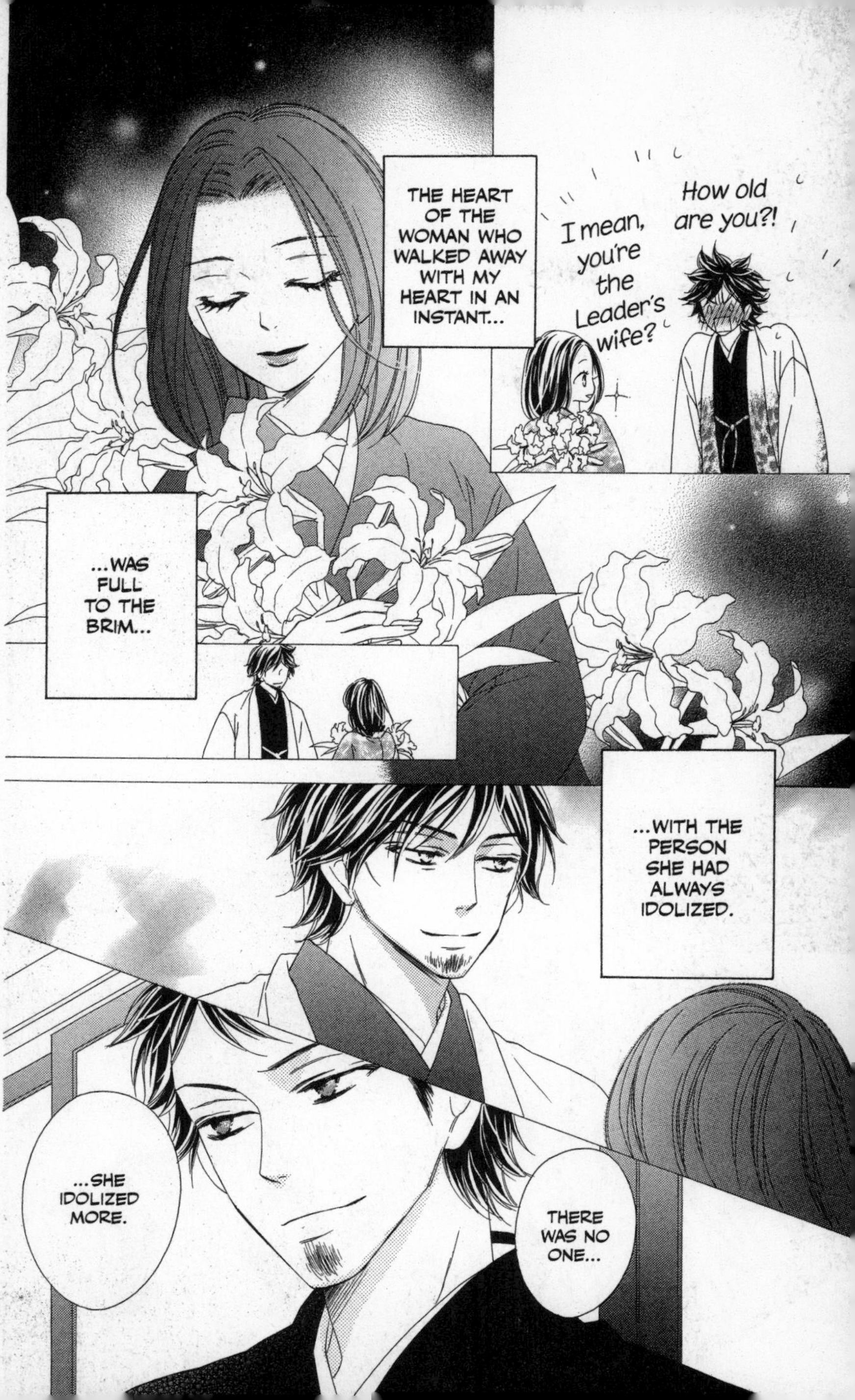
How old are you?!
I mean, you're the Leader's wife?
THE HEART OF THE WOMAN WHO WALKED AWAY WITH MY HEART IN AN INSTANT...
...WAS FULL TO THE BRIM...
...WITH THE PERSON SHE HAD ALWAYS IDOLIZED.
THERE WAS NO ONE...
...SHE IDOLIZED MORE.

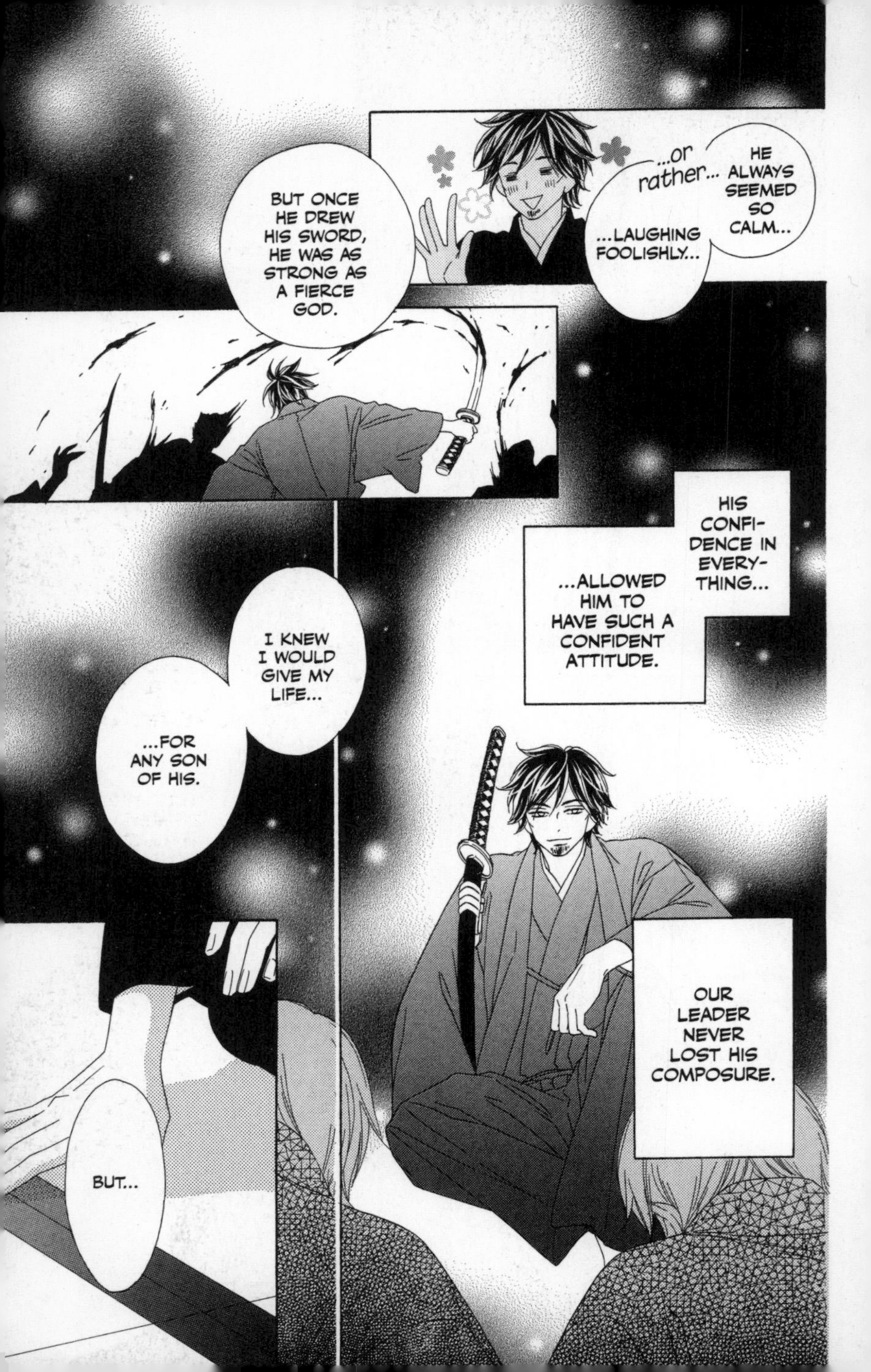
HE ALWAYS SEEMED SO CALM...
...or rather...
...LAUGHING FOOLISHLY...
BUT ONCE HE DREW HIS SWORD, HE WAS AS STRONG AS A FIERCE GOD.
HIS CONFIDENCE IN EVERYTHING...
...ALLOWED HIM TO HAVE SUCH A CONFIDENT ATTITUDE.
OUR LEADER NEVER LOST HIS COMPOSURE.
I KNEW I WOULD GIVE MY LIFE...
...FOR ANY SON OF HIS.
BUT...

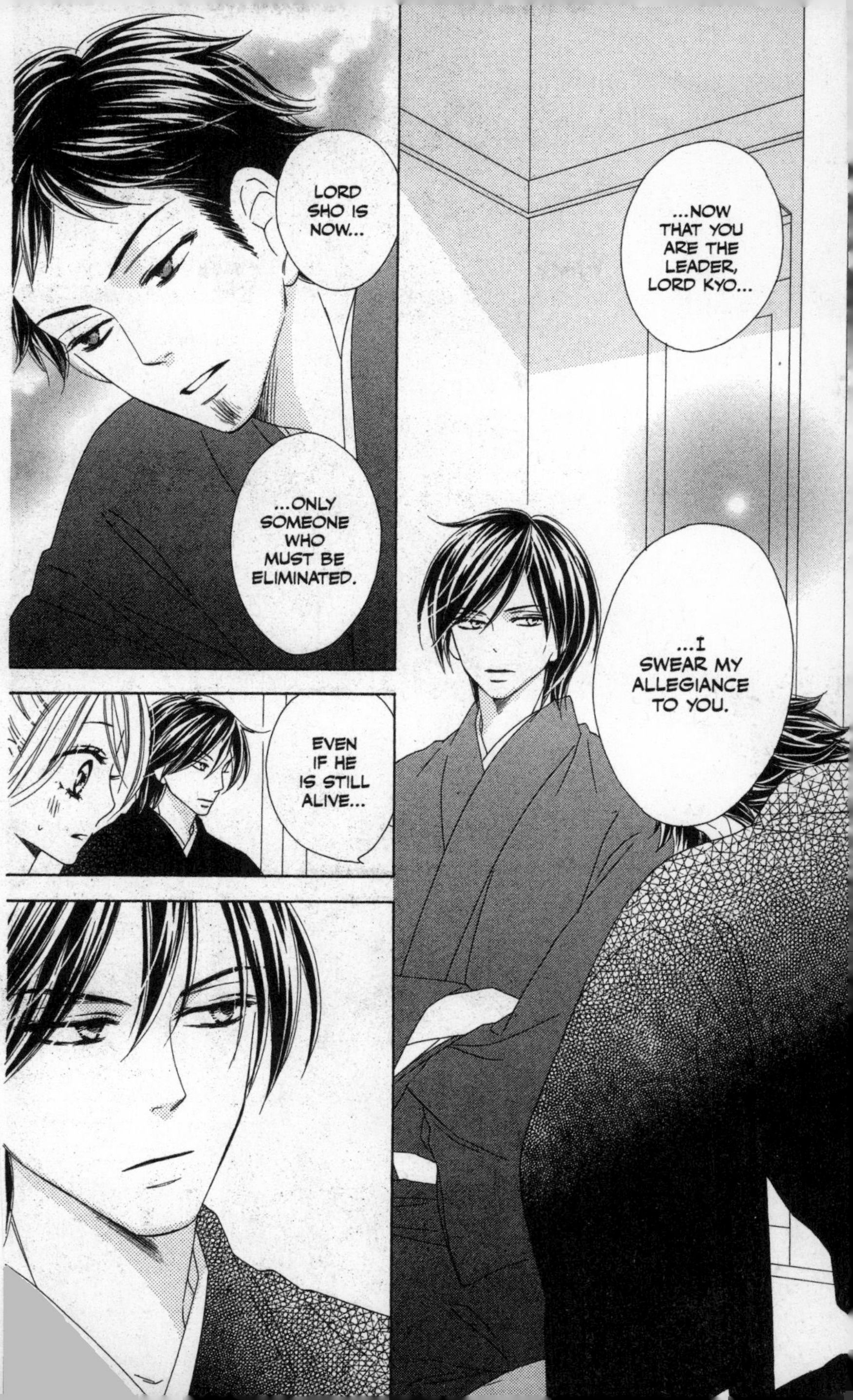
...NOW THAT YOU ARE THE LEADER, LORD KYO...
...I SWEAR MY ALLEGIANCE TO YOU.
LORD SHO IS NOW...
...ONLY SOMEONE WHO MUST BE ELIMINATED.
EVEN IF HE IS STILL ALIVE...

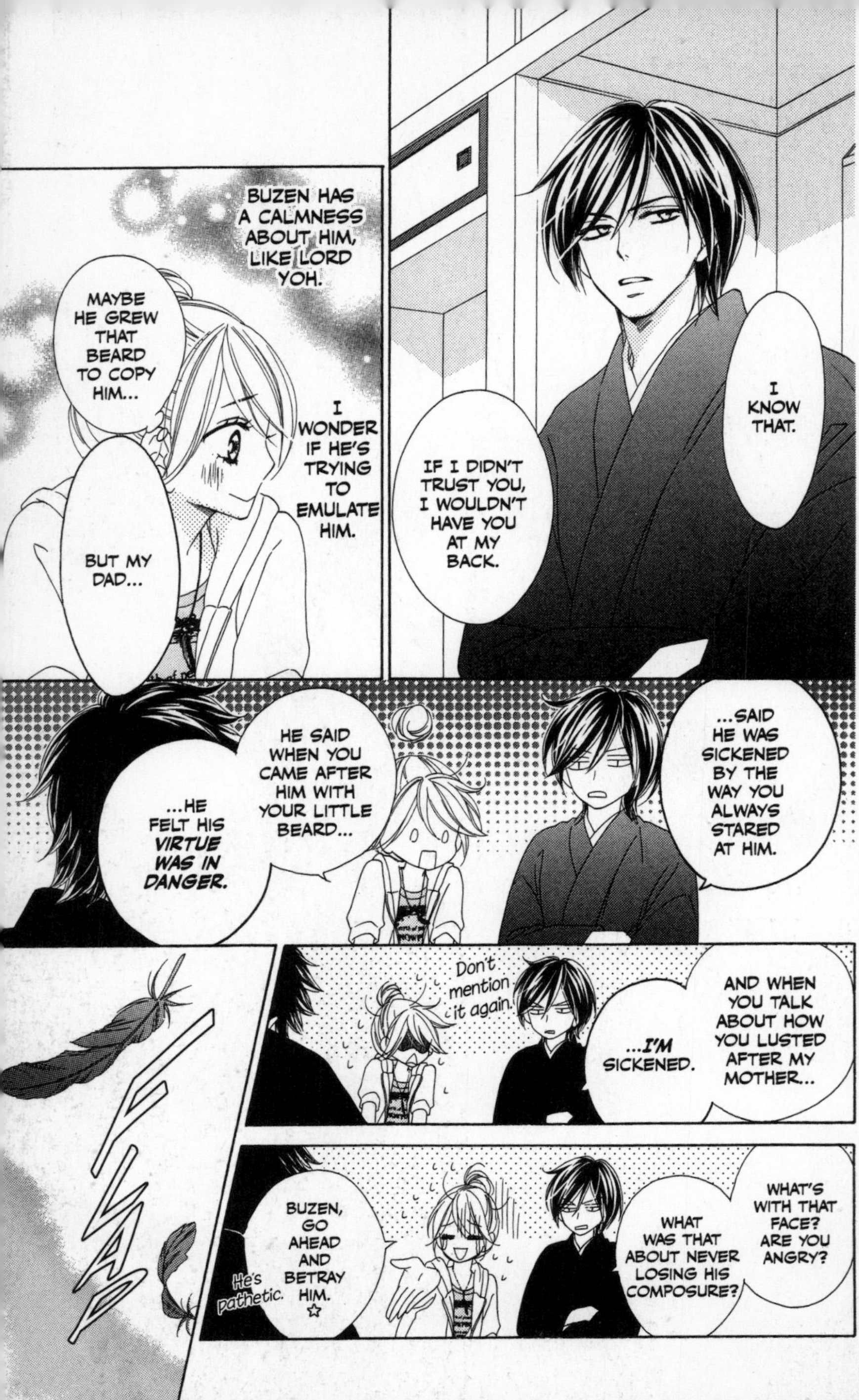
I KNOW THAT.
IF I DIDN'T TRUST YOU, I WOULDN'T HAVE YOU AT MY BACK.
BUZEN HAS A CALMNESS ABOUT HIM, LIKE LORD YOH.
MAYBE HE GREW THAT BEARD TO COPY HIM...
I WONDER IF HE'S TRYING TO EMULATE HIM.
BUT MY DAD...
...SAID HE WAS SICKENED BY THE WAY YOU ALWAYS STARED AT HIM.
HE SAID WHEN YOU CAME AFTER HIM WITH YOUR LITTLE BEARD...
...HE FELT HIS *VIRTUE WAS IN DANGER.*
AND WHEN YOU TALK ABOUT HOW YOU LUSTED AFTER MY MOTHER...
...*I'M* SICKENED.
Don't mention it again.
WHAT'S WITH THAT FACE? ARE YOU ANGRY?
WHAT WAS THAT ABOUT NEVER LOSING HIS COMPOSURE?
BUZEN, GO AHEAD AND BETRAY HIM. ☆
He's pathetic.

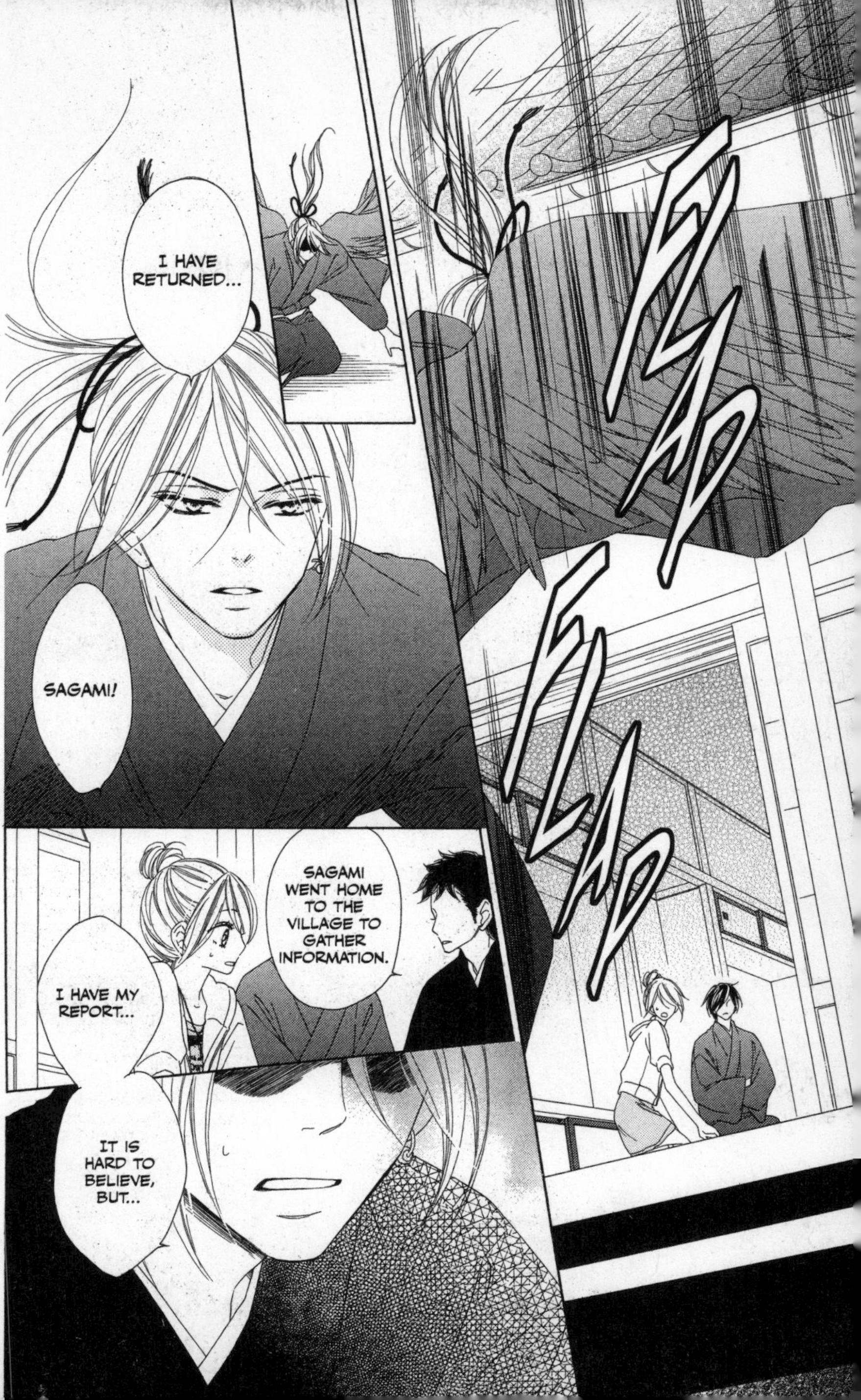
FLAP FLAP
I HAVE RETURNED...
SAGAMI!
SAGAMI WENT HOME TO THE VILLAGE TO GATHER INFORMATION.
I HAVE MY REPORT...
IT IS HARD TO BELIEVE, BUT...

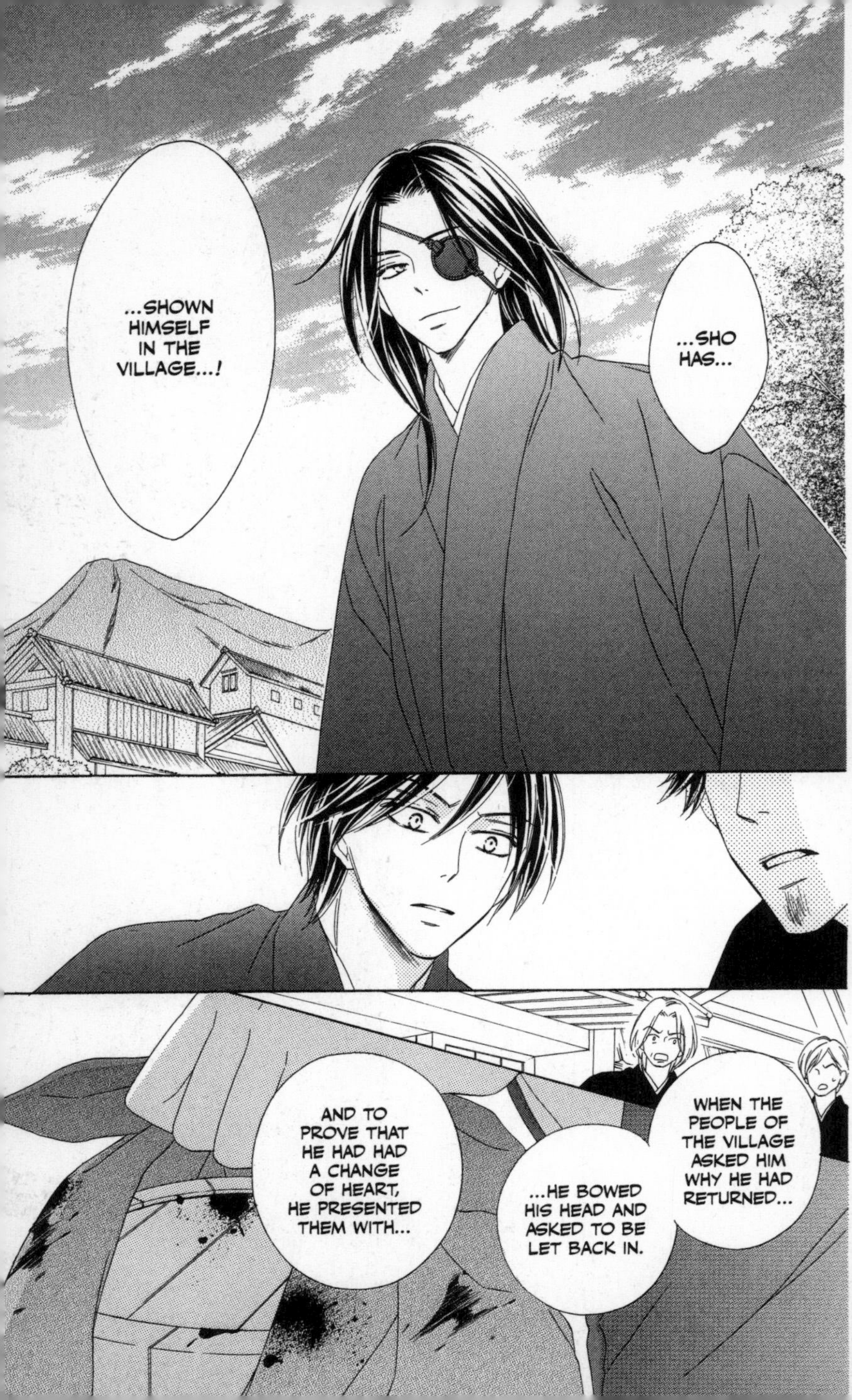
...SHO HAS...
...SHOWN HIMSELF IN THE VILLAGE...!
WHEN THE PEOPLE OF THE VILLAGE ASKED HIM WHY HE HAD RETURNED...
...HE BOWED HIS HEAD AND ASKED TO BE LET BACK IN.
AND TO PROVE THAT HE HAD HAD A CHANGE OF HEART, HE PRESENTED THEM WITH...

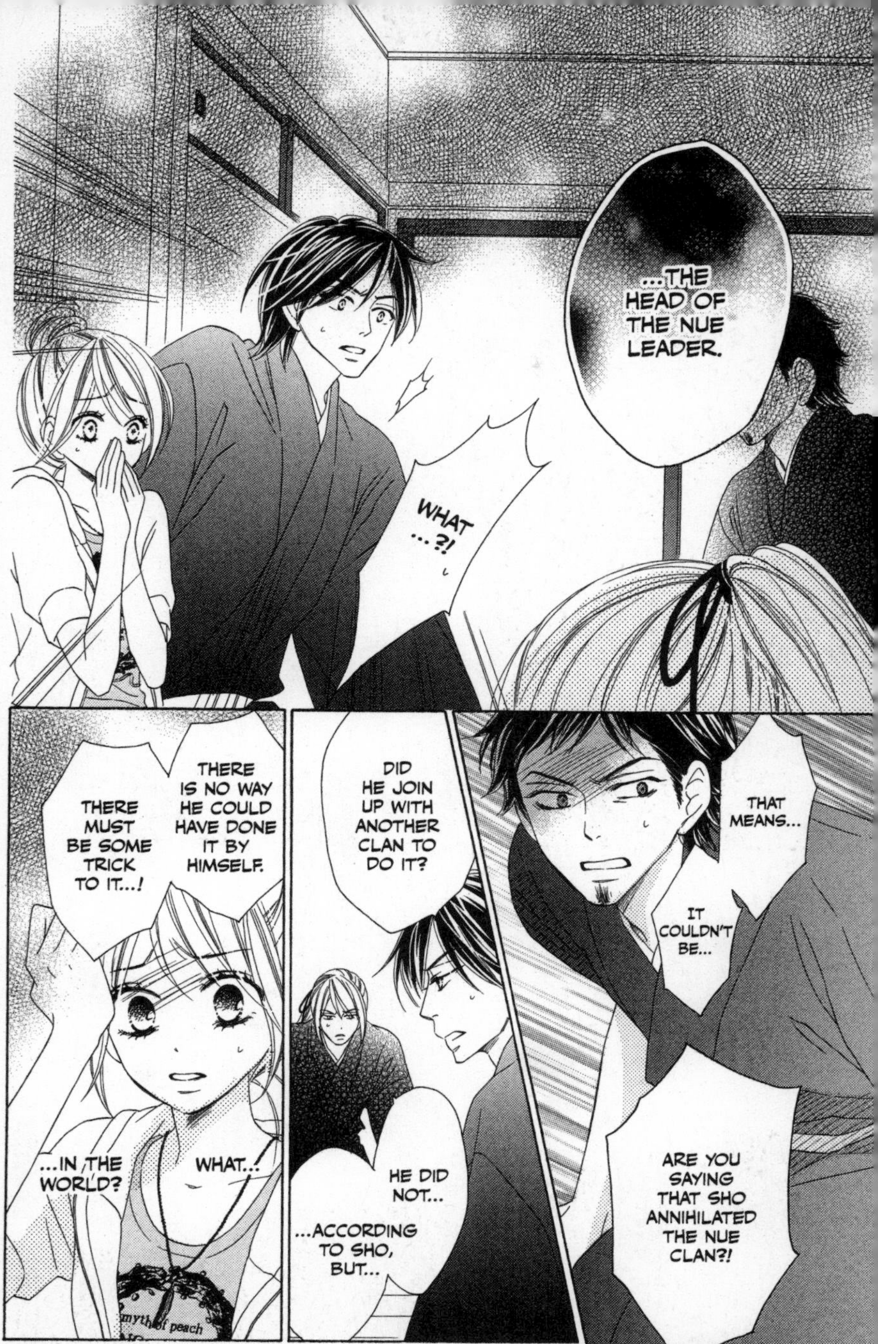
...THE HEAD OF THE NUE LEADER.
WHAT...?!
THAT MEANS...
IT COULDN'T BE...
ARE YOU SAYING THAT SHO ANNIHILATED THE NUE CLAN?!
DID HE JOIN UP WITH ANOTHER CLAN TO DO IT?
HE DID NOT...
...ACCORDING TO SHO, BUT...
THERE IS NO WAY HE COULD HAVE DONE IT BY HIMSELF.
THERE MUST BE SOME TRICK TO IT...!
WHAT...
...IN THE WORLD?
myth of peach

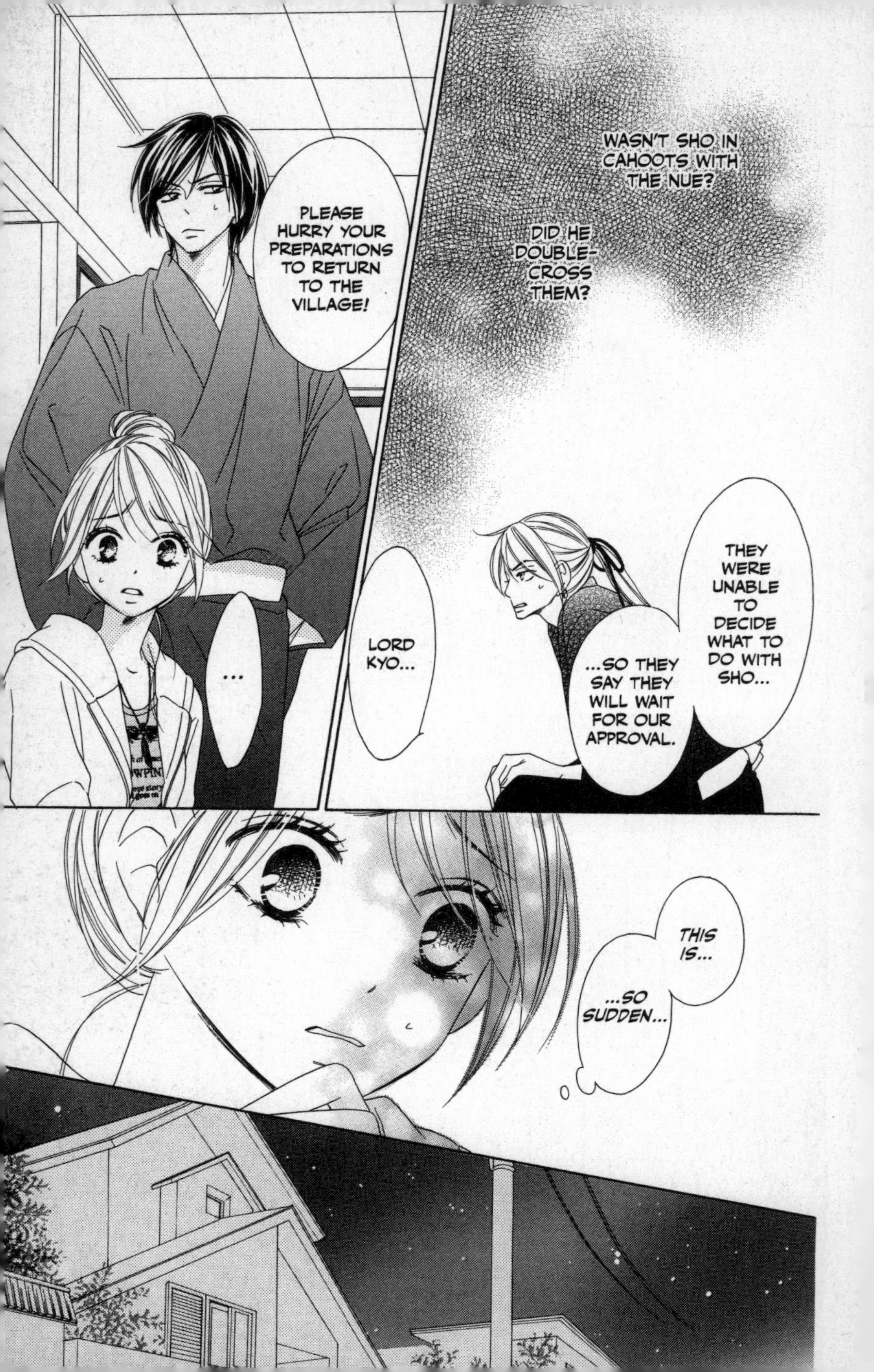
WASN'T SHO IN CAHOOTS WITH THE NUE?
DID HE DOUBLE-CROSS THEM?
THEY WERE UNABLE TO DECIDE WHAT TO DO WITH SHO...
...SO THEY SAY THEY WILL WAIT FOR OUR APPROVAL.
LORD KYO...
PLEASE HURRY YOUR PREPARATIONS TO RETURN TO THE VILLAGE!
...
THIS IS...
...SO SUDDEN...

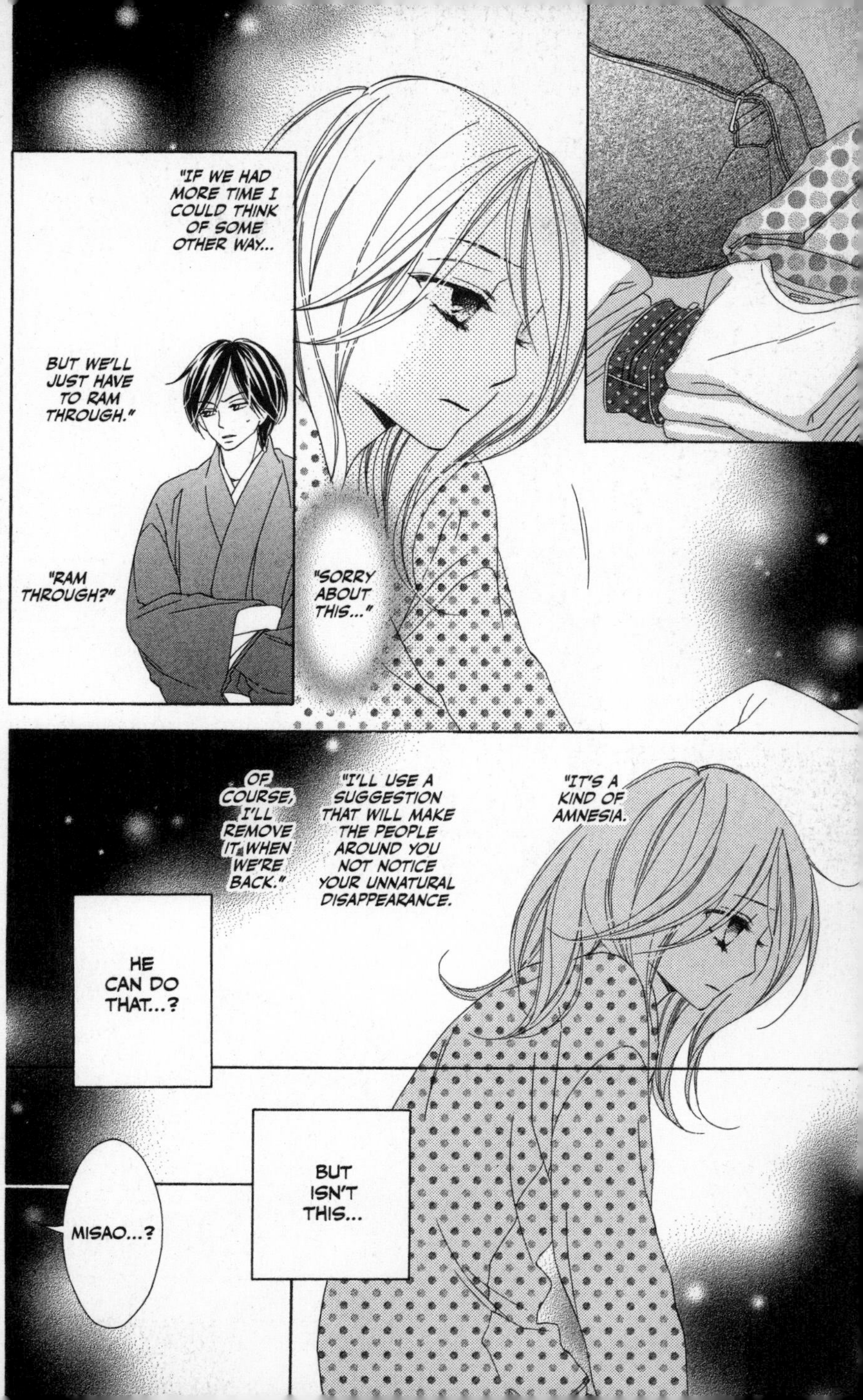
"IF WE HAD MORE TIME I COULD THINK OF SOME OTHER WAY...
BUT WE'LL JUST HAVE TO RAM THROUGH."
"RAM THROUGH?"
"SORRY ABOUT THIS..."
"IT'S A KIND OF AMNESIA.
"I'LL USE A SUGGESTION THAT WILL MAKE THE PEOPLE AROUND YOU NOT NOTICE YOUR UNNATURAL DISAPPEARANCE.
OF COURSE, I'LL REMOVE IT WHEN WE'RE BACK."
HE CAN DO THAT...?
BUT ISN'T THIS...
MISAO...?

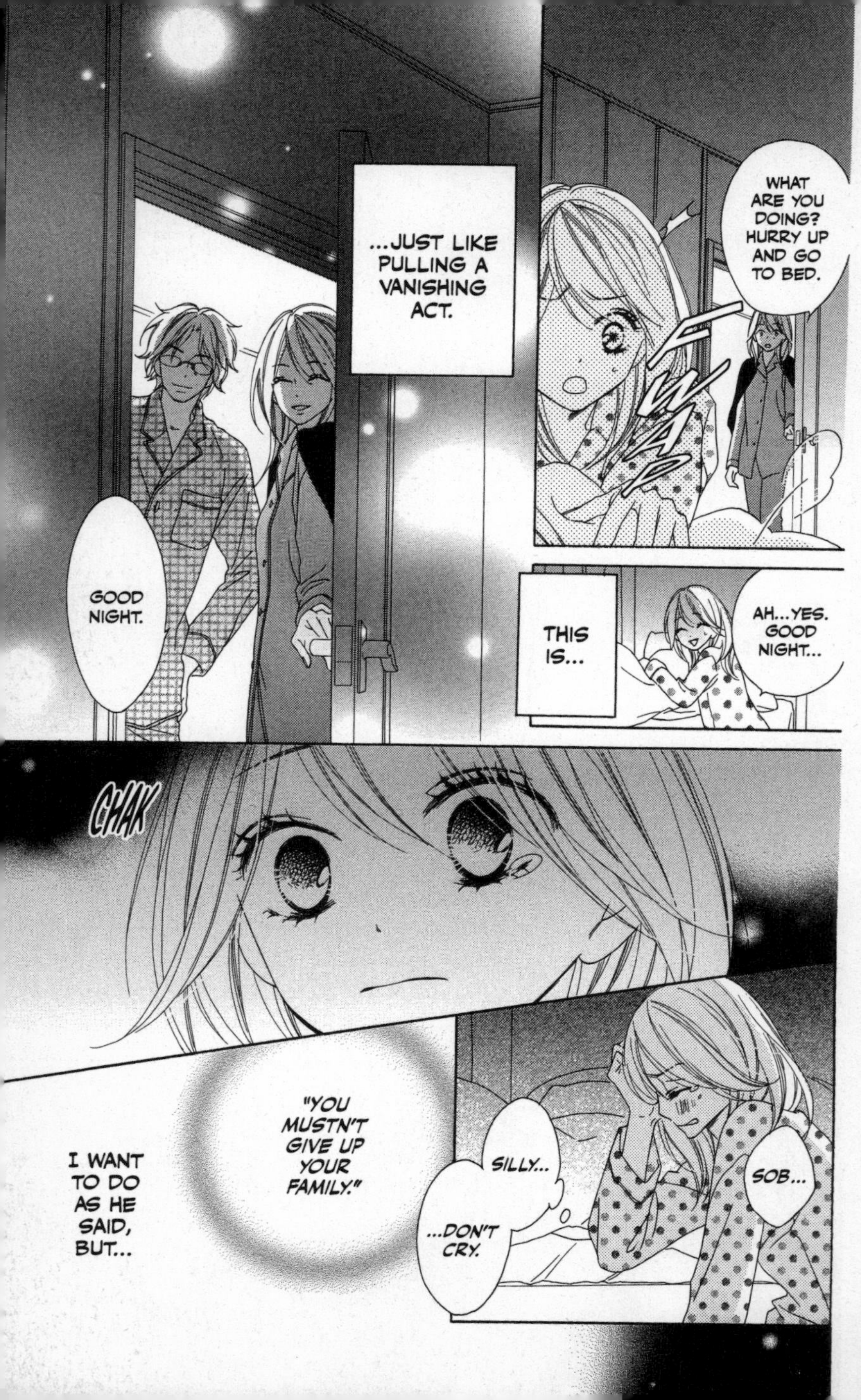
WHAT ARE YOU DOING? HURRY UP AND GO TO BED.
FWAP
AH...YES. GOOD NIGHT...
THIS IS...
...JUST LIKE PULLING A VANISHING ACT.
GOOD NIGHT.
CHAK
SOB...
SILLY...
...DON'T CRY.
"YOU MUSTN'T GIVE UP YOUR FAMILY."
I WANT TO DO AS HE SAID, BUT...

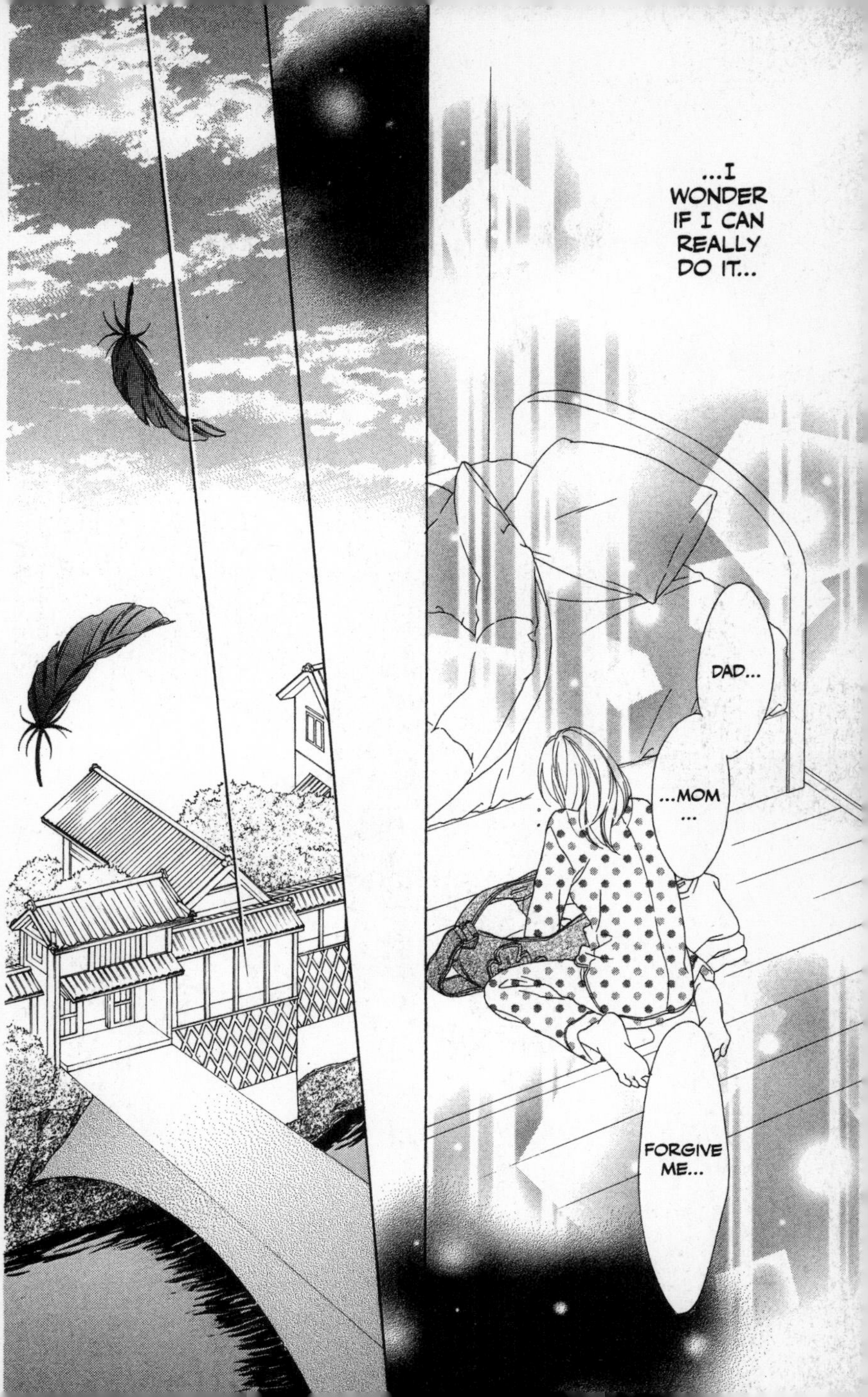
...I WONDER IF I CAN REALLY DO IT...
DAD...
...MOM...
FORGIVE ME...

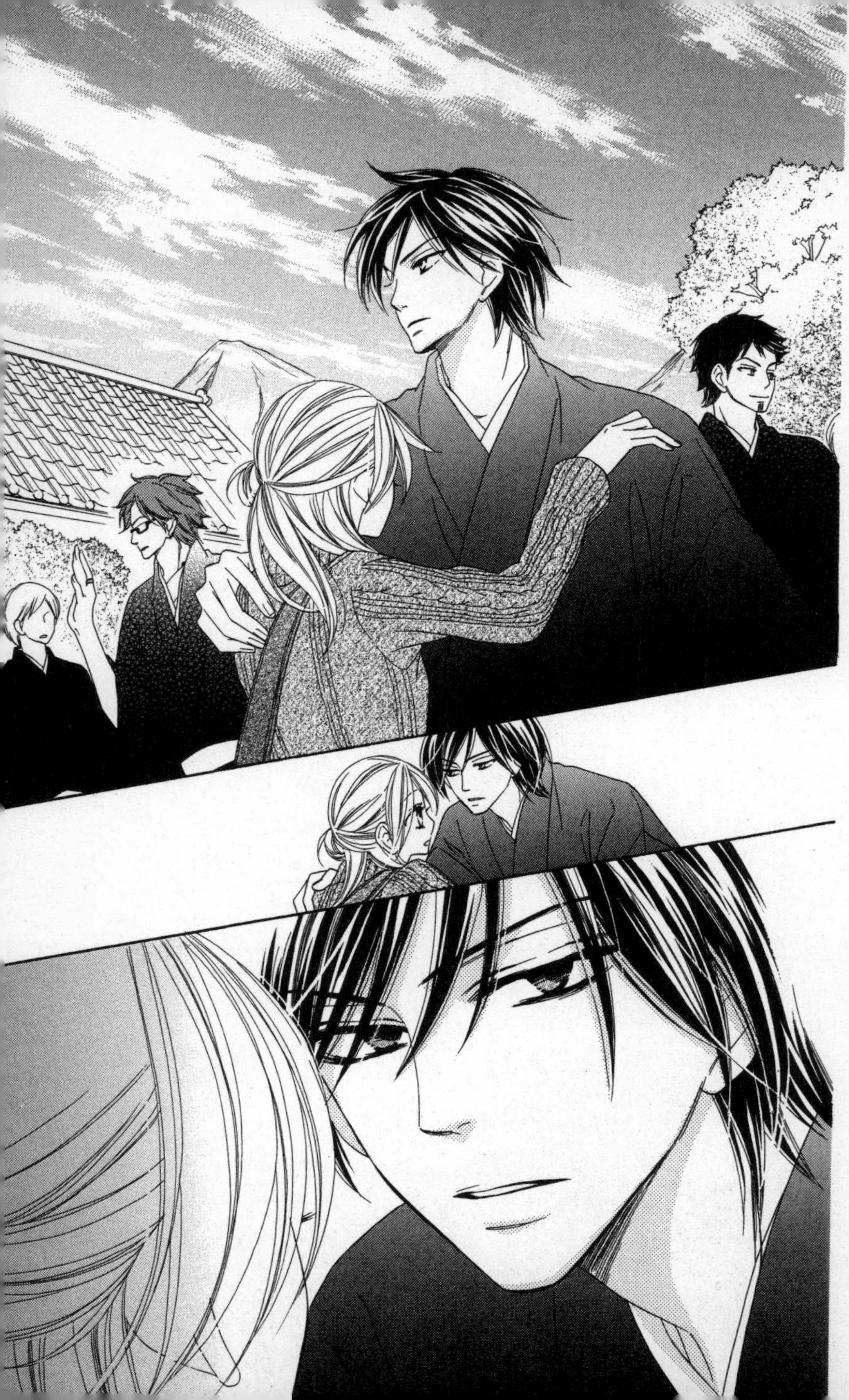

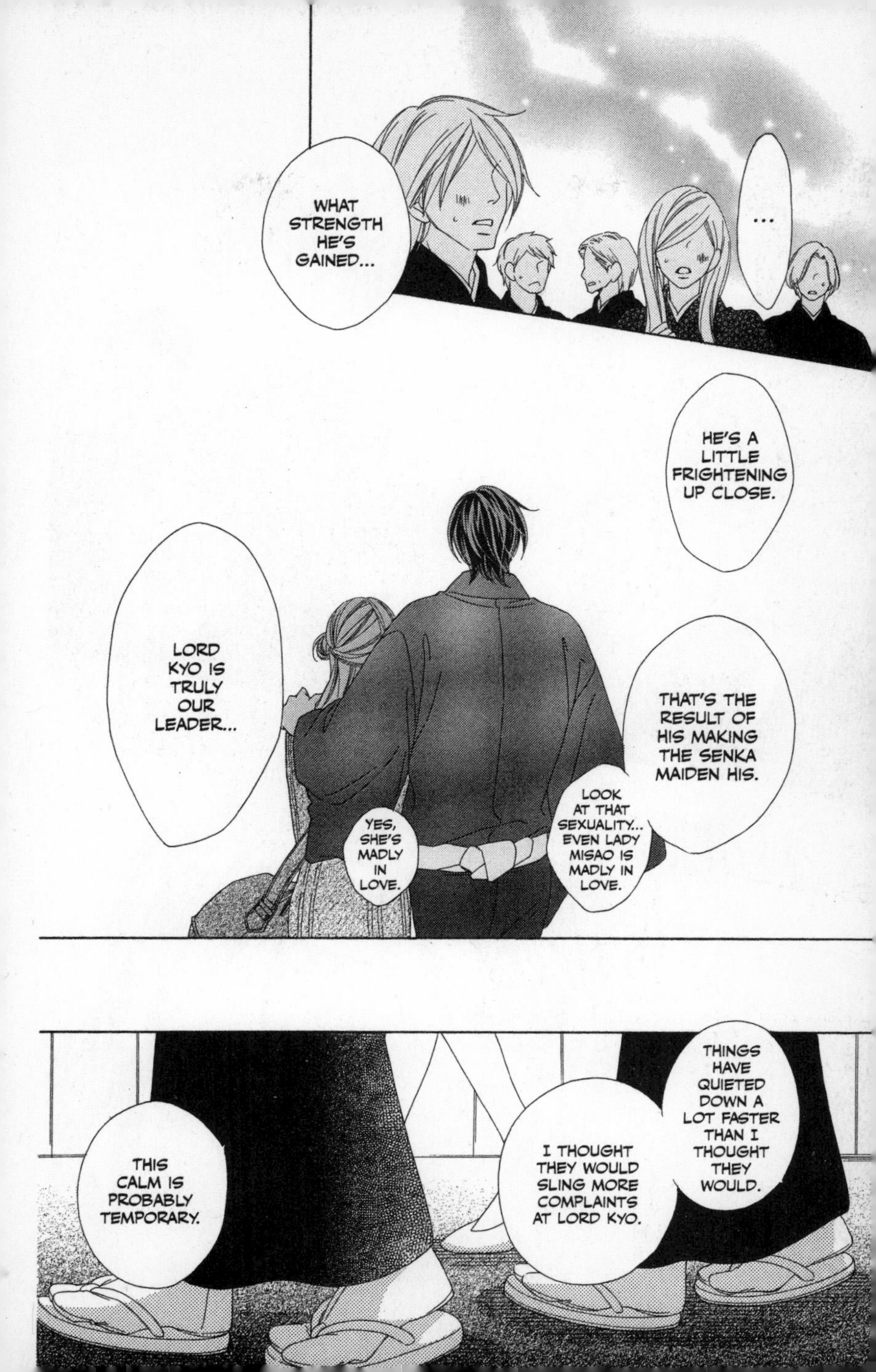
...
WHAT STRENGTH HE'S GAINED...
HE'S A LITTLE FRIGHTENING UP CLOSE.
LORD KYO IS TRULY OUR LEADER...
THAT'S THE RESULT OF HIS MAKING THE SENKA MAIDEN HIS.
LOOK AT THAT SEXUALITY... EVEN LADY MISAO IS MADLY IN LOVE.
YES, SHE'S MADLY IN LOVE.
THINGS HAVE QUIETED DOWN A LOT FASTER THAN I THOUGHT THEY WOULD.
I THOUGHT THEY WOULD SLING MORE COMPLAINTS AT LORD KYO.
THIS CALM IS PROBABLY TEMPORARY.

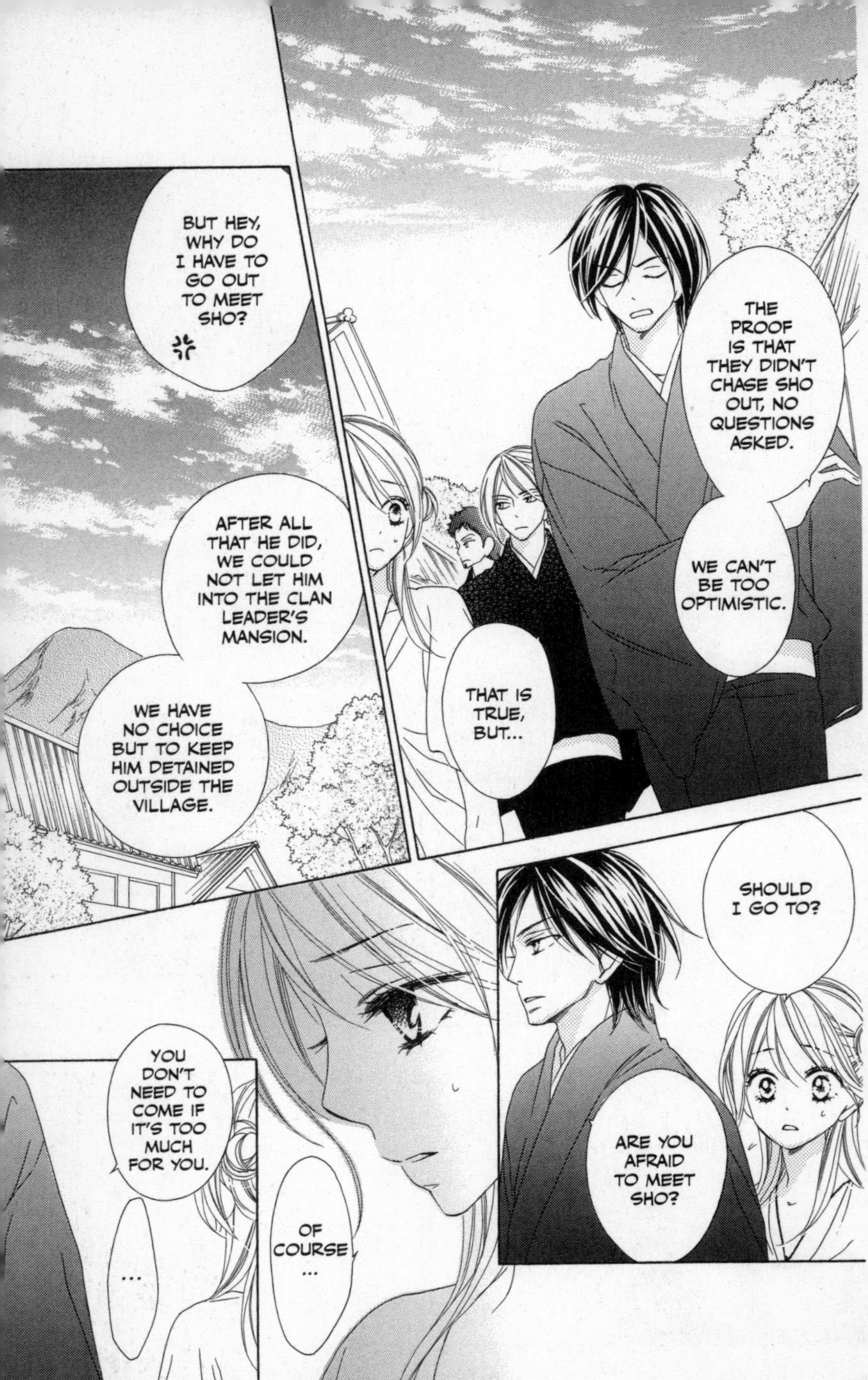
THE PROOF IS THAT THEY DIDN'T CHASE SHO OUT, NO QUESTIONS ASKED.
WE CAN'T BE TOO OPTIMISTIC.
THAT IS TRUE, BUT...
BUT HEY, WHY DO I HAVE TO GO OUT TO MEET SHO?
AFTER ALL THAT HE DID, WE COULD NOT LET HIM INTO THE CLAN LEADER'S MANSION.
WE HAVE NO CHOICE BUT TO KEEP HIM DETAINED OUTSIDE THE VILLAGE.
SHOULD I GO TO?
ARE YOU AFRAID TO MEET SHO?
OF COURSE ...
YOU DON'T NEED TO COME IF IT'S TOO MUCH FOR YOU.
...

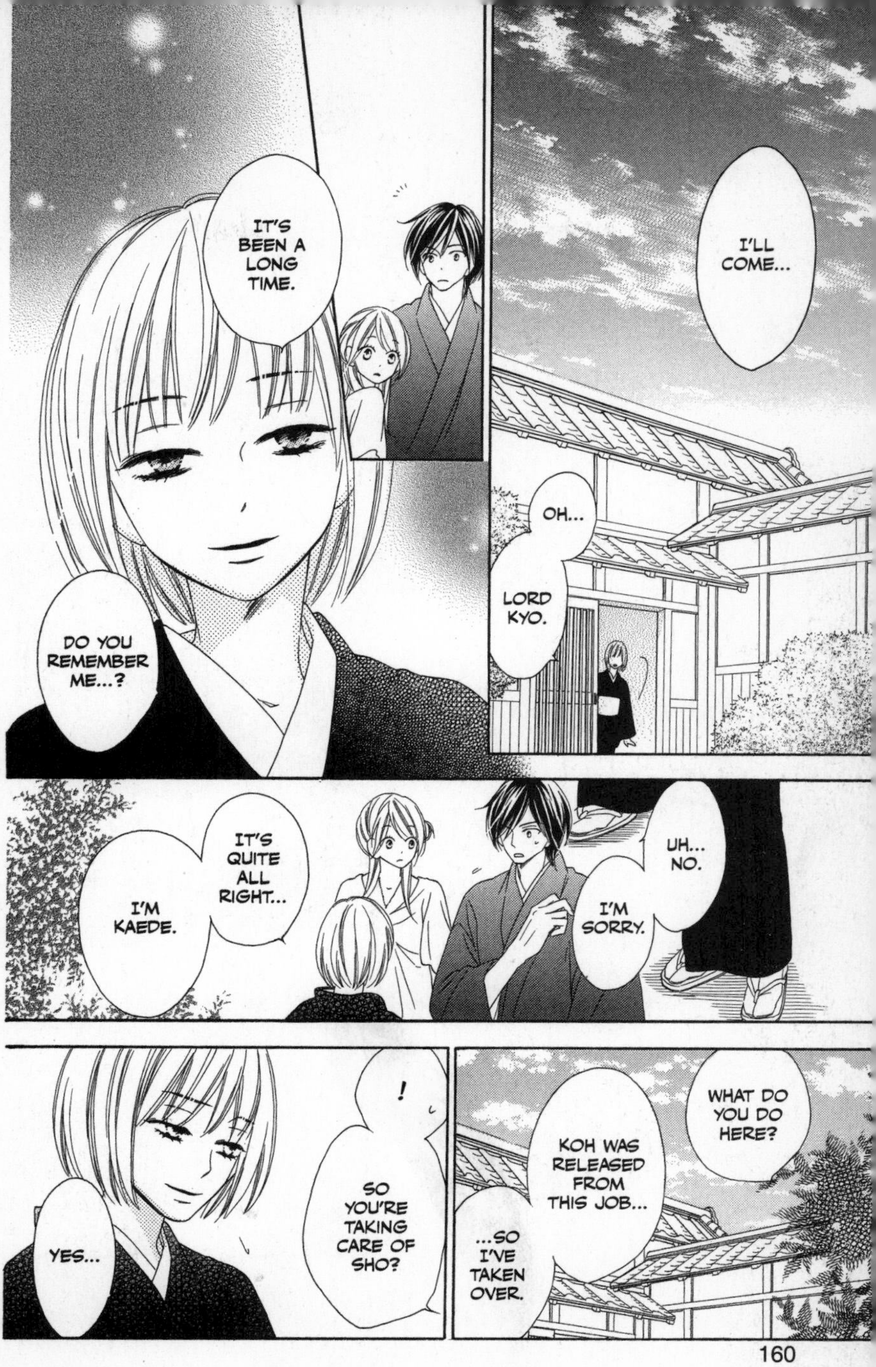
I'LL COME...
OH...
LORD KYO.
IT'S BEEN A LONG TIME.
DO YOU REMEMBER ME...?
UH... NO.
I'M SORRY.
IT'S QUITE ALL RIGHT...
I'M KAEDE.
WHAT DO YOU DO HERE?
KOH WAS RELEASED FROM THIS JOB...
...SO I'VE TAKEN OVER.
!
SO YOU'RE TAKING CARE OF SHO?
YES...

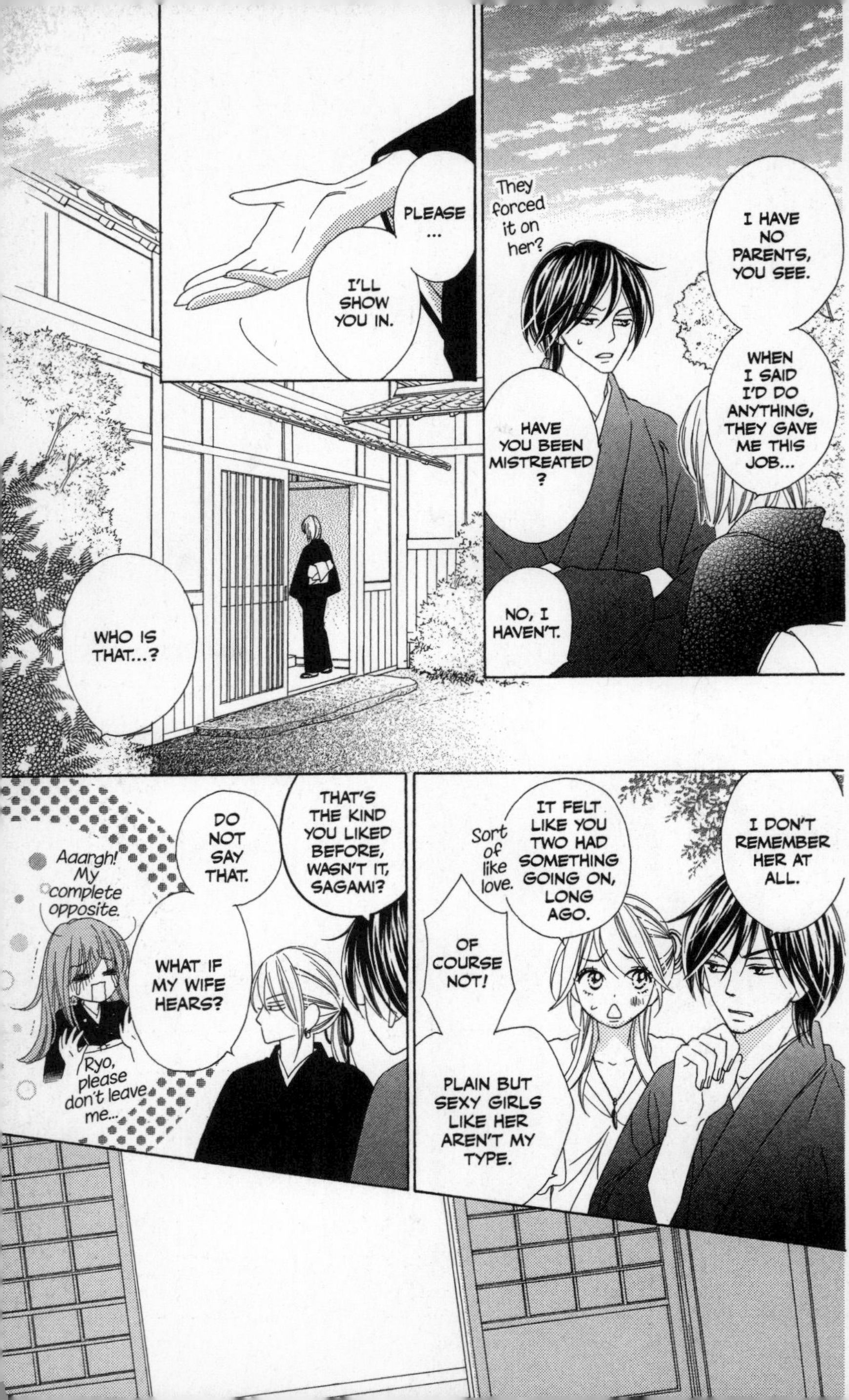
I HAVE NO PARENTS, YOU SEE.
WHEN I SAID I'D DO ANYTHING, THEY GAVE ME THIS JOB...
They forced it on her?
HAVE YOU BEEN MISTREATED?
NO, I HAVEN'T.
PLEASE...
I'LL SHOW YOU IN.
WHO IS THAT...?
I DON'T REMEMBER HER AT ALL.
IT FELT LIKE YOU TWO HAD SOMETHING GOING ON, LONG AGO.
Sort of like love.
OF COURSE NOT!
PLAIN BUT SEXY GIRLS LIKE HER AREN'T MY TYPE.
THAT'S THE KIND YOU LIKED BEFORE, WASN'T IT, SAGAMI?
DO NOT SAY THAT.
WHAT IF MY WIFE HEARS?
Aaargh! My complete opposite.
Ryo, please don't leave me...

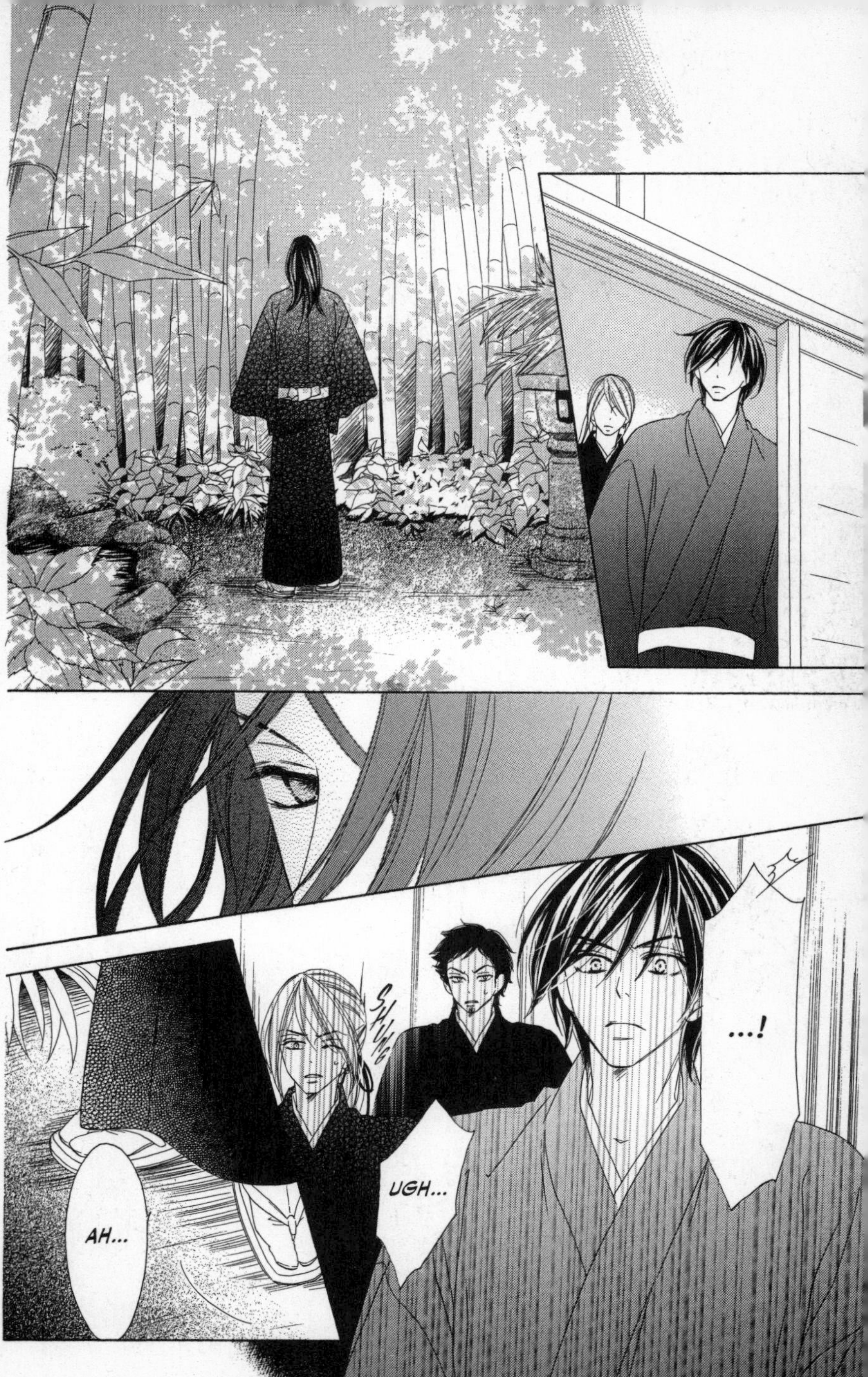
...!
SHUNG
UGH...
AH...

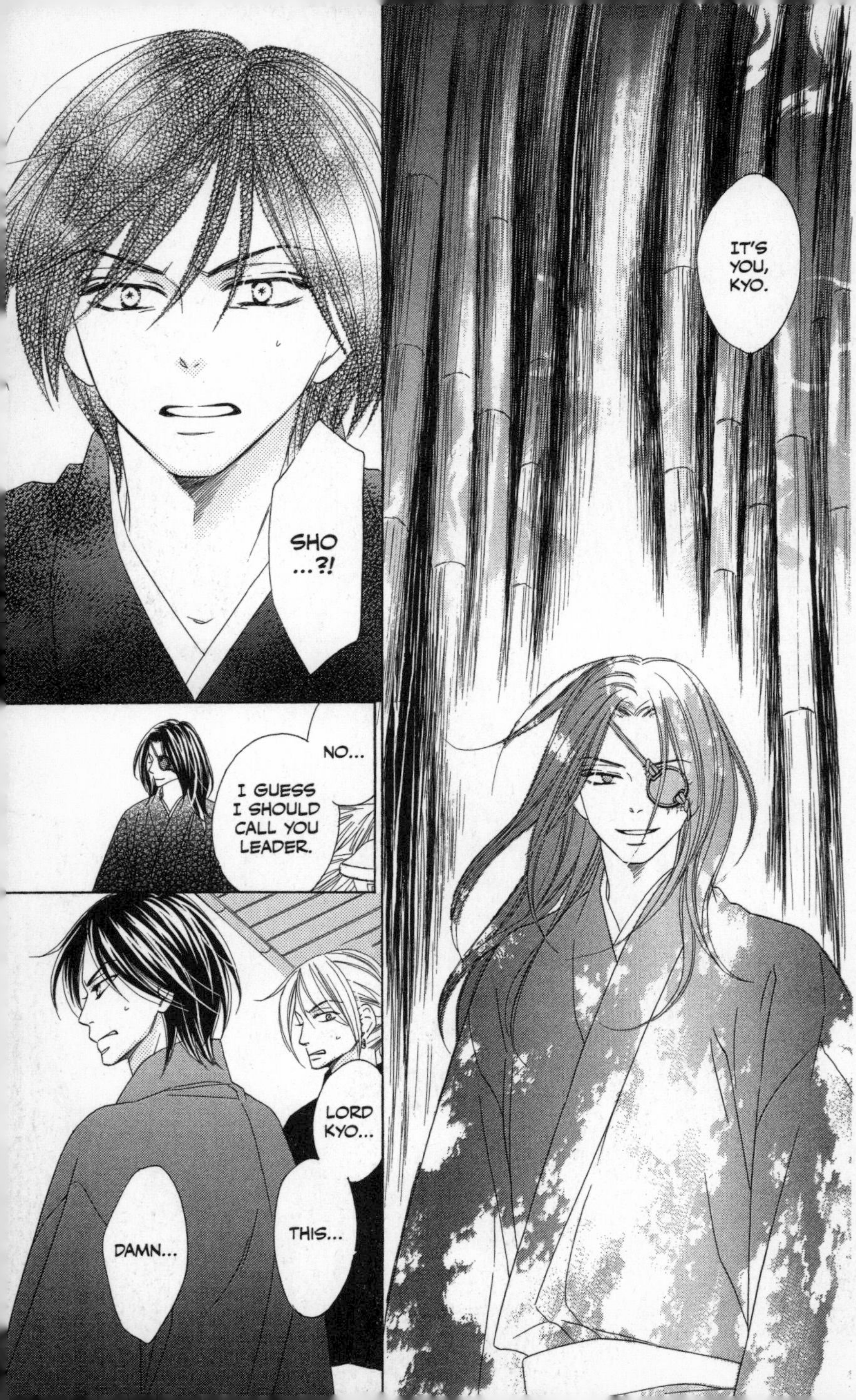
IT'S YOU, KYO.
SHO ...?!
NO...
I GUESS I SHOULD CALL YOU LEADER.
LORD KYO...
THIS...
DAMN...

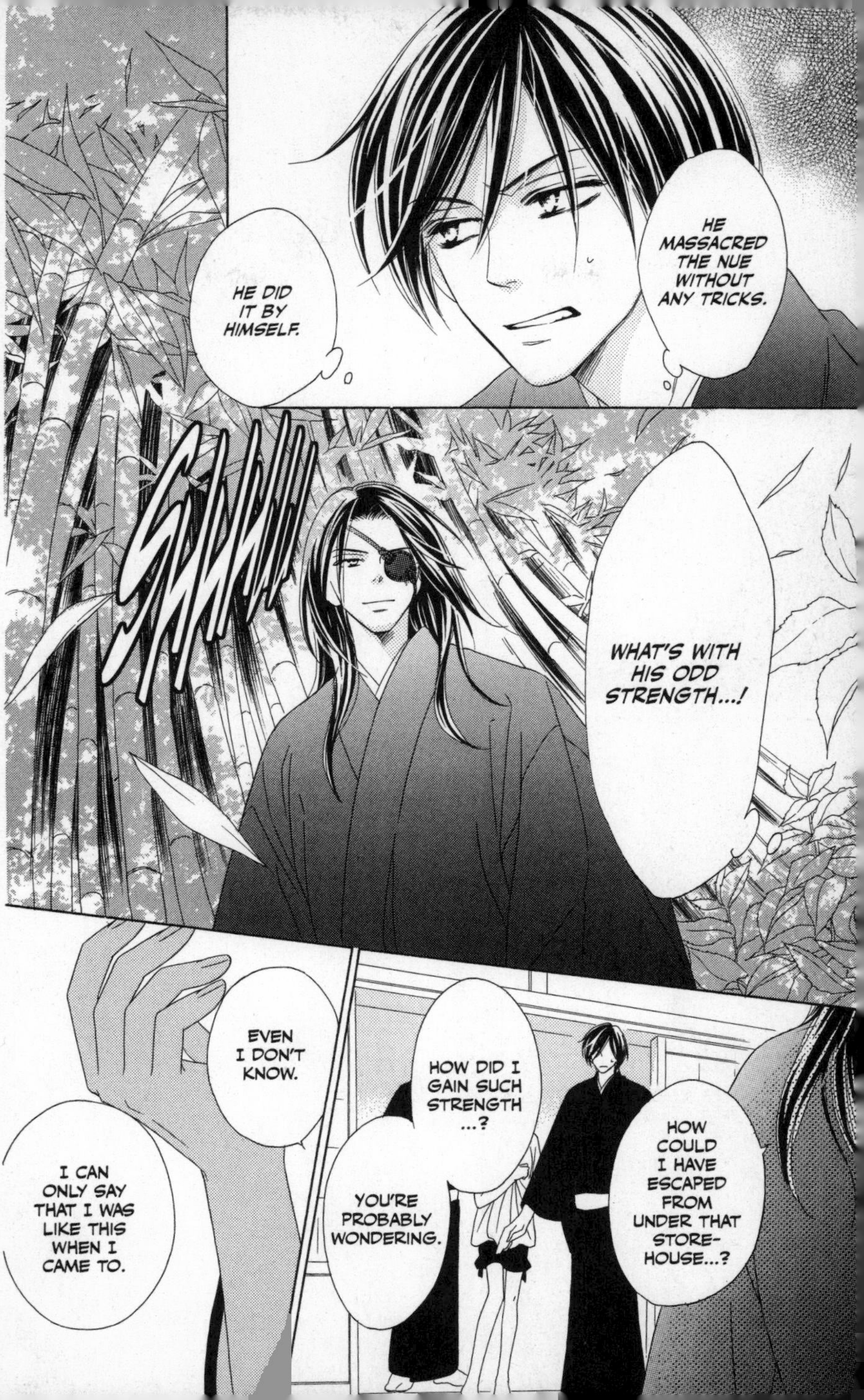
HE MASSACRED THE NUE WITHOUT ANY TRICKS.
HE DID IT BY HIMSELF.
WHAT'S WITH HIS ODD STRENGTH...!
HOW COULD I HAVE ESCAPED FROM UNDER THAT STORE-HOUSE...?
HOW DID I GAIN SUCH STRENGTH ...?
YOU'RE PROBABLY WONDERING.
EVEN I DON'T KNOW.
I CAN ONLY SAY THAT I WAS LIKE THIS WHEN I CAME TO.

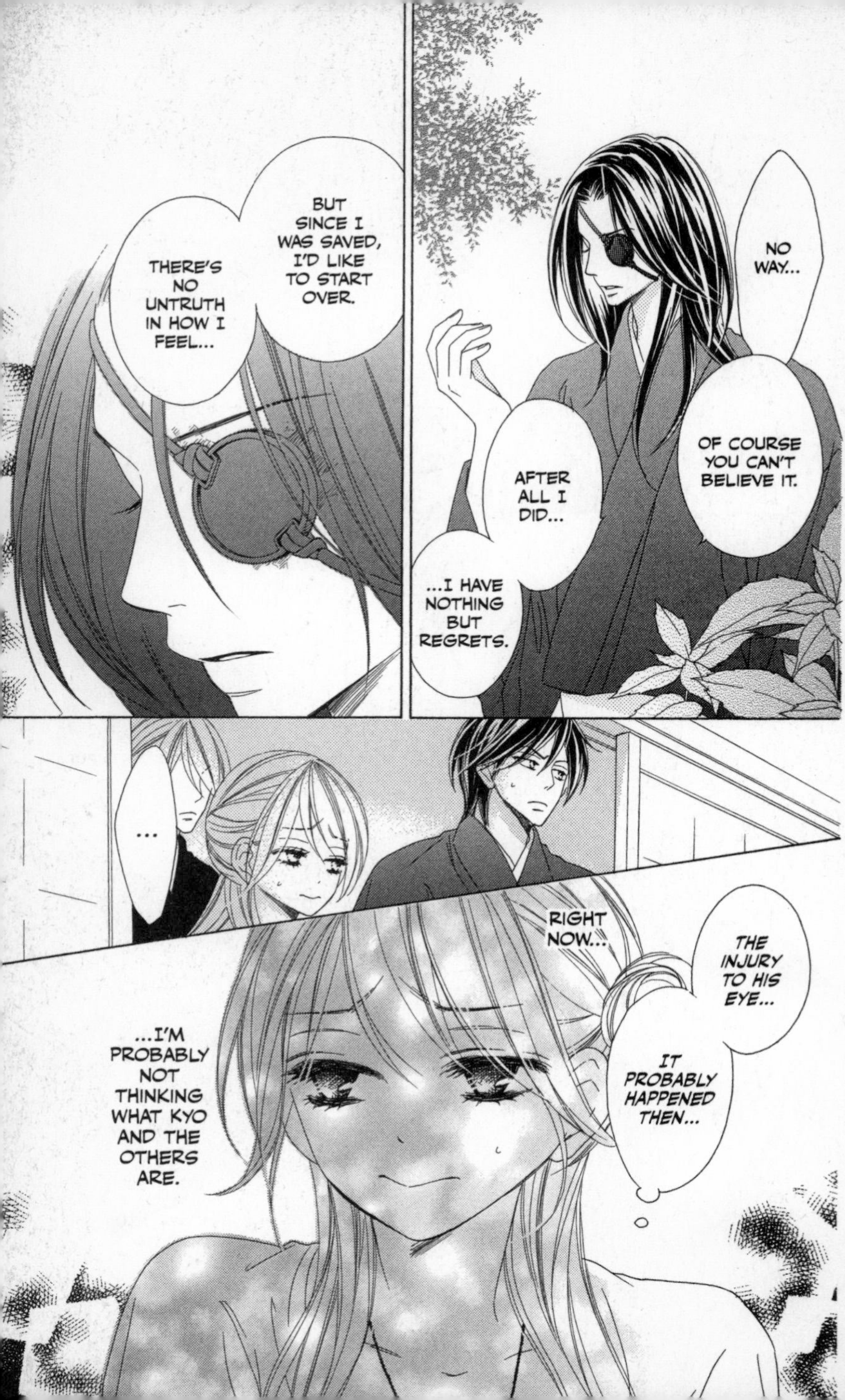
NO WAY...
OF COURSE YOU CAN'T BELIEVE IT.
AFTER ALL I DID...
...I HAVE NOTHING BUT REGRETS.
BUT SINCE I WAS SAVED, I'D LIKE TO START OVER.
THERE'S NO UNTRUTH IN HOW I FEEL...
...
THE INJURY TO HIS EYE...
IT PROBABLY HAPPENED THEN...
RIGHT NOW...
...I'M PROBABLY NOT THINKING WHAT KYO AND THE OTHERS ARE.

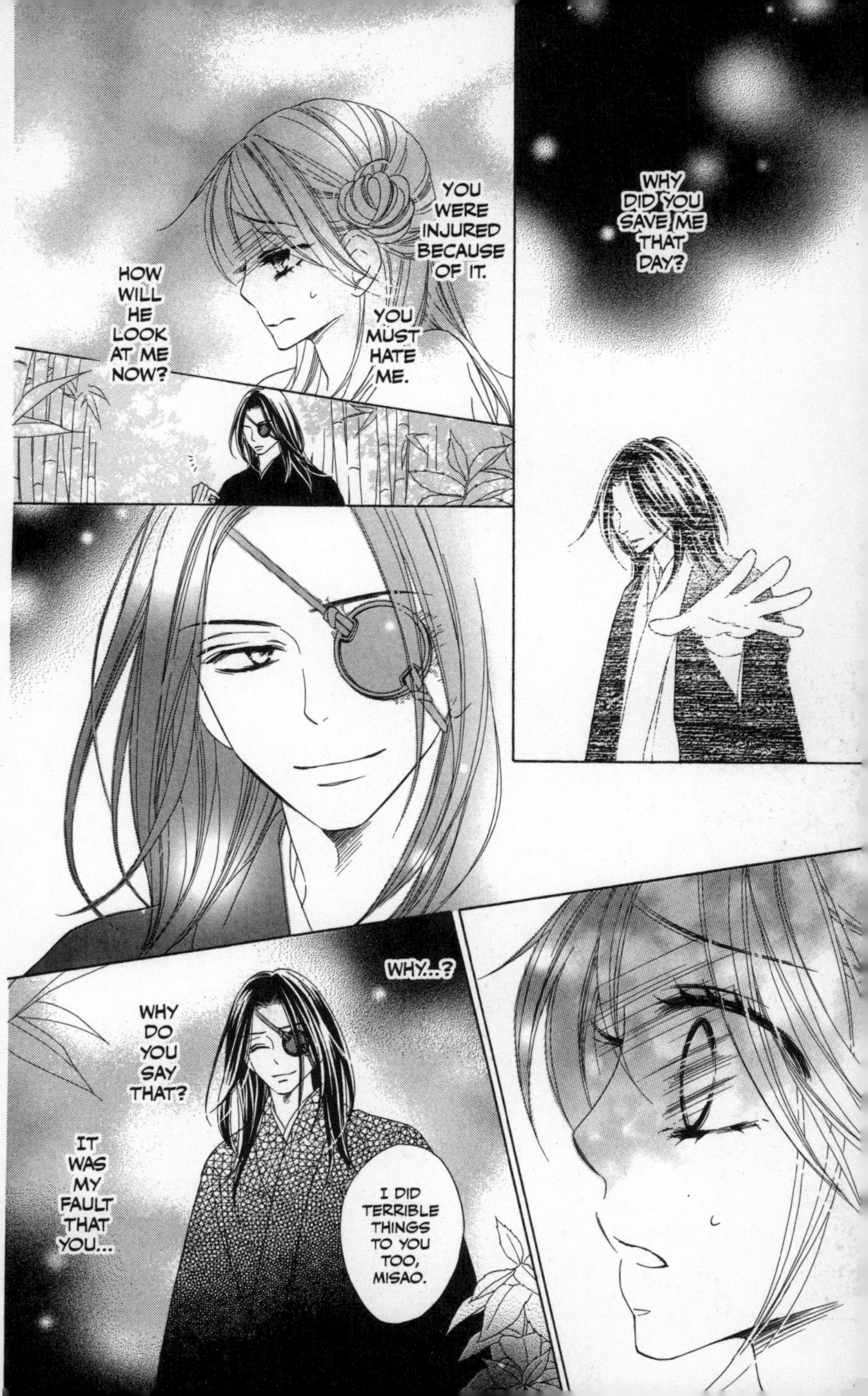
WHY DID YOU SAVE ME THAT DAY?
YOU WERE INJURED BECAUSE OF IT.
YOU MUST HATE ME.
HOW WILL HE LOOK AT ME NOW?
WHY...?
WHY DO YOU SAY THAT?
I DID TERRIBLE THINGS TO YOU TOO, MISAO.
IT WAS MY FAULT THAT YOU...

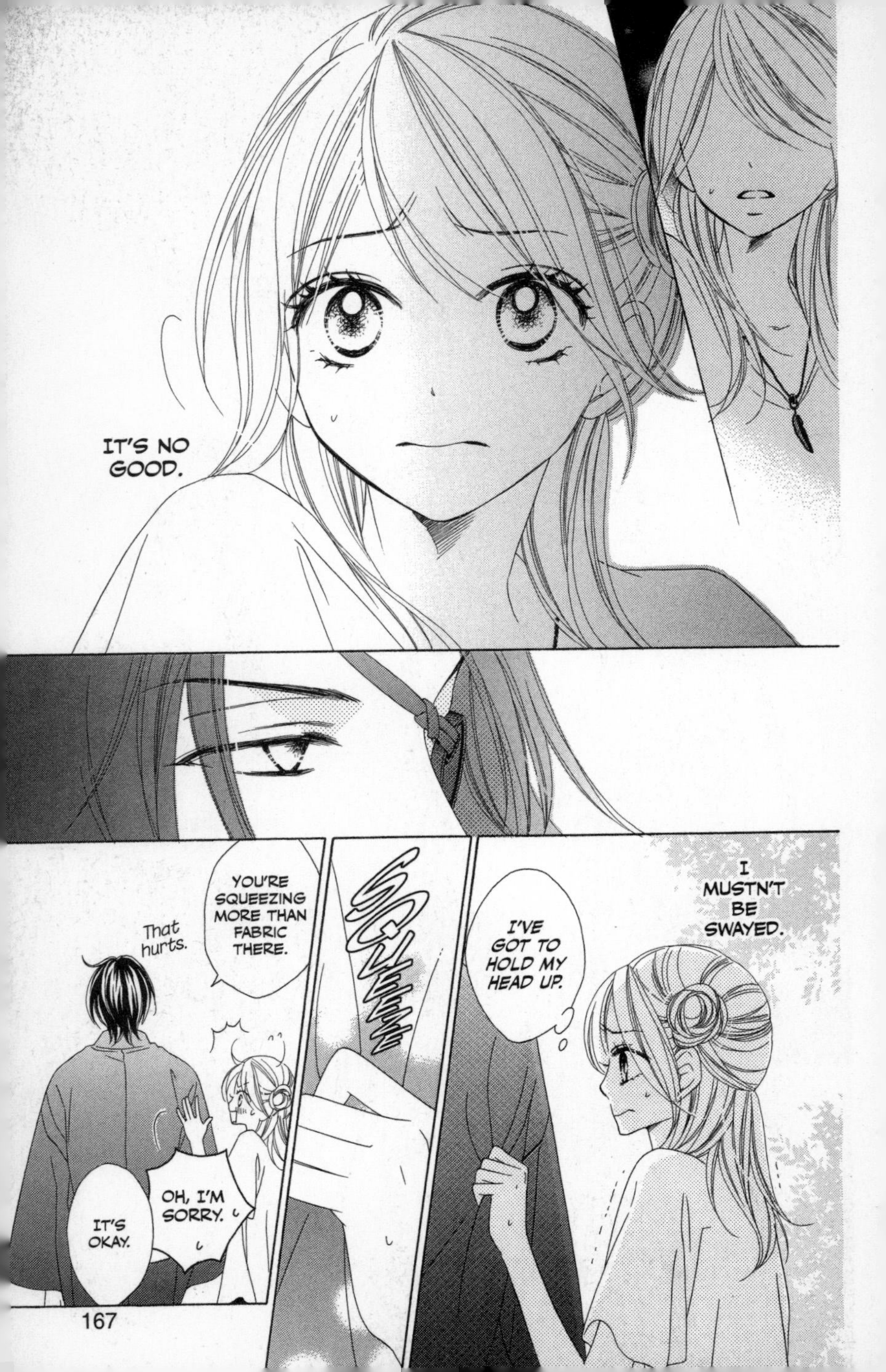
IT'S NO GOOD.
I MUSTN'T BE SWAYED.
I'VE GOT TO HOLD MY HEAD UP.
YOU'RE SQUEEZING MORE THAN FABRIC THERE.
That hurts.
OH, I'M SORRY.
IT'S OKAY.

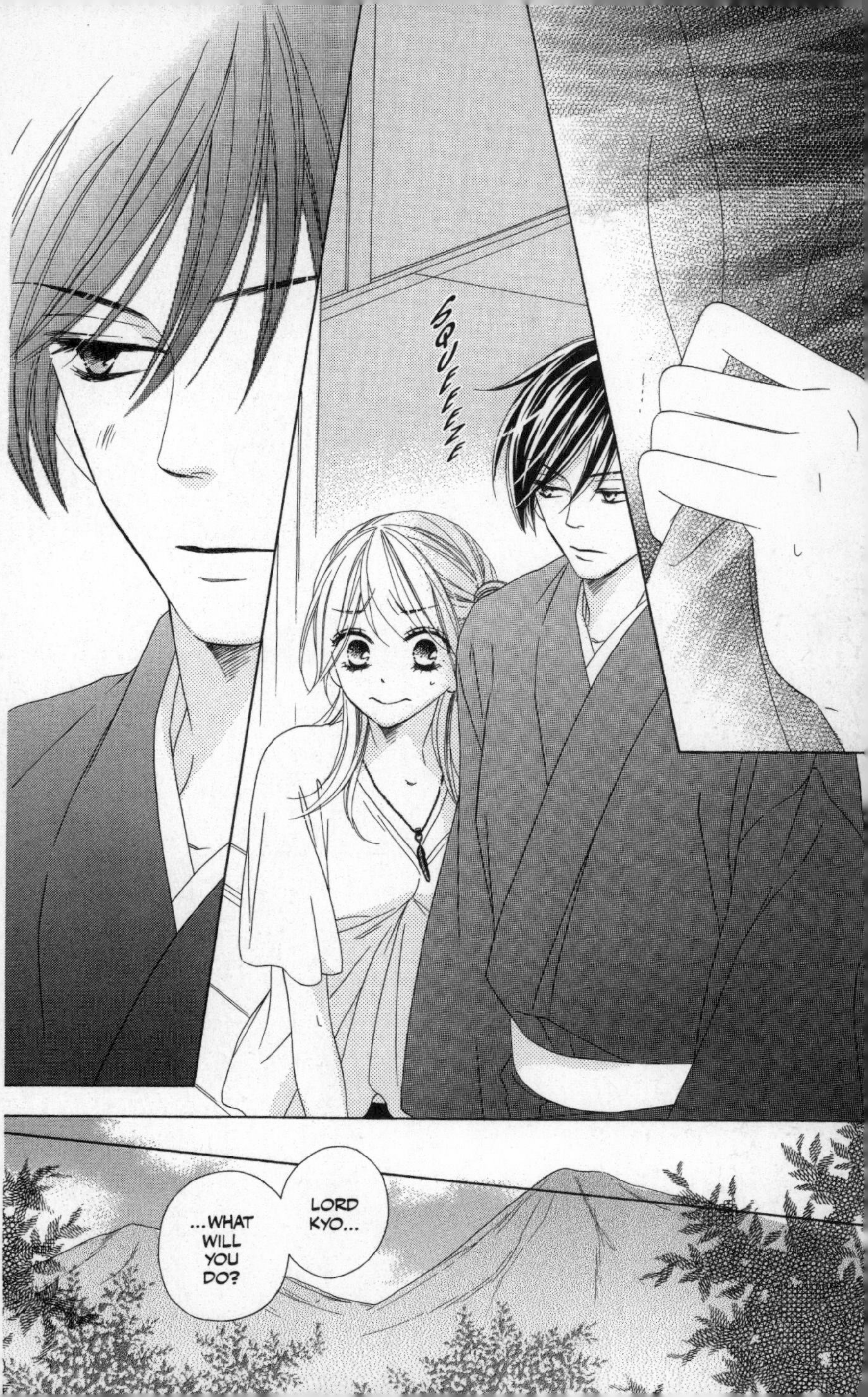
SQUEEEZE
LORD KYO...
...WHAT WILL YOU DO?

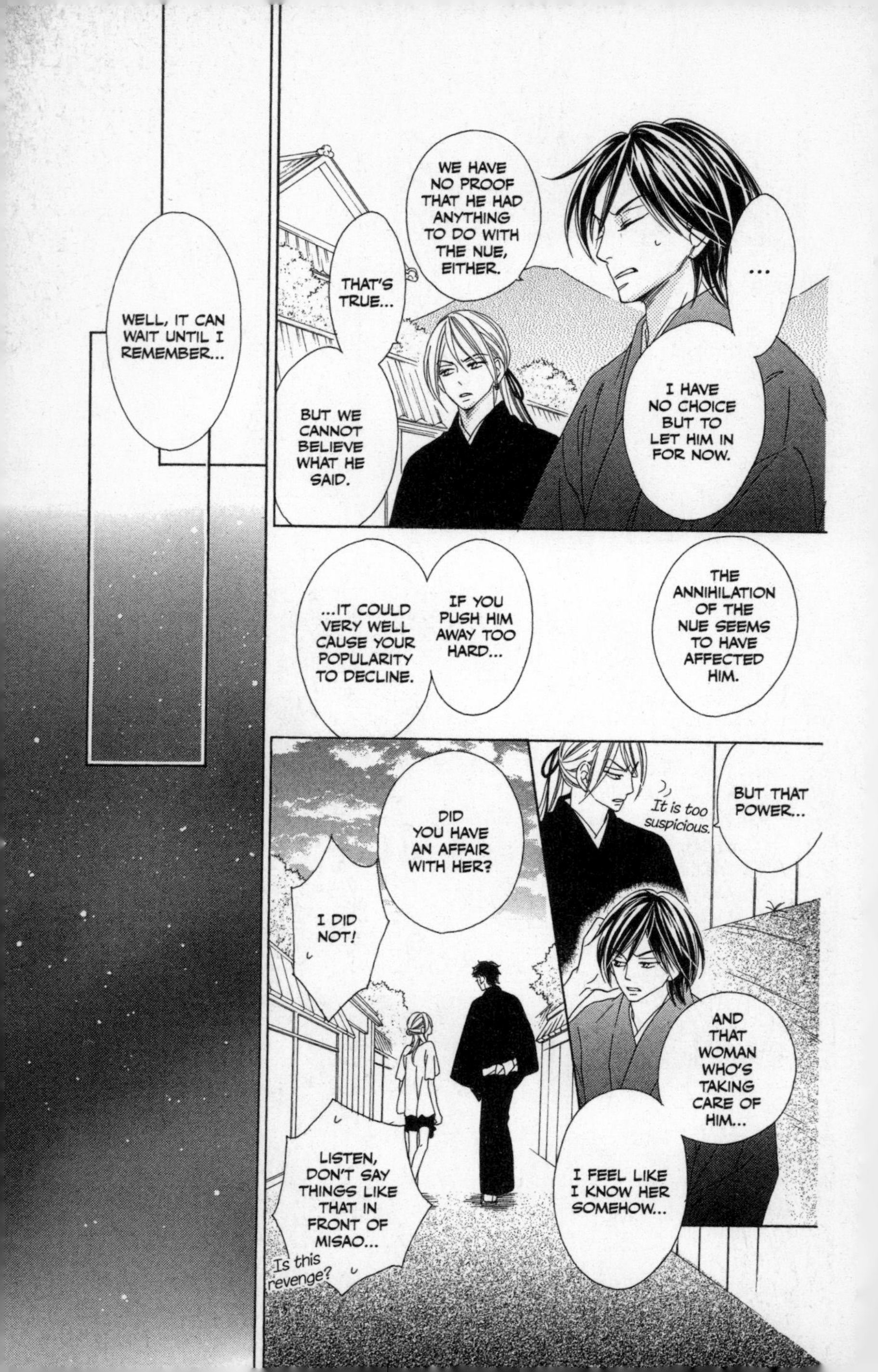
...
I HAVE NO CHOICE BUT TO LET HIM IN FOR NOW.
WE HAVE NO PROOF THAT HE HAD ANYTHING TO DO WITH THE NUE, EITHER.
THAT'S TRUE...
BUT WE CANNOT BELIEVE WHAT HE SAID.
THE ANNIHILATION OF THE NUE SEEMS TO HAVE AFFECTED HIM.
IF YOU PUSH HIM AWAY TOO HARD...
...IT COULD VERY WELL CAUSE YOUR POPULARITY TO DECLINE.
BUT THAT POWER...
It is too suspicious.
AND THAT WOMAN WHO'S TAKING CARE OF HIM...
I FEEL LIKE I KNOW HER SOMEHOW...
DID YOU HAVE AN AFFAIR WITH HER?
I DID NOT!
LISTEN, DON'T SAY THINGS LIKE THAT IN FRONT OF MISAO...
Is this revenge?
WELL, IT CAN WAIT UNTIL I REMEMBER...

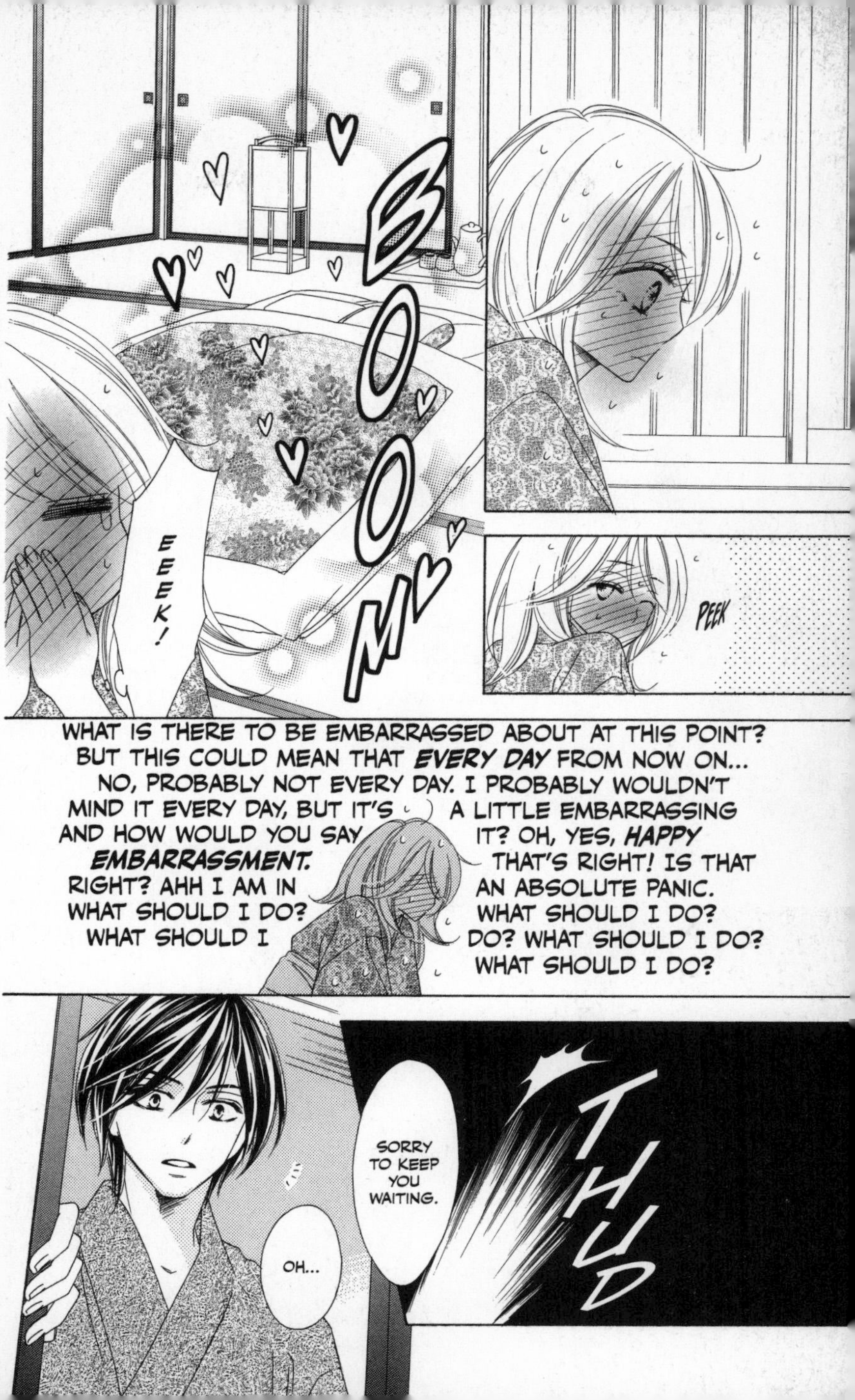
PEEK
BOOOM
EEEEK!
WHAT IS THERE TO BE EMBARRASSED ABOUT AT THIS POINT? BUT THIS COULD MEAN THAT EVERY DAY FROM NOW ON... NO, PROBABLY NOT EVERY DAY. I PROBABLY WOULDN'T MIND IT EVERY DAY, BUT IT'S A LITTLE EMBARRASSING AND HOW WOULD YOU SAY IT? OH, YES, HAPPY EMBARRASSMENT. THAT'S RIGHT! IS THAT RIGHT? AHH I AM IN AN ABSOLUTE PANIC. WHAT SHOULD I DO? WHAT SHOULD I DO? WHAT SHOULD I DO? WHAT SHOULD I DO? WHAT SHOULD I DO?
THUD
SORRY TO KEEP YOU WAITING.
OH...

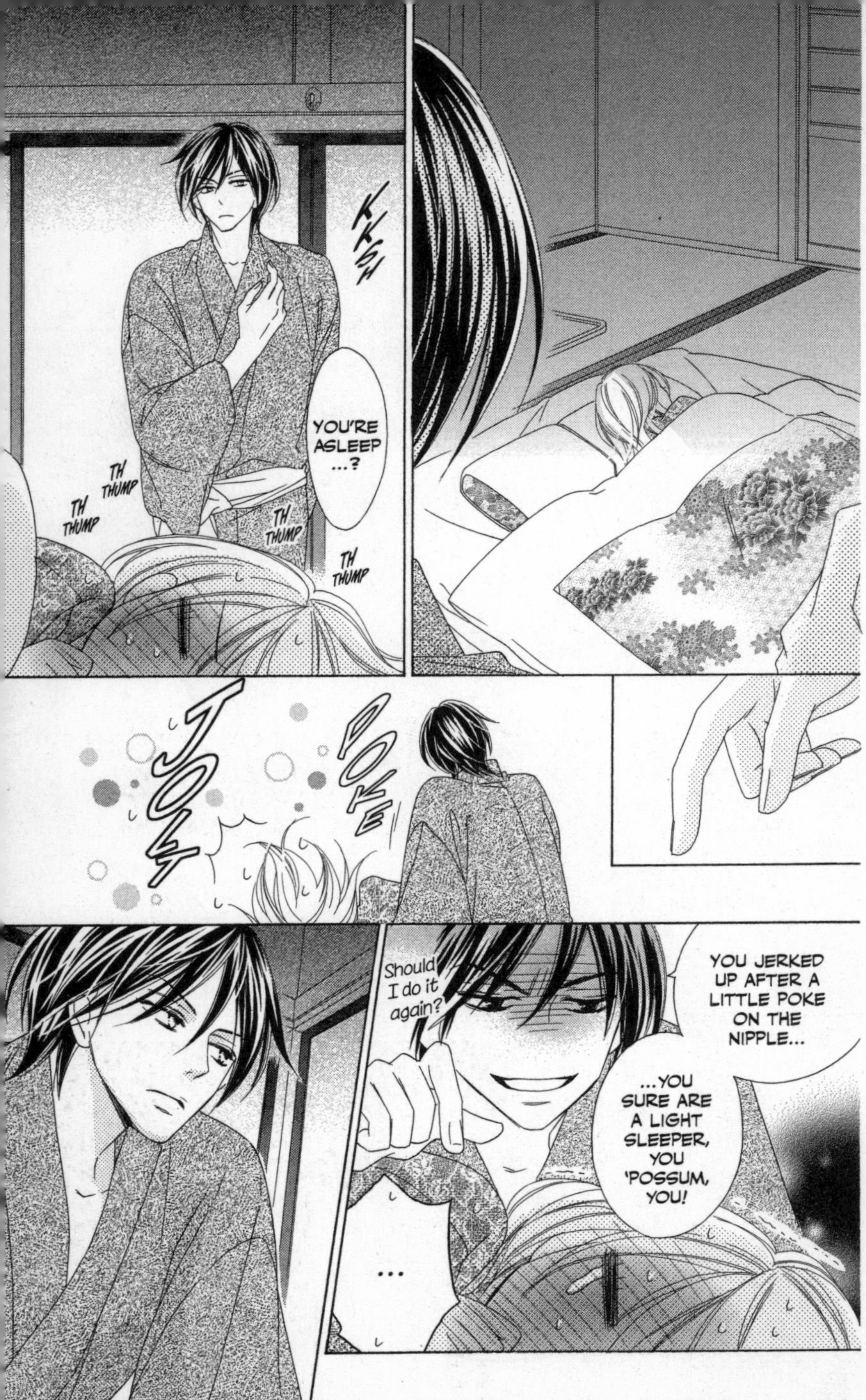
KKSH
YOU'RE ASLEEP ...?
TH THUMP
TH THUMP
TH THUMP
TH THUMP
POKE
JOLT
YOU JERKED UP AFTER A LITTLE POKE ON THE NIPPLE...
...YOU SURE ARE A LIGHT SLEEPER, YOU 'POSSUM, YOU!
Should I do it again?
...

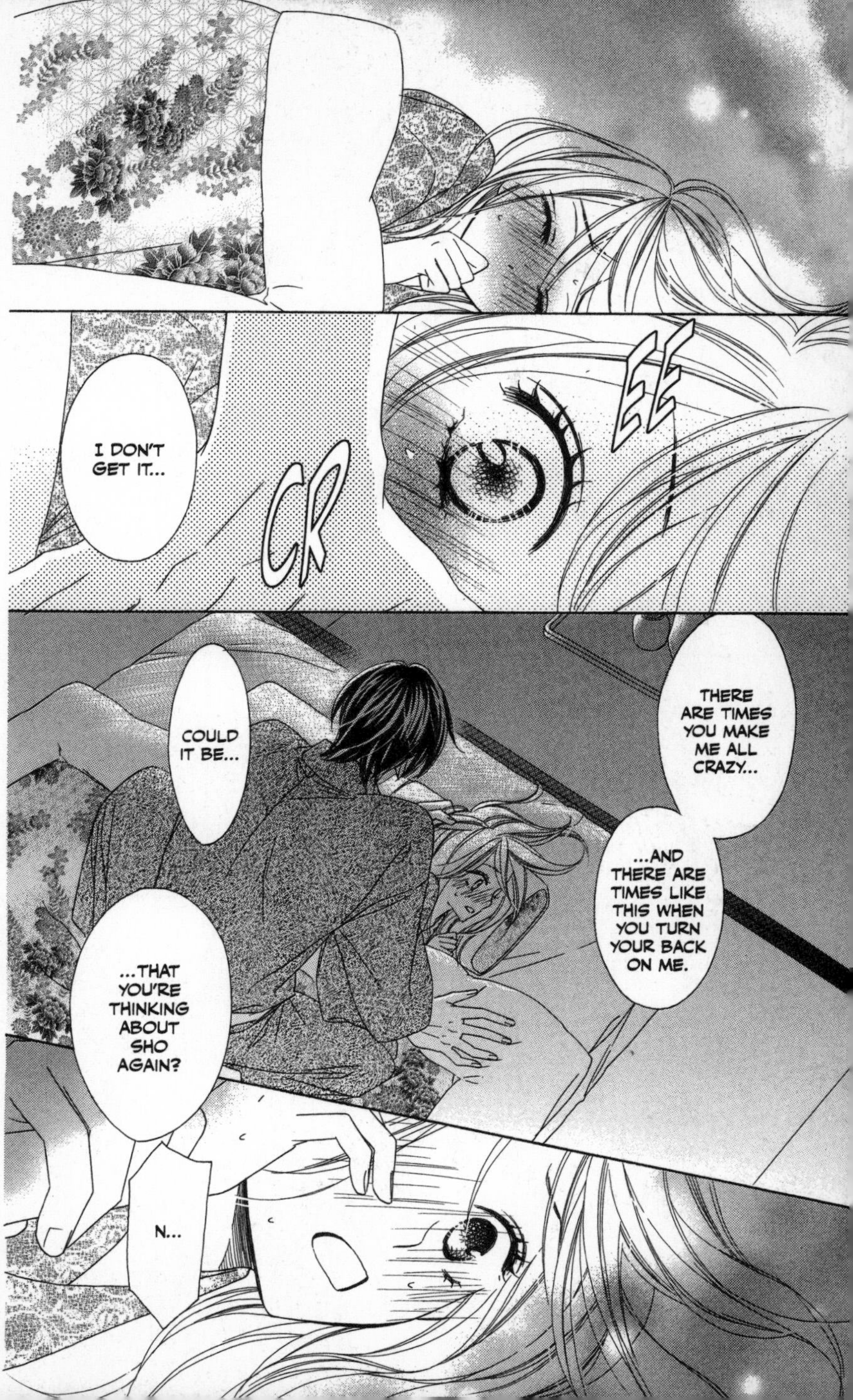
EE
I DON'T GET IT...
CR
THERE ARE TIMES YOU MAKE ME ALL CRAZY...
COULD IT BE...
...AND THERE ARE TIMES LIKE THIS WHEN YOU TURN YOUR BACK ON ME.
...THAT YOU'RE THINKING ABOUT SHO AGAIN?
N...

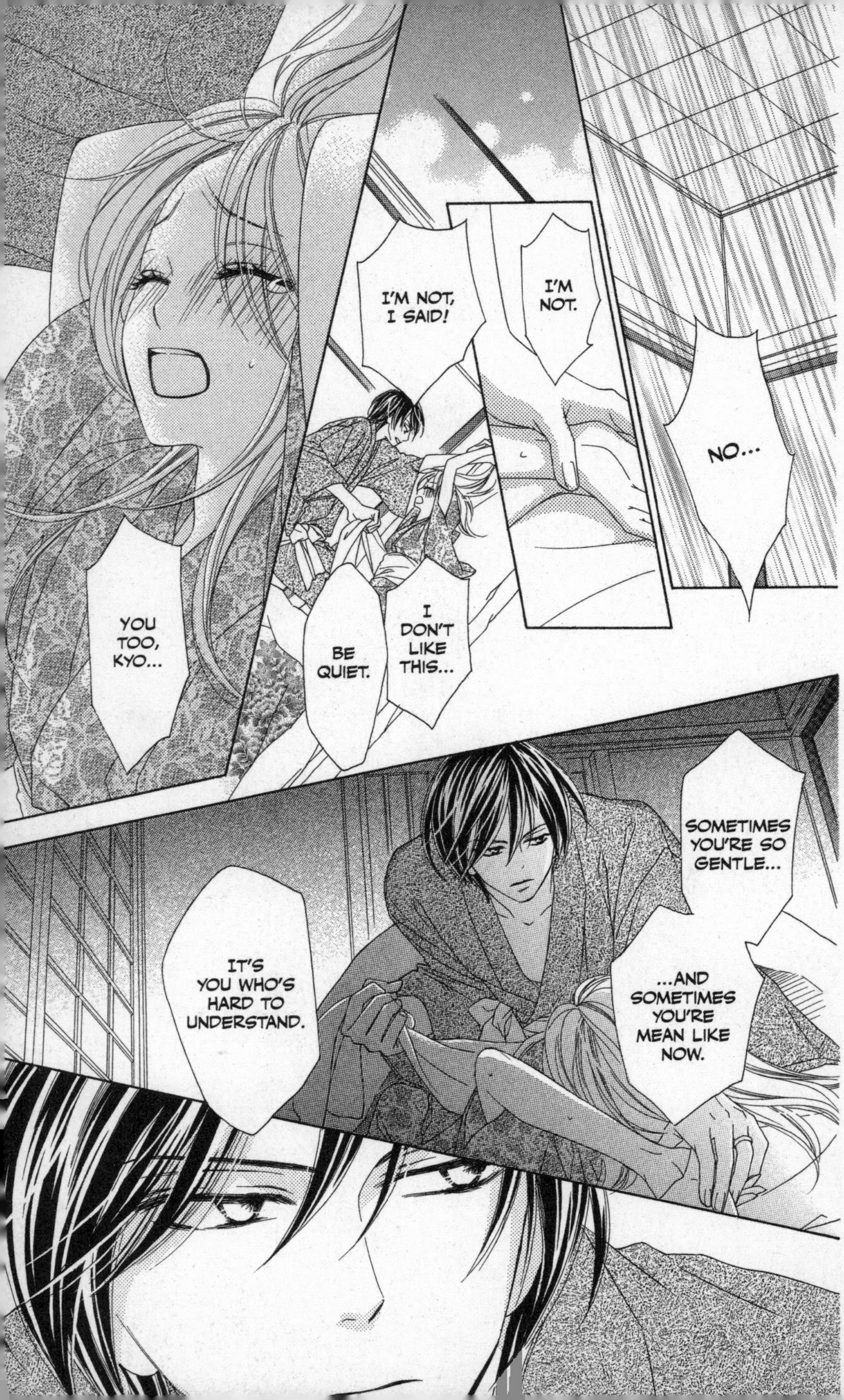
NO...
I'M NOT.
I'M NOT, I SAID!
I DON'T LIKE THIS...
BE QUIET.
YOU TOO, KYO...
SOMETIMES YOU'RE SO GENTLE...
...AND SOMETIMES YOU'RE MEAN LIKE NOW.
IT'S YOU WHO'S HARD TO UNDERSTAND.

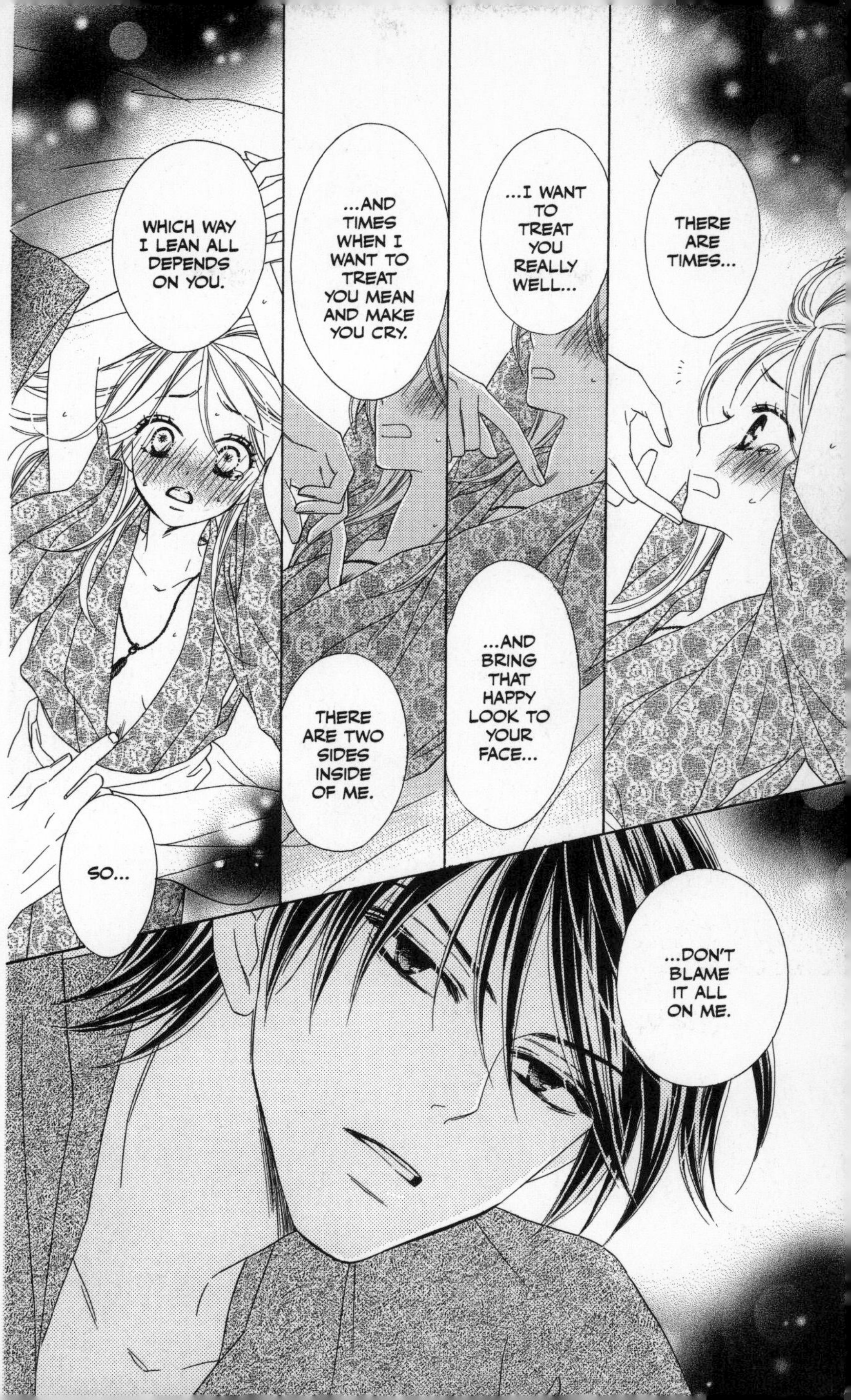
THERE ARE TIMES...
...I WANT TO TREAT YOU REALLY WELL...
...AND BRING THAT HAPPY LOOK TO YOUR FACE...
...AND TIMES WHEN I WANT TO TREAT YOU MEAN AND MAKE YOU CRY.
THERE ARE TWO SIDES INSIDE OF ME.
WHICH WAY I LEAN ALL DEPENDS ON YOU.
SO...
...DON'T BLAME IT ALL ON ME.

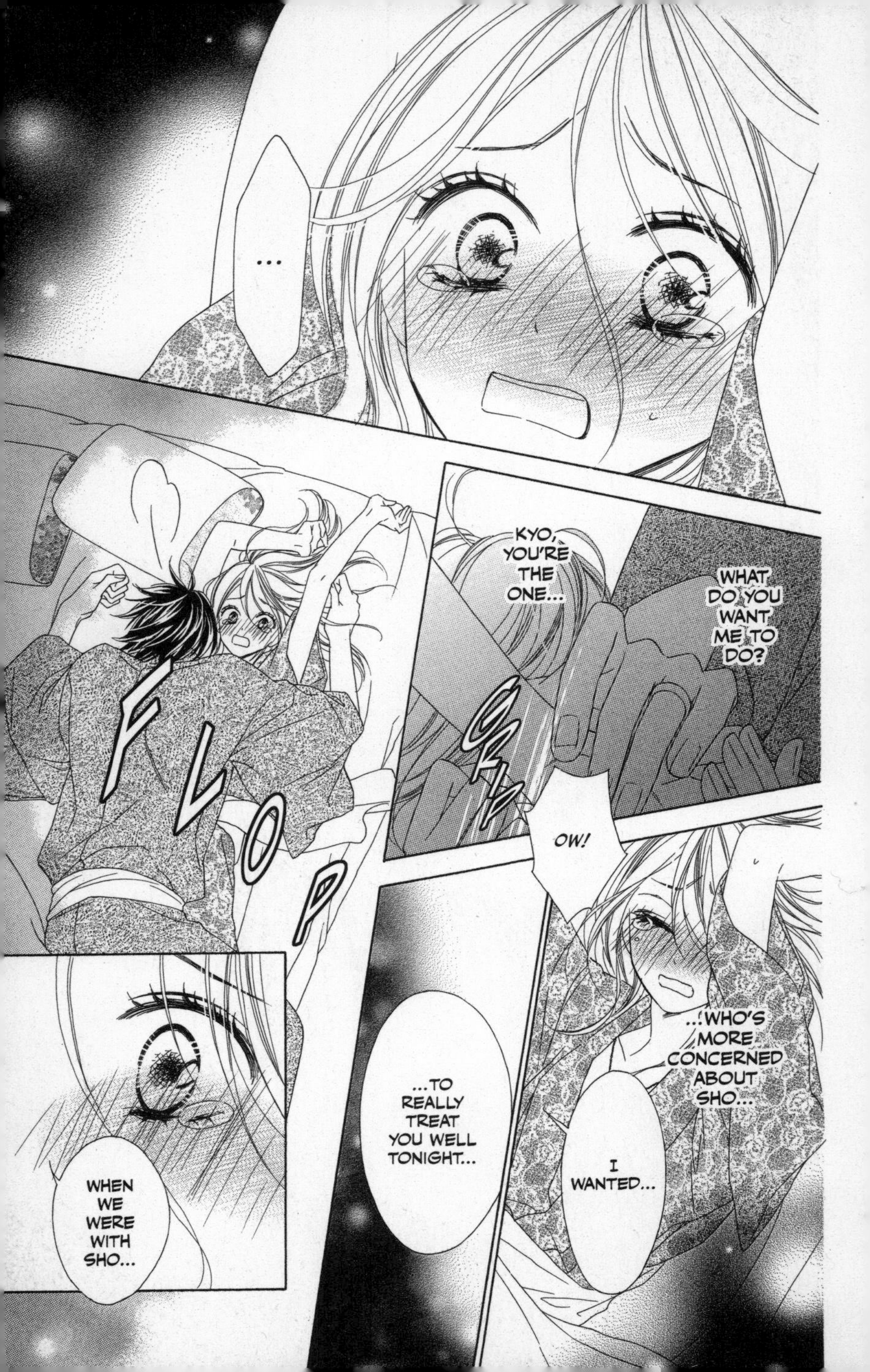
...
WHAT DO YOU WANT ME TO DO?
KYO, YOU'RE THE ONE...
FLOP
OW!
...WHO'S MORE CONCERNED ABOUT SHO...
I WANTED...
...TO REALLY TREAT YOU WELL TONIGHT...
WHEN WE WERE WITH SHO...

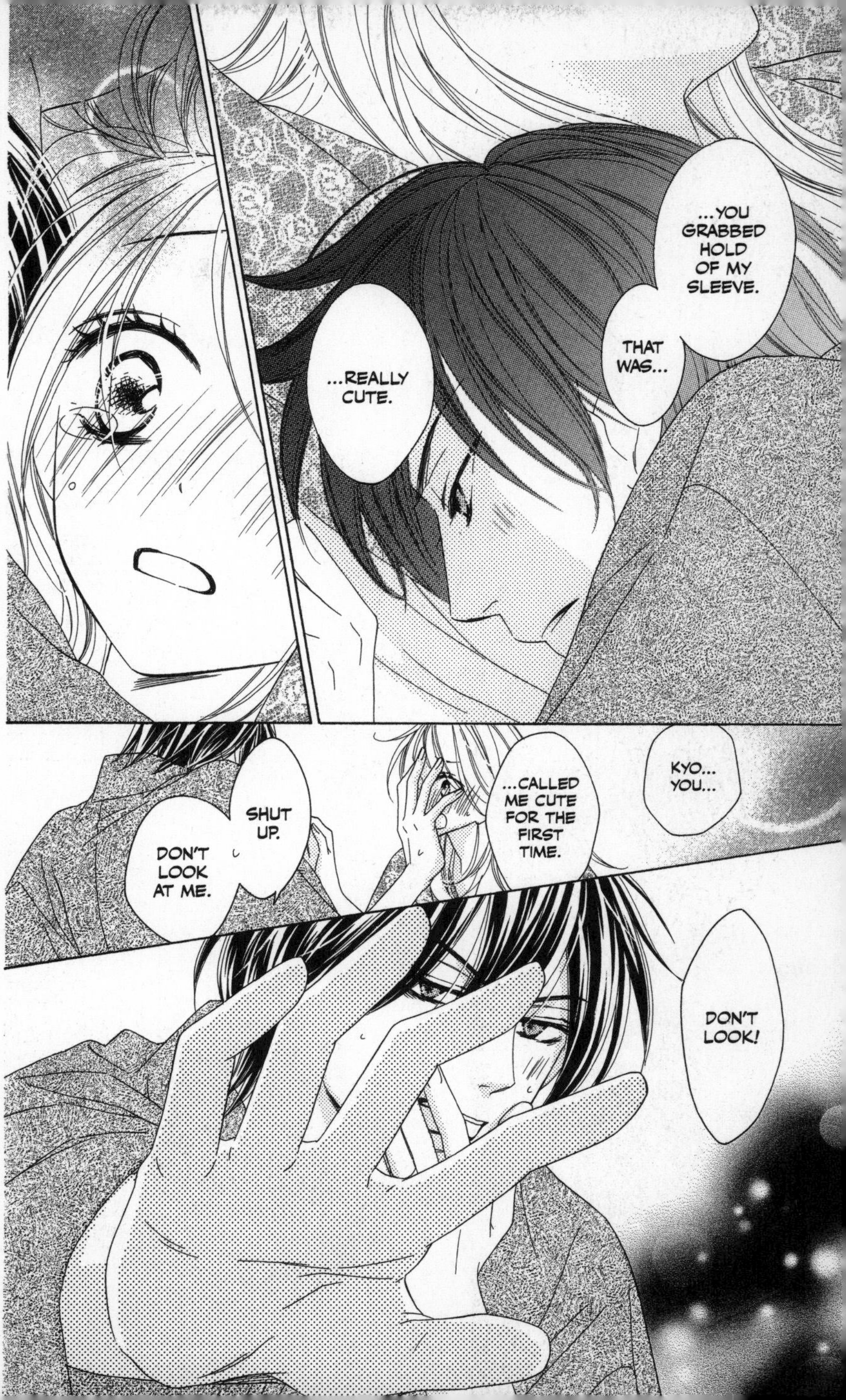
...YOU GRABBED HOLD OF MY SLEEVE.
THAT WAS...
...REALLY CUTE.
KYO... YOU...
...CALLED ME CUTE FOR THE FIRST TIME.
SHUT UP.
DON'T LOOK AT ME.
DON'T LOOK!

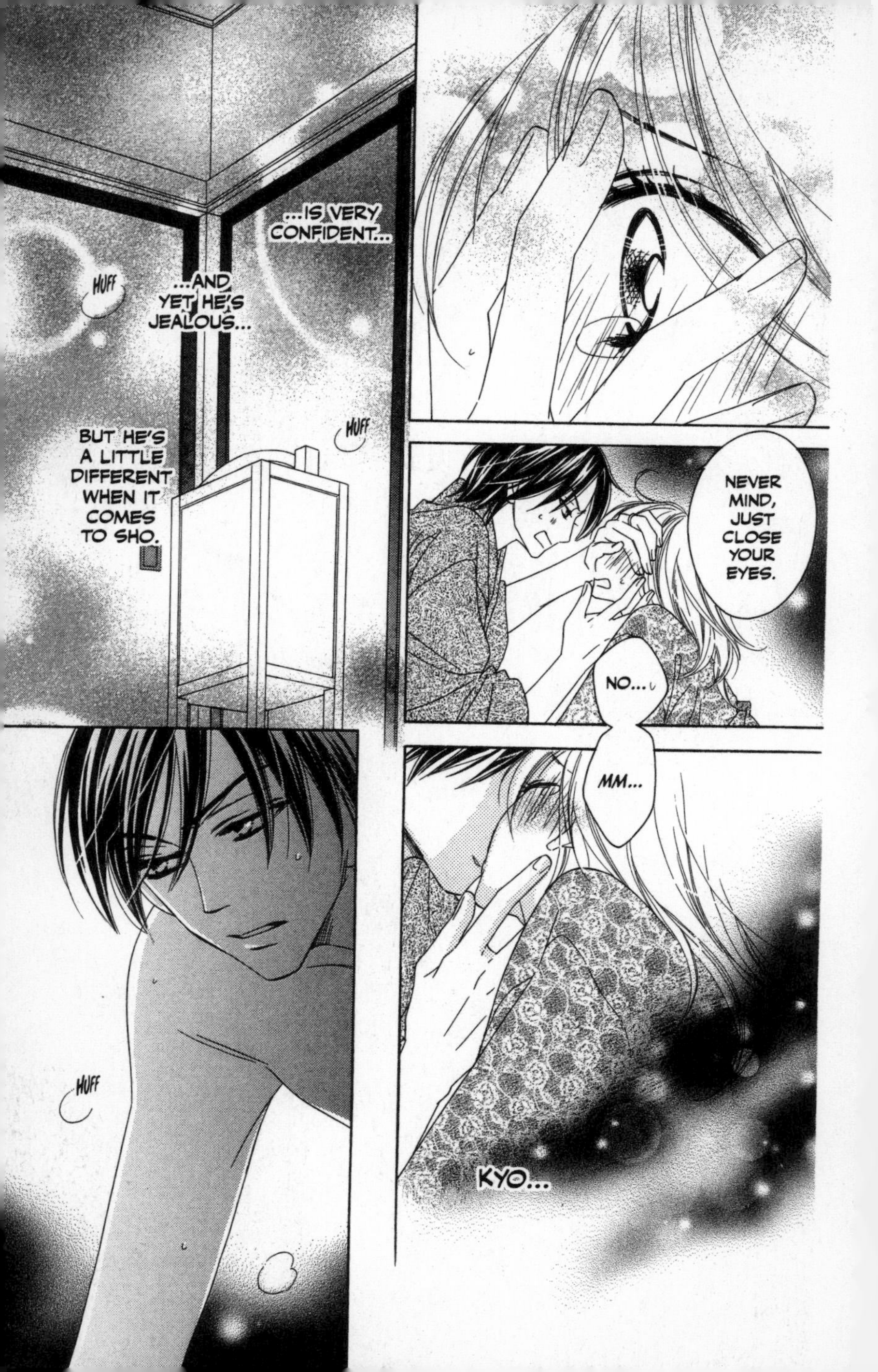
NEVER MIND, JUST CLOSE YOUR EYES.
NO...
...IS VERY CONFIDENT...
HUFF
...AND YET HE'S JEALOUS...
BUT HE'S A LITTLE DIFFERENT WHEN IT COMES TO SHO.
HUFF
MM...
KYO...
HUFF

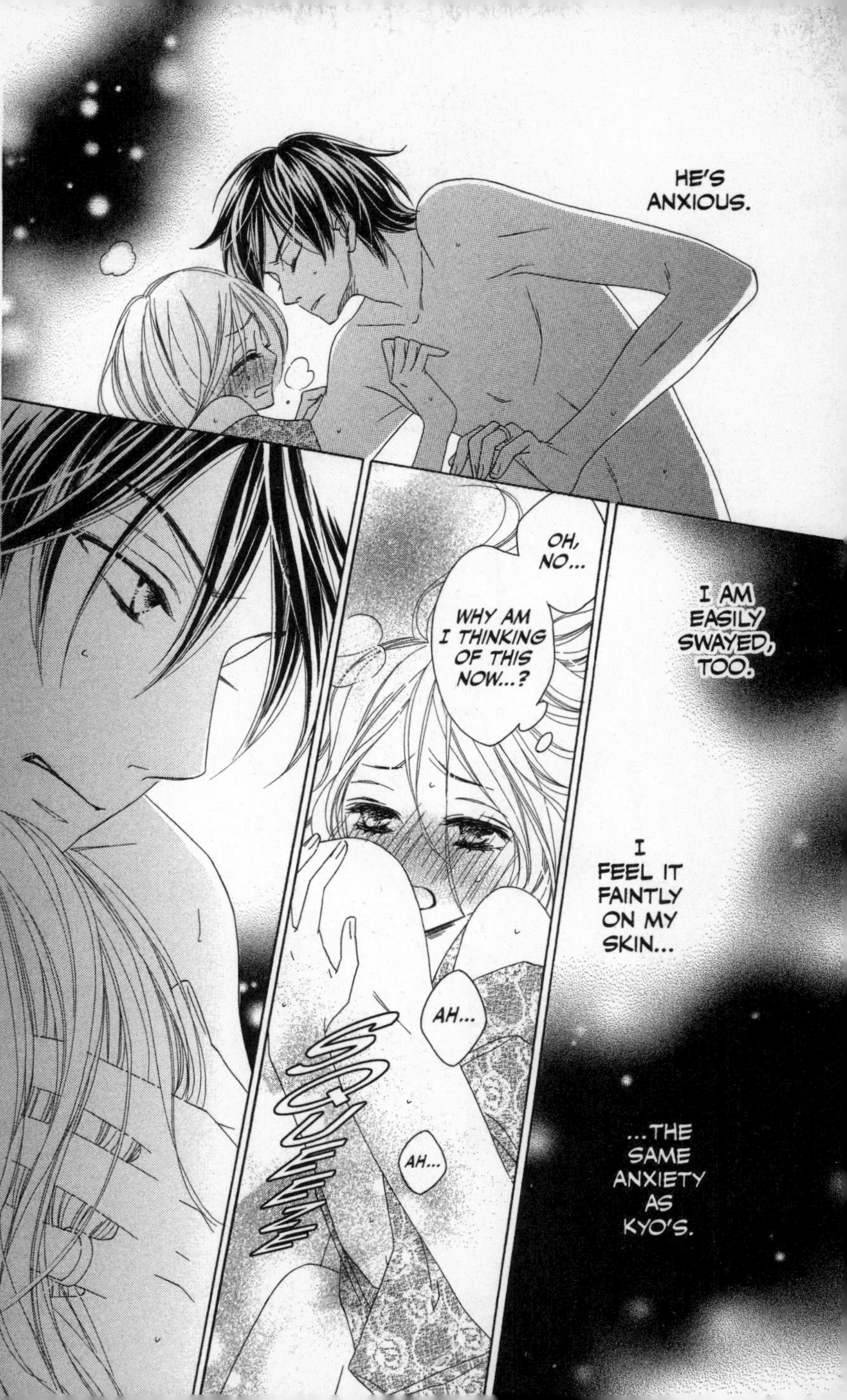
HE'S ANXIOUS.
I AM EASILY SWAYED, TOO.
OH, NO...
WHY AM I THINKING OF THIS NOW...?
I FEEL IT FAINTLY ON MY SKIN...
AH...
AH...
...THE SAME ANXIETY AS KYO'S.

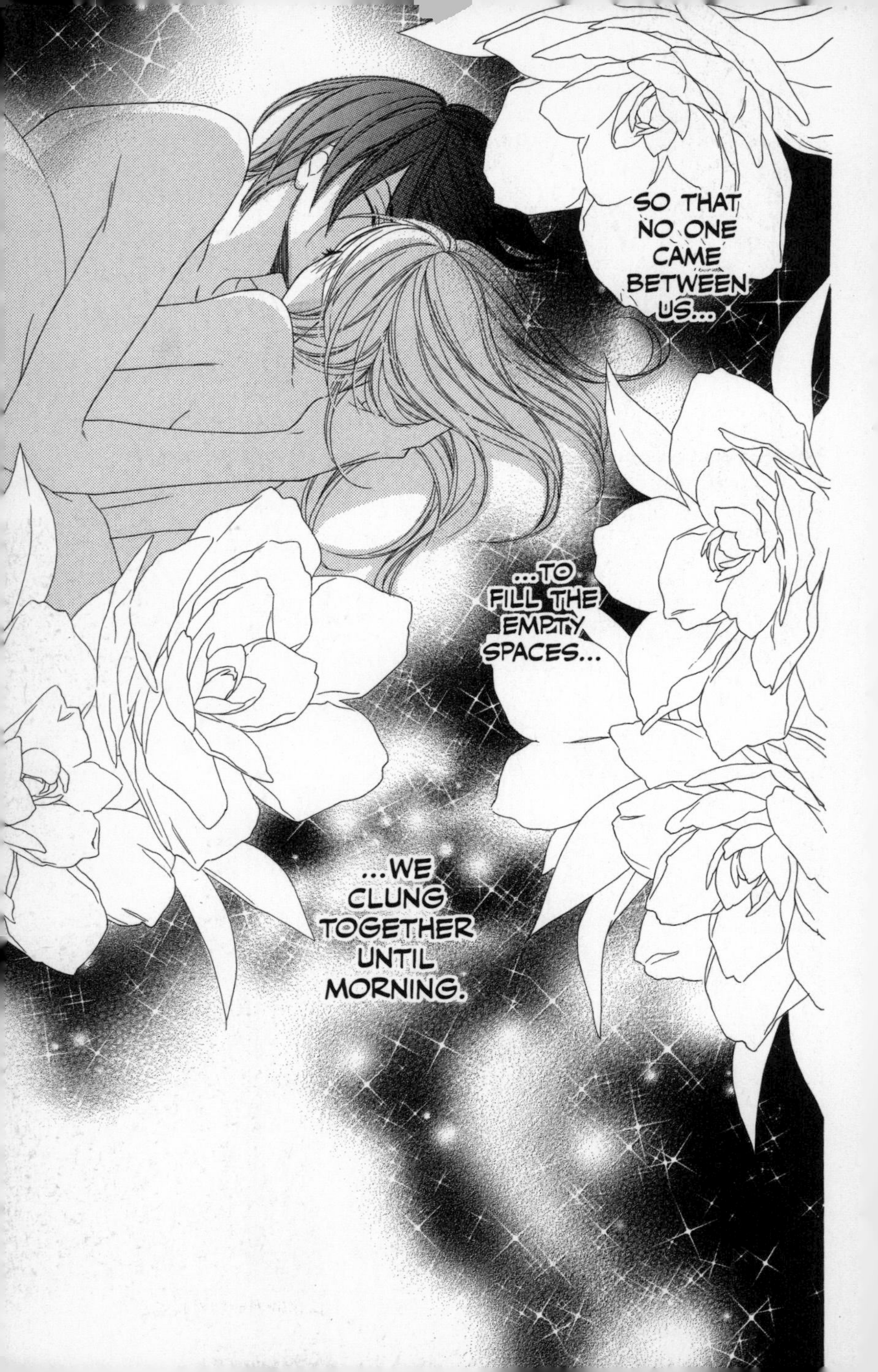
SO THAT NO ONE CAME BETWEEN US...
...TO FILL THE EMPTY SPACES...
...WE CLUNG TOGETHER UNTIL MORNING.

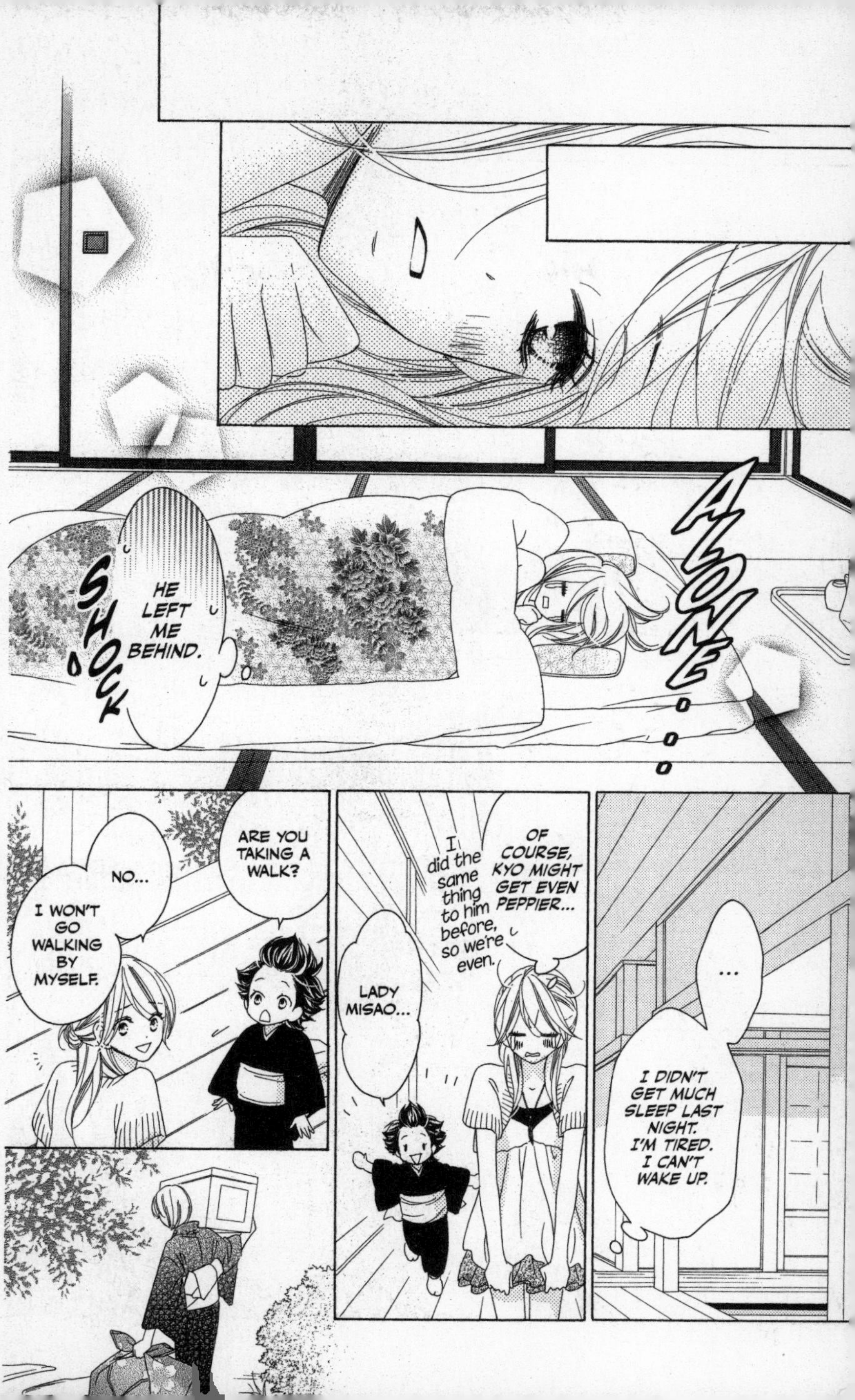
ALONE...
SHOCK
HE LEFT ME BEHIND.
...
I DIDN'T GET MUCH SLEEP LAST NIGHT. I'M TIRED. I CAN'T WAKE UP.
OF COURSE, KYO MIGHT GET EVEN PEPPIER...
I did the same thing to him before, so we're even.
LADY MISAO...
ARE YOU TAKING A WALK?
NO...
I WON'T GO WALKING BY MYSELF.

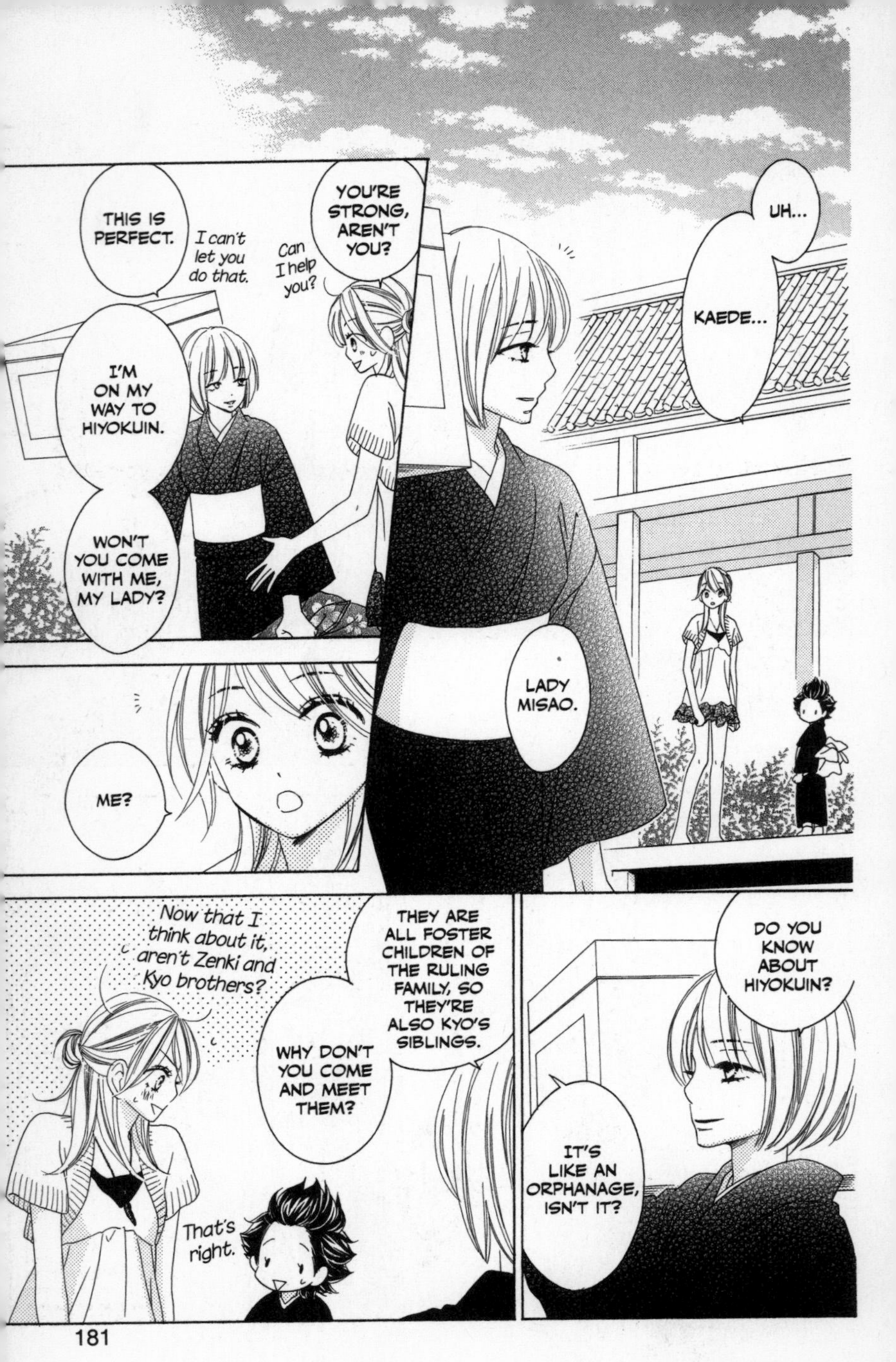
UH...
KAEDE...
LADY MISAO.
YOU'RE STRONG, AREN'T YOU?
Can I help you?
I can't let you do that.
THIS IS PERFECT.
I'M ON MY WAY TO HIYOKUIN.
WON'T YOU COME WITH ME, MY LADY?
ME?
DO YOU KNOW ABOUT HIYOKUIN?
IT'S LIKE AN ORPHANAGE, ISN'T IT?
THEY ARE ALL FOSTER CHILDREN OF THE RULING FAMILY, SO THEY'RE ALSO KYO'S SIBLINGS.
Now that I think about it, aren't Zenki and Kyo brothers?
WHY DON'T YOU COME AND MEET THEM?
That's right.

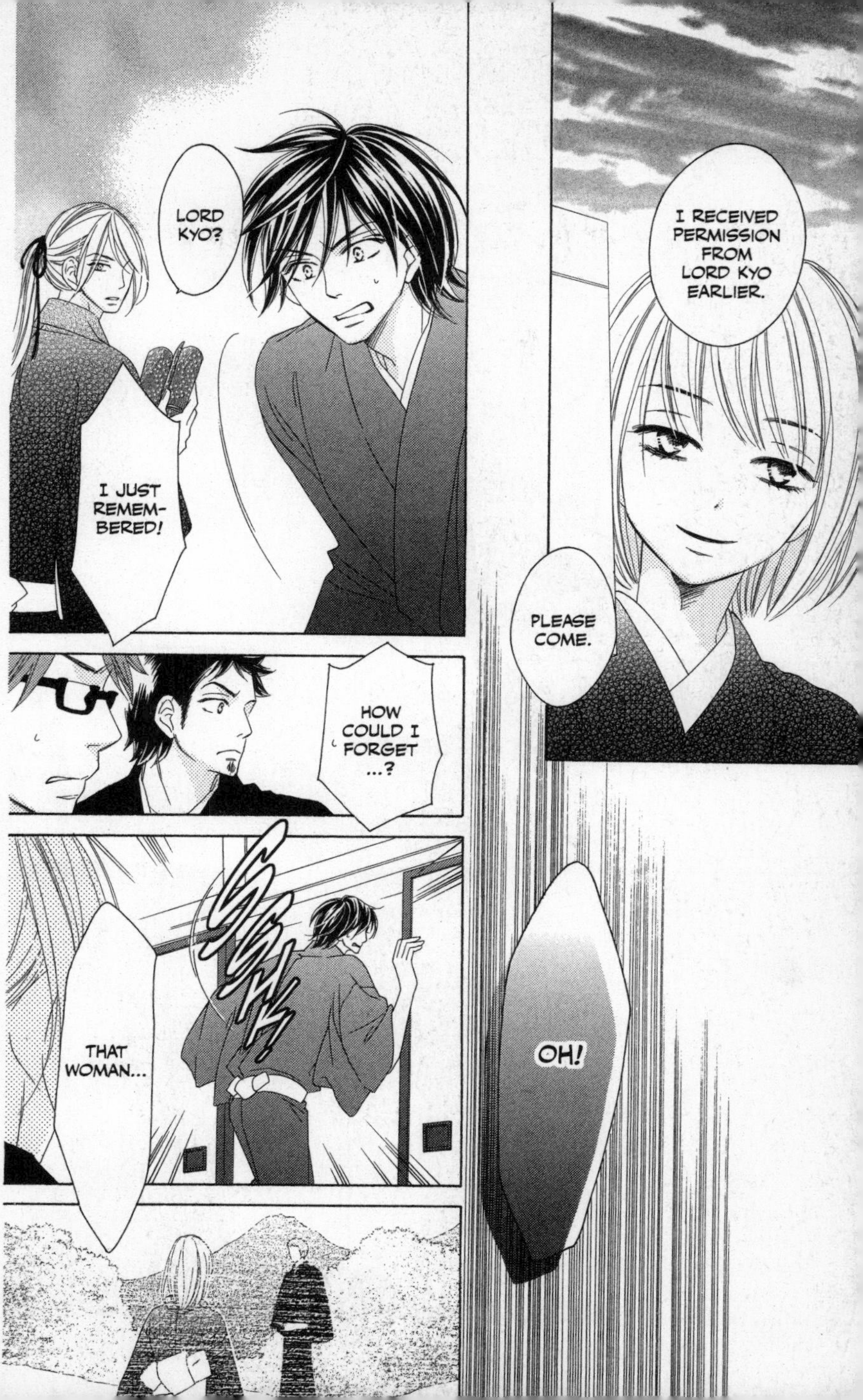
I RECEIVED PERMISSION FROM LORD KYO EARLIER.
PLEASE COME.
OH!
LORD KYO?
I JUST REMEMBERED!
HOW COULD I FORGET ...?
THAT WOMAN...

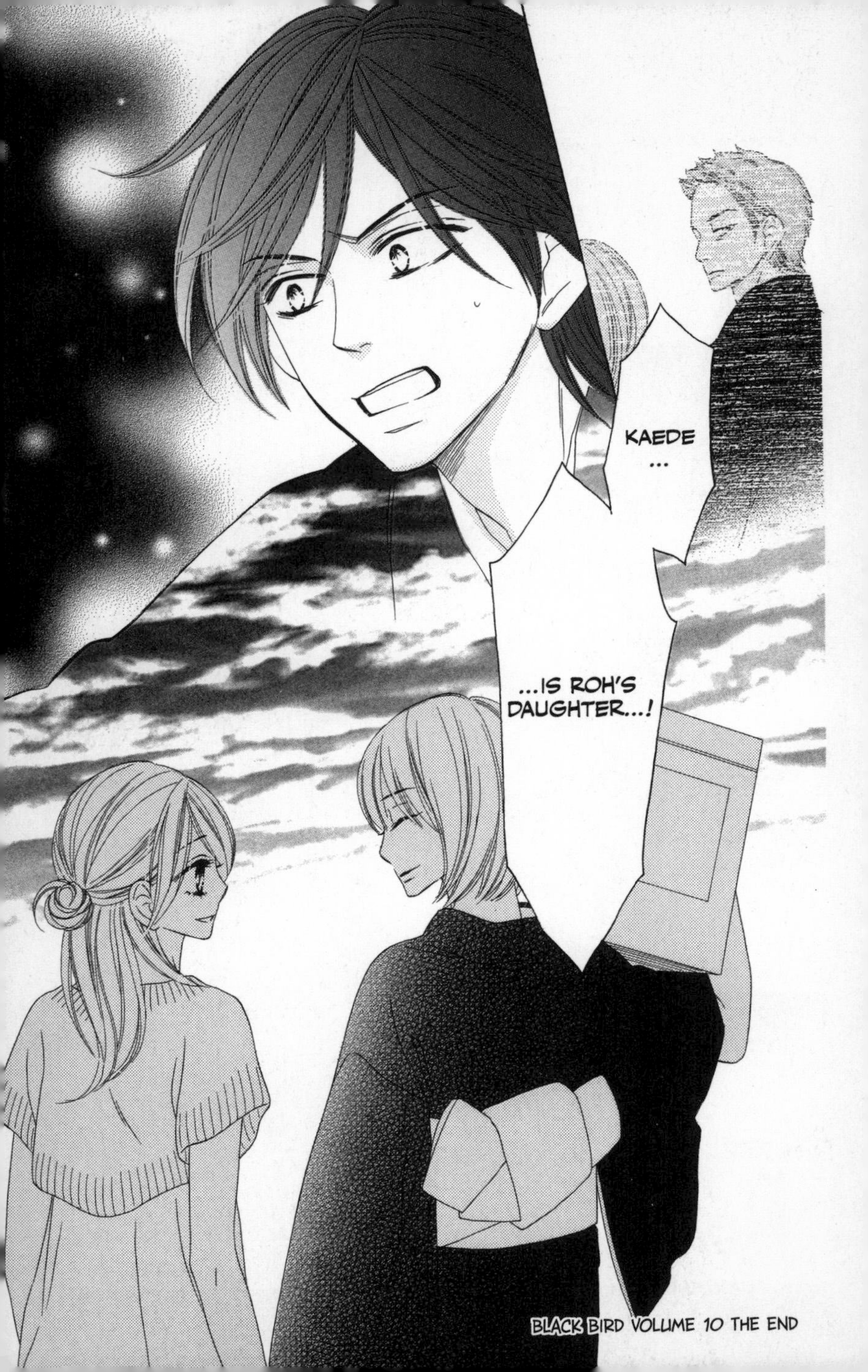
KAEDE
...
...IS ROH'S DAUGHTER...!
BLACK BIRD VOLUME 10 THE END

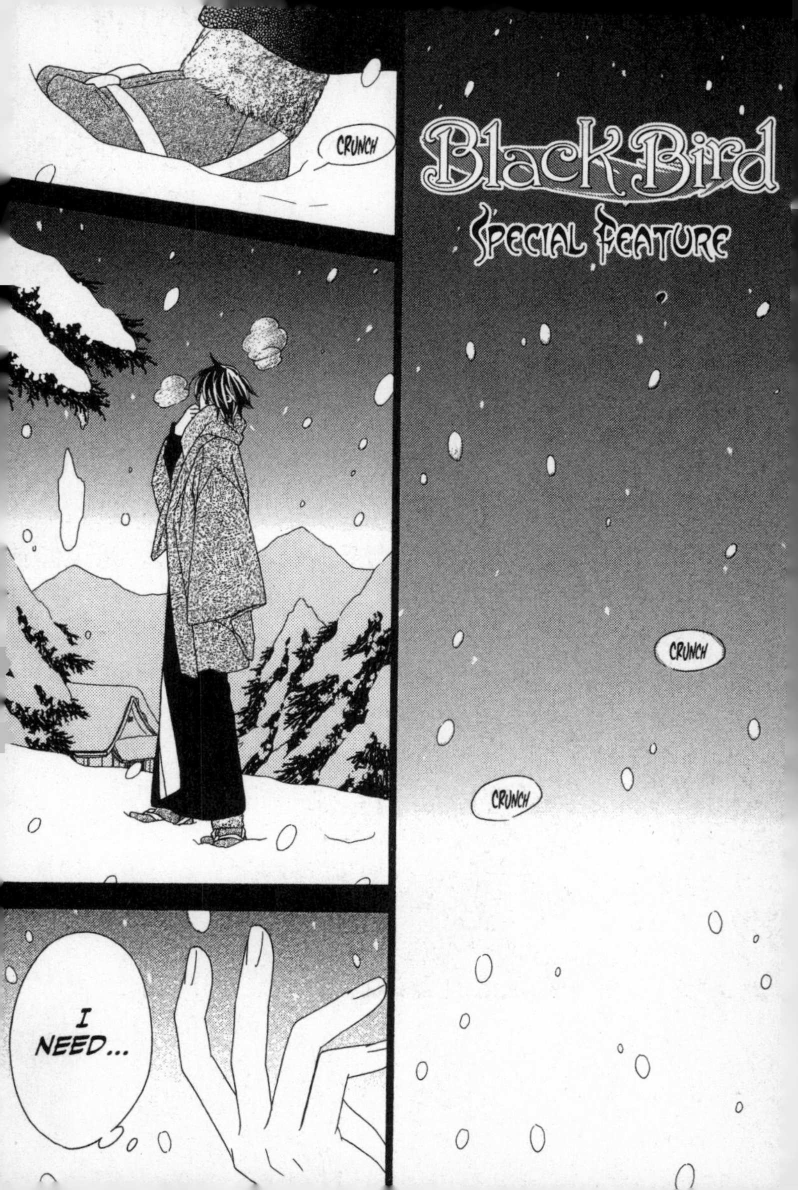
Black Bird
Special Feature
CRUNCH
CRUNCH
CRUNCH
I NEED...

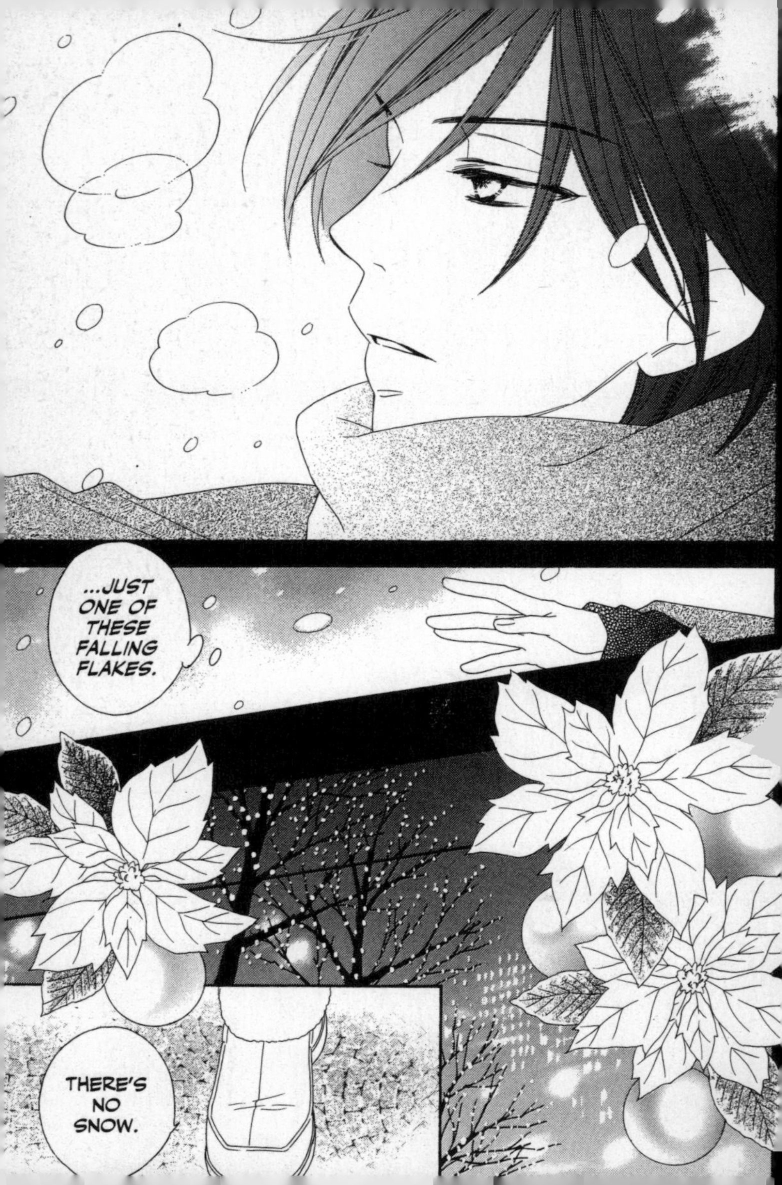
...JUST ONE OF THESE FALLING FLAKES.
THERE'S NO SNOW.

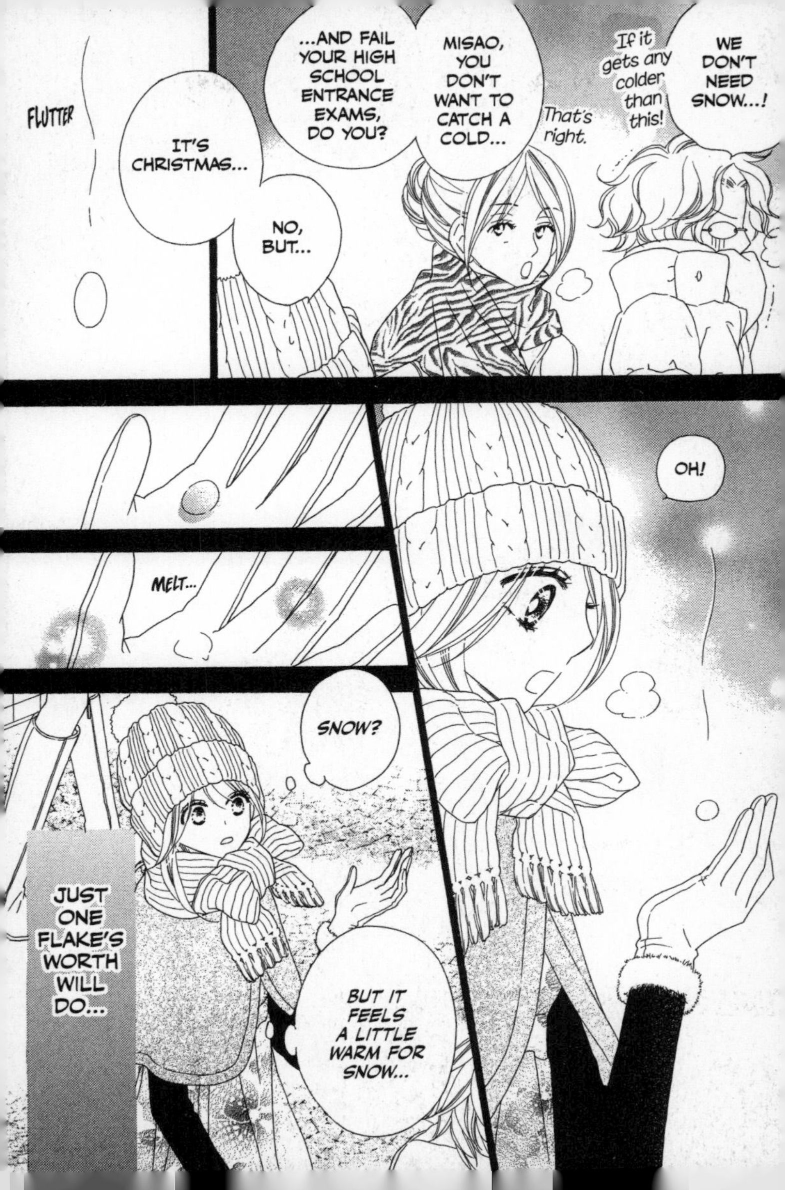
WE DON'T NEED SNOW...!
If it gets any colder than this!
That's right.
MISAO, YOU DON'T WANT TO CATCH A COLD...
...AND FAIL YOUR HIGH SCHOOL ENTRANCE EXAMS, DO YOU?
NO, BUT...
IT'S CHRISTMAS...
FLUTTER
OH!
MELT...
SNOW?
BUT IT FEELS A LITTLE WARM FOR SNOW...
JUST ONE FLAKE'S WORTH WILL DO...

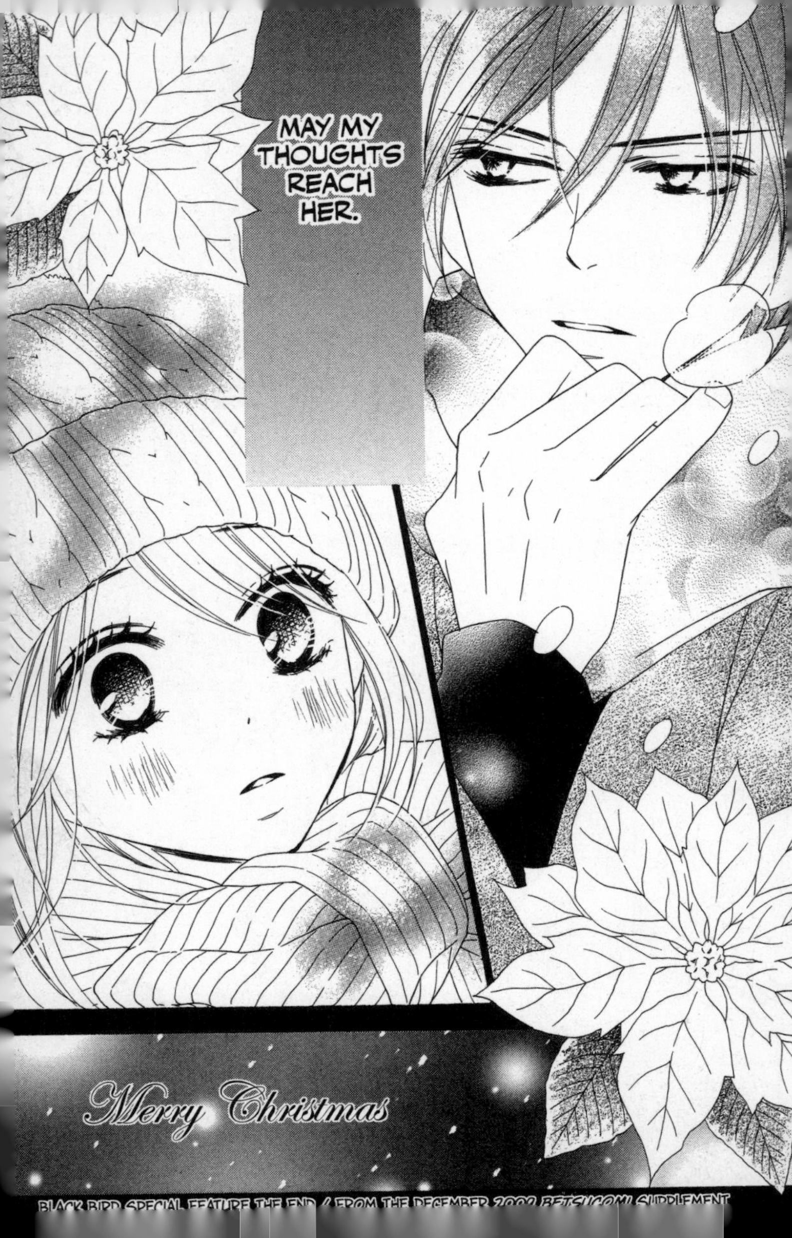
MAY MY THOUGHTS REACH HER.
Merry Christmas

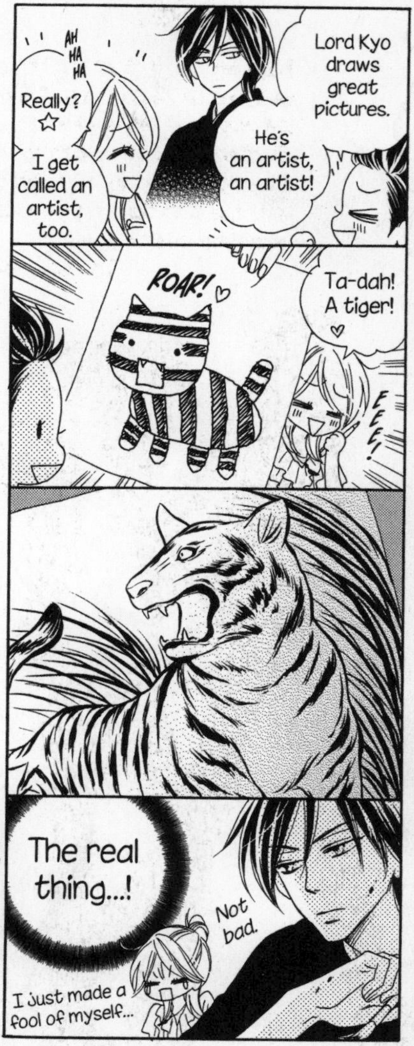
Lord Kyo draws great pictures.
He's an artist, an artist!
AH HA HA
Really? ☆
I get called an artist, too.
Ta-dah! A tiger! ♡
ROAR! ♡
EEE!
The real thing...!
Not bad.
I just made a fool of myself...

Kyo most likely received the usual education.

He can perform traditional Japanese dance & recite traditional Japanese poetry at the age of 20...

Because he's a tengu.

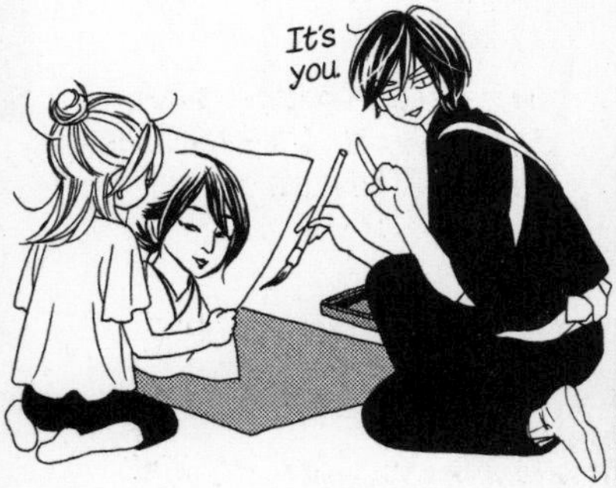
It's you.

February will make ten full years since I debuted at *Betsucomi*. The following month, Volume 10 of this series will come out in Japan. It all seems a little strange, but I'm very happy.♥ I would like to send my heartfelt thanks to all those who have supported me, and those who have loved my work!

Thank you very much!!

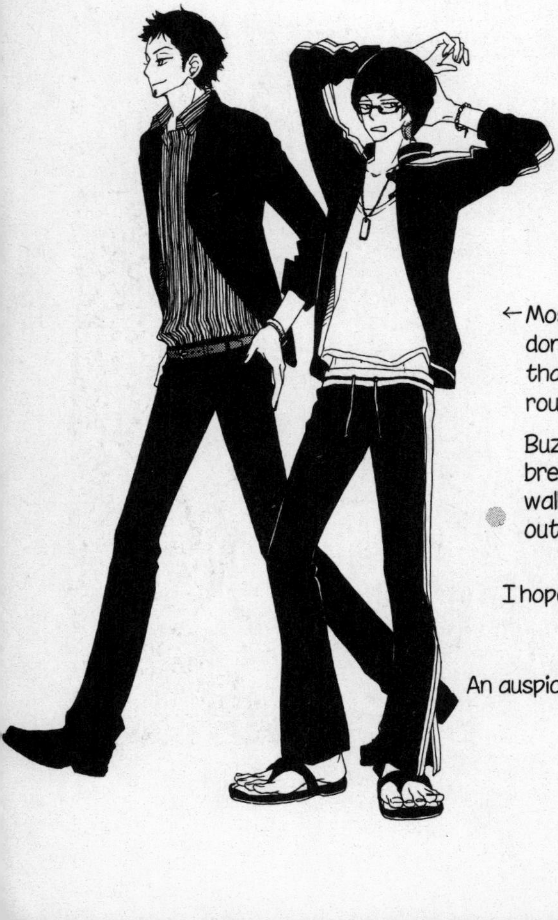

I will continue to do my best so that you will continue to support my work! In the next volume, I will also announce the results of the *Betsucomi* Character Popularity Contest.♥

←Mostly likely these two don't have anything that can be called daily routines...

Buzen's womanizing is like breathing to him. Zenki likes walking. They are both outdoorsmen.

I hope we'll meet again!♥♥

An auspicious day, January 2010

Kanoko Sakurakoji

桜小路 かのこ

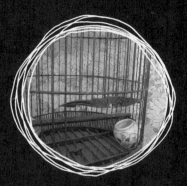

Kanoko Sakurakoji was born in downtown
Tokyo, and her hobbies include reading,
watching plays, traveling and shopping. Her
debut title, *Raibu ga Hanetara*, ran in *Bessatsu
Shojo Comic* (currently called *Bestucomi)* in
2000, and her 2004 *Bestucomi* title *Backstage
Prince* was serialized in VIZ Media's
Shojo Beat magazine. She won the 54th
Shogakukan Manga Award for *Black Bird*.

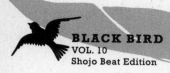

BLACK BIRD
VOL. 10
Shojo Beat Edition

Story and Art by KANOKO SAKURAKOUJI

© 2007 Kanoko SAKURAKOUJI/Shogakukan
All rights reserved.
Original Japanese edition "BLACK BIRD" published by SHOGAKUKAN Inc.

TRANSLATION JN Productions
TOUCH-UP ART & LETTERING Gia Cam Luc
DESIGN Amy Martin
EDITOR Pancha Diaz

The rights of the author(s) of the work(s) in this publication
to be so identified have been asserted in accordance with
the Copyright, Designs and Patents Act 1988. A CIP catalogue
record for this book is available from the British Library.

Printed in the U.S.A.

Published by VIZ Media, LLC
P.O. Box 77010
San Francisco, CA 94107

10 9 8 7 6 5 4 3 2 1
First printing, September 2011

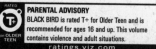